Mohammad Javad Ahmadian, María del Pilar García Mayo (Eds.)
Recent Perspectives on Task-Based Language Learning and Teaching

Trends in Applied Linguistics

Edited by
Ulrike Jessner
Claire Kramsch

Volume 27

Recent Perspectives on Task-Based Language Learning and Teaching

—

Edited by
Mohammad Javad Ahmadian
María del Pilar García Mayo

DE GRUYTER
MOUTON

ISBN 978-1-5015-1938-3
e-ISBN (PDF) 978-1-5015-0339-9
e-ISBN (EPUB) 978-1-5015-0329-0
ISSN 1868-6362

Library of Congress Cataloging-in-Publication Data
A CIP catalog record for this book has been applied for at the Library of Congress.

Bibliographic information published by the Deutsche Nationalbibliothek
The Deutsche Nationalbibliothek lists this publication in the Deutsche Nationalbibliografie;
detailed bibliographic data are available on the Internet at http://dnb.dnb.de.

© 2019 Walter de Gruyter Inc., Boston/Berlin
This volume is text- and page-identical with the hardback published in 2018.
Typesetting: RoyalStandard, Hong Kong
Printing and binding: CPI books GmbH, Leck
♾ Printed on acid-free paper
Printed in Germany

www.degruyter.com

Table of contents

Ali Shehadeh
Foreword: New Frontiers in Task-Based Language Teaching Research — vii

Mohammad Javad Ahmadian and María del Pilar García Mayo
Introduction: Recent Perspectives on Task-Based Language Teaching and Learning — 1

I Cognitive-Interactionist Perspective

María del Pilar García Mayo, Ainara Imaz Agirre and Agurtzane Azkarai
1 **Task Repetition Effects on CAF in EFL Child Task-Based Oral Interaction** — 9

Zhisheng (Edward) Wen
2 **Using Formulaic Sequences to Measure Task Performance: The Role of Working Memory** — 29

Laura Gurzynski-Weiss, Carly Henderson, and Daniel Jung
3 **Examining Timing and Type of Learner-Modified Output in Relation to Perception in Face-to-Face and Synchronous Task-Based Chat** — 53

II Sociocultural Theory Perspective

Rémi A. van Compernolle
4 **Dynamic Strategic Interaction Scenarios: A Vygotskian Approach to Focusing on Meaning and Form** — 77

Caroline Payant
5 **Effects of L3 Learner Proficiency and Task Types on Language Mediation: A Sociocultural Perspective** — 99

Lawrence Williams
6 **Task-Based Language Teaching and Concept-Based Instruction** — 121

III Complexity Theory Perspective

Martin Bygate
7 Dynamic Systems Theory and the Issue of Predictability in Task-Based Language: Some Implications for Research and Practice in TBLT —— 143

Hoa Nguyen and Diane Larsen-Freeman
8 Using Tasks to Teach Formulaic Sequences: Interindividual and Intraindividual Variation —— 167

Claire Kramsch and Jean-Paul Narcy-Combes
9 From Social Tasks to Language Development: Coping with Historicity and Subjectivity —— 195

IV Pedagogic and Educational Perspective

Martin East
10 "If it is All about Tasks, Will They Learn Anything?" Teachers' Perspectives on Grammar Instruction in the Task-Oriented Classroom —— 215

Andreas Müller-Hartmann and Marita Schocker
11 The Challenge of Thinking Task-Based Teaching from The Learners' Perspectives – Developing Teaching Competences Through an Action Research Approach to Teacher Education —— 233

Jonathan Newton and Trang Bui
12 Teaching with Tasks in Primary School EFL Classrooms in Vietnam —— 259

Index —— 279

Ali Shehadeh
Foreword: New Frontiers in Task-Based Language Teaching Research

1 Introduction

In the last 30+ years, there has been an enormous interest by researchers, language professionals and practicing teachers worldwide in task-based language teaching (TBLT) as an approach to second/foreign language (L2) learning and teaching and a teaching methodology in which classroom tasks constitute the main focus of instruction. This is evidenced by the numerous publications, symposiums, seminars, colloquiums, academic sessions, conference presentations, and indeed whole conferences that are specifically dedicated to TBLT (Van den Branden, Bygate, and Norris 2009). The most notable of these is the formation of the International Consortium on Task-based Language Teaching (ICTBLT) in 2005 which holds a biennial international conference on the topic, now transformed into a professional association, named International Association for Task-Based Language Teaching (IATBLT). The most recent TBLT conference was held in Barcelona, Spain, April (2017).

Virtually all of these publications, professionals, and academic/professional events speak of the potential value of TBLT for L2 learning and teaching. Based on insights from second language acquisition (SLA) research findings, empirical findings on effective instructional techniques, and cognitive psychology, it is strongly believed that TBLT facilitates SLA and makes L2 learning and teaching more principled and more effective. For instance, Van den Branden, Bygate, and Norris (2009: 11) state:

> ... there is widespread agreement that tasks, potentially at least, offer a uniquely powerful resource both for teaching and testing of language. In particular, they provide a locus for bringing together the various dimensions of language, social context, and the mental processes of individual learners that are key to learning. There are theoretical grounds, and empirical evidence, for believing that tasks might be able to offer all the affordances needed for successful instructed language development, whoever the learners might be, and whatever the context.

Van den Branden et al. have based these conclusions on the extensive and varied literature on task-based learning, teaching and assessment, which speaks to the potential of TBLT as an approach to L2 learning and teaching and as a teaching methodology (Van den Branden et al. 2009: 1).

In keeping with these statements, TBLT research and implementation has indeed in the last 10 years or so expanded substantially in range and scope to new boundaries. Three areas, in particular, stand out as having received researchers' special attention. These are TBLT in foreign language contexts, TBLT and L2 writing, and TBLT and technology.

The first area that has received researchers' good attention in recent years is TBLT in foreign language (FL), as against second language (SL), contexts, given that most of the TBLT research and implementation has until recently been conducted in SL contexts (for overviews and critiques, see, e.g., Manchón 2009; Ortega 2009; Shehadeh 2012). Towards this end, a number of studies and volumes have focused on research and implementation of TBLT in FL contexts. The former include, for instance, McDonough's research in Thailand (e.g., McDonough 2004; McDonough and Chaikitmongkol 2007, 2010), Robinson's work in Japan (e.g., Cadierno and Robinson 2009; Robinson 2007; Robinson Cadierno, and Shirai 2009), and the extensive work in Spain by García Mayo and her team – the Basque team (e.g., Alegría de la Colina and García Mayo 2009; Azkarai and García Mayo 2012, 2015; García Mayo 2002, 2014; García Mayo and Azkarai 2016) and by Gilabert and his team (e.g., Gilabert 2007; Gilabert, Baron and Llanes 2009), This research also includes studies in collections including Bygate, Skehan, and Swain (2001); Edwards and Willis (2005); Van den Branden (2006); Van den Branden, Van Gorp and Verhelst (2007); García Mayo (2007); and Shehadeh and Coombe (2010).

The latter include dedicated volumes to the issue including Leaver and Willis's (2004) volume titled *Task-based instruction in foreign language education: Practices and programs;* Shehadeh and Coombe's (2012) volume titled *Task-based language teaching in foreign language contexts: Research and implementation*; and Thomas and Reinders's (2015) volume titled *Contemporary task-based language teaching in Asia*.

It is clear from this review that TBLT research and implementation in FL contexts is firmly on the TBLT map and on the rise.

For TBLT and L2 writing, see for example, the recent volume specifically devoted to the topic by Byrnes and Manchón (2014) titled *Task-based language learning: Insights from and for L2 writing*, a number of articles in the volumes by Edwards and Willis (2005), García Mayo (2007), and Shehadeh and Coombe (2010, 2012), as well as a number of journal articles (e.g., Ellis and Yuan 2005; Kuiken and Vedder 2007a). For TBLT and technology, see for example, two volumes specifically devoted to the topic: the first one is by Thomas and Reinders (2010) titled *Task-based language learning and teaching with technology*; and the other is by González-Lloret and Ortega (2014) titled *Technology-mediated TBLT: Researching technology and tasks*, in addition to a number of articles in the volumes by Edwards and Willis (2005), García Mayo (2007), Leaver and Willis (2004), Shehadeh and Coombe (2010, 2012), and Thomas and Reinders (2015).

Other areas, however, have only received scant attention from TBLT researchers including (i) TBLT and content-based instruction, (ii) TBLT and learner-centered instruction, (iii) TBLT and English for specific purposes, and (iv) TBLT and languages other than English. The main purpose of this chapter is therefore to suggest directions that take TBLT research and implementation to new boundaries along these venues. Indeed, the full potential of TBLT as an approach to L2 learning and teaching and a teaching methodology is yet to be explored. This chapter is a step forward towards extending TBLT research and implementation to these new frontiers and vistas.

2 TBLT and content-based instruction

The first line of research to expand TBLT scholarship is to explore the links between TBLT and content-based instruction (CBI). CBI refers to an instructional approach that delivers non-linguistic curricular content (e.g., science, mathematics, geography, social studies, etc.) in the medium of the L2 which learners are learning. A lucid and concise dictionary definition of CBI is provided by Richards and Schmidt (2010: 125) who define CBI as "a method that integrates language instruction with subject matter instruction in the target language, for example, studying science, social studies or mathematics through the medium of English in a content-based ESL program." Similarly, Lyster and Ballinger (2011: 279) define CBI as "an instructional approach in which non-linguistic curricular content such as geography or science is taught to students through the medium of a language that they are concurrently learning as an additional language." Examples of CBI include language across the curriculum, content-based learning (CBL), content-based language teaching (CBLT), content and language integrated learning (CLIL), immersion programs in Canada, and sheltered second language education programs in the USA, UK and Australia.

Through its focus on both subject-matter *and* language teaching, CBI provides students with a context for meaningful and purposeful communication in the L2. García Mayo (2015b), for instance, states that "CBI is designed to help learners (i) construct knowledge and develop understanding about a [subject-matter] topic, (ii) use language meaningfully, and (iii) learn about language in the context of learning through language", which are all in line with the basic principles of TBLT. More significantly, the construct of task itself, which is intrinsic to TBLT, is also central to CBI through its integration of subject-matter and language teaching goals because CBI normally uses tasks that are engaging and cognitively challenging for the learners in order to achieve both content and language teaching goals (Brinton, Snow, and Wesche 1989, cited in García Mayo 2015b: 1).

In spite of that, the links between TBLT and CBI have been so rarely explored (Ortega 2015: 103). Only recently did researchers start to examine the TBLT-CBI interfaces (see, e.g., Basterrechea and García Mayo 2013, 2014; Basterrechea, García Mayo, and Leeser 2014; Van den Branden 2009; Van Houtven, Peters, and Van den Branden 2013). Based on studies carried out by himself and his team of researchers in the Belgian context, Van den Branden, for instance, maintains that supportive, long-term teacher training and teacher development might constitute the basis for the success of any TBLT-CBI innovations.

System's recent special issue (Vol. 54) however, guest-edited by García Mayo (García Mayo 2015a), constitutes the first serious attempt at exploring the links between TBLT and CBI. This thematic issue contains eight studies that have investigated task implementation in CBI/CLIL educational contexts in Canada (Lyster); Finland (Nikula); Belgium (Van Gorp and Van den Branden); Spain (García Mayo and Lázaro Ibarrola, and Pérez-Vidal and Roquet); Spain and Poland (Juan-Garau and Jacob); Austria, Finland and Spain (Llinares and Dalton-Puffer); and Japan (Butler). These studies explored the links between TBLT and CBI using quantitative and qualitative research methods, and taking as their participants children and adolescents from various L1 backgrounds learning Dutch, English and French as an L2.

The studies document the opportunities and challenges of utilizing TBLT in CBI contexts. They all attest to the deep commonalities between both of these two educational approaches, and the rise in implementing TBLT in CBI/CLIL contexts, in Europe in particular. For example, García Mayo and Lázaro Ibarrola (2015) examined differences in amount of negotiation for meaning on a spot-the-difference task between children at two age groups (8–9 vs. 10–11) in a CLIL context, as compared to an EFL context. Data were collected from 80 children who were paired to form 40 age- and proficiency-matched dyads (20 EFL, 20 CLIL). The researchers analyzed the children's oral production to identify the different strategies these two age groups used to complete the task. The investigators found that "CLIL learners negotiate more and resort to the L1 less frequently than EFL learners. On the other hand, older children in both contexts negotiate less and use the L1 more frequently than younger children" (p. 40). García Mayo and Lázaro Ibarrola suggest that the findings of their study show that the links between age (younger children vs. older children) and context (EFL vs. CLIL) are multifaceted and that all these four variables interact with one another in different and interesting ways to produce different results (see García Mayo and Lázaro Ibarrola, 2015 for complete discussion of these findings and their implications for TBLT-CLIL research and the classroom situation).

In her commentary on the eight articles comprising the special issue, Ortega (2015: 107) holds that "[A]ll the contributions in this special issue bear witness to the richness and multidimensionality of CLIL and TBLT learning" and therefore the benefits of TBLT-CBI/CLIL instruction must not be reduced to linguistic benefits only. She explains:

> The innovations offered when L2 instruction integrates language-and-content in well-designed task structures hold great promise for optimal linguistic learning, yes. But as many of the studies in the special issue show, they also aim at promoting the learning of (a) academic content, (b) social, contextual, interactional, and identity dimensions of using a new language, (c) transcultural learning, and (d) technological literacy learning (Ortega 2015: 107).

As mentioned above, *System's* special issue constitutes only a first step towards exploring the links between TBLT and CBI, but it also opens up for a number of future research directions in this venue as suggested by the guest-editor, Ortega's commentary on the special issue, and the investigators themselves. In her commentary on the various themes addressed by the eight articles, Ortega (2015), in particular, points to two other themes for researching the links between TBLT and CBI. The first theme relates to the roles of the teacher. Echoing Van den Branden's (2009) remark mentioned earlier that long-term teacher development might be the basis for the success of any TBLT-CBI innovations, Ortega argues that future research must address teachers' attitudes and views because some investigators examining the TBLT-CBI interfaces, in *System's* special issue and elsewhere, have found that "many CLIL teachers have misgivings about neglecting content-related learning goals when language learning goals, in their perception, are overemphasized" (p. 108). The second theme relates to the status of L1 in the TBLT-CBI/CLIL pedagogy. Citing a number of foreign language educators' views arising from the current special issue and other works in varied EFL and CLIL settings, which held different or seemingly opposing positions on the use of L1, Ortega reiterates Moore's (2013) conclusion that "the roles for the L1 are multiple and complex rather than wholesale deleterious or beneficial" (p. 108). Calling for more research in this area too, Ortega suggests that "researchers and teachers in CLIL and TBLT ought to find common ground in the argument that not all uses of the L1 are equal, nor are they all exclusively deleterious or beneficial out of context" (p. 108).

Finally, one might also like to know whether and to what degree CBI supports the development of wider student learning capacities including L2 learning, and conversely, whether and to what degree TBLT supports the development of wider student learning capacities including subject-matter learning.

3 TBLT and learner-centered instruction

The second direction to expand TBLT research and implementation is to explore whether and to what degree TBLT successfully utilizes the underlying principles of learner-centered instruction (LCI) in L2 teaching and learning.

In the last 20 years or so, there has been a noticeable shift towards learner-centered instruction (LCI) in education in general, and L2 teaching in particular. In L2 teaching, the consequence of this shift was a change from teacher-centered/directed instruction (a teaching situation in which most decisions are made and carried out by the teacher based on his/her priorities) to learner-centered instruction (a teaching situation that makes the learner "central to all aspects of language teaching, including planning teaching, and evaluation") (Richards and Schmidt 2010: 326–327). LCI promotes such concepts as learner independence, students' self-evaluation, individualized instruction, student-student interaction, pair and group work, and collaborative learning. More specifically, LCI is a teaching situation in which:

- Learners take part in setting goals and objectives of their learning.
- There is concern about learners' needs, likes, dislikes, feelings and values.
- There is concern about learners' prior knowledge.
- There is concern about learners' different learning styles and learning preferences.
- Learners are seen as active, rather than passive, participants in the learning/teaching process.
- Learners take much of the responsibility for their own learning.
- Learners are actively involved in shaping how they learn. They co-construct knowledge rather than just receive knowledge.
- There is ample teacher-student and student-student interaction.
- Self-corrections/repairs are favored over peer-corrections/repairs or teacher-corrections/repairs.
- There is an abundance of brainstorming activities, pair work and small group work.
- The teacher is seen as a facilitator of learning rather than an instructor or lecturer who spoon feeds learners with knowledge (see Benson 2007; Richards and Schmidt 2010).

As can be surmised, this shift in L2 learning and teaching from teacher-centered/directed instruction to learner-centered instruction fits well with TBLT, which also makes the learner central to all aspects of the learning and teaching process (see above). Viewed from this perspective, it is possible to argue that TBLT can potentially be an ideal platform for implementing the basic principles of LCI.

Indeed, research has shown that *task-based pair and group activities* that are generated by students themselves, or are sensitive to the students' preferences, ensure: (i) that students take on responsibility for much of the work, (ii) greater student involvement in the learning process, and (iii) that the teacher is free to focus on monitoring and providing relevant feedback (e.g., Shehadeh 2004, 2005), which are all major characteristics of LCI. Similarly, research has also shown that *task-based self-initiated, self-completed repairs* (a major characteristic of LCI) must be encouraged in the L2 classroom, not just because these are more prevalent and more frequent than other-initiated, other-completed repairs, but also because self-initiated self-completed repairs as internal attention-drawing devices, rather than other-initiated, other-completed repair as external attention-drawing devices, are more facilitative of L2 learning (Izumi 2002; Shehadeh 1999, 2001).

It follows that the second line of research to expand TBLT scholarship is to explore whether and to what degree TBLT successfully utilizes the underlying principles of LCI in L2 instruction. For instance, such research might investigate issues like: (i) Whether and to what degree students are actually taking part in setting the goals and objectives of their learning in a TBLT-based setting, (ii) Whether and to what degree students are taking much of the responsibility for their own learning, (iii) Whether and to what degree students are actively involved in shaping how they learn, and (iv) Whether and to what degree students are given sufficient time and opportunity for self-correction/repair before peer-correction/repair or teacher-correction/repair in the L2 classroom.

The last point, in particular, is quite important when we know that some classroom studies have observed that students are not given sufficient time or opportunity to self-correct in a classroom situation. For example, McHoul (1990) observed that teachers initiated corrections "either (a) immediately a trouble-source is over, with usually no gap occurring or (b) immediately the repairable [i.e., the trouble-source] itself is spoken/heard" (p. 375). McHoul goes on to say that "The latter cases of other-initiations either (i) overlap the trouble-source turn or (ii) interrupt it. In instances of (i), teacher and student can both be heard to be speaking, albeit briefly, at the same time. In instances of (ii), the student immediately yields the floor to the teacher" (McHoul 1990: 375).

4 TBLT and English for specific purposes

English for specific purposes (ESP) and its subsidiary fields of English for vocational/occupational purposes (EVP/EOP) and English for academic purposes (EAP), like LCI discussed above, also make the learner central to the learning and teaching process. ESP is a branch of English language teaching (ELT). The aim of an ESP course or program of study is to teach English to students in a *specific professional field* or *specific area of knowledge*. ESP instruction was first developed in the late 1960s in response to a need for targeted assistance for learners from non-English speaking countries who were studying or working in English-speaking countries. Instruction in ESP is determined by the specific needs of a particular group of learners. The concept of needs and needs analysis is perhaps the major component that distinguishes ESP from general English. For instance, Wette (in press) states that an ESP course is distinguished from a general English course by its "substantial emphasis on the necessity to establish and meet the needs of learners and other stakeholders through the selection of relevant genre exemplars, language items and instructional tasks from real-world contexts." Thus, ESP is based on designing courses that meet learners' needs by:

- meeting learners' target situation needs (product) and learning needs (process).
- meeting their specific learning goals.
- meeting their specific interests and likes/dislikes.
- using authentic language, materials, texts, examples, samples, demonstrations, illustrations, tasks, activities, projects, etc. from the learners' actual and specific professional field, domain of knowledge, or discipline like engineering, biology, medicine, business, tourism, banking, commerce, media, law, etc.

Since its inception, ESP has continued to expand in range and importance, in part due to the growth and expansion in the global use of English in trade, business, science, technology, education and research, and in part due to the increasing role of English as a lingua franca in international and intra-national communication (Paltridge and Starfield 2012; Wette, in press, for recent overviews of ESP history, development and scope). Nonetheless, in spite of that and in spite of the striking similarities between the underlying principles of ESP and TBLT (e.g., both put the learner at the centre of the learning-teaching process, both use authentic language, both use an abundance of tasks and activities, and both are guided by specific learning goals and objectives), surprisingly only very few studies to date have investigated ways of utilizing and implementing TBLT in ESP contexts (e.g., Alwi 2015; Hager and Lyman-Hager 2004; Horiba and Fukaya 2012; Macias 2004; Stark 2005; Weaver 2012; Widodo 2015).

For instance, Macias (2004) describes a task-based Spanish for Specific Purposes (SSP) program designed for professionals in the fields of healthcare and real estate in California, USA. The researcher documents the successes and challenges she faced in teaching this kind of student body. Stark (2005) describes a task-based syllabus she developed for her English business students in the

Faculty of Economics, University of Fribourg, Switzerland. Stark's findings show how task-based learning can be successfully achieved within a management context that enables learners to use English as a working language. In a recent study, Widodo (2015) explored the potential of designing and implementing a task-based framework for vocational English (VE) materials in the secondary education sector in Indonesia. Findings of the study show that task-based materials successfully promote active engagement in language learning by VE secondary school students.

The third line to expand TBLT scholarship is therefore to move towards the world of ESP and its subsidiary fields of EVP/EOP and EAP. These can constitute interesting and rich educational environments and venues for investigating the potential of designing, utilizing, and implementing the principles of TBLT in authentic educational settings.

5 TBLT and languages other than English

The fourth and final line of research proposed in this chapter for moving the TBLT field forward is exploring TBLT research and implementation in languages other than English. As stated in the introduction to this chapter, TBLT is an approach to L2 learning and teaching and a teaching methodology. So in theory, TBLT principles should apply to the teaching and learning of *any* second or foreign language, not just English. For example, Leaver and Willis (2004: 47) argue that "task-based instruction can be used successfully for nearly any language" (see also, for example, the quote by Van den Branden et al. (2009) cited in the introduction to this chapter). Nonetheless, most of TBLT scholarship comes from settings in which *English* is the second or foreign language. For instance, Shehadeh (2012: 4), commenting on existing TBLT research, points out that "most of the scholarship on TBLT ... comes from *English* as a second and/or foreign language contexts" (italics in origin). Shehadeh based his conclusion on a thorough review of existing literature on TBLT that has appeared across many journals, edited volumes, monographs, and special issues in refereed journals. It must be admitted, however, that this is not unexpected because *English* is currently the most widely taught and learnt language in the world, and is certainly the one in which there exists most research on virtually any field of study or discipline.

Nonetheless, many other languages in the world are taught and learnt as a second or foreign language, and therefore are worthy of investigation by TBLT researchers. Some researchers did explore the potential of researching and implementing TBLT in languages other than English (e.g., Alosh 2004 (Arabic); Fernández García 2007; Macias 2004; Ortega 2005; Toth 2008; Van Altena 2004

(Spanish); Hager and Lyman-Hager 2004; Kuiken and Vedder 2007b; Swain and Lapkin 1998 (French); Leaver and Kaplan 2004 (Slavic languages); Peters 2007 (German); Saito-Abbott 2004 (Japanese). For example, Saito-Abbott (2004) describes a task-based Japanese program in the Japanese Department at California State University, USA. The study describes the use of task-based teaching at very beginning levels of instruction and documents the advantages and challenges of using tasks in such programs. Kuiken and Vedder (2007b) investigated the cognitive complexity of the task and the complexity of the linguistic output. The researchers collected data from 76 Dutch university learners of French as a second language. Results of the study show that students did not perform significantly better on the cognitively less complex tasks than the cognitively more complex tasks used in their study. On the other hand, the researchers did find greater linguistic accuracy on more complex tasks than less complex tasks. Toth (2008) compared quantitative and qualitative results for task-based L2 grammar instruction conducted as whole-class, teacher-led discourse (TLD) and small-group, learner-led discourse (LLD). The researcher collected data from 78 university low-level English-speaking learners of L2 Spanish. Results of the study showed stronger performance by TLD learners, suggesting a potential for teachers to facilitate L2 learning by directing learners' attention to specific target language structures.

As can be deduced from this review, however, the number of studies exploring TBLT in languages other than English is still very low and the field is in need of more extensive TBLT research in this area, too. This is important if TBLT is to be considered a comprehensive approach to L2 learning and teaching whose underlying principles and assumptions can apply to *any* L2 learning and teaching situation, not just English as an L2.

6 Conclusion

Task-based language teaching has stood the test of time for over 3 decades. During these 30+ years, it has expanded and still expands in range, scope, complexity and importance as an approach and a methodology to second/foreign language learning, teaching and assessment. No wonder many teachers around the world are shifting their teaching practices toward TBLT based on the strong belief that TBLT facilitates SLA and makes L2 learning and teaching more successful and more effective. Indeed, it is now well-established that TBLT represents an innovation in L2 learning and teaching at both theoretical and methodological levels. From a theoretical perspective, TBLT views SLA as a process not directly influenced by formal instruction but which is fostered through the meaningful use of language. At the methodological level, TBLT considers students as language users rather than learners, with the explicit analysis of language structures and forms emerging from difficulties experienced during the completion of tasks (Ogilvie and Dunn, 2010: 162; and Bygate 2015; Long 2015, for recent overviews of the field).

Notwithstanding that, it was argued in this chapter that TBLT is yet to exploit its full potential. Four research directions were proposed as potential venues for expanding TBLT scholarship. These were (i) TBLT and content-based instruction, (ii) TBLT and learner-centered instruction, (iii) TBLT and English for specific purposes, and (iv) TBLT and languages other than English. It is hoped that these venues are a step forward towards taking task-based language teaching research to new levels and extending its research agenda to new boundaries.

References

Alegría de la Colina, A. & M.P. García Mayo. 2009. Oral interaction in task-based EFL learning: The use of the L1 as a cognitive tool. *International Review of Applied Linguistics* 47(3–4). 325–345.

Alosh, M. 2004. Learning Arabic: From language functions to tasks in a diglossic context. B.L. Leaver & J. Willis (eds.), *Task-based instruction in foreign language education: Practices and programs*, 96–121. Washington, DC: Georgetown University Press.

Alwi, N.A. 2015. Language learning performance using engineering-based tasks via text chat. In M. Thomas & H. Reinders (eds.), *Contemporary task-based language teaching in Asia*, 193–210. London: Bloomsbury.

Azkarai, A. & M. P. García Mayo. 2012. *Does gender influence task performance in EFL? Interactive tasks and language-related episodes*. In. E. Alcón & P. Safont (eds.), *Discourse and language learning across L2 instructional settings*, 249–278. Amsterdam: Rodopi.

Azkarai, A. & M. P. García Mayo. 2015. Task modality and L1 use in EFL oral interaction. *Language Teaching Research* 19(5). 550–571.

García Mayo 2015b. EFL task-based interaction: Does task modality impact on language-realted episodes? In M. Sato & S. Ballinger (eds.), *Peer interaction and second language learning: Pedagogical potential and research agenda*, 241–266. Amsterdam: John Benjamins.

Basterrechea, M. & M. P. García Mayo. 2013. Language-related episodes during collaborative tasks: A comparison of CLIL and EFL learners. In K. McDonough & A. Mackey (eds.), *Second language interaction in diverse educational contexts*, 25–43. Amsterdam: John Benjamins.

Basterrechea, M. & M. P. García Mayo. 2014. Dictogloss and the production of the English third person -s by CLIL and mainstream learners: A comparative study. *International Journal of English Studies* 14(2). 77–98.

Basterrechea, M., M. P. García Mayo & M. Leeser. 2014. Pushed output and noticing in a dictogloss: Task implementation in the CLIL classroom. *Porta Linguarum* 22. 7–22.

Benson, P. 2007. Autonomy in language teaching and learning. *Language Teaching* 40(1). 21–40.

Brinton, D. M., M. A. Snow & M. B. Wesche. 1989. *Content-based second language instruction*. New York: Newbury House.

Bygate, M. (ed.). 2015. *Domains and directions in the development of TBLT: A decade of plenaries from the international conference*. Amsterdam: John Benjamin's.

Bygate, M., P. Skehan & M. Swain (eds.). 2001. *Researching pedagogic tasks: Second language learning, teaching, and testing*. Harlow, England: Longman.

Byrnes, H. and R.M Manchón. (eds.). 2014. *Task-based language learning: Insights from and for L2 writing*. Amsterdam: John Benjamin's.

Cadierno, T. & P. Robinson. 2009. Language typology, task complexity and the development of L2 lexicalization patterns for describing motion events. *Annual Review of Cognitive Linguistics* 6. 245–277.

Edwards, C. & J. Willis (eds.). 2005. *Teachers exploring tasks in English language teaching*. London: Palgrave Macmillan.

Ellis, R. & Y. Yuan. 2005. The effects of careful within-task planning on oral and written task performance. In R. Ellis (ed.), *Planning and task performance in a second language*, 167–192. Amsterdam: John Benjamins.

Fernández García, M. 2007. Tasks, Nnegotiation and L2 learning in a foreign language context. In M.P. García Mayo (ed.), *Investigating tasks in formal language learning*, 69–90. Clevedon, UK: Multilingual Matters.

García Mayo, M.P. 2002. The effectiveness of two form-focused tasks in advanced EFL pedagogy. *International Journal of Applied Linguistics* 12(2). 156–175.

García Mayo, M.P. (ed.). 2007. *Investigating tasks in formal language learning*. Clevedon, UK: Multilingual Matters.

García Mayo, M.P. 2014. Collaborative tasks and their potential for grammar instruction in second/foreign language contexts. In C. Lavale & M. Arche (eds.), *The grammar dimensions in instructed second language learning: Theory, research and practice*, 82–102. London: Continuum.

García Mayo, M.P. 2015a. Learning language and content through tasks: Exploring the interfaces. [Special issue]. *System* 54.

García Mayo, M.P. 2015b. The interface between task-based language teaching and content-based instruction. *System* 54. 1–3.

García Mayo, M.P. & A. Lázaro Ibarrola. 2015. Do children negotiate for meaning in task-based interaction? Evidence from CLIL and EFL settings. *System* 54. 40–54.

Gilabert, R. 2007. The simultaneous manipulation of task complexity along planning time and [± Here-and-Now]: Effects on L2 oral production. In M.P. García Mayo (ed.), *Investigating tasks in formal language learning*, 44–68. Clevedon, UK: Multilingual Matters.

Gilabert, R., J. Baron & M. Llanes. 2009. Manipulating task complexity across task types and its influence on learners' interaction during oral performance. *International Review of Applied Linguistics* 47. 367–395.

González-Lloret, M. & L. Ortega (eds.). 2014. *Technology-mediated TBLT: Researching technology and tasks*. Amsterdam: John Benjamins.

Hager, W.R. & M.A. Lyman-Hager. 2004. Bridging the gap between the sciences and humanities: French for engineers and other technical professions. In B.L. Leaver & J. Willis (eds.), *Task-based instruction in foreign language education: Practices and programs*, 161–177. Washington, DC: Georgetown University Press.

Horiba, Y. & K. Fukaya. 2012. Effects of task instructions on text processing and learning in a Japanese EFL college nursing setting. In A. Shehadeh & C. Coombe (eds.), *Task-based language teaching in foreign language contexts: Research and implementation*, 89–107. Amsterdam: John Benjamin's.

Izumi, S. 2002. Output, input enhancement, and the noticing hypothesis: An experimental study on ESL relativization. *Studies in Second Language Acquisition* 24. 541–577.

Kuiken, F. & I. Vedder. 2007a. Task complexity and measures of linguistic performance in L2 writing. *International Review of Applied Linguistics in Language Teaching (IRAL)* 45. 261–284.

Kuiken, F. & I. Vedder. 2007b. Cognitive task complexity and linguistic performance in French L2 writing. In M.P. García Mayo (ed.), *Investigating tasks in formal language learning*, 117–135. Clevedon, UK: Multilingual Matters.

Leaver, B.L. & M.A. Kaplan. 2004. Task-based instruction in U.S. government Slavic language programs. In B.L. Leaver & J. Willis (eds.), *Task-based instruction in foreign language education: Practices and programs*, 47–66. Washington, DC: Georgetown University Press.

Leaver, B. L. & J. Willis (eds.). 2004. *Task-based instruction in foreign language education: Practices and programs*. Washington, DC: Georgetown University Press.

Long, M. 2015. *Second language acquisition and task-based language teaching*. London: Wiley-Blackwell.

Lyster, R. 2015. Using form-focused tasks to integrate language across the immersion curriculum. *System* 54. 4–13.

Lyster, R. & S. Ballinger. 2011. Content-based language teaching: Convergent concerns across divergent contexts. *Language Teaching Research* 15. 279–288.

Macias, C. 2004. Task-based instruction for teaching Spanish to professionals. In B.L. Leaver & J. Willis (eds.), *Task-based instruction in foreign language education: Practices and programs*, 142–160. Washington, DC: Georgetown University Press.

Manchón, R. 2009. Introduction: Broadening the perspective of L2 writing scholarship: The contribution of research on foreign language writing. In R. Manchon (ed.), *Writing in foreign language contexts*, 1–22. Clevedon, UK: Multilingual Matters.

McDonough, K. 2004. Learner-learner interaction during pair and small group activities in a Thai EFL context. *System* 32. 207–224.

McDonough, K. & W. Chaikitmongkol. 2007. Teachers' and learners' reactions to a task-based EFL course in Thailand. *TESOL Quarterly* 41(1). 107–132.

McDonough, K. & W. Chaikitmongkol. 2010. Collaborative syntactic priming activities and EFL learners' production of wh-questions. *The Canadian Modern Language Review* 66(6). 817–842.

McHoul, A. 1990. The organization of repair in classroom talk. *Language in Society* 19. 349–377.

Moore, P. J. 2013. An emergent perspective on the use of the first language in the English-as-a-foreign-language classroom. *Modern Language Journal* 97. 239–253.

Ogilvie, G. & W. Dunn. 2010. Taking teacher education to task: Exploring the role of teacher education in promoting the utilization of task-based language teaching. *Language Teaching Research* 14. 161–181.

Ortega, L. 2005. What do learners plan?: Learner-driven attention to form during pre-task planning. In R. Ellis (ed.), *Planning and task performance in a second language*, 77–109. Amsterdam: John Benjamins.

Ortega, L. 2009. Studying writing across EFL contexts: Looking back and moving forward. In R. Manchon (ed.), *Writing in foreign language contexts*, 209–231. Clevedon, UK: Multilingual Matters.

Ortega, L. 2015. Researching CLIL and TBLT interfaces. *System* 54. 103–109.

Paltridge, B. & S. Starfield (eds.). 2012. *The handbook of English for specific purposes*. Malden, MA: Wiley.

Peters, E. 2007. L2 vocabulary acquisition and reading comprehension: The influence of task complexity. In M.P. García Mayo (ed.), *Investigating tasks in formal language learning*, 178–198. Clevedon, UK: Multilingual Matters.

Richards, J. & R. Schmidt. 2010. *Longman dictionary of language teaching and applied linguistics* (4th edn.) London: Longman.

Robinson, P. 2007. Task complexity, theory of mind, and intentional reasoning: Effects on L2 speech production, interaction, uptake and perceptions of task difficulty. *International Review of Applied Linguistics* 45. 193–214.

Robinson, P., T. Cadierno & Y. Shirai. 2009. Time and motion: Measuring the effects of the conceptual demands of tasks on second language production. *Applied Linguistics* 28. 533–554.

Saito-Abbott, Y. 2004. Designing an outcomes-based TBI Japanese language program. In B.L. Leaver & J. Willis (eds.), *Task-based instruction in foreign language education: Practices and programs*, 122–141. Washington, DC: Georgetown University Press.

Shehadeh, A. 1999. Non-native speakers' production of modified comprehensible output and second language learning. *Language Learning* 49(4). 627–675.

Shehadeh, A. 2001. Self- and other-initiated modified output during task-based interaction. *TESOL Quarterly* 35. 433–457.

Shehadeh, A. 2004. Modified output during task-based pair interaction and group interaction. *Journal of Applied Linguistics* 1. 351–382.

Shehadeh, A. 2005. Task-based language learning and teaching: Theories and applications. In C. Edwards & J. Willis (eds.), Teachers exploring tasks in English language teaching, 13–30. London: Palgrave Macmillan.

Shehadeh. A. 2012. Broadening the perspective of task-based language teaching scholarship: The contribution of research in foreign language contexts. In A. Shehadeh & C. Coombe (eds.), *Task-based language teaching in foreign language contexts: Research and implementation*, 1–20. Amsterdam: John Benjamins.

Shehadeh, A. & C. Coombe (eds.). 2010. *Applications of task-based learning in TESOL*. Alexandria, VA: TESOL.

Shehadeh, A. & C. Coombe (eds.). 2012. *Task-based language teaching in foreign language contexts: Research and implementation*. Amsterdam: John Benjamins.

Stark, P.P. 2005. Integrating task-based learning into a business English programme. In C. Edwards & J. Willis (eds.), *Teachers exploring tasks in English language teaching*, 40–49. London: Palgrave Macmillan.

Swain, M. & S. Lapkin. 1998. Interaction and second language learning: Two adolescent French immersion students working together. *The Modern Language Journal* 82(3). 320–337.

Thomas, M. & H. Reinders (eds.). 2010. *Task-based language learning and teaching with technology*. London and New York: Continuum.

Thomas, M. & H. Reinders (eds.). 2015. *Contemporary task-based language teaching in Asia*. London: Bloomsbury.

Toth, P.D. 2008. Teacher-and learner-led discourse in task-based grammar instruction: Providing procedural assistance for L2 morphosyntax development. *Language Learning* 58(2). 237–283.

Van Altena, A.M. 2004. Using media-based tasks in teaching Spanish. In B.L. Leaver & J. Willis (eds.), *Task-based instruction in foreign language education: Practices and programs*, 67–82. Washington, DC: Georgetown University Press.

Van den Branden, K. (ed.). 2006. *Task-based language education: From theory to practice*. Cambridge: Cambridge University Press.

Van den Branden, K. 2009. Mediating between predetermined order and chaos: The role of the teacher in task-based language education. *International Journal of Applied Linguistics* 19. 264–285.

Van den Branden, K., M. Bygate & J. Norris (eds.). 2009. *Task-based language teaching: A reader*. Amsterdam: John Benjamins.

Van Houtven, T., E. Peters & K. Van den Branden. 2013. Analyzing student teachers' academic literacy needs: A qualitative analysis of Flemish first-year teacher trainees' needs. *Language Learning in Higher Education* 3. 267–292.

Van den Branden, K., K. Van Gorp & M. Verhelst (eds.). 2007. *Tasks in action: Task-based language education from a classroom-based perspective*. Newcastle: Cambridge Scholars Publishing.

Weaver, C. 2012. Incorporating a formative assessment cycle into task-based language teaching in a university setting in Japan. In A. Shehadeh & C. Coombe (eds.), *Task-based language teaching in foreign language contexts: Research and implementation*, 287–309. Amsterdam: John Benjamins.

Wette, R. in press. English for specific purposes (ESP) and English for academic purposes (EAP). *The TESOL encyclopaedia of English language teaching*. Wiley.

Widodo, P. 2015. Designing and implementing task-based vocational English materials: Text, language, task, and context in Indonesia. In M. Thomas & H. Reinders (eds.), *Contemporary task-based language teaching in Asia*, 291–312. London: Bloomsbury.

Mohammad Javad Ahmadian and María del Pilar García Mayo
Introduction: Recent Trends in Task-Based Language Teaching and Learning

Task-based Language Teaching (TBLT) constitutes both an innovative language teaching method and a thriving area of investigation in the field of Second Language Acquisition (SLA). The past three decades have witnessed a surge of interest in TBLT which is evidenced by numerous published monographs, edited volumes, and articles and special issues in major SLA and Language Teaching journals (Ahmadian 2016; Bygate 2015; Bygate 2016; East 2012; Ellis 2003; García Mayo 2007, 2015; Jackson and Burch 2017; Long, 2015; Samuda and Bygate 2008; Sato and Ballinger 2016; Newton 2016; Shehadeh and Coombe 2012; Van den Branden 2006 to name but a few). Whilst, since the 1980's, some significant progress has been made in TBLT research and a plethora of theoretical positions have been put forth to explain SLA-related phenomena, these theories have predominantly been construed as "oppositional and incommensurable" (Ellis 2008: 925) and therefore no single monograph, edited volume, or special issue has addressed TBLT from the perspective of these diverse but, in our view, mutually-informing theories (see García Mayo, Gutierrez Mangado, and Martínez Adrián 2013 for a recent attempt at covering all main theoretical approaches to SLA).

The main impetus for this edited volume has been to reflect epistemological diversity in SLA and TBLT by bringing together distinct but complementary theoretical frameworks for task-based research, namely cognitive-interactionist theory, sociocultural theory (SCT), complexity theory, and education and pedagogy. These perspectives have been selected for a good reason. "Cognitive-interactionist" and "educational and pedagogical" perspectives have been the focus of much task-based research during the past decades but these constitute two of the most fruitful areas of research in TBLT and, therefore, we still need further research to enhance our understanding of: (a) the way in which manipulating tasks would affect cognitive mechanisms and in turn L2 acquisition and production; (b) whether and how we can manipulate task design features or implementation conditions to level the field for learners with different degrees of cognitive abilities; and (c) the challenges and benefits of implementing task-based or task-supported curricula in various parts of the world. Sociocultural theory and complexity theory perspectives have been selected for the novel lens that they offer for revisiting

Mohammad Javad Ahmadian, University of Leeds
María del Pilar García Mayo, Universidad del País Vasco (UPV/EHU)

DOI 10.1515/9781501503399-001

and researching TBLT which could address some of the longstanding and difficult phenomena in this area. Although there is a wealth of research from both perspectives on various dimensions of L2 acquisition, such studies are rather scarce in TBLT. The underpinning belief is that "engagement with, rather than dismissal of, multiple views and voices produces not only more socially useful and ethically responsible knowledge but also better and more valid knowledge" (Ortega 2012: 210). This, we believe, provides a better understanding of how teaching and learning occur by dint of tasks and opens up new avenues of exploration which could help the field mature. TBLT, in general, and the notion of task, in particular, are context sensitive and open to interpretation; therefore, we have attempted to solicit papers from different parts of the world (i.e. China, France, Germany, Indonesia, New Zealand, Russia, Spain, United Arab Emirate, the United Kingdom and United States) which, in a way, is in alignment with the volume's pluralistic approach to TBLT and SLA.

In this volume, whilst various chapters have adopted different theoretical perspectives and/or methodological approaches, they have all capitalized on a more or less similar definition of task. All contributors have, explicitly or implicitly, defined tasks as meaningful, outcome-oriented activities which induce learners to incidentally pay attention to form.

In the opening chapter, Ali Shehadeh discusses four directions in TBLT which are rather under-researched. He mentions "TBLT and content-based instruction" (see Samuda and Bygate 2008), "TBLT and learner-centred instruction", "TBLT and English for specific purposes", and "TBLT and languages other than English" as the four venues which have attracted scant attention compared to other areas. Shehadeh rightly points out that although TBLT has stood the test of time for over three decades, its full potential, as an approach to L2 learning and teaching and a teaching methodology, is yet to be explored. This introductory chapter is followed by four sections which address TBLT from different perspectives.

Section One explores TBLT from a cognitive-interactionist perspective with an emphasis on input, output, task-based procedures and internal cognitive mechanisms. This epistemology, according to Ortega (2012), has been the predominant approach to answering questions about SLA and a review of TBLT literature reveals that most of the TBLT studies have viewed, investigated, and evaluated tasks and their effects with reference to this perspective. In addition, as Long (2015: 61) suggests, this theory and the related empirical findings afford "the main psycholinguistic underpinnings for TBLT". Three carefully designed and robust empirical studies comprise this section. In **Chapter 1**, María del Pilar García Mayo, Ainara Imaz Agirre and Agurtzane Azkarai report on a study which investigates the effects of task repetition on the oral production of 120 young learners of English as a Foreign Language in Spain. This study is interesting and important for at least two reasons. First, whereas most previous research had adults as participants, this study features a sample of fairly young participants (7–9 years old). Second, most of the previous studies have used very small samples (see Bygate, 1999 and 2001 for example) which makes utilizing inferential statistics and thereby generalizing the results somewhat difficult. This study, however, has a relatively large sample of participants and therefore addresses one of the most important shortcomings of previous work. Its results provide evidence for the effects of task repetition on fluency and accuracy as well as trade-offs between different dimensions of L2 performance in young language learners.

In the next chapter (**Chapter 2**), Edward Wen reports on the preliminary results of an exploratory study into the main and interaction effects between working memory (WM) and pre-task planning on different dimensions of L2 formulaic sequences produced by EFL learners during retelling of narrative tasks. Wen argues for incorporating formulaic sequences as an additional dimension into the current complexity, accuracy, lexis, and fluency (CALF) tradition. In addition, focusing on WM capacity, which is now considered as one of the cornerstones of cognitive psychology (Conway et al. 2005), he proposes to conceptualize and operationalize cognitive mechanisms underlying L2 task performance from a WM perspective couched within the postulations of the Phonological/Executive model of WM in SLA. Therefore, Wen's chapter is of both theoretical and empirical importance.

In **Chapter 3**, Laura Gurzynski-Weiss, Carly Henderson and Daniel Jung investigate different types (full, partial, and none) as well as the timing (immediate and delayed) of modified output in relationship to learners' correct perception of feedback in face-to-face and synchronous task-based chats. Results of this study corroborate the findings of previous research that there is a statistically significant relationship between learners' correct noticing of feedback and their immediate modified output. That is, learners who produced immediate partial-modified output were more accurate than those who did not produce modified output at all. However, no significant relationship was found between full/partial delayed modified output and learners' correct feedback perception. Finally, the findings suggest that full/partial delayed modified output related more to learners' correct noticing in task-based chat (as compared to no delayed modified output), but this relationship did not turn out to be statistically significant.

Section Two takes on a sociocultural perspective to address TBLT. Since the publication of Frawley and Lantolf's (1985) paper, SCT has attracted SLA researchers' attention and over the years it has grown into an important and established part of SLA and language teaching research (van Compernolle and Williams 2013). One of the principal tenets of SCT is that higher level human psychological processes are organized or 'mediated' by three cultural factors: activities (e.g. play), artefacts (e.g. books), and symbols (e.g. language) (Lantolf 2006). From a SCT perspective, both dialogue and monologue (in the form of private speech) are of particular import in the process of 'mediation'. Therefore, tasks, which by definition induce learners to draw on their linguistic and cognitive resources in producing language (either monologically or dialogically), may prove appropriate instruments for fostering mediation and in turn internalization. Section Two includes three papers framed within SCT perspective.

First, Remi A. van Compernolle (**Chapter 4**) introduces dynamic strategic interaction scenarios (DSIS) tasks as useful pedagogic tools to facilitate developing learners' conscious knowledge of L2 forms and meaning and to accelerate learners' access to L2 knowledge during online processing. van Compernolle's argument for bringing together form and meaning and doing away with the form-meaning dichotomy is reminiscent of Long's (2015) notion of "analytic approach with a focus on form". Therefore, DSIS tasks could be construed as viable tools for realizing Long's third option in language teaching, namely analytic focus on form, which he believes is most efficient and effective for L2 acquisition (for an extensive discussion of these three options see Long 2015).

In **Chapter 5**, Caroline Payant adopts a sociocultural perspective to investigate whether and how two different task types – story completion and text reconstruction – create opportunities for collaborative dialogue between learners of French as a third language (L3) when paired with more and less proficient peers. One of the most interesting aspects of Payant's study is that it explores how learners' use of their L1, L2 or L3 while they negotiate language-related issues, i.e. Language Related Episodes – LREs (Swain and Lapkin 1998) correlates with their level of proficiency. The results of her study provided evidence that L3 learners engage in collaborative dialogue while jointly doing story completion gap tasks and text reconstruction tasks and that proficiency plays a significant role as a mediating variable. This study also shows that performing these two tasks could afford authentic opportunities for learners to discuss the language that they needed to successfully communicate with their peers as well as to integrate different skills (i.e. listening, reading, speaking and writing). Lawrence Williams, in **Chapter 6**, investigates the implementation of Concept-Based Instruction (CBI) within a model for TBLT used in the context of the French curriculum at a large, public university in the USA. The purpose of Williams' chapter is two-fold: first, it aims to demonstrate the ways in which CBI is compatible with and can promote TBLT and, second, it supports the notion that SLA and pedagogy are interdependent.

All three chapters in **Section Three** adopt a complexity theory (CT) approach to investigating TBLT. In 1997, Diane Larsen-Freeman argued that owing to the complex, dynamic, and non-linear nature of the process of L2 acquisition, viewing SLA-related phenomena from a complexity theory perspective would shed new light on many different conundrums. Since then, scores of articles, dissertations and books have been devoted to investigating and theorizing SLA from a complexity theory (or Dynamic Systems Theory) perspective (see Larsen-Freeman and Cameron 2007; Verspoor, de Bot, and Lowie 2011). Complex dynamic systems are characterized as being, inter alia, dependent on initial conditions, entailing various and fully interconnected elements and agents, non-linear, and context sensitive. This conceptualisation of learning and teaching widely differs from the reductionist and post-positivist accounts of SLA which have been around for decades now. Despite the wealth of research into SLA as a complex dynamic system, there is paucity of research into TBLT from a complexity theory perspective. In **Chapter 7**, Martin Bygate adopts a Dynamic Systems theory to revisit the notion of 'predictability'. One of his principal arguments is that, despite what some TBLT researchers and theoreticians might suggest, there is always some degree of predictability inherent in task-based teaching which enables teachers and materials developers to make useful and reasonable predictions about the language and learning that is likely to arise on given tasks without sacrificing the learners' personal agenda. He utilises the concept of 'useful trajectory' from dynamic systems theory to demonstrate how students might negotiate their way through a task. **Chapter 8**, by Hoa Nguyen and Diane Larsen-Freeman, reports on an empirical study which aims to unravel the interindividual and intraindividual variability in English as a Second Language learners' performance and acquisition of 30 English formulaic sequences in the classroom context. Using a pretest, posttest, delayed-posttest design, the results of the study show that TBLT is a useful approach to teaching not only grammatical features, as suggested by previous research, but also for teaching formulaic sequences. In addition, and in line with complexity theory, this study suggests that the process of developing knowledge, be it grammar or formulaic sequences, is unique in that different individuals retain, attrite or develop their receptive and productive knowledge in different and unique ways. In **Chapter 9**, Claire Kramsch and Jean-Paul Narcy-Combe present specific example to make a case for an ecologically conceived TBLT. Their suggested approach is squarely in line with a complexity theory perspective in that it emphasizes the interconnectedness of a wide range of variables (such as context, contents, cultures, discourse, individual learners' freedom, etc.) in the process of learning and teaching. They argue that language teaching courses will be effective only if 'freedom to learn' and learner reflexivity and responsibility go hand in hand with respect of who the learners are, where they come from and where they would like to go, and if a compromise is found between institutional demands and the learners' personal objectives and values.

One of the aims of TBLT is to integrate three important dimensions of language education, namely the cognitive, socio-cultural, and professional/pedagogical (Bygate this volume; Long 2015). In 2006, Kris Van den Branden argued that much of TBLT research has been conducted under laboratory and/or controlled conditions and that far less attention has been paid to whether and how tasks could be used as the basic units of language teaching syllabi. This state of affairs has not changed much since 2006 and there are still significant gaps in our knowledge of whether and how tasks, and TBLT for that matter, work for language learners and teachers. The fourth section of this volume addresses the pedagogical and educational aspects of TBLT.

Martin East, in **Chapter 10**, addresses the ways in which teachers reconcile grammar instruction with the task-oriented classroom. East attempts to answer two important questions: (a) how language teachers conceptualize effective language learning; and (b) how language teachers conceptualize and enact attention to grammar. In order to answer these two questions, he revisits his data for a research project arising from the context of curriculum reform in New Zealand in which TBLT was being encouraged in foreign language classrooms. His data reveals that teachers who are new to TBLT make clear links between communicative experience and a grammar pedagogy that contains several explicit and directly taught elements. Another interesting finding which emerges from East's analysis is that teachers tap into different dimensions of the forms-meaning-form trichotomy in reaction to what they see as their students' needs at the time. **Chapter 11**, by Andreas Müller-Hartmann and Marita Schocker report on the findings from a collaborative national research project in Germany. Based on action research, they have collaborated with twenty teachers for three years to develop competences in designing, implementing and researching tasks. The authors report on teachers learning how to document, reflect on and share their experiences in video-recorded case studies. The also show that exploratory practice allows teachers to work together and develop an understanding of TBLT. Their data analysis also shows how teachers negotiate the principles of tasks in their professional discourses when they reflect on their appropriateness for their use in groups in the classroom.

In **Chapter 12**, the final chapter, Jonathan Newton and Trang Bui focus on primary school classrooms in Vietnam where a new curriculum aimed at improving communicative skills has recently been initiated. In essence, their study aims to explore the curriculum and evaluate its congruence with the agreed-upon principles of TBLT. The results of the study show that despite the fact that the curriculum purports to be communicative and task-based, teachers who were constrained to follow textbooks, implemented a PPP approach in the classroom. One of the most interesting findings of this study is that teachers had basically gone beyond textbooks and had fostered task-supported approaches in the classroom. Obviously, this study could have implications for policy makers, materials developers, and teachers.

We hope that the wide range of topics addressed in this volume will be of interest to both experienced and novice TBLT researchers and that the volume opens up some new avenues of research. We are sincerely grateful to the series editors Ulrike Jessner and Claire Kramsch and to the following colleagues for their invaluable help in reviewing chapters for this collection: Cristina Escobar, Marta González-LLoret, YouJin Kim, Achilleas Kostoulas, James Lantolf, Patsy Lightbown, Ana Llinares, Mike Long, Wander Lowie, Andrea Revesz, Neomy Storch, Marjoline Verspoor, Martin Weddel, and David Wood. We also thank Shiva Ghominejad for preparing the index. García Mayo would like to acknowledge the financial support of the Basque Goverment [grant number IT904-16] and of the Ministerio de Economía y Competitividad [grant number FFI2012-32212].

References

Ahmadian, Mohammad Javad (ed.). 2016. Task-based language teaching. [Special issue]. *The Language Learning Journal* 44(4). 377–518.
Bygate, Martin. 1999. Quality of language and purpose of task: Patterns of learners' language on two oral communication tasks. *Language Teaching* Research 3. 185–214.
Bygate, Martin. 2001. Effects of task repetition on the structure and control of language. In Martin Bygate, Peter Skehan & Merrill Swain (eds.), *Researching pedagogic tasks: Second language learning, teaching and testing*, 23–48. Harlow: Longman
Bygate, Martin (ed.). 2015. *Domains and directions in the development of TBLT*. Philadelphia: John Benjamins.
Bygate, Martin. 2016. TBLT through the lens of applied linguistics. Engaging with the real world of the classroom. *International Journal of Applied Linguistics* 167(1). 3–15.
Conway, Andrew, Michael Kane, Michael Bunting, Zack Hambrick, Oliver Wilhelm & Randall Kane. 2005. Working memory span tasks: A methodological review and user's guide. *Psychological Bulletin & Review* 12. 769–786.
East, Martin. 2012. *Task-based language teaching from the teachers' perspectives: Insights from New Zealand*. Philadelphia: John Benjamins.
Ellis, Rod. 2003. *Task-based language learning and teaching*. Oxford: Oxford University Press.
Ellis, Rod. 2008. *The study of second language acquisition*. Oxford: Oxford University Press.
Frawley, William & James Lantolf. 1985. Second language discourse: A Vygotskyan perspective. *Applied Linguistics* 6. 19–44.
Garcia Mayo, María del Pilar (ed.). 2007. *Investing tasks in formal language learning*. Philadelphia: Multilingual Matters.
Garcia Mayo, María del Pilar (ed.). 2015. The interface between task-based language teaching and content-based instruction [Special issue]. *System* 54(3).

García Mayo, María del Pilar, María Junkal Gutierrez Mangado & María Martínez Adrián (eds.). 2013. *Contemporary approaches to second language acquisition*. Philadelphia: John Benjamins.

Jackson, Daniel & Alfred Burch (eds.). forthcoming. Complementary perspectives on task-based classroom realities. [Special issue]. *TESOL Quarterly*.

Lantolf, James. 2006. Sociocultural theory and L2: state of the art. *Studies in Second Language Acquisition* 28(1). 67–109.

Larsen-Freeman, Diane & Lynne Cameron. 2007. *Complex systems and applied linguistics*. Oxford: Oxford University Press.

Long, Michael H. 2015. *Second language acquisition and task-based language teaching*. West Sussex: John Wiley & Sons.

Newton, Jonathan (ed.). 2016. Researching tasks. [Special issue]. *Language Teaching Research* 20(3).

Ortega, Lourdes. 2012. Epistemological diversity and moral ends of research in instructed SLA. *Language Teaching Research* 16(2). 206–226.

Samuda, Virgina & Martin Bygate. 2008. *Tasks in second language learning*. New York: Palgrave McMillan.

Sato, Masatoshi & Susan Ballinger (eds.). 2016. *Peer interaction and second language learning Pedagogical potential and research agenda*. Amsterdam: John Benjamins.

Shehadeh, Ali & Christine A. Coombe (eds.). 2012. *Task-based language teaching in foreign language contexts: Research and implementation*. Philadelphia: John Benjamins.

Swain, Merrill & Susan Lapkin. 1998. Interaction and second language learning: two adolescent French immersion students working together. *The Modern Language Journal* 82. 320–337.

van Compernolle, Remi A & Lawrence Williams. 2013. Sociocultural theory and second language pedagogy. *Language Teaching Research* 17(3). 277–281.

Van den Branden, Kris (ed.). 2006. *Task-based language education: From theory to practice*. Cambridge: Cambridge University Press.

Verspoor, Marjoline, Kees de Bot & Wander Lowie (eds). 2011. *A dynamic approach to second language development*. Philadelphia: John Benjamins.

I Cognitive-Interactionist Perspective

María del Pilar García Mayo, Ainara Imaz Agirre and Agurtzane Azkarai
1 Task Repetition Effects on CAF in EFL Child Task-Based Oral Interaction

1 Introduction

Tasks have been widely used in second language acquisition (SLA) research as relevant tools to explore language learning opportunities available to second/foreign language (L2/FL) learners (García Mayo 2007; Samuda and Bygate 2008). Some of that research has focused on the effects of task repetition on learners' oral production and has shown the benefits of this task implementation variable for subsequent L2 learning (Bygate 2001; Kim and Tracy-Ventura 2013 – but see Kim 2013 for a different view). Research on task repetition has mainly focused on adult and adolescent populations but research with young learners is scarce. Previous SLA research has highlighted the cognitive, social, emotional and contextual factors that make young L2 learners differ from adult L2 learners (see Philp, Oliver and Mackey 2008 for details). Although there are features that occur in adult and child interaction (off-task behaviour, disagreements, etc.), these are qualitatively different and often less confrontational among adults because "children are less bound by the constraints of task conditions in their interaction, as well as by social norms" (Philp, Oliver and Mackey 2008: 8). Clearly, there is a need for detailed descriptions of the characteristics of children's L2 development and of those task implementation features that might enhance their language learning opportunities.

Research on task repetition is scarce and more so in English as a Foreign Language (EFL) settings (Pinter 2007; Shintani 2012, 2014) where exposure to the target language is limited to the classroom. As recently pointed out by Collins and Muñoz (2016), children in EFL contexts are a relevant group to consider. Most European countries have mandated an early exposure to the foreign language and teachers should be informed about valuable pedagogical tools they may want to use to increase their students' chances to improve their competence in the target language in low-input conditions. Two recent studies (Bret

---
María del Pilar García Mayo, Universidad del País Vasco/Euskal Herriko Unibertsitatea (UPV/EHU)
Ainara Imaz Agirre, Mondragon Unibertsitatea (MU)
Agurtzane Azkarai, Universidad del País Vasco/Euskal Herriko Unibertsitatea (UPV/EHU)

Blasco 2014; Sample and Michel 2014) have focused on the impact of task repetition on young learners' oral complexity, accuracy and fluency. They have reported a significant increase of fluency through task repetition but mixed findings regarding complexity and accuracy, which were probably due to the small sample of participants in their studies. The present study is an attempt to shed more light on previous findings by analysing the effects of task repetition on the oral production of a large number (n = 120) of child EFL learners in Spain. Our findings point to a significant impact of task repetition on fluency and accuracy and mixed findings regarding trade-off effects (Skehan 2009) in those two constructs as well.

2 Literature review

Within task-based language teaching there is a growing interest in the potential of pair and small group work (Fernández Dobao 2012) and in the interaction generated when learners complete communicative tasks within those groupings. Research has documented the effect of different task variables on learners' performance and language development and task repetition has been one of the most frequently studied. The potential benefits of task repetition on learners' oral performance have traditionally been explained on the basis of Levelt's (1989) speech production model, proposed for monolingual speakers. According to his model, speech processing proceeds in three overlapping stages. During the *conceptualization stage*, communicative goals/intentions are generated and elaborated in the form of a preverbal message. In the second stage, *formulation*, the preverbal message is translated into linguistic structures, which will be encoded as speech in the third stage, the *articulation stage*. When repeating a task, learners can retrieve traces of the conceptualization stage and, therefore, generating meaning will require less attentional resources and increases in learners' fluency and complexity in oral production will ensue. Ellis (2003) points out that this is so because if learners are familiar with what they have to deal with in a task "they have more processing space available for formulating the language needed to express their ideas" (2003: 246). It is well known that human attentional and processing capacity is restricted and that L2 learners cannot focus on both form and meaning, especially at beginning stages (VanPatten 1990). If learners repeat a task, they are likely to access content more easily and devote time to access formal aspects of the language more effectively.

Although there has been an increase in research on the topic since Bygate's (1996) initial study, it is true that most work has been done on L2 contexts and with adult learners and little has been done on foreign language contexts and with adolescents and children. In what follows, we briefly summarize the main findings of previous work on the topic and identify gaps that need to be addressed by studies to be carried out.

2.1 Task repetition and its effects on general L2 performance

Plough and Gass' (1993) was one of the first studies that analysed the effects of task repetition, in this case on the use of discourse markers and negotiation strategies (Long 1996). Their data came from 18 dyads of adult English as a Second Language (ESL) learners, who were divided on the basis of their familiarity with the task procedure through task repetition (same task, different content). The findings of the study showed that the group familiar with task procedure used more interactional features and fewer interruptions, whereas the group unfamiliar with the task produced more interruptions. Gass, Mackey, Álvarez-Torres and Fernández-García (1999) analysed the production of 103 undergraduate American university students learning Spanish as a Foreign Language. The learners were assigned to three groups, namely, same content group, different content group and a control group. The researchers reported a positive relationship between the repetition of the same exact task and the learners' overall performance, lexical sophistication and morphosyntax (i.e. more accuracy in the use of some of the linguistic targets). These findings were supported by Bygate and Samuda (2005), this time in an ESL setting. In their study the participants were 14 adult learners from different first language (L1) backgrounds and different proficiency levels and they produced more elaborate language the second time they worked on a story. They also narrated more coherent stories and considered different perspectives.

Overall, the above-mentioned studies seem to point to beneficial effects of task repetition on participants' oral production: by repeating a task learners are already familiar with either content or procedure and may devote their processing capacity to a richer (more lexical resources) and more accurate production, or even display more interactional features in their oral output (cf. Plough and Gass 1993). However, studies on the influence of task repetition on young learners' oral production are scarce. In what follows we briefly refer to those which, to the best of our knowledge, have considered the issue in ESL and EFL contexts. Mackey, Kanganas and Oliver (2007) undertook a study with 40 ESL children aged 7.0–8.5 who carried out communicative tasks in pairs. By manipulating familiarity with task procedure and task content, the researchers reported that children familiar with task procedure were able to express ideas and concepts more fluently than learners who were unfamiliar with the procedure. Children unfamiliar with the task were less certain about how to proceed, had a greater incidence of false starts and lexical errors and needed to negotiate with their partner more frequently. Pinter (2007) carried out a study with a pair of 10 year-old Hungarian boys, who repeated similar STD tasks. She assessed the changes from the first to the last repetition and reported that there were obvious benefits even for low-level learners as they moved from less effective to more effective ways of handling the task and from seeing it as a joint game instead of as an individual challenge. More recently, García Mayo and Imaz Agirre (2016) could not find any statistically significant difference between the interactional strategies used by a group of 120 Spanish EFL children (age 8–10) completing a spot-the-difference (STD) task at Time 1 (T1) and Time 2 (T2): neither same task repetition nor procedural repetition increased the frequency of the children's negotiation strategies, actually used to a lesser extent at T2. However, the authors reported more engagement (Storch 2002) among the younger learners at T2, as they used some language-related episodes (LREs) (Swain and Lapkin 1998) and showed interest in task completion.

2.2 Task repetition and complexity, accuracy and fluency (CAF)

This section will briefly review some studies that have considered the impact of task repetition on complexity, accuracy and fluency (CAF), first concentrating on those in ESL/EFL settings with adults to then move to studies in both settings with children as participants.

Bygate (1996) started a line of research whose goal was to analyse the effect of task repetition on oral production. In this first study he used a monologic task (story retelling) and analysed the changes in the production of a single ESL learner when he repeated the task with a 3-day interval. The findings pointed to an increase in fluency and accuracy. Bygate (2001) compared the performance of 48 learners on a narrative and an interview on two occasions with a 10-week interval. He found that task repetition had a significant effect on fluency and complexity but not so on accuracy.

Probably the first study carried out on the effects of task repetition in an EFL setting was Patanasorn (2010). He investigated the effects of procedural, content, and task repetition on accuracy and fluency. A total of 92 adult Thai EFL learners were assigned to three groups: a procedural repetition group, a content repetition, and a task repetition. Each group was given a pre-test, three treatment tasks, an immediate and a delayed post-test, all designed to elicit the past simple tense. The findings of the study showed that there was a clear task effect. Thus, the procedural repetition group improved on the accuracy of the target feature, the content repetition group improved global fluency but accuracy declined, and the task repetition group did not show any major changes. As Kim (2013: 7) observes, Patanasorn's was the first study to examine the effect of task repetition over time using collaborative tasks but he did not focus on the actual learner interaction but, rather, on the outcome of repetition in the three conditions. Ahmadian and Tavakoli (2011) carried out a laboratory study whose main aim was to assess the effects of simultaneous use of careful online planning and task repetition on CAF in the oral production of 60 adult intermediate-level Iranian EFL learners. Their findings pointed to an improvement in CAF when the same exact task was repeated. More recently, Saeedi and Kazerooni (2014) considered whether inherent narrative structure had an impact on the way task repetition influenced CAF. In their study 60 adult Iranian EFL learners recounted a loosely-structured and a tightly-structured narrative. Findings pointed to a clear influence of narrative structure; thus, repeating a loosely–structured narrative benefited the learners' oral complexity and fluency but did not make a significant difference in accuracy, whereas repeating a tightly-structured narrative improved the complexity, accuracy and also fluency.

Also in an EFL context, in this case in Japan, Hawkes (2012) considered task repetition as a post-task activity to direct learners' attention to form. Data obtained from three classes (16–20 students in each) of 13–14 year old students at a private school showed that more attention to form was being placed when the task was repeated. As was the case with Pinter's (2007) pair, the learners were more confident when they carried out the task a second time. Kim and Tracy-Ventura (2013) studied the impact of task and procedural repetition on Korean's EFL learners' development of L2 performance when carrying out collaborative tasks. The participants in their study were 36 13-year old female Korean students, who were divided into a task repetition and a procedural repetition group. After analysing the learners' oral production on a pre-test and two post-tests in terms of CAF, the findings showed that procedural repetition promoted syntactic complexity. None of the groups featured differences in accuracy and fluency decreased in the last post-test in both.

More recently, two studies, Sample and Michel (2014) and Bret Blasco (2014) considered CAF from the perspective of Skehan's Trade-off Hypothesis (Skehan 1998, 2009). Skehan's proposal is based on the assumption that humans' attentional capacity is limited and, therefore, how attentional resources are divided during L2 performance will depend on task characteristics. He claims that performance in CAF "entails competition for attentional resources (1998: 168), in other words, attention devoted to one of the members of the CAF triad may trigger a negative impact on another. Sample and Michel (2014) reported on an exploratory study which considered the performance of six young learners (mean age 9.5) over three repetitions of a STD task within three weeks with the aim of establishing the interrelations between CAF. The children worked with an original base picture, which was slightly modified for each of the performances (i.e. other differences were introduced). According to the authors, the design required the learners to consider the same problem and type of language within each task. Sample and Michel's findings supported earlier work on task repetition and its positive impact on fluency but mixed findings were reported for complexity and accuracy. The authors concluded that "by the third performance [...] these trade-off effects disappeared, suggesting that as the students became familiar with the task they were able to focus their attention on all three CAF areas simultaneously (2014:43)". A qualitative analysis of the data led the authors to conclude that learner cooperation increased with task repetition, there was more negotiation and knowledge co-construction. Besides, task repetition appeared to positively influence learners' motivation and confidence.

Bret Blasco (2014) analysed oral data from 52 learners (age 9–10 at the study onset), 20 enrolled in a mainstream EFL program (3.50 hours/week of EFL instruction) and 32 in a Content and Language Integrated (CLIL) program (Dalton-Puffer 2011) (1 hour CLIL/week + 3.50 hours/week EFL instruction). The data from an interview (with seven questions related to the learners' families, personal lives and routines) and a picture-elicited narrative (six pictures of a mother with her two children and a dog preparing food for a picnic) were collected at four points in time (T0, T1, T2 and T3) over a two-year period – every six months. The findings showed that both groups of learners featured a constant improvement of syntactic complexity and fluency from T0 to T3. Accuracy, however, displayed a gradual decrease throughout the four data collection times. According to Bret Blasco "these findings confirm Skehan and Foster's (Extended) Trade-off Hypothesis (2012) which claims that greater fluency will be accompanied by greater accuracy or complexity (but not both) due to the fact that attentional resources are limited and, thus, high levels of complexity, accuracy, and fluency are unlikely to take place simultaneously (2014: 339)".

As this brief review of previous studies on the effects of task repetition on CAF measures has shown, there seems to be some positive influence of task repetition on the three constructs but with clear trade-off effects. Besides, other variables such as the type of task repetition, task type, narrative structure and time from first to last task performance seem to be playing an important role in the learners' performance.

3 The present study

The main goal of the present study is to investigate the extent to which task repetition impacts CAF in the oral production of young Spanish EFL learners. As, to the best of our knowledge, only Sample and Michel (2014) and Bret Blasco

(2014) have addressed this topic with young EFL learners, we were interested in considering whether a much larger population sample than the one in their studies would support or refute their findings. Besides, we also wanted to consider whether different types of task repetition might affect CAF in the same way they did in Patanasorn's (2010) study with EFL adult learners. The two research questions we entertained were the following:
1. Do same task and procedural task repetition impact CAF in the oral production of young EFL learners during task performance?
2. Is there any trade-off effect among the three CAF measures at each testing time?

3.1 Participants

One hundred and twenty (n = 120) EFL children, paired in 60 dyads, participated in this study. Fifty-four (n = 54) children (36 males, 18 females) were in 3rd year primary (8–9 years old) (mean age = 8) and 66 children (44 males/22 females) in 4th year primary (9–10 years old) (mean age = 9.02). All of them attended a semi-private school in a major city in Spain and had started learning English at the age of 4. They received five hours of instruction in English per week, two of mainstream EFL classes and three of Science in English, as they were following a CLIL program. Participants completed the Young Learners of English Starters Cambridge Test, which determined that they were all beginner-level learners.

3.2 Task and procedure

Before the actual data collection procedure started, the researchers obtained written permission both from the school headmaster and teachers and from the children's parents. Data collection was carried out at two points in time. At Time 1 (henceforth T1) all participants completed a STD task. All the participants were at the same proficiency level, and were paired up randomly. As for the type of task, the STD task, which they had used in their foreign language classes, was chosen because previous work has claimed that it fosters collaborative work as each participant in the pair needs to exchange part of the information they hold in order to complete the task (Pica, Kang and Sauro 2006). Furthermore, the tasks were agreed upon between teachers and researchers and followed the criteria specified in Ellis (2009): the children focused on meaning, there was a gap in their knowledge (each member of the dyad had to identify the differences in the other member's drawing), the children had to rely on their linguistic resources and there was clear outcome of the task other than the use of language.

As Table 1 shows, at T1, all participants completed the same task: 'the cowboy task'. This task included a picture of a cowboy in a desert surrounded by different items, such as a snake, a vulture, a cactus or a palm tree. These items and the cowboy's clothes differed and learners had to guess what those differences were. The only element that distinguished the task completed by 3rd and 4th year learners was the number of differences in each drawing, five differences for the former and eight differences for the latter. At T2, three months later, 21 dyads (eleven in 3rd year, ten in 4th year) repeated exactly the same task in the 'same task repetition condition', that is, they repeated both the same procedure and the same content. Sixteen (n = 16) dyads (five in 3rd year and eleven in 4th year) repeated the same type of task but with different content in the 'procedural task repetition' condition. In this case the drawing showed a boy laying on a green field next to a rock. There were elements surrounding the boy such as flowers and birds. Again, there were differences in the number of certain flowers, or different animals, and the boy's clothes. Finally, 23 dyads (eleven in 3rd year and twelve in 4th year) completed a totally different task, a guessing game. For this task, learners had to choose a card and describe it. The options were a hamburger, a monkey, Bart Simpson, Spiderman, Harry Potter and an apple.

Table 1: Procedure of task completion at both testing times

Year	Time 1	Time 2	Dyad number
3rd	Spot-the-differences task (5 differences)	Task repetition group (STD Cowboy)	11
		Procedural repetition group (STD Boy)	5
		Control group (Guessing game)	11
4th	Spot-the-differences task (8 differences)	Task repetition group (STD Cowboy)	10
		Procedural repetition group (STD Boy)	11
		Control group (Guessing game)	12

3.3 Measures

The video-recorded oral production of the children (approximately 17 hours) was transcribed in CHILDES (McWhinney 2000). All c-units, "utterances (i.e. words, phrases or sentences, grammatical or ungrammatical) which provided referential or pragmatic meaning" were coded following Foster, Tonkyn and Wigglesworth (2000). This measure was chosen considering participants' level of English and age range.

Different studies have used different measures to assess CAF. Ellis (2005, 2008) provides a fairly comprehensive list of such measures. He also points out that using multiple measures to assess each dimension of language performance may result in a more valid assessment but that using different measures by different researchers may decrease the comparability of the results obtained. In this study, to enhance both the validity of the assessments and the comparability of the results, we decided to adapt some of the measures used by Wendel (1997), Yuan and Ellis (2003) and Ellis and Yuan (2004). In what follows we briefly describe such measures.

Complexity measures: the first measure was *syntactic complexity*, where we considered the amount of coordination. This was measured considering the ratio of clauses to c-units in participants' production. The rationale behind choosing coordination units rather than subordination was learners' proficiency level. As it was low, participants could not produce subordinate sentences. Therefore, the use of coordinated units was interpreted to be a more complex production (Bret Blasco 2014). A second complexity measure was *syntactic variety*, where we counted the total number of different grammatical verb forms used in participants' performances. The forms we considered were tense (e.g. simple present, simple past, etc.), modality (e.g. should, must, etc.) and subject-verb agreement. The final complexity measure was *lexical complexity*. We measured participants' lexical variety with the D value (Jarvis 2002). Only the first 50 items produced by each child were measured.

Accuracy measures: these were counted as the percentage of the clauses that were not erroneous (henceforth error-free clauses). All syntactic, morphological and lexical errors were taken into consideration.

Fluency measures: two rates were considered A, and B. For rate A we counted the number of syllables produced per minute of speech. This was measured considering the number of syllables within each narrative, divided by the number of seconds used to complete the task. In the case of rate B we counted the number of meaningful syllables per minute of speech. In order to measure this, we followed the same procedure as with rate A, but in this case we excluded all syllables, words, phrases that were repeated, reformulated, or replaced.

Moreover, task completion scores were calculated. A maximum score of five was given to 3rd year dyads, and of eight to 4th year dyads, as those were the number of differences in their respective drawings.

4 Results

Our first research question addressed the issue of whether same task repetition and procedural task repetition would impact CAF in the oral production of

Table 2: Descriptive statistics. 3rd year primary EFL children

Measure		Group	Time 1				Time 2			
			Mean	SD	Min.	Max.	Mean	SD	Min.	Max.
Complexity	Clauses/CU	Same	1.45	3.17	0	11.11	1.55	1.45	0	1.55
		Procedural	1.58	3.11	0	9.67	0.23	0.07	0	0.23
		Control	2.18	4.25	0	10.34	1.10	0.47	0	1.10
	D	Same	19.12	8.37	3.33	35.33	15.94	7.01	5.48	33.24
		Procedural	19.91	9.01	4.82	31.29	16.76	7.67	6.34	24.44
		Control	15.79	7.48	9.11	29.34	22.70	8.30	4.34	27.53
Accuracy	Error-free CU	Same	66.54	4.5	61.43	70.64	68.50	4.23	64.54	72
		Procedural	84.54	3.4	81.43	79.45	81.32	3.42	78.43	82
		Control	68.67	2.4	66	70	69.43	5.60	74.33	79.10
Fluency	Rate A	Same	12.15	4.07	4.32	16.56	13.88	5.31	8.45	32.42
		Procedural	13.73	5.12	4.53	24.43	22.72	9.15	14.55	36.65
		Control	14.45	5.43	3.24	32.44	13.13	6.07	3.56	24.55
	Rate B	Same	10.83	4.89	5.45	24.22	12.34	6.07	6.43	25.23
		Procedural	12.33	5.45	6.34	31.42	21.12	10.07	14.45	52.22
		Control	9.48	4.58	5.53	24.55	10.04	6.07	13.24	32.43
Completion scores		Same	3	0.57	2	3	3	0.64	3	4
		Procedural	4	0.10	4	5	5	0.56	4	5
		Control	3.20	1.32	2	4	1.54	0.32	1	2

young EFL learners while they completed a STD task. The transcribed data were submitted to Wilcoxon Signed Ranks tests to identify any statistically significant differences ($\alpha = .05$). Non-parametric tests were used due to the sample size in some of the groups. Tables 2 and 3 display the descriptive statistics of CAF measures in the production of 3rd and 4th year primary learners, respectively.

Lexical complexity in the production of 3rd year children decreased significantly from T1 to T2 in the task repetition group ($z = 2.094$; $p = .036$), whereas in the control condition children used a wider range of lexical items at T2 ($z = 2.334$; $p = .020$). Regarding syntactic complexity, learners in the task repetition condition as well as in the control condition produced significantly fewer coordinated units: task repetition condition: ($z = 2.028$; $p = .043$); control condition: ($z = 2.366$; $p = .018$) at T2. In the 4th year group, lexical ($z = 3.229$; $p = .001$) and syntactic complexity ($z = 2.638$; $p = .020$) increased in the control condition.

Regarding accuracy, a comparison between T1 and T2 showed that the only children who produced more error-free units at T2 were those in 4th year in the procedural repetition group ($z = 2.321$; $p = .020$). The analyses for fluency revealed that 3rd year learners were more fluent in the procedural repetition condition

Table 3: Descriptive statistics. 4th year primary EFL children

Measure		Group	Time 1				Time 2			
			Mean	SD	Min.	Max.	Mean	SD	Min.	Max.
Complexity	Clauses/CU	Same	0.82	1.82	0	5.55	0.97	1.79	0	4.87
		Procedural	0.45	1.31	0	5.55	0.40	1.78	0	3.33
		Control	0.57	1.62	0	5.88	2.86	3.37	0	8.88
	D	Same	19.16	7.79	7.74	30.92	18.59	6.94	11.27	26.95
		Procedural	18.32	7.91	9.65	34.12	20.95	9.71	9.63	33.04
		Control	20.60	8.72	11.19	36.61	29.58	11.91	15.48	34.84
Accuracy	Error-free CU	Same	65	17.50	41.02	95.65	67,68	18.97	35.29	82.05
		Procedural	48.91	13.80	28.57	70.37	59,57	12.85	48.38	92.14
		Control	57.71	14.52	43.75	86.04	61,71	17.03	45	69.23
Fluency	Rate A	Same	15.18	5.51	14.83	21.60	13.47	4.38	7.26	20.56
		Procedural	16.05	7.55	5.72	35.73	13.60	4.43	9.82	23.73
		Control	16.32	7.23	8.49	24.49	12.60	3.71	8.20	16.23
	Rate B	Same	11.08	5.06	4.76	16.81	10.87	5.10	3.08	15.30
		Procedural	12.05	7.24	3.65	20.66	11.46	5.65	9.40	23.73
		Control	11.95	7.41	4.70	20.86	11.68	3.92	8.20	13.46
Completion scores		Same	3.63	0.57	3	4	4.42	0.64	4	4
		Procedural	4.01	0.10	4	5	5.53	0.56	4	7
		Control	3.98	1.32	3	5	1.28	0.32	1	2

($z = 2.803$; $p = .005$) at T2. All other comparisons yielded statistically non-significant results. Table 4 summarizes our findings:

Table 4: Impact of task repetition on CAF measures at T2

		Complexity		Accuracy	Fluency
		Syntactic	Lexical		
Year 3	Same	Decrease	Decrease	=	=
	Procedural	=	=	=	Increase
	Control	Decrease	Increase	=	=
Year 4	Same	=	=	=	=
	Procedural	=	=	Increase	=
	Control	Increase	Increase	=	=

The second research question focused on trade-off effects between the different dimensions of task performance (Skehan 2009). Spearman correlational analyses between measures of complexity (lexical: D value; syntactic: clauses/C unit and words/C unit), accuracy (total number of errors/C unit) and fluency (number of filled pauses/C unit, words/minute, completion time) as well as the completion score (number of differences spotted) were performed ($\alpha = 0.05$). Given that the procedural repetition group in 3rd year was comprised of only five dyads, these findings need to be interpreted with caution.

The production of each group was analysed individually in order to examine trade-off effects at each testing time. At T1, no significant correlation effects were found between task completion and CAF measures. In contrast, at T2 CAF measures revealed interesting results with regard to task completion. The production of the 3rd year learners who repeated exactly the same task (same procedure, same content) displayed negative correlation effects in lexical ($r_s = -.80$; $p = .007$) and syntactic ($r_s = -.76$; $p = .012$) complexity. That is, those learners who had more difficulties in completing the task and could not spot all the differences were those who used a more varied range of lexical items as well as more coordinated units. In the control group (guessing game task), strong positive correlation effects were found for lexical complexity ($r_s = .84$; $p = .001$): those dyads that completed the task used more varied lexical items. In the production of 4th year learners, however, an opposite correlation effect ($r_s = .77$; $p = .023$) was found. Participants with lower task completion rates used a wider vocabulary range. Regarding the use of coordinated units, negative correlation effects were found for syntactic complexity in 3rd year ($r_s = -.82$; $p = .001$) and 4th year ($r_s = -.75$; $p = .030$).

In the procedural repetition groups, that is, those groups who repeated the same task procedure but with different content, significant correlation effects were found between fluency and task completion ($r_s = .86$; $p = .001$) in 3rd year and error-free clauses and task completion ($r_s = .79$; $p = .011$) in 4th year. Our findings indicated that those dyads who found most (or all) differences were the most fluent participants in 3rd year and the ones who made fewer errors in 4th year.

5 Discussion

The main goal of this study was to assess the potential impact of task repetition on CAF in the oral production of 120 EFL children who completed the same STD task at T1 and who either repeated the very same task or carried out a procedural task repetition (same task type, different content) at T2. The only significant differences on CAF measures upon task repetition were found in the procedural repetition group regarding fluency among 3rd year learners and accuracy among 4th year learners. However, no significant benefits could be reported for lexical or syntactic complexity, which actually decreased in the task repetition condition in 3rd year. As mentioned above, the children participating in this study repeated the task once after a 3-month interval. In Bret Blasco's (2014) study, also carried out in a classroom setting, the children repeated the task three times with a six-month interval. When reviewing research in which participants repeat tasks, one should consider that there is a great deal of variation not only in the number of repetitions (four in Gass et al. (1999), eleven in Ahmadian (2011)) but also in the repetition intervals (from one week in Sample and Mitchel to ten weeks in Bygate (2001) and six months in Bret Blasco (2014)). It is important then that our data partially corroborate findings in the two recent studies (Bret Blasco (2014) and Sample and Michel (2014)) with EFL children repeating a task in the sense that task repetition seems to have a different impact on each of the CAF measures.

A possible explanation for why there was a decrease in complexity, both lexical and syntactic, among 3rd year learners in the task repetition condition at T2 could be that, even after three months, the children were able to recall both procedure and the lexical items they needed and, thus, could complete the task using shorter and more direct utterances, which were also less syntactically complex. Most children seemed to be very motivated with the tasks but, at this point, we can only speculate that it was that motivation that allowed them to recall both the tasks and the vocabulary needed. Examples (1) and (2) below display excerpts of the first minute of interaction by the same dyad at T1 and at T2. As can be observed, c-units are longer at T1 and both children seem to be more interested in task completion, both of them asking questions even when one of them, Child B, acknowledges that the lexical item his partner needs (*snake*, *cactus*) is not in his drawing. He shows his interest in locating where the element is (*where is the snake*? / *where is the cactus*?) to make sure that, in fact, it is not in his drawing. At T2, however, turns are shorter and the overall impression is that both members want to finish the task soon because they remember the items they are looking for.

Example (1)
Child B: no.
Child A: there is a snake in your picture?
Child B: no.
Child B: where is the snake?
Child A: next to the [/] to the person.
Child B: have you got a cactus in your picture?
Child A: no.
Child A: where is the cactus?

Child B: under the hand of the [/] of the pers [/] of the person.
Child B: have you got two (.) how do you say in English flechas@spa?
Child A: yes, I've got.
Child A: the person has got next to the.
Child A: what do you say palmera@spa?
Child B: I don't know.   (Dyad 3_Group A. T1)

Example (2)
Child A: you has got a snake?
Child B: no.
Child B: has you got two cloudy?
Child A: yes.
Child A: has you got a what do you a palmera@spa?.
Child B: I don't know but no.
Child A: where is the palmera@spa?.
Child B: is next to the person.
Child B: how do you say in English fleche@spa?.
Child A: I don't know.   (Dyad 3_Group A.T2)

Our second research question addressed the issue of whether there were any trade-off effects among CAF measures triggered by task repetition. Our data revealed different findings for each of the two experimental groups and for the control group. In the procedural repetition group, positive correlation effects were found between fluency in 3rd year and accuracy in 4th year and task completion. These findings indicated that the dyads that spotted the largest number of differences were the most fluent in 3rd year and the most accurate ones in 4th year. As pointed out by Mackey et al. (2007) 'learning the task discourse', that is, being familiar with task procedure positively affected fluency and accuracy in each of the groups but complexity, whether lexical or syntactic, was not affected. As was the case with adult participants in ESL settings, Pinter (2005, 2007) and Sample and Michel (2014) also pointed out that children who were familiar with the task could organize it more effectively, thus benefiting fluency and accuracy. Our findings in the procedural repetition group seem to corroborate previous research in the sense that young learners who are familiar with the procedure of the task, even though its content is different, display significant gains in fluency and accuracy. Our findings also seem to support Skehan's Trade-off Hypothesis since learners devote their attention to one of the CAF measures at the expense of the other two.

Moreover, in the interaction between task completion scores and CAF measures, age seems to be a relevant factor since 3rd year learners show trade-off effects in fluency, whereas 4th year learners display those effects in accuracy. This was not the case in the task repetition group, though. Negative correlation effects were found for lexical and syntactic complexity when learners completed a task with the same procedure and content, thus indicating that when learners repeated the very same task their lexical richness decreased and fewer coordinated units were used. It seems that learners who obtained the highest task completion rates used fewer lexical items and coordinated units in comparison to children who did not complete the whole task. High achiever dyads, that is, those who completed the task, systematically targeted the differences already spotted at T1, whereas low achiever dyads had to resort to a wider variety of lexical items to find all the differences. Findings seem to indicate that language was used more effectively by high achievers who provided the essential information in order to complete the task.

In the control condition correlation effects were only found between lexical complexity and task completion. Third year learners that completed the task used a wider range of vocabulary whereas 4th year learners used fewer lexical items. Younger learners were more talkative and engaged when completing the task than 4th year participants (García Mayo and Imaz Agirre, 2016) probably because the task was more motivating for them. As no motivation questionnaire was administered, this statement is speculative at this point. Our findings indicated that learners mainly focused on content rather than on form. However, the differences in terms of positive and negative correlation effects in each age group could be explained on the basis of the easiness of the task for the older group or the lack of engagement of this group.

6 Conclusion

This exploratory study aimed at investigating the effect of two types of task repetition, namely same task repetition, and procedural repetition, on CAF measures in the oral production of young EFL learners while they completed a STD task. Our findings seem to indicate that, for this group of young EFL learners, procedural task repetition positively impacts fluency and accuracy at T2. Specifically, participants in 3rd year were more fluent, whereas learners in 4th year were more accurate. The different outcomes in each measure and in each age group provided evidence in favor of Skehan's Trade-off hypothesis and were in line with recent work on the effect of task repetition and CAF on young learners' oral production. Moreover, task completion seems to be a strong predictor of fluency and accuracy outcomes. We see this study as a contribution to the topic of the impact of task repetition on the oral production of a foreign language, English, among a group of young learners in a low-input context in which teachers welcome advice on any task that may help improve their student's foreign language competence.

We are aware of the limitations of the study but all of them can be considered as lines for further research. Thus, because of the difficulty in accessing real classrooms, the time interval between the two task performances was longer than usual in most task repetition research (but see Bygate (2001) and Bret Blasco (2014)). Further research should consider whether a shorter time interval would lead to different results. As mentioned above, although our database is comprised of 120 participants, one of the groups, the 3rd year procedural repetition group, has only data from five dyads and, therefore, our findings should be considered with care. Future studies should aim at having the same number of pairs in the different groups. Another issue worth of further research is to widen the age gap of the participants. In the current study there was only one-year gap between the children and that might have made it difficult to assess significant changes. On a different front, studies should be carried out considering whether children's motivation toward task repetition might play a role in how they complete the task. The impact of task repetition should also be explored from a more qualitative and microgenetic perspective as we might find out that upon repetition young learners develop cooperative strategies that will foster positive attitudes towards foreign language learning.

Acknowledgement

We gratefully acknowledge the funding from research grants FFI2012-32212 (Spanish Ministry of Economy and Competitiveness) and IT904-16 (Basque Government). We also express our sincere thanks to the school that allowed us to gather the data reported in this chapter and to the children who participated in the study.

References

Ahmadian, Mohammad Javad & Mansoor Tavakoli. 2011. The effects of simultaneous use of careful online planning and task repetition on accuracy, fluency, and complexity of EFL learners' oral production. *Language Teaching Research* 15(1). 35–59.

Bret Blasco, Anna. 2014. *L2 English young learners' oral production skills in CLIL and EFL settings: A longitudinal study.* Barcelona: Universitat Autònoma de Barcelona dissertation.

Bygate, Martin. 1996. Effects of task repetition: Appraising the developing language of learners. In Jane Willis & Dave Willis (eds.), *Challenge and change in language teaching*, 136–146. Oxford: Heinemann.

Bygate, Martin. 2001. Effects of task repetition on the structure and control of language. In Martin Bygate, Peter Skehan & Merrill Swain (eds.), *Researching pedagogic tasks: Second language learning, teaching and testing*, 23–48. Harlow: Longman.

Bygate, Martin & Virginia Samuda. 2005. Integrative planning through the use of task repetition. In Rod Ellis (ed.), *Planning and task performance in a second language*, 34–74. Amsterdam: John Benjamins.

Collins, Laura & Carmen Muñoz. 2016. The foreign language classroom: Current perspectives and future considerations. *The Modern Language Journal* 100. 133–147.

Dalton-Puffer, Christiane. 2011. Content and language integrated learning: From practice to principles? *Annual Review of Applied Linguistics* 31. 182–204.

Ellis, Rod. 2003. *Task-based language learning and teaching*. Oxford: Oxford University Press

Ellis, Rod. 2005. Planning and task-based performance: Theory and research. In Rod Ellis (ed.), *Planning and task performance in second language*, 3–34. Amsterdam: John Benjamins.

Ellis, Rod. 2008. *The study of second language acquisition*. Oxford: Oxford University Press.

Ellis, Rod. 2009. Task-based language teaching: Sorting out the misunderstandings. *International Journal of Applied Linguistics* 19. 221–246.

Ellis, Rod & Fangyuan Yuan. 2004. The effects of planning on fluency, complexity, and accuracy in second language narrative writing. *Studies in Second Language Acquisition* 26. 59–84.

Fernández Dobao, Ana. 2012. Collaborative writing tasks in the L2 classroom: Comparing group, pair, and individual work. *Journal of Second Language Writing* 21(1). 40–58.

Foster, Pauline, Anton Tonkyn & Gillian Wigglesworth. 2000. Measuring spoken language: A unit for all reasons. *Applied Linguistics* 21. 353–375.

García Mayo, M.P. 2007. Investigating tasks in formal language learning. Clevedon: Multilingual Matters.

García Mayo, M.P. and Imaz Agirre, A. 2016. Task repetition and its impact on EFL children's negotiation of meaning strategies and pair dynamics. An exploratory study. *The Language Learning Journal* 44. 451–466.

Gass, Susan M., Alison Mackey, María José Álvarez-Torres & Marisol Fernández-García. 1999. The effects of task repetition on linguistic output. *Language Learning* 49. 549–580.

Hawkes, Martin L. 2012. Using task repetition to direct learner attention and focus on form. *English Language Teaching* 66. 327–336.

Jarvis, Scott. 2002. Short texts, best-fitting curves and new measures of lexical diversity. *Language Testing* 19(1). 57–84.

Kim, YouJin. 2013. Promoting attention to form through task repetition in a Korean EFL context. In Kim McDonough & Alison Mackey (eds.), *Second language interaction in diverse educational settings*, 3–24. Philadelphia, PA: John Benjamins.

Kim, YouJin. & Nicole Tracy-Ventura. 2013. The role of task repetition in L2 performance development: What needs to be repeated during task-based interaction? *System* 41. 829–840.

Levelt, William. 1989. *Speaking: From intention to articulation*. Cambridge, MA: MIT Press.

Long, Michael H. 1996. The role of linguistic environment in second language acquisition. In William C. Ritchie & Tej K. Bhatia (eds.), *Handbook of research on language acquisition*, 413–468. New York: Academic Press.

Mackey, Alison, Alec Peter Kanganas & Rhonda Oliver. 2007. Task familiarity and interactional feedback in child ESL classrooms. *TESOL Quarterly* 41. 285–312.

McWhinney, Brian. 2000. *The CHILDES project: tools for analyzing talk*. Mahwah, NJ: Lawrence Erlbaum Associates.
Patanasorn, Chomraj. 2010. *Effects of procedural content and task repetition on accuracy and fluency in an EFL context*. Flagstaff: Northern Arizona University dissertation.
Philp, Jenefer, Rhonda Oliver & Alison Mackey (eds.). 2008. *Second language acquisition and the younger learner. Child's play?* Amsterdam: John Benjamins.
Pica, Teresa, Hyun-Sook Kang & Shannon Sauro. 2006. Information gap tasks: Their multiple roles and contributions to interaction research methodology. *Studies in Second Language Acquisition* 28. 301–338.
Pinter, Annamaria. 2005. Task repetition with 10-year-old children. In Corony Edwards & Jane Willis (eds.), *Teachers exploring tasks in English language teaching*, 113–126. London: Palgrave Macmillan.
Pinter, Annamaria. 2007. Some benefits of peer-peer interaction: 10-year old children practicing with a communication task. *Language Teaching Research* 11. 189–207.
Plough, India & Susan Gass. 1993. Interlocutor and task familiarity: Effects on interactional structure. In Graham Crookes & Susan Gass (eds.), *Language learning: Integrating theory and practice*, 35–56. Philadelphia: Multilingual Matters.
Saeedi, Masoud & Shirin Rahimi Kazerooni. 2014. The influence of task repetition and task structure on EFL learners' oral narrative retellings. *Innovation in Language Learning and Teaching* 8(2). 116–131.
Sample, Evelyn & Marije Michel. 2014. An exploratory study into trade-off effects of complexity, accuracy and fluency in young learners' oral task repetition. *TESL Canada Journal* 31. 23–46.
Samuda, Virginia & Martin Bygate. 2008 *Tasks in second language learning*. Basingstoke: Palgrave Macmillan.
Shintani, Natsuko. 2012. Repeating input-based tasks with young beginner learners. *RELC Journal* 43(1). 39–51.
Shintani, Natsuko. 2014. Using tasks with young beginner learners: The role of the teacher. *Innovation in Language Learning and Teaching* 8(3). 279–294.
Skehan, Peter. 1998. *A cognitive approach to language learning*. Oxford: Oxford University Press.
Skehan, Peter. 2009. Modelling second language performance: Integrating complexity, accuracy, fluency, and lexis. *Applied Linguistics* 30(4). 510–532.
Skehan, Peter & Pauline Foster. 2012. Complexity, accuracy and lexis in task-based performance. A synthesis of the Ealing research. In Alex Housen, Folkert Kuiken & Ineke Vedder (eds.), *Dimensions of L2 performance and proficiency: Complexity, accuracy and fluency*, 199–220. Amsterdam: John Benjamins.
Storch, Neomy. 2002. Patterns of interaction in ESL pair work. *Language Learning* 5. 119–158.
Swain, Merrill & Sharon Lapkin. 1998. Interaction and second language learning: Two adolescent French immersion students working together. *The Modern Language Journal* 82. 320–337.
VanPatten, Bill. 1990. Attending to form and content in the input. *Studies in Second Language Acquisition* 12. 287–301.
Wendel, J. 1997. *Planning and second language narrative production*. Unpublished doctoral dissertation, Temple University, Japan.
Yuan, Fangyuan & Rod Ellis. 2003. The effect of pre-task planning and online planning on fluency, complexity, and accuracy in L2 oral production. *Applied Linguistics* 24. 1–27.

Zhisheng (Edward) Wen
2 Using Formulaic Sequences to Measure Task Performance: The Role of Working Memory

1 Introduction

In the realms of second language acquisition (SLA), research into task-based language teaching (TBLT) has made significant progress in recent decades (Long, 2015). Within TBLT research streams, task planning and performance has occupied a unique position gathering increasing enthusiasm among SLA scholars since the seminal paper by Rod Ellis (1987). So far, significant progress has been made on both theoretical and methodological fronts (Bygate, 2015). In terms of the theoretical framework, for example, Rod Ellis' taxonomy of planning (e.g., offering L2 learners the opportunity to prepare for completing the task; 2005 and 2009) is quite firmly established as an operational framework, in which he conceptualizes that task planning conditions can be implemented via (a) pretask or strategic task planning, (b) online planning and (c) task repetition and/ or task rehearsal Meanwhile, on the methodological fronts, TBLT researchers have generally followed Peter Skehan's (1998; Skehan and Foster, 1997, 1999) tri-partite taxonomy to assess participants' L2 task performance under the three dimensions of (a) fluency, (b) accuracy, and (c) complexity; which becomes increasingly known as the 'CAF' framework (Ellis and Barkhuizen, 2005; Housen and Kuiken 2009; Housen, Kuiken, and Vedder 2012).

Despite these obvious achievements, however, task planning and performance research is still beset with many unresolved issues concerning both theoretical underpinnings and methodology paradigms (e.g., Révész, 2014). To begin with methodology, the existing list of specific measures to be adopted under each dimension of the 'CAF' framework indexing L2 task performance is far from exhaustive and definitive. As such, continued efforts are being made to either refine existing measures (e.g., Gilabert, 2007; Ortega and Norris, 2009), or to add new members to the list. For example, Skehan (2009) has added a 'lexical dimension' (i.e., Lambda) to the CAF taxonomy and thus argued for an expanded 'CAFL' framework. Recently, Bei (2011) and Wen (2016a) also included a measure of 'formality index' (i.e., FI) to the existing CAFL framework. Table 1 lists all these

Zhisheng (Edward) Wen, Macao Polytechnic Institute

old and new task performance measures together with their descriptions and specific indices.

Table 1: Existing L2 Task Performance Measures (Based on Wen, 2016a)

Measures	Specific Indices	Description
Fluency	words per minute (WPM)	Total number of words produced divided by total number of minutes
Accuracy	Error-free clauses (Accu)	Percentage of error-free clauses over the total number of all clauses in all AS units
Complexity	Syntactic complexity (Complex)	Ratio of subordinate clauses to the total number of AS units
Lexis	Lexical D (D); Llambda	Based on a mathematical formula that corrected for sample size (as opposed to the simple Type-Token-Ratio)
Stylistic variations	Formality Index	Formality = (noun freq. + adj. freq. + art. freq. − pron. freq. − verb freq. − adv. freq. − interjection freq. + 100) /2.

Key: freq. = frequency, adj. = adjective, art. = article, pron. = pronoun, adv. = adverb

Notwithstanding, there are still other possibilities for adding new measures to index L2 task performance. More relevantly, as I will argue in this chapter, previous and existing measures of L2 task performance have failed to give adequate consideration to the *developmental* aspects of participants' L2 proficiency and in particular, to the fact that most participants in typical task planning studies belong to either intermediate or post-intermediate proficiency levels (but not L2 beginners, for practical reasons of completing the task). To that effect, I will further argue that *formulaic sequences* (FSs), that is, the multi-word units/chunks produced by L2 learners (e.g., while retelling narrative tasks), may serve as a useful index for measuring L2 task-based speech performance and therefore can be incorporated into future TBLT research of task performance (also see Nguyen and Larsen-Freeman, this volume for advocating using tasks to teach formulaic sequences).

In terms of theoretical aspects then, a thorny issue in L2 task planning and performance research relates to the on-going debate on the implicated cognitive mechanisms underlying observable variations in L2 learners' task-based performance. Towards this goal, two major theoretical proposals have been available in current TBLT literature (Bygate, 2015). On the one hand, Skehan (1998, 2014, 2015) subscribes to a '*limited attention capacity*' (LAC) hypothesis that portrays the competition for limited cognitive resources that can be simultaneously allocated to different performance areas during task execution, thus postulating trade-off relationships between them (e.g., in particular, the see-saw effects between complexity and accuracy in L2 task performance). Alternatively, Robinson (2011, 2015) hypothesized in his 'cognition hypothesis' that different dimensions of task performance (e.g., complexity, accuracy, and fluency) may all be improved if the cognitive demands of a certain task are complex enough to push for such increment all round.

These two contrastive positions in TBLT have remained disparate, giving rise to the '*Trade-off vs. Cognition*" debate in current TBLT, as demonstrated in the two chapters in Bygate (2015). To help resolve this dispute, in this chapter I will opt for a third approach to explaining variations in L2 task performance instead, by proposing a working memory (WM) perspective on interpreting the cognitive mechanisms underlying L2 task planning and performance. The major thrust is to illuminate possible effects of distinctive WM components and functions, independently or in combination with task planning conditions (in particular, pre-task planning), on the production of L2 formulaic sequences during narrative task performance by L2 speakers at an intermediate level of English as a foreign language (EFL) or above.

To reiterate, drawing upon these recent developments in SLA and TBLT, the current chapter aims to push further into L2 task planning and performance research into two new directions, with dual objectives of advancing both its theoretical underpinnings and its methodological paradigms. First of all, in terms of measuring L2 task performance, the chapter argues for incorporating formulaic sequences (FSs) as an additional dimension into the current 'CAFL' framework. Second, it proposes to conceptualize and operationalize cognitive mechanisms underlying L2 task performance from a WM perspective couched within the postulations of the Phonological/Executive model of WM in SLA (Wen, 2012, 2014a, 2015, 2016b). Then in light of these two arguments, the chapter reports preliminary results from an exploratory investigation into the main and interaction effects between WM and pre-task planning on different dimensions of L2 formulaic sequences produced by EFL learners during retelling of narrative tasks. The chapter concludes by further outlining the theoretical and methodological implications of the study's results and findings within the broader context of TBLT.

2 Measuring formulaic sequences as L2 task performance

2.1 An overview of research into formulaic sequences in SLA

In recent years, considerable research in the multiple fields of phraseology, corpus linguistics and (developmental) psychology has pointed out that formulaic sequences (FSs) are pervasive in first and second language (N. Ellis, 2012; N. Ellis et al., 2015; Erman and Warren 2000; Foster 2001; Moon 1998; Nattinger and DeCarrico 1992; Schmitt and Carter 2004; Wood, 2015), and that they serve many important functions in L2 learners' interlanguage development in terms of how the target language is *acquired*, *processed* and *used* (Schmitt and Carter, 2004; Weinert, 1995; Wen, 2014b; Wray, 2000 and 2002; Wray and Perkins, 2000). Other SLA researchers have argued for including the ability of using formulaic sequences effectively, i.e., collocational proficiency or native-like fluency and native-like selection (Pawley and Syder, 1983) as another key component of the L2 proficiency construct (Bolibaugh and Foster, 2013; Foster et al., 2014; Skrzypek, 2009; Wen, 2016b).

Notwithstanding, an unresolved issue in existing studies of formulaic sequences in SLA has been inconsistency in taxonomy and consequently, a standardized procedure for identification and measurement. The term and its relatives have appeared in so many different forms and have so many synonyms (e.g. fifty as listed in Wray 2002, p. 9) that it is usually difficult just to come up with a comprehensive definition. For example, the same phenomenon has been under discussion of holophrases, prefabricated routines and patterns, formulaic speech, memorized sentences and lexicalized stems, formulas, linguistic sequences or chunks and lexical patterns and collocational knowledge (Wen, 2014b; also see Wood, 2010a, 2010b, 2015). However, the present study will adopt Wray's definition due to its consideration of both linguistic and psycholinguistic criteria (Schmitt and Carter 2004; Siyanova-Chaturia and Martinez, 2014; Wray, 2008). Adopted in this way, a formulaic sequence in the present study refers to:

> *"a sequence, continuous or discontinuous, of words or other meaning elements, which is, or appears to be, prefabricated: that is, stored and retrieved whole from memory at the time of use, rather than being subject to generation or analysis by the language grammar."* (Wray, 2000, p. 465)

That is to say, the formulaic sequences which underlie language are not accessed as analyzable syntactic structures during real-time performance. Instead, they are drawn on as "stored and retrieved wholes" so that speed of processing (i.e., fluency) is enhanced and computational demands on the L2 learner can thus be greatly reduced (cf. Siyanova-Chanturia, 2015). Given this definition, issues still remain as how to identify and operationalize formulaic sequences in SLA research (also see; Wood, 2015). For example, in terms of identifying formulaic sequences, Foster (2001) has instructed native speakers to intuitively rate the native-likeness in terms of memory retrieval (i.e., whether they retrieved as memory wholes) and psychological reality. An example of speech elicited from a decision-making task is presented below (Figure 1), with each bracket representing the marking of 'formulaicity' by one native speaker (Foster, 2001, p. 83). In other words, the more brackets for a certain linguistic chunk, the more 'idiomatic' or 'formulaic' it was perceived to be by native speakers. This study represented the first attempt to incorporate formulaic sequences into task-based performance research. It thus has shed important light on identifying formulaic sequences in L2 task planning research, an area that I wish to pick on and push further in this current chapter.

> (((((((it doesn't matter))))))) (((((what the circumstances,))))) (((((she didn't have the right to))))) (((((take his life))))). If she was that er emotionally (((((((you know))))))) er distressed, then she should have- (((((((I don't know))))))) – (got out of the situation). (((((It's difficult to say))))) when you are not (((((in the situation))))) but (((((((at the end of the day))))))) she did (((((take another human life))))). ((((((There you go)))))).

Figure 1: An example of formulaic sequences in task-based performance

Addressing these relevant methodological issues, Nick Ellis and colleagues (N. Ellis, 2012; N. Ellis and Simpson, 2009; N. Ellis, Simpson and Maynard, 2008; also see O'Donnell, Römer and Ellis, 2012; N. Ellis, et al., 2015) put forward a theoretical framework for identifying and measuring formulaic sequences that effectively integrates research insights from corpus linguistics, psycholinguistics, computer science, and TESOL practitioners. As the authors cogently demonstrated in a series of empirical studies, four criteria (i.e., N-gram, frequency, mutual information score, native norm; as shown in Table 2) are divergent and complementary

Table 2: Dimensions of Formulaic Sequences

Criteria	Description/Characteristics	Operationalization and Supports
N-Gram	Number of words in the multi-unit sequence	Retrieved and stored in memory as a whole (Wray, 2000, 2008)
Frequency	Most sensitive to L2 learners	Formulas are recurrent sequences (e.g., Research by Biber and colleagues)
Mutual Information (MI) Score	Most sensitive to native speakers	Psycholinguistically salient sequences cohere much more than would be expected by chance (Manning and Schutze, 1999; Oakes, 1998)
Native Norms	Most sensitive to native speakers	Native-like fluency or Native-like selection (e.g., collocational proficiency) (Foster, 2001; Foster et al., 2014; Pawley and Syder, 1983)

(Based on N. Ellis, 2012; O'Donnell, Römer and Ellis, 2012)

and should represent a viable assessment framework for identifying the different dimensions of formulaic sequences.

Adopting this model as theoretical basis, I now turn to discuss possible advantages of using formulaic sequences as an additional dimension to the existing 'CAFL' framework (Skehan, 2009) to approximate L2 task-based performance. More importantly, based on this model, it is hypothesized that among the four criteria (i.e., N-gram, frequency, MI score, and native norms), it is the 'frequency' dimension that is postulated to be most sensitive to L2 learners (as opposed to the other dimensions for L1 speakers). I will further look into this particular aspect of formulaic sequences in the current study.

2.2 Formulaic sequences as an L2 task performance measure

Compared with existing measures (Table 1) in current CAFL framework in L2 task performance, there should be quite a number of perceivable advantages from also adopting formulaic sequences to approximate L2 task performance. First of all, as discussed above, the definition of formulaic sequences as adopted here is based on multiple perspectives from research insights of phraseology, corpus linguistics, psychology and TESOL, this will not just allow this measure to rest on a more solid theoretical basis than most existing indices (e.g., the CAFL framework), but also further complements the unresolved issues regarding theoretical cognitive underpinnings of L2 task planning.

Secondly, as the mastery of an effective repertoire of native-like formulaic sequences is increasingly deemed to represent a significant marker of advanced proficiency in the target language (Boers et al, 2006; Boers et al., 2014; Wood, 2015; Wray, 2010), the adoption of formulaic sequences should offer an unparalleled choice of measure for assessing task performance particularly among intermediate or post-intermediate L2 learners who are typical participants in most current TBLT studies (to be discussed further in the next section; also see Wen, 2016b for a similar argument). As far as I see it, this 'developmental' perspective associated with formulaic sequences represents its biggest advantage as an L2 task performance measure as most existing measures in the CAFL framework have not taken L2 proficiency into account.

Last but not least, as will be further demonstrated in the next chapter by Nguyen and Larsen-Freeman in this same volume, language teachers can and should use various task types to improve L2 learners' formulaic sequences. This represents a new direction of TBLT that will likely have significant implications not just for TBLT itself, but also for the whole field of applied linguistics and language education. In other words, from now on, formulaic sequences or collocational proficiency (Skrzypek, 2009) should constitute another component in future TBLT curriculum.

Putting these reasons together then, adopting formulaic sequences as a task performance measure is not just possible and feasible, but also viable and advantageous in both theoretical and methodological aspects. Therefore, the current study will adopt this multi-faceted framework (as presented in Table 2) as guidelines to identify and measure formulaic sequences produced by L2 learners during narrative task performance. More specifically, it will seek to further explore possible effects of working memory (WM) and pre-task planning, both independently and in combination, on different dimensions of formulaic sequences (e.g., in particular, its frequency dimension that is assumed to be most sensitive to L2 learners) during L2 task performance. These become the dual objectives of the current project in the first place. With that, I now turn to the theoretical aspects of L2 task planning research and will argue for adopting a WM perspective to interpret cognitive mechanisms underpinning observable variations in L2 task-based speech performance.

3 The role of working memory in L2 task performance and formulaic sequences

3.1 The phonological/executive model of WM and SLA

Among the various cognitive individual difference factors likely influence different aspects of SLA, working memory (WM) has been increasingly recognized as playing an important role in either directly influencing or through mediating instruction that likely impacts upon L2 ultimate learning outcomes (Linck et al., 2014; Wen, 2015, 2016b, 2017). In terms of the association between WM and SLA, two major theoretical proposals are in position, with each targeting at two key functions of the WM construct and their respective implications for L2 acquisition and processing.

The first is the theoretical proposal by Nick Ellis (1996, 2012) and colleagues who have cogently argued that the phonological short-term store and the articulatory rehearsal mechanism that are associated with the phonological WM component (i.e., PWM) play a critical role in the *chunking* procedure and subsequently the *consolidating* process of linguistic sequences into long-term knowledge. These linguistic sequences or chunks can range from lexis (or vocabulary) and formulaic sequences (or phrases), to morpho-syntactic constructions (or grammatical structures). Such a *connectionist* view on language acquisition (L1 and L2) as accumulating linguistic sequences and on the fundamental role of PWM in this process echoes the classical and standard conception of this phonological WM component as a *'language learning device'* by most Europe-based cognitive psychologists (Baddeley et al., 1998; also see Baddeley 2003, 2015).

On the other hand, there are other SLA researchers (e.g., Harrington, 1992; McLaughlin, 1995; Skehan, 1998, 2014, 2015) who opt for interpreting the WM effects on SLA from an (information) *processing* perspective, in which they postulate that the limited resources of attention control or executive aspects of WM (i.e., EWM) should have important consequences for some cognitively demanding processes implicated in various L2 comprehension and production processes. These normally include more finer-grained cognitive processes during L2 listening, speaking, reading, writing, and interpreting. Depending on the specific domains, task demands and participants' L2 proficiency, these processes can be either automatic, parallel at times but they can also be controlled, pressured and cognitively demanding processes at other times and naturally require more of cognitive resources of WM. This processing oriented perspective on the WM-SLA nexus (Wen, 2012, 2016b) is resonated largely with the North America-based attention and control views of WM (Bunting and Engle, 2015; Cowan, 2005, 2015). Interpreted this way, executive WM (EWM), becomes a *'language processing device'*, or simply a *'language processer'* (Lu, 2011, as cited in Wen, 2016b).

These above two portrayals of the WM-SLA association are complementary in contributing to a unified understanding of fractionated WM functions as they relate to various facets of SLA learning domains and processes. Reconciling these two views gives rise to an integrated conceptual framework to theorize and measure the WM construct in nuanced SLA research that culminates in the Phonological/Executive Hypothesis (i.e., the P/E model; Wen, 2012, 2015, 2016b). As discussed above, a major tenet of the P/E model lies in its theoretical alignment of the distinctive functions and mechanisms embedded within the PWM component (composed of a phonological short-term store and articulatory rehearsal mechanism; generally measured by the simple serial recall span tasks) and the EWM component (comprised of such executive functions as memory retrieval, updating, task switching, inhibition etc.; usually indexed by complex versions of storage plus processing memory span tasks) with corresponding SLA domains and processes that are likely to be specifically affected by each component (albeit to a varying degree).

Another feature of the P/E model is its incorporation of long-term memory (LTM) effects that have not been adequately addressed in most current WM-SLA studies (Wen, 2016b). To that end, LTM as conceptualized in the P/E model is sub-serving both L1 competence (including mental lexicon and grammar) and L2 knowledge/proficiency (lexis, formulae, grammatical rules and metalinguistic knowledge). More importantly, the model takes into account of the dynamic interactions between L1 and L2 as a function of L2 proficiency developments. In other words, it is hypothesized that L2 proficiency assumes a significant role in attenuating both the PWM-SLA relations and the EWM-SLA relationships described above. For example, it postulates that *ceteris paribus* (other things being equal), PWM is likely to play a more relevant role at initial stages of SLA (e.g., among *ab initio* L2 learners or learners of artificial languages; Sanz et al., 2014; Serefini and Sanz, 2015); while EWM is believed to weigh in gradually as participants' L2 proficiency progresses, with its effects becoming more obvious among intermediate and post-intermediate L2 learners (Wen, 2016b). Interpreted this way, it is EWM rather than PWM, as we will argue later, that should be more relevant for L2 task planning research given that most participants in these studies belong to these relatively more advanced levels of SLA (to enable a demanding task to be completed).

Following this logic then, after L2 learners' proficiency becomes so advanced and gradually approaches native-like L1 level, WM effects as a whole (either of PWM or EWM) can be expected to become less obvious (at least as measured by existing assessment procedures such as the simple memory span tasks and the complex memory span tasks). That is to say, at this high-level SLA stage, WM effects may turn implicit or undetectable in more aspects of SLA learning domains and processes, a view that is receiving increasing empirical evidence (e.g., Hummel, 2009; Sanz et al., 2014; Winke, 2013; Verhagen et al., 2015). Having said so, it can be argued that, at such late SLA stages, the distinctive roles or the subtle effects between PWM and EWM should be considered in light of those witnessed in first language acquisition (i.e., with monolinguals), such as those conceived in Levelt's (1989) model of L1 speaking and Kellogg's WM-based L1 writing model (1996, 1999).

Overall, these articulated hypotheses regarding the fractionated and dichotomous view of WM components/functions and multi-faceted SLA domains as laid out in the P/E model have been increasingly recognized and empirically supported in current cognitive psychology and SLA research alike. In terms of the specific contributions of PWM, for example, previous research in both fields has lent strong support to its significant role in L2 vocabulary acquisition and development (e.g., Atkins and Baddeley, 1998; Service, 1992), and its role in learning L2 formulaic sequences or collocational proficiency (e.g., Skrzypek, 2009; Bolibaugh and Foster, 2013; Foster et al., 2014) as well as L2 grammar (e.g., Martin and Ellis 2012; Tagarelli et al., 2011; Verhagenand et al., 2015) is also emerging. Regarding EWM then, most empirical studies (see Juffs and Harrington, 2011; Linck et al., 2014; Williams, 2011) have generally endorsed its role in major albeit selective aspects of L2 sub-skills learning (e.g., listening, reading, speaking, writing, and translation/interpreting), particularly among L2 learners at their intermediate or post-intermediate proficiency levels (Wen, Mota and McNeill, 2013, 2015).

Other recent larger-scale and more systematic reviews of WM-SLA studies are lending further support to these hypothetic links formulated in the P/E model. Among these, a recent meta-analytical study conducted by Linck et al. (2014) based on 79 sample studies (involving 748 effect sizes, totaling a number of 3,707 adult participants) not only points to a significant and positive relationship between WM and overall L2 proficiency development and outcomes (with an estimated effect size of 0.255), but, more intriguingly, it has demonstrated greater effect sizes for the executive control component of WM (i.e., EWM; as opposed to the storage component, i.e. PWM) in affecting L2 learning among college-level intermediate proficiency students. As we have argued elsewhere (Wen et al., 2017), such a strong link can complement previous findings pointing to language aptitude as more closely related to L2 learning among high school students (Li, 2015).

Given this cumulative evidence in support of the basic tenets and specific hypotheses of the P/E model, such a conceptual framework may serve as a departure point for further explorations into the specific and distinctive roles of PWM and EWM on other more specific aspects of SLA domains and processes. In this chapter, we aim to further explore their purportedly distinctive effects on L2 task-based speech performance, and particularly their separate main effects and interaction effects on production of formulaic sequences by L2 learners when retelling narrative tasks under planned or unplanned conditions.

3.2 The P/E model and L2 task planning and performance

So far, some empirical studies have already adopted Rod Ellis' typology of task planning conditions as a theoretical basis and investigated the main effects of WM, as well as its interaction effects with internal and external task design/structure and task planning conditions on L2 learners' speech performance. Task planning conditions are usually implemented as pre-task or strategic planning (e.g., Fortkamp, 1999, 2003; Guará-Tavares, 2008; Wen, 2016a; cf. Nielson, 2014), online-planning (Ahmadian, 2012, 2015) and task repetition (Ahmadian, 2013). Table 3 summarizes some of these studies.

In line with the above hypothesis regarding WM and L2 task performance, most of these studies point to positive main effects of EWM as well as its interaction effects with task planning (e.g., pre-task planning, online planning) on various measures indexing different dimensions of L2 speech (i.e., fluency, accuracy, complexity and lexis, as well as formality scores). Despite this generally positive links, EWM effects were not detected for all L2 performance measures,

Table 3: Empirical Studies of WM and L2 Task Performance

Authors	Participants' Age (children vs. adult) and L2 Proficiency Level	WM Components and Measures	Task Design/ Feature	WM effects on aspects of L2 task performance
Fortkamp (1999)	Adults/ intermediate	EWM (SST, OST in L2)	A description task; and a narrative task	EWM effects: +C,A,F -Lexis
Fortkamp (2003)	Adults/ intermediate	EWM (SST in L2)	A description task; and a narrative task	EWM effects: +C,A,F -Lexis
Guará-Tavares (2008)	Adults/ intermediate	EWM (SST in L2)	A narrative task/ pre-task planning	EWM effects: +C, F (cf. planning effects: +A, C)
Ahmadian (2012)	Adults/ intermediate	EWM (LST in L1)	A narrative task/ (Careful) Online planning	EWM effects: +A, F
Révész (2012)	Adults/ intermediate	PWM (Digit span, Nonword span); EWM (RST)	An oral narrative task; A written narrative task/ recast	PWM effects on oral task; while EWM effects on written task
Ahmadian (2013)	Adults/ intermediate	EWM (LST in L1)	A narrative task/ Task repetition	EWM effects: +A, F
Nielson (2014)	Adults/ intermediate	Online Visuo-spatial WM Tasks (Block-span & Shape-builder)	Two narrative tasks/ Pre-task planning	No WM effects on L2 speech performance (though planning effects on: +C, F)
Mojavezi & Ahmadian (2014)	Adults/ intermediate	EWM (LST in L1 & L2)	A narrative task/ Online planning	EWM effects: +L2 self-repairs
Ahmadian (2015)	Adults/ intermediate	EWM (LST in L1)	A narrative task/ Online planning	EWM effects: +L2 self-repairs
Wen (2016a)	Adults/ intermediate	PWM (L2) +EWM (in L1 & L2)	A narrative task/ Pre-task planning	EWM effects: +FS

Note: NWR = Nonword Repetition Span Task; RST = Reading Span Task; LST = Listing Span Task; SST = Speaking Span Task; EWM = Executive Working Memory; CAF = Complexity, Accuracy, Fluency; FS = Formality Score.

but were rather selective, generally pointing to certain degree of 'trade-off' relationships (Skehan, 2014, 2015) among L2 speech performance measures (most obviously in the two studies by Fortkamp, 1999, 2003; which indicated a trade-off between CAF and lexical diversity). Also in line with the hypothesis laid out above, PWM effects were generally not recorded in these studies (except in Révész, 2012 which showed a positive relationship between PWM and the developmental gains in participants' oral task performance). Then, in another study (Nielson, 2014) in which two visuo-spatial WM span tasks were implemented, it should not be too surprising to see their effects on L2 task performance were not detected as both WM span tasks were not considered as EWM measures in the P/E model (Wen, 2016b). Taken as a whole, these results can be interpreted as providing evidence to the relevant hypotheses laid out in the P/E model within the context of L2 task performance (more details are provided in Chapter 8 of Wen, 2016b).

That is to say, as predicted in the P/E model being applied in accounting for L2 task performance, most current studies described here had targeted participants who were mostly adult learners at intermediate level of their L2 development. As I have argued earlier (Wen, 2016b), this was reasonable as the completion of these supposedly rather demanding tasks (e.g., description or narrative tasks) usually requires participants to have an adequate level of L2 proficiency (such as college students). Following this, as I shall further argue in the next section that the measure of formulaic sequences is poised to be a viable tool for assessing L2 task performance among these relatively more advanced L2 participants.

4 The empirical study

4.1 The research question

Based on the above reviews, it should be revealing and worthwhile to incorporate both the cognitive aptitude factor of WM and the measure of formulaic sequences into L2 task planning and performance research. Following the hypotheses of the P/E model, the current project sets out to further investigate the distinctive roles of PWM and EWM in the production of formulaic sequences by a group of college-level Chinese learners of English as a Foreign Language (EFL) when retelling narrative tasks under the planned and unplanned conditions.

More specifically, it aims to answer the research question: *What is the possible relationship between learners' WM (operationalized as consisting of PWM and EWM), independently and interplaying with pre-task planning, on the formulaic sequences produced while narrating tasks in L2?* In particular, based on the above discussion, it is hypothesized that EWM will be more relevant given that learners' L2 proficiency already reached intermediate level.

4.2 Participants

The participants in the study came from the same pool of Wen (2016a), who were college-level (adult) learners of English (N = 40) attending a credit-bearing English program at a tertiary institute in Southern China. As demonstrated by their National Test for English Majors Level 4 (TEM4), these participants had similar English proficiency at the intermediate level.

4.3 Test instruments and materials

The test instruments and materials were the same as in Wen (2016a). Briefly, three WM span tasks were administered, including a nonword repetition span task (based on participants' L2 English) tapping into PWM, and two speaking span tasks (constructed based on participants' L1 Chinese and L2 English respectively) indexing EWM. The narrative tasks adopted in the present study were based on retellings of Mr. Bean video clips following Skehan and Foster (1999) and Wen (2016a). Then, the construct of planning was operationalized at two levels: (a) no planning (NoPlan; in which L2 learners were instructed to retell the story by speaking to the microphone once they finished watching the video clip, i.e., the "Watch and Retell" condition), (b) 10 minutes pre-task planning (i.e., in which L2 learners first finished watching the video clip, planned the story for 10 minutes with a blank sheet of paper, and then retold the story without referring to the notes; i.e., the "Watch, Plan and Retell" condition; more details on these test materials were discussed in Wen (2016a). I now turn to the identification and measure of formulaic sequences.

Speech samples from 40 participants carrying out the narrative tasks entered the main study, with 10 participants randomly assigned to each planning condition and task type. That is to say, the first group of 10 participants did the 'MR. Bean having a meal' task (about Mr. Bean going to a fancy restaurant having a meal) under the no planning condition and a second group of 10 participants did the same task under the 10 minutes planning condition. Then, a third group of 10 participants did the Mr. Bean 'golf' task (about Mr. Bean playing a round of crazy golf) under the no planning condition. Finally, a fourth group of 10 participants did the same narrative task under the 10 minutes planning condition. In other words, all participants did only one task in only one planning condition, thus making the study follow a strict between-subject research design.

The target formulaic sequences were taken from the self-constructed small-scale corpora of these 40 speech samples (with a total number of words = 22047; Types: 1439). These target formulaic sequences were chosen with "*Collocate*" (developed by Michael Barlow) following four main criteria described above (Table 1), including (a) N-Gram lengths between 3–6 (i.e., the number of words per multi-word unit), (b) frequency (that is to say, all target formulaic sequences also need to have a certain degree of frequency in language use that is based on corpus reference data (with a frequency threshold = 13); (c) Mutual Information (MI) score threshold = 8, with N-Gram lengths also set at between 3–6. Please take note that the fourth criterion of native norm was not yet implemented in the current study as I mainly focused on comparing WM effects on the two dimensions of 'frequency' and 'MI' score. In particular, as suggested by Ellis et al. (2008), it can be hypothesized that the frequency aspect of formulaic sequences is related to L2 learners (as opposed to MI, which is more related to native speakers).

Following these, "*AntConc*" (Version .3.2.3; developed by Anthony) was run to get the formulaic sequences profile for each individual speaker (N = 40). In addition, multiple occurrences were counted as 1 in each speaker. As a result, 49 formulaic sequences entered the statistical analysis (8 failed to run). The top 20 most frequent formulaic sequences are shown in Table 4 by the order of frequency (Fre.) vs. their corresponding mutual information (MI) scores (as reference), together with the standard deviation (SD) score among L2 speakers.

Table 4: Top 10 Formulaic Sequences by Frequency vs. MI

Fre.	MI	SD	FSs
1.	58	7.946214	out of the
2.	54	6.327181	and then he
3.	41	5.860279	the ball was
4.	37	5.332490	the bus and
5.	34	8.372074	Mr. bean was
6.	31	6.877084	and Mr. bean
7.	29	9.185084	Mr. bean went
8.	27	5.231267	went to the
9.	27	6.300106	the ball went
10.	26	6.802887	of the bus
11.	26	8.773974	the bus stop
12.	25	11.926015	at that time
13.	25	8.706619	so Mr. bean
14.	25	5.048673	he put the
15.	24	10.865628	the ice cream
16.	24	9.018556	he took out
17.	23	5.806388	he found the
18.	22	8.170660	hit the ball
19.	21	5.773485	he went to
20.	21	8.466532	on the table

4.4 Statistical procedures and analyses

After all the scores (PWM and EWM span scores, frequency scores of formulaic sequences) were ready, they were run through SPSS (version 16) for data analyses. These included a series of correlation analyses between each WM component and frequency of formulaic sequences and a step-wise regression analysis (with PWM and EWM as predictors and frequency score of formulaic sequences as dependent variables). Specifically, a series of correlational analyses were run to identify the association between each of the two WM components and their respective relationships with the frequency dimension of formulaic sequences.

4.5 Results and discussion

4.5.1 Main effects of PWM and EWM on formulaic sequences

The major objective of the present paper relates to the theoretical argument for conceptualizing and measuring PWM and EWM as they relate to the frequency dimension of L2 formulaic sequences. Table 5 displays the descriptive statistics for the three WM measures and the frequency of formulaic sequences adopted in the current study. As shown in Table 5, L2 learners' mean scores for the nonword repetition span task were lower than either one of the speaking span tasks (22.50 vs. 26.70 and 26.58), while the mean scores for the two speaking span tasks were quite close to each other.

Table 5: Descriptive Statistics

	N	Range	Minimum	Maximum	Mean	Std. Deviation	Skewness		Kurtosis	
nonscore	40	16	13	29	22.50	3.955	−.338	.374	−.374	.733
SST-E	40	19	20	39	26.70	3.488	.837	.374	2.707	.733
SST-C	40	17	15	32	26.57	3.768	−.713	.374	.719	.733
comspsp	40	15.00	19.00	34.00	26.6375	3.071	−.109	.374	.093	.733
formula frequency	40	25.00	2.00	27.00	12.3750	7.102	.538	.374	−.799	.733

Table 6: Correlations

	nonscore	SST-E	SST-C	comspsp
SST-E	.052 .750			
SST-C	.051.756	.433** .005		
comspsp	.061 .710	.833** .000	.859** .000	
formula frequency	.092 .573	.184 .256	.653** .000	.505** .001

** Correlation is significant at the 0.01 level (2-tailed); N = 40

In order to further probe into the inter-relationship of these independent (IV) and dependent variables (DVs), an inter-correlation analysis was carried out (as shown in Table 6). First of all, Table 8 shows that the participants' nonword repetition span scores correlated with neither the L1-based nor the L2-based speaking span task. These results further corroborate the theoretical conceptualizations of the P/E model of WM and SLA (Wen, 2016b). That is to say, the phonological WM component (PWM; as indexed by the nonword repetition span task) and the executive WM component (EWM; as indexed by the bilingual speaking span tasks) are regarded as two distinctive WM components as they are not correlated and are unrelated to each other. This result, despite its preliminary nature, suggests that combining PWM and EWM into a composite WM Z-score (as in some previous studies such as Mackey et al., 2002; Mizera, 2006) may blur or even confound the distinction between the two separate WM components. Therefore, as proposed by the P/E model, it is necessary to incorporate the PSTM-EWM distinction in future WM-SLA explorations (Wen, 2015, 2016b).

Then, in terms of the relationship between WM functions and formulaic sequences, it was found that both L1-based speaking span score (SST-C) and the composite/bilingual speaking span (comspsp) are significantly correlated with the frequency dimension of formulaic sequences, while PWM (as measured by nonword span task) and L2-based speaking span task (SST-E) are not. These results seem to further confirm the distinctive roles of PWM and EWM, as well as lending initial support to the hypothesis of the P/E model postulating L2 proficiency as a LTM factor mediating the WM-SLA interactions (Wen, 2016b). That is, when participants' L2 proficiency reaches intermediate and post-intermediate levels (such as those participants in the current study), their EWM tends to play a bigger role in L2 processes than PWM does.

To further probe into the predictive roles of PWM and EWM in the production of formulaic sequences, a stepwise regression analysis was conducted with PWM and EWM as predictors and the frequency dimension of formulaic sequences as dependent variables. Using the "enter" method, a significant model emerged ($F_{2,37} = 6.449$, $P < 0.05$, Adjusted $R^2 = .218$). Among the two predictors (PWM vs. EWM), it was found that PWM effects were not significant, while EWM effects were. These results again suggest a separate role for the two WM components in relation to formulaic sequences produced in L2 task performance, as well as corroborating the above hypothesis of the P/E model (also see Wen, 2016b) that EWM (as opposed to PWM) is more relevant for L2 task performance among those participants at intermediate or post-intermediate levels (who are typical participants in most L2 task planning research).

4.5.2 PWM, EWM and pre-task planning on formulaic sequences

It should be noted that the above statistical analyses of main effects of WM had collapsed the data of both planning conditions. To probe into the interaction effects of WM and pre-task planning, the data file was split into two separate groups, namely, between the 10 minutes planning group (N=20) and the no-planning group (N=20). Two more rounds of regression analyses were then run to further determine the predictive roles of PWM and EWM in relation to the frequency of formulaic sequences under these two different planning conditions.

In terms of results, a similar pattern to the whole cohort was detected. More specifically, for the '10 minutes planning' group, a significant model emerged ($F_{2,17}$ = 4.931, $P < 0.05$, Adjusted R^2 = .293) and again, only EWM (as indexed by the bilingual speaking span tasks) was a significant predictor ($P = 0.007 < 0.005$) while PWM was not. The same pattern was detected for the nonplanning group, with only EWM being the significant predictor ($F_{2,17}$ = 5.609, $P < 0.05$, Adjusted R^2 = 0.327).

Following these, a series of analyses of variance (ANOVAs) were also conducted to check if there were any interaction effects between PWM and pre-task planning, and between EWM and pre-task planning on the frequency dimension of formulaic sequences. None of these analyses produced any significant results (despite the significant main effects of pre-task planning). In other words, pre-task planning seems to write off EWM effects regarding the frequency aspect of formulaic sequences in L2 task performance. Of course, more empirical studies are needed in the future to tease out the complex relationships between WM functions (PWM and EWM), planning conditions (pre-task planning, online planning, and task repetition), and L2 task performance measures (CAFL, formality score, and formulaic sequences).

5 Implications and conclusion

It is hoped that the current project will have some theoretical and pedagogical ramifications for both TBLT and SLA. First of all, in terms of theoretical advancement, the study should be able to help raise awareness among SLA researchers and TBLT practitioners that the ultimate goals of second/foreign language teaching and learning should not just include the learning of vocabulary and grammatical knowledge (as emphasized in most current ELT curriculum), but also should incorporate the learning and teaching of an adequate repertoire of phrasal knowledge, i.e., formulaic sequences that can help reduce processing cost during

L2 use and performance, allowing L2 learners to approach native-like fluency with native-like selection (Pawley & Syder, 1990), thus facilitating effective communication (Segalowitz, 2010; Wood, 2010, 2015).

Secondly, the current study has also explored the distinctive roles of two key WM functions in the production of formulaic sequences during L2 task performance. It is hoped that such insights should prove beneficial for L2 educators/teachers to make more informed decisions by taking into account L2 learners' cognitive individual differences underlying observable variations in aspects of L2 task performance. Gradually, the ultimate goal is to arrive at tailor-made teaching pedagogy and classroom instruction suited to L2 learners' individuality (Gregersen and MacIntyre, 2014). That said, further research is needed to investigate the relationships between other cognitive (e.g., language aptitude) and social (such as learning context) factors purported to influence various facets of L2 acquisition and processing (Granena, Yilmaz and Jackson, 2016).

Finally, regarding pedagogical implications, the current study should have implications for language policy making, textbook compilation and language classroom practice. Its results and findings will likely push language educators/practitioners (e.g., policy makers, curriculum designers and/or language teachers) to reexamine their current practice in TBLT. Influenced by the outcome of the current study, they will likely feel the need to incorporate an additional component of *'collocational proficiency'* (the ability to use formulaic sequences effectively; Foster et al., 2014; Siyanova-Chanturia, 2015; Skrzypek, 2009) along with other existing goals of lexical fluency and grammatical accuracy. Given the fact that the focus of most contemporary language policy and classroom instruction has been (mis)placed on the learning of single vocabulary items or on the knowledge of grammatical rules, the current study should help to rectify this (mal)practice and put ELT onto its right track (by incorporating formulaic sequences as an important component).

Indeed, an increasing number of studies in recent years have indicated that, besides and between vocabulary and grammar, L2 learners also need to acquire a substantial number of routine-like formulaic sequences that are selected and used idiomatically by the native speakers (Bolibaugh and Foster, 2013; Foster, 2001; Foster et al., 2014; Pawley and Syder, 1983). It is therefore hoped that, through this study and the next chapter by Nguyen and Larsen-freeman in this volume, formulaic sequences will not only become a topic to be pursued in L2 task planning and performance research, but also enter the mainstream syllabus and curriculum design in both TBLT and SLA.

References

Ahmadian, M.J. 2012. The relationship between working memory and oral production under task-based careful online planning condition. *TESOL Quarterly* 46/1. 165–175.

Ahmadian, M.J. 2013. Working memory and task repetition in second language oral production. *Asian Journal of English Language Teaching* 23(1). 37–55.

Ahmadian, M.J. 2015. Working memory, online planning, and L2 self-repair behavior. In Z. Wen, M.B. Mota & A. McNeill (eds.), *Working memory in second language acquisition and processing*, 160–174. Bristol, UK: Multilingual Matters.

Baddeley, A.D. 2003. Working memory and language: An overview. *Journal of Communication Disorders* 36. 189–208.

Baddeley, A.D. 2015. Working memory in second language learning. In Z. Wen, M.B. Mota & A. McNeill (eds.), *Working memory in second language acquisition and processing*, 17–28. Bristol, UK: Multilingual Matters.

Baddeley, A. D. & G. Hitch. 1974. Working memory. In G.A. Bower (ed.), *The psychology of learning and motivation*, Vol. 8, 47–89. New York: Academic Press.

Baddeley, A., S. E. Gathercole & C. Papagno. 1998. The phonological loop as a language learning device. *Psychological Review* 105. 158–173.

Bei, G. X. 2011. Formality in second language discourse: Measurement and performance. *Interdisciplinary Humanities* 28(1). 32–41.

Bolibaugh C. & P. Foster. 2013. Memory-based aptitude for nativelike selection: The role of phonological short-term memory. In Gisela Granena & Mike Long (eds.), *Sensitive periods, language aptitude, and ultimate L2 attainment*, 203–228. Amsterdam: John Benjamins.

Boers, F., M. Demecheleer, A. Coxhead & S. Webb. 2014. Gauging the effects of exercises on verb-noun collocations. *Language Teaching Research* 18/1. 54–74.

Boers, F, J. Eyckmans, J. Kappel, H. Stengers & M. Demecheleer. 2006. Formulaic sequences and perceived oral proficiency: Putting a lexical approach to the test. *Language Teaching Research* 10. 245–261.

Bunting, M.F. & R. Engle. 2015. Foreword. In Z. Wen, M. Mota & A. McNeill (eds.), *Working memory in second language acquisition and processing*. Bristol, UK: Multilingual Matters.

Bygate, M. 2015. *Domains and directions in the development of TBLT: A decade of plenaries from the international conference*. Amsterdam: John Benjamins.

Cowan, N. 2005. *Working memory capacity*. New York and Hove: Psychology Press.

Cowan, N. 2015. Second language use, theories of working memory and the Vennian mind. In Z. Wen, M. Mota & A. McNeill (eds.), *Working memory in second language acquisition and processing*, 29–40. Bristol, UK: Multilingual Matters.

Ellis, N.C. 1996. Sequencing in SLA: Phonological memory, chunking and points of order. *Studies in Second Language Acquisition* 18. 91–126.

Ellis, N. C. 2012. Formulaic language and second language acquisition: Zipf and the phrasal Teddy Bear. *Annual Review of Applied Linguistics* 32. 17–44.

Ellis, N. C. 2013. Second language acquisition. In G. Trousdale & T. Hoffmann (eds.), *Oxford handbook of construction grammar*, 365–378. Oxford: Oxford University Press.

Ellis, N. C., R. Simpson-Vlach, U. Römer, M. O'Donnell & S. Wulff. 2015. Learner corpora and formulaic language in SLA. In Sylviane Granger, Gaëtanelle Gilquin & Fanny Meunier (eds.), *Cambridge handbook of learner corpus research*, 357–378. Cambridge: Cambridge University Press.

Ellis, R. 1987. Interlanguage variability in narrative discourse: Style in the use of past tense. *Studies in Second Language Acquisition* 9. 12–20.

Ellis, R. 2005. *Planning and task-based performance in a second language*. Amsterdam: John Benjamins.

Ellis, R. 2009. The differential effects of three types of task planning on the fluency, complexity, and accuracy in L2 oral production. *Applied Linguistics* 30(4). 474–509.

Ellis, R. & G. Barkhuizen. 2005. *Analyzing learning language*. Cambridge: Oxford University Press.

Erman, B. & B. Warren. 2000. The idiom principle and the open-choice principle. *Text* 20. 29–62.

Fortkamp, M.B.M. 1999. Working memory capacity and aspects of L2 speech production. *Communication and Cognition* 32. 259–296.

Fortkamp, M.B.M. 2003. Working memory capacity and fluency, accuracy, complexity and lexical density in L2 speech production. *Fragmentos* 24. 69–104.

Foster, P. 2001. Rules and routines: A consideration of their role in the task-based language production of native and non-native speakers. In M. Bygate, P. Skehan & M. Swain (eds.), *Researching pedagogic tasks: Second language learning, teaching and testing*, 75–94. Harlow: Longman.

Foster, P., C. Bolibaugh & A. Kotula. 2014. Knowledge of nativelike selections in an L2: The influence of exposure, memory, age of onset and motivation in foreign language and immersion settings. *Studies in Second Language Acquisition* 36(01). 101–132.

Granena, G., D. Jackson & Y. Yilmaz (eds.). forthcoming. *Cognitive individual differences in L2 processing and acquisition*. Amsterdam: John Benjamins.

Gregersen, T. & P. D. MacIntyre. 2014. *Capitalizing on language learners' individuality: from premise to practice*. Bristol, UK: Multilingual Matters.

Guará-Tavares, M. G. 2008. *Pre-task planning, working memory capacity and L2 speech performance*. Unpublished doctoral thesis, Universidade Federal de Santa Catarina, Brazil.

Harrington M. 1992. Working memory capacity as a constraint on L2 development. In R. J. Harris (ed.), *Cognitive processing in bilinguals*, 123–135. Amsterdam: North Holland.

Housen, A. and F. Kuiken. 2009. Complexity, accuracy, and fluency in second language acquisition. *Applied Linguistics* 30(4). 461–473.

Housen, A., F. Kuiken & I. Vedder. 2012. *Dimensions of L2 performance and proficiency: Complexity, accuracy and fluency in SLA*. Amsterdam: John Benjamins.

Hummel, K. M. 2009. Aptitude, phonological memory, and second language proficiency in nonnovice adult learners. *Applied Psycholinguistics* 30. 225–249.

Jiang, N. & T. Neckrasova. 2007. The processing of formulaic sequences in a second language. *The Modern Language Journal* 91. 433–445.

Kellogg, R. 1996. A model of working memory in writing. In Levy C. and S. Ransdell (eds.), *The science of writing*. Mahwah, NJ: Erlbaum.

Kellogg, R. 1999. Components of working memory in text production. In M. Torrance & G.C. Geffery (eds.), *The cognitive demands of writing*. Amsterdam: Amsterdam University Press.

Larsen-Freeman, D. 2015. Saying what we mean: Making a case for 'language acquisition' to become 'language development'. *Language Teaching* 48/4. 491–505.

Levelt, W. J. M. 1989. *Speaking: From intention to articulation*. Cambridge, MA: The MIT Press.

Levelt, W. J. M. 1999. Producing spoken language: A blueprint of the speaker. In C. Brown & P. Hagoort (eds.), *The neurocognition of language*, 83–154. Oxford: Oxford University Press.

Lewis, M. 1993. *The lexical approach*. Hove: Teacher Training Publications.

Li, S. 2015. The associations between language aptitude and second language grammar acquisition: A meta-analytic review of five decades of research. *Applied Linguistics* 36(3). 385–408.

Linck, J.A., P. Osthus, J.T. Koeth & M.F. Bunting. 2014. Working memory and second language comprehension and production: A meta-analysis. *Psychonomic Bulletin and Review* 21/4. 861–883.

Long, M. H. 2015. *Second language acquisition and task-based language teaching*. Oxford: Wiley-Blackwell.

Mackey, A., J. Philp, T. Egi, A. Fujii & T. Tatsumi. 2002. Individual differences in working memory, noticing of interactional feedback and L2 development. In P. Robinson (ed.), *Individual differences and second language instruction*, 181–209. Philadelphia: John Benjamins.

Martin, K. I. & N. C. Ellis. 2012. The roles of phonological STM and working memory in L2 grammar and vocabulary learning. *Studies in Second Language Acquisition* 34(3). 379–413.

McLaughlin, B. 1995. Aptitude from an information processing perspective. *Language Testing* 11. 364–381.

Mizera, G. J. 2006. *Working memory and L2 oral fluency*. Unpublished PhD dissertation, University of Pittsburgh.

Mojavezi, A. & M. Ahmadian. 2014. Working memory capacity and self-repair behavior in first and second language oral production. *Journal of Psycholinguistic Research* 43(3). 289–97.

Moon, R. 1998. *Fixed expressions and idioms in English*. Oxford: Clarendon Press.

Nattinger, J.R. & J.S. DeCarrico. 1992. *Lexical phrases and language teaching*. Oxford: Oxford University Press.

Nielson, K. B. 2014. Can planning time compensate for individual differences in working memory capacity? *Language Teaching Research* 18(3). 272–293.

O'Donnell, M. B., U. Römer & N. C. Ellis. 2013. The development of formulaic language in first and second language writing: Investigating effects of frequency, association, and native norm. *International Journal of Corpus Linguistics* 18(1). 83–108.

Pawley, A. & F.H. Syder. 1983. Two puzzles for linguistic theory: Nativelike selection and nativelike fluency. In J.C. Richards & R.W. Schmidt (eds.), *Language and communication*, 191–226. New York: Longman.

Révész, A. 2012. Working memory and the observed effectiveness of recasts on different L2 outcome measures. *Language Learning* 62(1). 93–132.

Révész, A. 2014. Towards a fuller assessment of cognitive models of task-based learning: Investigating task-generated cognitive demands and processes. *Applied Linguistics* 35(1). 87–92.

Robinson, P. 2005. Aptitude and second language acquisition. *Annual Review of Applied Linguistics* 25. 46–73.

Robinson, P. 2011. Task-based language learning: A review of issues. *Language Learning* 61. 1–36.

Robinson, P. 2012. Individual differences, aptitude complexes, SLA processes, and aptitude test development. In M. Pawlak (ed.), *New perspectives on individual differences in language learning and teaching*, 57–75. Berlin/Heidelberg: Springer-Verlag.

Robinson, P. 2015. The cognition hypothesis, second language task demands and the SSARC model of task sequencing. In Martin Bygate (ed.), *Domains and directions in the development of TBLT: A decade of plenaries from the international conference*, 87–122. Amsterdam/Philadelphia: John Benjamins.

Sanz, C., H.-J. Lin, B. Lado, C. A. Stafford & H. W. Bowden. 2014. One size fits all? Learning conditions and working memory capacity in ab initio language development. *Applied Linguistics*. First published online 29 October 2014.

Schmitt N. (ed.). 2004. *Formulaic sequences*. Amsterdam/Philadelphia: John Benjamins.

Schmitt, N., Z. Dornyei, S. Adolph & V. Durow. 2004. Knowledge and acquisition of formulaic sequences: A longitudinal study. In N. Schmitt (ed.), *Formulaic sequences*. Amsterdam/Philadelphia: John Benjamins.

Schmitt N. & R. Carter. 2004. Formulaic sequences in action: An introduction. In N. Schmitt (ed.), *Formulaic sequences*. Amsterdam/Philadelphia: John Benjamins.

Segalowitz, N. 2010. *Cognitive bases of second language fluency*. New York: Routledge.

Serafini, E. J. & C. Sanz. 2015. Evidence for the decreasing impact of cognitive ability on second language development as proficiency increases. *Studies in Second Language Acquisition*, 1–40. FirstView

Service, E. 1992. Phonology, working memory and foreign-language learning. *Quarterly Journal of Experimental Psychology* 45(1). 21–50.

Siyanova-Chanturia, A. 2015. On the 'holistic' nature of formulaic language. *Corpus Linguistics and Linguistic Theory*.

Siyanova-Chanturia, A. & R. Martinez. 2014. The idiom principle revisited. *Applied Linguistics*.

Sinclair, J. 1991. *Corpus, concordance, collocation*. Oxford: Oxford University Press.

Skehan, P. 1998. *A cognitive approach to language learning*. Oxford: Oxford University Press.

Skehan, P. 2014. *Processing perspectives on task performance*. Amsterdam: John Benjamins.

Skehan, P. 2015. Working memory and second language performance. In Z. Wen, M. Mota & A. McNeill (eds.), *Working memory in second language acquisition and processing*, 189–201. Bristol, UK: Multilingual Matters.

Skehan, P. & P. Foster. 1997. Task type and task processing conditions as influences on foreign language performance. *Language Teaching Research* 1/3. 1–27.

Skehan, P. & P. Foster. 1999. The influence of task structure and processing conditions on narrative retellings. *Language Learning* 49. 93–120.

Skehan, P. & P. Foster. 2012. Complexity, accuracy, fluency and lexis in task-based performance: A synthesis of the Ealing research. In A. Housen, F. Kuiken & I. Vedder (eds.), *Dimensions of L2 performance and proficiency: Complexity, accuracy and fluency in SLA*. Amsterdam: John Benjamins.

Skrzypek, A. 2009. Phonological short-term memory and L2 collocational development in adult learners. *EUROSLA Yearbook* 9. 160–184.

Tagarelli, K., M. B. Mota & P. Rebuschat. 2011. The role of working memory in implicit and explicit language learning. In L. Carlson, C. Hölscher & T. Shipley (eds.), *Proceedings of the 33rd Annual Conference of the Cognitive Science Society*, 2061–2066. Austin, TX: Cognitive Science Society.

Verhagen, J., M. H. Messer & P. P. M. Leseman. 2015. Phonological memory and the acquisition of grammar in child L2 learners. *Language Learning* 65/2. 417–448.

Weinert, R. 1995. The role of formulaic language in second language acquisition: A review. *Applied Linguistics* 16(2). 180–205.

Wen, Z. 2009. *Effects of working memory capacity on L2 task-based speech planning and performance*. Unpublished PhD dissertation, The Chinese University of Hong Kong.

Wen, Z. 2012. Working memory and second language learning. *International Journal of Applied Linguistics* 22/1. 1–22.

Wen, Z. 2014a. Theorizing and measuring working memory in first and second language research. *Language Teaching* 47/2. 173–190.
Wen, Z. 2014b. Comfortable fossilization: Chinese EFL learners' acquisition and use of formulaic sequences in L2 writing. *Estudos Anglo-Americanos* 42. 37–52.
Wen, Z. 2015. Working memory in second language acquisition and processing: The Phonological/Executive model. In Z. Wen, M.B. Mota & A. McNeill. (eds.), *Working memory in second language acquisition and processing*, 41–62. Bristol, UK: Multilingual Matters.
Wen, Z. 2016a. Phonological and executive working memory in L2 task-based speech planning and performance. *The Language Learning Journal* 44(4). 418–435.
Wen, Z. 2016b. *Working memory and second language learning: An integrated framework*. Bristol, UK: Multilingual Matters.
Wen, Z. (forthcoming). *Cognitive individual differences in second language acquisition: Theories, assessment and pedagogy*. Berlin: De Gruyter Mouton.
Wen, Z., A. Biedron & P. Skehan. 2017. Foreign language aptitude theory: Yesterday, today and tomorrow. *Language Teaching*. 50(1). 1–31.
Wen, Z, B. M. Mota & A. Mcneill. 2013. Working memory and SLA: Innovations in theory and research [Special Issue]. *Asian Journal of English Language Teaching* 23. 1–102.
Wen, Z, B. M. Mota & A. Mcneill. 2015. *Working memory in second language acquisition and processing*. Bristol, UK: Multilingual Matters.
Winke, P. 2013. An investigation into L2 aptitude for advanced Chinese language learning. *The Modern Language Journal* 97(1). 109–130.
Wood, D. 2010. *Formulaic language and second language speech fluency: Background, evidence, and classroom applications*. London/New York: Continuum.
Wood, D. 2015. *Fundamentals of formulaic language: An introduction*. London/New York: Bloomsbury.
Wray, A. 2000. Formulaic sequences in second language teaching. *Applied Linguistics* 21(4). 463–489.
Wray, A. 2002. *Formulaic language and the lexicon*. Cambridge: Cambridge University Press.
Wray, A. 2008. *Formulaic language: Pushing the boundary*. Oxford: Oxford University Press.
Wray, A. 2012. What do we (think we) know about formulaic language? An evaluation of the current state of play. *Annual Review of Applied Linguistics* 32. 231–254.
Wray, A. & M. Perkins. 2000. The functions of formulaic sequences: An integrated model. *Language and Communication* 20. 1–28.

Laura Gurzynski-Weiss, Carly Henderson, and Daniel Jung

3 Examining Timing and Type of Learner-Modified Output in Relation to Perception in Face-to-Face and Synchronous Task-Based Chat

1 Introduction

Decades of research within the cognitive-interactionist framework have demonstrated that corrective feedback can have facilitative effects for second language (L2) development, provided that learners notice and utilize the feedback given within meaning-based interaction. While this is largely agreed upon in L2 research, several more nuanced questions, including how to most effectively measure learners' noticing and use of feedback, however, have been the focus of much discussion. Recently, researchers have turned their critical attention to the ways learner noticing has been operationalized, such as modified output, seeking more specific definitions to describe how learners notice the corrective nature of feedback, the target of feedback, and how this relates (or does not) to what they do with the feedback they are given. Additionally, studies have turned their attention to examinations of the factors that mediate the facilitative nature of feedback, including the mode in which feedback is provided.

The current study examines these issues and expands upon research initiated by Gurzynski-Weiss and Baralt (2014, 2015), investigating learners' use of feedback, operationalized as full, partial and no modified output, in tasks completed face-to-face and via synchronous computerized chat. Specifically, the aforementioned earlier work demonstrated a significant relationship between type of learner-modified output (partial > full > none) produced immediately following feedback, and learners' correct noticing of immediate feedback, with no significant difference according to the mode of interaction (face-to-face or chat). In other words, when learners parsed out only the corrected mistake, and reformulated it, they were significantly more likely to correctly notice the feedback as feedback, and to notice the target of that feedback.

The current study extends this research by examining (a) both the type (full, partial, and none) and timing (immediate and delayed) of modified output in

---

Laura Gurzynski-Weiss, Carly Henderson and Daniel Jung, Indiana University

DOI 10.1515/9781501503399-004

relationship to learners' correct perception of feedback and (b) if these relationships differ according to the mode of interaction. Examining these potential relationships between learners' visible responses to feedback in the form of modified output and their cognitive processing of said feedback provides valuable information for theorists, researchers, and pedagogues alike.

2 The role of feedback and noticing in L2 learning

Theoretically, noticing is posited to be necessary for second language (L2) acquisition to occur, as it encourages learners to connect form and meaning (Schmidt 1990, 1995, 2001). Particularly important for the current study, feedback provided during interaction by more competent interlocutors is seen as beneficial for learning as it may facilitate learners' noticing of the mismatch between their erroneous production and target-like forms when learners are already engaged in meaningful exchanges (Long 1996). Empirically, meta-analyses highlight research attesting to the facilitative role that feedback plays in second language acquisition (SLA) (Keck, Iberri-Shea, Tracy-Ventura, and Wa-Mbaleka 2006; Li 2010; Lyster and Saito 2010; Mackey and Goo 2007; Russell and Spada 2006). As a result, research has turned to the investigation of factors potentially mediating learners' noticing of feedback including cognitive and affective learner-internal factors (e.g., Goo 2012), task complexity (e.g., Baralt 2013), and mode of interaction (synchronous computer-mediated chat or face-to-face) (e.g., Gurzynski-Weiss and Baralt 2014, 2015; Lai and Zhao 2006).

A central challenge in this line of research is measuring learners' noticing, investigated in the current study as learners' perception of feedback reported during stimulated recalls[1]. While research has often claimed links between learners' noticing and use of feedback within task-based interaction, operationalized as language-related episodes, (Storch 2008; Swain and Lapkin 2001), uptake (Loewen 2005; Lyster and Ranta 1997; Mackey and Philp 1998; Nuevo 2006; Panova and Lyster 2002; Révész, Sachs, and Mackey 2011), or modified output (Egi 2010; Gurzynski-Weiss and Baralt 2014, 2015; McDonough 2005; Nuevo, Adams, and Ross-Feldman 2011), whether or not these constructs correspond to learners' cognitive perceptions of feedback, or are the interpretation of the researcher, has not always been empirically verified. For this reason, recent

---

[1] By perception of feedback, we mean whether or not learners reported having cognitively registered both the corrective nature of a specific feedback episode, and the target of the feedback, explained in more detail in the methods section. Other studies, such as Leow (1997) have utilized learners' comments during think-alouds to operationalize noticing.

research has paired examinations of learner feedback use along with retrospective methodology, in particular, stimulated recall protocols (Gurzynski-Weiss and Baralt 2014, 2015; Mackey, Gass, and McDonough 2000).

In this study, we adopt one of the more narrow operationalizations of learner use of feedback as modified output. We follow Gurzynski-Weiss and Baralt (2014, 2015), where learner-modified output occurs following corrective feedback and is a reformulation by the learner of her original non-targetlike production incorporating the feedback.[2]

3 Relationships between modified output and noticing

Theoretically, modified output is believed to promote cognitive processing beneficial for learning. As modifying one's output immediately following feedback involves reprocessing the original non-targetlike production, this may lead to continued hypothesis testing about the targetlike form and can ultimately result in the learner incorporating those modifications into her interlanguage (Nuevo, Adams, and Ross-Feldman 2011; Swain 1995). Several studies empirically investigating a link between modified output and learners' perception of feedback have found a positive relationship (e.g., Egi 2010; Gurzynski-Weiss and Baralt 2014, 2015; Mackey, Gass and McDonough. 2000), and even between learner use of feedback and learning (e.g., Havranek 2002; Loewen 2005; referred to as uptake in these studies). Despite this empirical support, others have suggested that learners' immediate response to feedback may be merely a parroting of such feedback in which no conscious noticing of its corrective nature took place (Mackey and Philp 1998; McDonough and Mackey 2006). However, these two studies did not measure noticing in relationship with learner use of feedback.

Egi (2010) and Mackey, Gass, and McDonough (2000) did examine learners' use of feedback in relationship to noticing, measured via learner verbal reports from stimulated recalls. Egi (2010) found that learners noticed feedback significantly more often when they produced uptake. Results from Mackey, Gass, and McDonough (2000) also demonstrated that the feedback target was accurately perceived in two-thirds of feedback episodes containing uptake as compared to one-third of episodes containing no uptake. Importantly, these studies were limited to examining the relationship between learner-modified output and

---

[2] For additional discussion on this operationalization choice, and how it differs from other terminology, see Gurzynski-Weiss and Baralt (2015).

noticing in the face-to face mode. These studies demonstrate evidence that learner use of feedback is related to their perception of feedback, and leave questions for additional research to address, particularly if this relationship between noticing and modified output may be affected by additional variables, including mode and type of modified output.

4 Factors found to influence the relationship between modified output and noticing

4.1 Mode

One of the factors believed to influence modified output and noticing has been mode. Originally conceived as potentially heightening the likelihood that learners would notice feedback, synchronous computer-mediated chat (henceforth "chat") has been heavily and comparatively investigated with face-to-face interaction (e.g., Gurzynski-Weiss and Baralt 2014; Lai and Zhao 2006; Lai, Fei, and Roots 2008; Long 2007; Sauro 2009; Yilmaz and Yuksel 2011). However, despite claims that learners would have more time in chat to notice forms within meaning, be able to return to previous exchanges to look for targetlike form, and have access to a more salient feedback (as compared to face-to-face), the latter hypothesis, with respect to the increase in learners' noticing, has not been empirically supported. While research has demonstrated that learners have additional time and opportunity to return to previous exchanges in chat (Baralt and Gurzynski-Weiss 2011, Gurzynski-Weiss and Baralt 2014; Lai and Zhao 2006), most studies have found no significant difference in learner noticing of feedback or modified output according to the mode of interaction, face-to-face or chat (Gurzynski-Weiss and Baralt 2014, 2015).[3]

An interesting trend was identified by Gurzynski-Weiss and Baralt's (2014) study, which examined noticing of feedback across face-to-face and chat modes by intermediate learners of Spanish. While the study found no significant mode differences for noticing of feedback as reported during a stimulated recall, the

---

[3] Lai and Zhao (2006) found that learners reported being more aware of their output during chat tasks, and having significantly more self-corrections. However, the study contained methodological limitations that prohibit a full contribution to the research domain. Smith (2009) also found German learners to engage in more self-repair over grammatical items than lexical items in a chat environment, although this was not compared to their self-corrections in a face-to-face task.

authors found that the opportunities for modified output were significantly different according to mode and type of feedback. Specifically, the face-to-face mode afforded more opportunities for modified output following feedback on lexis and morphosytnax. The researchers also found that learners took advantage of these opportunities more in this mode, contrary to results by Lai and Zhao (2006). In a subsequent study, Gurzynski-Weiss and Baralt (2015) analyzed a subset of the (2014) data, investigating the relationship between type of modified output, noticing of feedback, and mode. The researchers found that in spite of the additional opportunities for modified output in face-to-face, there was no statistical difference in learner use of feedback according to mode.

4.2 Type of modified output

Drawing on earlier hypotheses that the type of learner use of feedback may provide insight into the nature of learner noticing (Loewen 2005; Robinson 1995), Gurzynski-Weiss and Baralt (2015) empirically operationalized learner-modified output as tertiary: full modified output, partial modified output, and no modified output, positing that partial modified output might be most predictive of correct noticing of feedback, given that learners demonstrate having parsed out the non-targetlike forms within a larger context. In this study, full modified output was learners' complete use (repetition) of the instructor interlocutor's correction. Partial modified output was the learners' partial use (repetition) of the correction, using only the corrected portion of the feedback. No modified output referred to learners not using any of the correction, including responses such as "yes," "no" or "okay." Gurzynski-Weiss and Baralt (2015), which examined the aforementioned subset of their (2014) data where feedback was noticed correctly, demonstrated a significant relationship between the type of learner-modified output (partial > full > none) produced immediately following feedback, and learners' correct noticing of immediate feedback, with no significant difference according to the mode of interaction. In other words, regardless of mode, learners' production of partial modified output was most predictive of their correct noticing of feedback, followed by the production of full modified output; both were significantly related to learners' correctly noticing feedback as compared to no production of modified output. In this initial study examining immediate modified output as full, partial, and none, Gurzynski-Weiss and Baralt (2015) demonstrated, as hypothesized, that when learners isolate a correction, they are more likely to notice the feedback as corrective, and accurately notice the target of the feedback.

4.3 Timing

Finally, an additional potentially intervening variable in the relationship between learner use of feedback and noticing are comparisons of the nature of interaction timing in face-to-face and chat. Some researchers (González-Lloret 2009; Henshaw 2011; Long 2007; Sauro 2007) have commented that mode differences have the potential to differentially affect interaction and, thus, relationships such as modified output and noticing. However, simple mode comparisons may no longer be sufficient, with many studies beginning to break down potential differences between modes, such as their effect on anxiety (Baralt and Gurzynski-Weiss 2011), timing of feedback (Arroyo and Yilmaz 2014) and turn-taking (González-Lloret 2009), with the aim of more thoroughly understanding the nature of interaction and the relationship between learner use of feedback, noticing, and eventually, learning in different interactional modes.

Timing has been investigated in relationship to feedback provision and learning, less so with respect to learner use of feedback and noticing. Researchers have commonly investigated the differences between feedback given immediately after the error and delayed feedback, which is given at the end of the task, lesson, or even several days later. While some hold immediate feedback as being optimally efficient because it promotes cognitive comparisons between the error and the correct form (Doughty 2001), others view delayed feedback as more beneficial due to the limited processing abilities of learners (Skehan 1998). Results from empirical research are split, with some studies finding no difference (e.g., Dabaghi 2006; Henshaw 2012; Nakata, 2015; Quinn 2014), and others finding an advantage for immediate feedback (Arroyo and Yilmaz 2015; Aubrey and Shintani 2014). A particular challenge to investigating the timing of feedback and, of particular relevance for this study, the timing of learner use of feedback, is the difficulty in measuring opportunity for immediate feedback as compared to delayed, and operationalizing turn-taking (for categorizing use of feedback), particularly in synchronous chat. As mentioned previously, it has been noted that turn-taking follows different patterns in face-to-face and chat communication due to mode differences (García and Jacobs 1999; Herring 1999), and many traditional methods used to define turns (such as the Turn Construction Unit, from Conversation Analysis [Sacks, Schegloff, and Jefferson 1974]) are unsuitable for describing chat conversations, where turns frequently overlap (González-Lloret 2009). In synchronous chat, this problematizes categorizations of feedback that depend on the definition of a turn, which influence potential coding of opportunity for and learner use of feedback as immediate or delayed.

To the best of our knowledge, immediate and delayed learner use of feedback has not been investigated in relationship to type of modified output. An additional contribution of the current study is the examination of learners' use of modified output in both immediate and delayed turns in face-to-face and chat.

5 The current study

Noticing is largely held to be an important if not necessary precursor for language learning. As previously discussed, recent research into the relationship between learners' immediate modified output and noticing (as measured by stimulated recalls) has demonstrated that partial modified output may be the best predictor of correct feedback perception, when compared to full modified output and no modified output, regardless of whether the task-based interaction occurs in face-to-face or chat (Gurzynski-Weiss and Baralt 2014, 2015). However, the timing of modified output, a potentially critical component of these mode differences, has not been empirically considered in relationship to type of modified output. This study builds upon this line of work by examining the type (full, partial, none) as well as the timing (immediate and delayed) of learners' modified output in relationship to their accurate perception of feedback in face-to-face and chat task-based interaction.

5.1 Research questions

1. Is learner-modified output (immediate and/or delayed; as well as none, partial, or full) indicative of their accurate perception of feedback?
2. Are these relationships different in face-to-face or chat task-based interactions?

5.2 Participants

The participants in this study were 16 intermediate-level Spanish learners, 4 male and 12 female, recruited from two sections of an introductory course in Hispanic Linguistics, one in the spring and a second section during the summer semester in the U.S. These courses are accessible only through placement testing or completion of five semesters of university-level Spanish in a task-supported language department. Participants reported using technology, such as word processing, chat, and social media, for an average of 31.5 hours per week. Of these, 3.3 hours were spent interacting in Spanish, while the remaining 28.2 hours were spent interacting in English. The majority of participants ($n = 13$) reported not speaking additional languages. Three reported speaking additional languages (French, Italian, or Arabic); these languages were studied for less than two semesters at the college level. Participants were provided extra credit in their course for completion of the study. The interlocutor was one of the authors. At the time of the study, he was a 25-year-old male doctoral student in Hispanic Linguistics who was a near-native speaker of Spanish. The interlocutor had taken classes in Applied Linguistics, including corrective feedback and teaching methodology, and had experience teaching university-level beginning and intermediate Spanish.

5.3 Procedure

This study largely replicated the methodology employed by Gurzynski-Weiss and Baralt (2014, 2015). Participants interacted one-on-one with the interlocutor in both face-to-face and chat interactions during which they received corrective feedback while they completed a task. After each interaction, learners engaged in a mode-specific stimulated recall session to measure their noticing of the corrective feedback they received.[4]

5.4 Materials

Materials used in the current study included two experimental information-gap tasks, stimulated-recall questions targeting learners' perceptions during the task, and a background questionnaire to elicit demographic information. The tasks met Ellis's (2009) criteria for what constitutes a task, in that they had a focus on meaning (rather than form), there was a 'gap' creating a need for communication, learners had to rely on their own resources to complete the task, and there was a non-linguistic, communicative outcome (p. 223). Complete copies of all materials used in this experiment can be found via www.IRIS-database.org.

5.4.1 Background questionnaire

Participants completed a background questionnaire to obtain information about basic demographics, computer use (in both English and Spanish), impressions of the study, perceptions of language practice in the two different modes, experience with Spanish at the college level, and motivation for studying Spanish. The questionnaires were used to ensure that learners had comparable experience with interaction via chat and face-to-face and to provide a more qualitative picture of any patterns indicated by the quantitative analysis.

---

[4] Additionally, the current study employed pre- and post-test measures to compare noticing of feedback in relation to learning. The pre, post-, and delayed post-test materials and data are not considered here.

5.4.2 Information-gap tasks

Learners engaged in two information-gap tasks with the interlocutor. These tasks were taken from Gurzynski-Weiss and Baralt (2014, 2015), given their success in eliciting interaction between participants and their interlocutors. Learners were given a picture depicting either a kitchen scene or a living room scene, with 12 items (furniture, appliances, etc.) highlighted. They were told their interlocutor had the same picture, but was missing the highlighted items, and they had to explain to him where to place the cut-out of each item. During the face-to-face interaction, learners were unable to see the interlocutor's picture and were told to avoid using gestures and to rely on their words. During the chat interaction, participants interacted with the interlocutor from another room using Skype.

5.4.3 Stimulated recall protocol

After completing each information-gap task with the interlocutor, participants completed the mode-specific stimulated recall with one of the other researchers. During the recall focusing on the chat, participants viewed a screen capture video of the interaction captured with iShowYou recording software, and during the face-to-face recall they viewed a video recording of the interaction. Both recall recordings were seen on the same MacBook Pro laptop. During each stimulated recall, learners were shown ten interaction episodes in which there was (a) an error, (b) an interlocutor response, and (c) the participant response, if any. The interaction episodes were chosen to ensure an even mix of feedback that learners responded to and did not respond to, and further divided based on the type of error (lexis, grammar) and whether or not it was the first time the error had been committed during the interaction or if it was an error that had been produced earlier. After being shown each interaction episode, learners were asked to comment on what they remembered thinking at the time.

6 Coding and analysis

6.1 Coding

The chat and face-to-face transcripts were coded for: (1) error type; (2) type of feedback; (3) opportunity for modified output; (4) type of modified output (none, partial, or full); and (5) timing of modified output (immediate or delayed[5]). The

---

[5] The delayed data was also coded for the number of turns delayed, to be discussed in depth in a separate paper.

stimulated recall protocol comments were coded for learner accurate noticing of feedback as feedback, as well as feedback target.

Opportunity for immediate modified output was a binary variable, coded as *yes* or *no*, depending on whether or not the interlocutor provided time and space for learner-modified output in the turn immediately following feedback. In the chat mode, if the interlocutor provided feedback and then stopped typing, this was coded as an opportunity for modified output. However, if the interlocutor provided feedback and then continued entering text, thus not allowing time or space in the discourse for the learner to modify her output, this was coded as no opportunity for immediate modified output. It was considered that there was always at least one opportunity[6] for delayed modified output, defined as time and space for the learner to modify their output in later turns during the interaction.

Type of modified output was operationalized as none, partial, or full. When the learner did not produce modified output for a particular correction, it was coded as no modified output, as were acknowledgements and repetitions of the original error without correction. If the learner incorporated the exact feedback provided by the interlocutor it was coded as full modified output. If a learner isolated and repeated only the corrected element, including incorporating it into a new utterance, it was coded as partial modified output.

Finally, timing of modified output was also a binary variable, coded as immediate or delayed. Immediate modified output was coded as modified output immediately following feedback, while delayed was coded as any modified output that occurred with at least one intervening turn between the feedback and the modified output. Operationalizations and examples of opportunity for, type and timing of modified output and learner accurate noticing of feedback can be found in Appendix A.[7]

6.2 Analysis

For research question 1, examining the type and timing of modified output in relationship to correct noticing of feedback, we ran a generalized estimated

---

6 As mentioned in the previous footnote, we originally coded the number of turns delayed. To facilitate statistical analyses, it was necessary to only consider the first opportunity for delayed modified output, so as not to have too many empty cells.

7 Due to space limitations, operationalizations for error type, feedback type, stimulated recall comment categorization, and learner noticing of feedback are not provided in the current paper. The reader is referred to Gurzynski-Weiss and Baralt (2015) for detailed operationalizations and examples.

equation[8] with binary outcome to account for a correlation within subject (e.g., the fact that each participant had multiple entries, ranging from 7–27 errors per participant). In other words, for each opportunity for modified output, learner-modified output was analyzed as both a type (full, partial, or none) as well as having occurred at a specific time (immediate or delayed) in relationship to learners' noticing (correct or incorrect noticing of feedback). For research question 2, examining potential differences between these relationships in face-to-face as compared to chat, we ran a generalized estimated equation with partial and full modified output collapsed. This was necessary as some of the cells were zero (for example, there were no instances of immediate full modified output in the chat mode). Importantly, when interpreting the generalized estimated equation, the means (percentages), not effect sizes, are the common predictive value of the strength of relationship.

7 Results

Prior to running the generalized estimated equation, we ran cross-tabs to describe the data set. As seen in Table 1, there were 554 task-based interactions analyzed in the current study, with comparable numbers of interactions taking place in face-to-face (264) and chat (290).

7.1 Descriptives: Face-to-face

When learners had opportunities for immediate modified output in face-to-face task-based interaction, they most often did not produce modified output, followed by partial, then full modified output. When it came to learners noticing feedback correctly or not immediately following feedback, the largest difference noted was between immediate partial modified output (noticed correctly 72.0% of the time, as compared to when they did not notice or were incorrect in their perception of the target of feedback, 28.0% of the time). With respect to opportunities for delayed modified output in face-to-face, learners followed the same pattern: they most often did not produce modified output, followed by partial then full modified output. With respect to noticing feedback correctly or not following opportunities for delayed modified output, the largest difference was between

---

[8] Generalized estimated equation (GEE) is the appropriate statistical test to use when data violate the independency assumed in binary logistic regression.

learners noticing correctly (58.5%) or incorrectly (41.5%) when they did not produce delayed modified output. For delayed partial and full, the numbers were too close to draw conclusions.

7.2 Descriptives: Chat

When learners had opportunities for immediate modified output in chat, they overwhelmingly did not produce modified output, followed by partial then full modified output. When it came to learners noticing feedback correctly or not immediately in chat, the largest difference noted was between immediate partial (noticed correctly 93.3% of the time, as compared to when they did not notice/

Table 1: Learner noticing in relationship to modified output timing and type

	Not noticed/not correct	Noticed correctly	Total
Face-to-face (264 episodes)			
No Delayed	34 (41.5%)	48 (58.5%)	82 (100.0%)
Delayed Partial	22 (48.9%)	23 (51.1%)	45 (100.0%)
Delayed Full	2 (40.0%)	3 (60.0%)	5 (100.0%)
Totals Delayed	58 (43.9%)	74 (56.1%)	132 (100.0%)
No Immediate	40 (48.2%)	43 (51.8%)	83 (100.0%)
Immediate Partial	7 (28.0%)	18 (72.0%)	25 (100.0%)
Immediate Full	11 (45.8%)	13 (54.2%)	24 (100.0%)
Totals Immediate	58 (43.9%)	74 (56.1%)	132 (100.0%)
Chat (290 episodes)			
No Delayed	42 (48.8%)	44 (51.2%)	86 (100.0%)
Delayed Partial	22 (39.3%)	34 (60.7%)	56 (100.0%)
Delayed Full	1 (33.3%)	2 (66.7%)	3 (100.0%)
Totals Delayed	65 (44.8%)	80 (55.2%)	145 (100.0%)
No Immediate	64 (50.8%)	62 (49.2%)	126 (100.0%)
Immediate Partial	1 (6.7%)	14 (93.3%)	15 (100.0%)
Immediate Full	0 (0.0%)	4 (100.0%)	4 (100.0%)
Totals Immediate	65 (44.8%)	80 (55.2%)	145 (100.0%)
Overall across modes (554 episodes)			
No Delayed	76 (45.2%)	92 (54.8%)	168 (100.0%)
Delayed Partial	44 (43.6%)	57 (56.4%)	101 (100.0%)
Delayed Full	3 (37.5%)	5 (62.5%)	8 (100.0%)
Totals Delayed	123 (44.4%)	154 (55.6%)	277 (100.0%)
No Immediate	104 (49.8%)	105 (50.2%)	209 (100.0%)
Immediate Partial	8 (20.0%)	32 (80.0%)	40 (100.0%)
Immediate Full	11 (39.3%)	17 (60.7%)	28 (100.0%)
Totals Immediate	123 (44.4%)	154 (55.6%)	277 (100.0%)

were incorrect in their perception of the target of feedback, 6.7% of the time). With respect to opportunities for delayed modified output in chat, learners followed the same pattern: they most often did not produce modified output, followed by partial then full modified output. When it came to learners noticing chat-based feedback correctly or not following opportunities for delayed modified output, however, the largest difference noted was between delayed partial (noticed correctly 60.7% of the time, as compared to when they did not notice/ were incorrect in their perception of the target of feedback, 39.3% of the time). For no delayed and full delayed modified output, the numbers were too close to draw conclusions.

7.3 Research question one: Type and timing of learner-produced modified output in relationship to perception

The reader is reminded that research question one asked: Is learner-modified output (immediate and/or delayed; none, partial, full) indicative of their accurate perception of feedback? Results revealed that the type of immediate modified output is significantly related to learner feedback perception, χ^2 (2) = 8.291, p = .02. Specifically, 80.0% of immediate partial-modified output is perceived correctly by learners as compared to a 50.2% chance of correctly perceiving feedback with no immediate modified output ($p < .01$), averaging across modes. 60.7% of immediate full modified output is perceived correctly by learners (as compared to a 50.2% chance of correctly perceiving feedback with no immediate modified output), though this relationship was not significant ($p = .75$).

Full or partial delayed modified output was not predictive of perception of feedback, again averaging across both modes, χ^2 (2) =.037, $p = .98$. Delayed partial is 56.4% predictive (as compared to 54.8% of correctly perceiving feedback with no delayed modified output produced), and delayed full is 62.5% predictive (as compared to 54.8% of correctly perceiving feedback with no delayed modified output).

7.4 Research question two: Potential differences in face-to-face and chat

The second research question asked: Are these relationships (type and timing of learner-modified output and their accurate perception of feedback) different in face-to-face and chat modes? For the generalized estimated equation analysis for this second research question, we had to collapse partial and full modified output, as some cells were zero. Thus, for this research question, we isolated our examination specifically on immediate and delayed modified output according to mode. To facilitate this reading, we will denote this collapse as full/partial when reporting results for this second research question.

When the data was split according to mode, there were significant differences: the effect of full/partial immediate modified output depends on mode, χ^2 (1) = 7.89, p = .01. Learner production of full/partial immediate modified output was predictive in both modes but stronger in chat: 94.7% of the time learners correctly perceived feedback when they produced full/partial immediate modified output in chat (as compared to 49.2% with no immediate full or partial modified output produced, p < .01). In face-to-face learners accurately perceived feedback 63.3% of the time when they produced full/partial immediate modified output (as compared to 51.8% with no immediate modified output produced, p = .15).

The effect of full/partial delayed modified output was also found to depend on mode, χ^2 (1) = 4.11, p = .04. This effect was found to be predictive in both modes but stronger again in chat: 61.0% of the time learners correctly perceived feedback when they produced full/partial delayed modified output in chat (as compared to 51.2% with no full/partial delayed modified output produced, p = .17). In contrast, in face-to-face learners more often correctly perceived feedback when they did not produce delayed modified output, 58.5%, as compared to when they produced full/partial delayed modified output, 52.0%, p = .19.

8 Discussion

To facilitate the most robust interpretation of the data, the discussion will be divided as follows: (a) relationships between learner immediate modified output and accurate perception of feedback across modes (research question 1, part 1); (b) relationships between learner immediate modified output according to mode (research question 2, part 1); (c) relationships between learner delayed modified output and accurate perception of feedback across modes (research question 1, part 2); followed by (d) relationships between learner delayed modified output according to mode (research question 2, part 2). A reminder that this study is situated within the cognitive-interactionist strand of research, which views feedback provided within meaning-based interaction as potentially beneficial for L2 learning, provided that learners cognitively register the feedback as corrective and understand the target of the feedback. In this study we examined both learners' noticing and use of feedback, to see if relationships between noticing and modified output found in earlier work (Gurzynski-Weiss and Baralt 2014, 2015) are found in another learning context. We also examined whether or not learners' partial and full modified output was more or less likely to demonstrate their noticing if it was produced immediately following feedback, or produced later on in the interactions, which took place both in face-to-face and computer-mediated modes.

In this study, learner-modified output was found to be indicative of their accurate perception of feedback (as corrective in nature as well as with respect to the specific target of feedback) overall across modes, at least with respect to turns immediately following feedback provision. Specifically, 80.0% of immediate partial modified output was perceived correctly by learners (as compared to 50.2% chance of correctly perceiving feedback with no immediate modified output). While immediate full modified output was also more predictive of correctly noticing feedback (60.7%) as compared to no immediate modified output (50.2%), this relationship was not significant. The current results corroborate findings from Gurzynski-Weiss and Baralt (2015), which found both partial and full immediate modified output to significantly relate to learner noticing as compared to no immediate modified output, with a greater effect for partial. We concur with their argumentation that partial immediate modified output, at least in these two studies, provides evidence that the learner has noticed the feedback as corrective, and accurately focused on the nature of the error. The learner must parse out the error from the remainder of the utterance and choose to use it. Additionally, in producing partial immediate modified output, the learner demonstrates a commitment to utilize the task-based interaction as a learning opportunity. When learners produce comments such as "yes" or "ok," coded in this (and the earlier) study as no modified output, this could be taken equally as evidence of their desire to move on in the interaction and/or more of a social response than a willingness to focus once again on form, as is the case with partial immediate modified output. Other studies have similarly cautioned that acknowledgments render it difficult if not impossible to determine whether learners have processed the targeted structure, referring to these instances as "unsuccessful uptake" (Loewen 2004, 2005) or "continue" (Mackey and Philp 1998), among other classifications. In other words, in this and previous research, for learners' interaction to be beneficial for further use, learners must go beyond simply speaking or typing – they need to engage with the information and use it in specific ways. The fact that this study (and Gurzynski-Weiss and Baralt 2015) found learners' noticing to relate to their observable behavior is promising news for instructors, in addition to researchers. If additional studies find similar results, this research may be able to inform in-class practices for learner use of feedback.

Examining the patterns more closely according to mode, interpretations are inherently limited by the required collapse of full and partial modified output (a reminder to the reader that this is written as full/partial). As with the first, results for the second research question demonstrated significant relationships between full/partial immediate modified output in relationship to learners' correct noticing. This relationship was significantly stronger in chat: 94.7% of the time that learners correctly perceived feedback was when they produced full/partial immediate modified output, as compared to no immediate modified output (49.2%). This relationship corroborates results from the only other study to examine full and partial modified output. Gurzynski-Weiss and Baralt (2015) also found partial modified output to be a stronger indicator of accurate noticing in chat as compared to face-to-face, and argued that the juxtaposition of the incorrect and correct form, followed by the learners' production of immediate modified output, provided an abundance of information for the learners to adjust their interlanguage (p. 1410); this opportunity is perhaps not as salient in face-to-face. Additionally, while previous research has not compared types of modified output in face-to-face and chat, synchronous chat in general has been described often as talking "in slow motion," providing additional time and opportunity for learners to notice feedback (Beauvois 1992). There is the possibility that learners were experiencing additional opportunities to notice feedback given the greater time taken to complete the tasks in SCMC, as has been a consistent finding across studies (see, for example, greater timing found for SCMC interaction in Baralt 2013; Baralt and Gurzynski-Weiss 2011; Gurzynski-Weiss and Baralt 2014, etc.). Importantly, these results speak to the potential differences inherent in modes of interaction. Despite the push for online language learning, this study, like others (Jepson 2005; Kaneko 2009; Roushad, Wigglesworth, and Storch 2015; Sim, Har, and Luan 2010; Yanguas 2010), demonstrates that there may be differences in learning opportunities that are mode-specific and interactive task design should be considered with these potential processing differences in mind. The empirically researched benefits of interaction that have been found in face-to-face cannot be assumed to extend as-is to chat.

When investigated across modes, these relationships did not hold for delayed modified output: neither full (62.5%) nor partial (56.4%) delayed modified output was significantly predictive of learners' perception of feedback as compared to no modified output (54.8%). First, it is important to mention that there were only eight instances of delayed full modified output in both modes; five of which were noticed correctly and three which were not noticed/noticed incorrectly. This is considerably lower than the 101 instances of delayed partial and the 168 instances of no delayed, and such notable differences, as well as the previous lack of research examining this potentially mediating factor of timing, preclude any strong statements regarding the data interpretation. Future research is needed following this initial study on this variable of timing, a recent focus of feedback research that has found inconclusive results to date, both in face-to-face (Quinn 2014) and in chat, (Arroyo and Yilmaz 2015).[9]

Splitting the data according to mode proved useful for deeper investigations into full/partial delayed modified output. Full/partial delayed modified output was also found to be predictive of learners' noticing of feedback (61.0%) as compared to no delayed modified output (51.2%), and this relationship was stronger in chat. Surprisingly, in face-to-face, learners most often correctly perceived feedback when no delayed modified output was produced (58.5%), as compared to producing full/partial delayed modified output (52.0%), although this relationship was not significant. The finding that delayed full/partial modified output is more predictive of noticing in chat is perhaps evidence that some of the hypothesized mode differences (e.g., Ortega 2009) are in fact borne out when investigated in enough detail. For example, due to the utilization of screen capture software, we were able to watch learners scroll back up to consult previous feedback, which happened often. At times, learners even copy-and-pasted their interlocutor's correction. This option was of course unavailable in face-to-face. Instead, in the face-to-face mode, learners frequently asked the interlocutor to supply the word they had learned earlier (with questions such as, "¿*Cómo se dice* 'counter'?" 'How does one say counter?'), or attempted something that approximated the word. Often in face-to-face interaction it was clear that learners were frustrated with their inability to remember the new words, sighing loudly or making faces. Other studies have also reported this type of emotional response that potentially influenced face-to-face interaction (e.g., Baralt, Gurzynski-Weiss, and Kim 2016; Kim and Tracy-Ventura 2011; Sheen 2008). Despite the finding in this study that delayed modified output was more predictive of noticing in chat than in face-to-face, more research is needed with respect to the lasting effect of delayed modified output. For example, while it may be more accessible for learners interacting in chat to consult and/or copy-and-paste feedback from an earlier interaction, their cognitive involvement is arguably limited, particularly compared to retyping the correction from memory. In these cases, one would anticipate a more lasting effect for delayed modified output depending on how learners produced it, and how many turns later. It would be interesting, too, to see if there were different relationships observed for learners with greater working memory, in relationship to mode (perhaps face-to-face being more difficult and presumably more possible for those with greater working memory), type (partial modified output perhaps more possible compared to those with less working

---

9 Both Quinn 2014 and Arroyo and Yilmaz 2015 studied the timing of feedback only, without considering modified output.

memory) and timing (delayed modified output being more accessible to those with greater working memory).

9 Limitations and future research directions

The current study is not without limitations. A particular drawback was the necessity of collapsing full and partial modified output into a single category, which was unavoidable due to the modest sample size. As has been established in prior research, full and partial modified output have significant differences in terms of the noticing they indicate (Gurzynski-Weiss and Baralt 2015), and these differences should be examined in the context of delayed and immediate modified output, as well. Additionally, a measurement of acquisition should be employed to see if noticing of feedback correlates with acquisitional gains. This data was collected, but was not analyzed in the present study. Establishing whether a relationship between noticing of corrective feedback and acquisitional gains exists, and describing the extent of this relationship, is an important next step in understanding how perception of feedback and the production of modified output figures into the acquisition process. Additionally, more research into the chat modality, specifically from a discourse structure perspective, would allow for more impartial and more consistent operationalizations of turn-taking, which in turn would assist in feedback research which seeks to examine the effect of immediate and delayed feedback and modified output. Future studies should also take care to recruit a greater sample size; having 16 participants without doubt influenced the results and limited the generalizability of our findings. Finally, a fifth area for future research efforts would include investigations into type of task, particularly tasks that have a focus other than lexis. In this study, as with Gurzynski-Weiss and Baralt (2014, 2015), the information-gap tasks were designed to focus on prepositional and furniture vocabulary, with a secondary linguistic focus on the Spanish copula *ser* and *estar*. Future studies would do well to examine if these patterns of partial modified output > full modified output > no modified output extend to other linguistic domains, as well.

10 Conclusions

The current study extended work by Gurzynski-Weiss and Baralt (2014, 2015), examining if the relationship between type of modified output (full, partial, and none) and noticing (as measured via stimulated recall) would be replicated in task-based interactions in face-to-face and chat in a second Spanish FL context. The study also provided an initial investigation into the relationship between type and timing of modified output (operationalized as immediate and delayed) in relationship to learner noticing of feedback.

Largely corroborating results from Gurzynski-Weiss and Baralt (2015), we found learners' correct noticing of feedback to significantly relate to their immediate modified output: learners were most accurate in perceiving feedback when they produced immediate partial- modified output, compared to producing no modified output. Unlike the earlier study, this relationship was found to be more predictive in chat as compared to face-to-face. With respect to the novel contribution of the study, investigating delayed full, partial, and no modified output in relationship to learner noticing of feedback, no significant relationship was found between full/partial delayed modified output and learners' correct feedback perception. While full/partial delayed modified output related more to learners' correct noticing in chat (as compared to no delayed modified output), this relationship was not significant. In face-to-face, full/partial delayed modified output trended towards learners' incorrect feedback perception as compared to no production of delayed modified output.

References

Arroyo, Diana & Yucel Yilmaz. 2015. The effect of feedback timing on the acquisition of spanish gender agreement through synchronous computer-mediated communication. Paper presented at the meeting of the American Association of Applied Linguistics, University of Toronto, 21–24 March.
Aubrey, Scott & Natsuko Shintani. 2014. The effects of synchronous and asynchronous written corrective feedback on grammatical accuracy in a computer-mediated environment. Paper presented at the meeting of the American Association of Applied Linguistics, University of Portland, 22–25 March.
Baralt, Melissa. 2013. The impact of cognitive complexity on feedback efficacy during online versus face-to-face interactive tasks. *Studies in Second Language Acquisition* 35(4). 689–725.
Baralt, Melissa & Laura Gurzynski-Weiss. 2011. Comparing learners' state anxiety during task-based interaction in computer-mediated and face-to-face communication. *Language Teaching Research* 15(2). 201–229.
Baralt, Melissa, Laura Gurzynski-Weiss, & YouJin Kim. 2016. The effects of task type and classroom environment on learners' engagement with the language. In Masatoshi Sato & Susan Ballinger (eds.), *Peer interaction and L2 learning*, 209–239. Amsterdam/Philadelphia, PA: John Benjamins.
Beauvois, Margaret. 1992. Computer-assisted classroom discussion in the foreign language classroom: Conversation in slow motion. *Foreign Language Annals* 25(5). 455–464.

Doughty, Catherine. 2001. Cognitive underpinnings of focus on form. In Peter Robinson, Michael Long, & Jack Richards (eds.), *Cognition and second language instruction*, 206–257. Cambridge: Cambridge University Press.

Dabaghi, Azizollah. 2006. Error correction: Report on a study. *Language Learning Journal* 34(1). 10–13.

Egi, Takako. 2010. Uptake, modified output, and learner perceptions of recasts: Learner responses as language awareness. *Modern Language Journal* 94. 1–21.

Ellis, Rod. 2009. Task-based language teaching: Sorting out the misunderstandings. *International Journal of Applied Linguistics* 19(3). 221–246.

Ellis, Rod, Helen Basturkmen & Shawn Loewen. 2001. Learner uptake in communicative ESL lessons. *Language Learning* 51(2). 281–318.

García, Angela C. & Jennifer Baker Jacobs. 1999. The eyes of the beholder: Understanding the turn-taking system in quasi-synchronous computer-mediated communication. *Research on Language and Social Interaction* 32(4). 337–367.

González-Lloret, Marta. 2009. CA for computer-mediated interaction in the Spanish L2 classroom. In Gabriele Kasper & Hanh thi Nguyen (eds.), *Conversation analytic studies of L1 and L2 interaction, learning, and education*, 281–316. Honolulu, HI: University of Hawaii Press.

Goo, Jaemyung. 2012. Corrective feedback and working memory capacity in interaction-driven L2 learning. *Studies in Second Language Acquisition* 34(03). 445–474.

Gurzynski-Weiss, Laura & Melissa Baralt. 2014. Exploring learner perception and use of task-based interactional feedback in FTF and CMC modes. *Studies in Second Language Acquisition* 36(1). 1–37

Gurzynski-Weiss, Laura & Melissa Baralt. 2015. Does type of modified output correspond to learner noticing of feedback? A closer look in face-to-face and computer-mediated task-based interaction. *Applied Psycholinguistics* 36. 1393–1420.

Havranek, Gertraud. 2002. When is corrective feedback most likely to succeed? *International Journal of Educational Research* 37. 255–270.

Henshaw, Florencia. 2011. Effects of feedback timing in SLA: A computer assisted study on the Spanish subjunctive. In Ronald P. Leow & Cristina Sanz (eds.), *Implicit and explicit language learning: Conditions, processes, and knowledge in SLA and bilingualism*, 85–99. Washington, DC: Georgetown University Press.

Herring, Susan. 1999. Interactional coherence in CMC. *Journal of Computer-Mediated Communication* 4(4).

Jepson, Kevin. 2005. Conversations – and negotiated interaction – in text and voice chat rooms. *Language Learning & Technology* 9. 79–98.

Kaneko, Aki. 2009. *Comparing computer mediated communication (CMC) and face-to-face (FTF) communication for the development of Japanese as a foreign language*. Perth, Australia: The University of Western Australia dissertation.

Keck, Casey, Gina Iberri-Shea, Nicole Tracy-Ventura, & Safary Wa-Mbaleka. 2006. Investigating the empirical link between task-based interaction and acquisition. In John Norris & Lourdes Ortega (eds.), *Synthesizing Research on language learning and teaching*, 91–132. Amsterdam/Philadelphi, PA: John Benjamins.

Kim, YouJin & Nicole Tracy-Ventura. 2011. Task complexity, language anxiety and the development of past tense. In Peter Robinson (ed.), *Task complexity: Researching the Cognition Hypothesis of language learning and performance*, 287–306. Philadelphia, PA: John Benjamins.

Lai, Chun & Yong Zhao. 2006. Noticing and text-based chat. *Language Learning & Technology* 10(3). 102–120.

Lai, Chun, Fei Fei & Robin Roots. 2008. The contingency of recasts and noticing. *CALICO* 26(1). 70–90.
Leow, Ron. 1997. Attention, awareness, and foreign language behavior. *Language Learning* 47(3). 467–505.
Li, Shaofeng. 2010. The effectiveness of corrective feedback in SLA: A meta-analysis. *Language Learning* 60(2). 309–365.
Loewen, Shawn. 2004. Uptake in incidental focus on form in meaning-focused ESL lessons. *Language Learning* 54(1). 153–187.
Loewen, Shawn. 2005. Incidental focus on form and second language learning. *Studies in Second Language Acquisition* 27(3). 361–86.
Long, Michael H. 1996. The role of linguistic environment in second language acquisition. In William Ritchie, Tej K. Bhatia (eds.), *Handbook of second language acquisition*, 413–468. San Diego, CA: Academic Press.
Long, Michael H. 2007. *Problems in SLA*. Mahwah, NJ: Lawrence Erlbaum.
Lyster, Roy & Leila Ranta. 1997. Corrective feedback and learner uptake: negotiation of form in communicative classrooms. *Studies in Second Language Acquisition* 19(1). 37–66.
Lyster, Roy & Kazuya Saito. 2010. Oral feedback in classroom SLA. *Studies in Second Language Acquisition* 32(2). 265–302.
Mackey, Alison & Jenefer Philp. 1998. Conversational interaction and second language development: Recasts, responses, and red herrings? *Modern Language Journal* 82(3). 338–356.
Mackey, Alison, Susan Gass & Kim McDonough. 2000. How do learners perceive interactional feedback? *Studies in Second Language Acquisition* 22(4). 471–497.
Mackey, Alison & Jaemyung Goo. 2007. Interaction research in SLA: A meta-analysis and research synthesis. In Alison Mackey (ed.), *Conversational interaction in SLA: A collection of empirical studies*, 408–452. New York, NY: Oxford University Press.
McDonough, Kim. 2005. Identifying the impact of negative feedback and learners' responses on ESL question development. *Studies in Second Language Acquisition* 27(1). 79–103.
McDonough, Kim & Alison Mackey. 2006. Responses to recasts: Repetitions, primed production and linguistic development. *Language Learning* 56(4). 693–720.
Nakata, Tatsuya. 2015. Effects of feedback timing on second language vocabulary learning: Does delaying feedback increase learning? *Language Teaching* 19(4). 416–434.
Nuevo, Ana-María. 2006. *Task complexity and interaction: L2 learning opportunities and interaction*. Washington, DC: Georgetown University dissertation.
Nuevo, Ana-María, Rebecca Adams, & Lauren Ross-Feldman. 2011. Task complexity, modified output, and L2 development in learner–learner interaction. In Peter Robinson (ed.), *Second language task complexity: Researching the cognition hypothesis of language learning and performance*, 175–202. Amsterdam/Philadelphia, PA: John Benjamins.
Ortega, Lourdes. 2009. Interaction and attention to form in L2 text-based computer-mediated communication. In Alison Mackey & Charlene Polio (eds.), *Multiple perspectives on interaction*, 226–253. New York, NY: Routledge.
Panova, Liliana & Roy Lyster. 2002. Patterns of corrective feedback and uptake in an adult ESL classroom. *TESOL Quarterly* 36. 573–595.
Quinn, Paul. 2014. *Delayed versus immediate corrective feedback on orally produced passive errors in English*. Toronto, ON: University of Toronto dissertation.
Révész, Andrea, Rebecca Sachs & Alison Mackey. 2011. Task complexity, uptake of recasts, and L2 development. In Peter Robinson (ed.), *Second language task complexity: Researching the Cognition Hypothesis of language learning and performance*, 203–238. Amsterdam/Philadelphia, PA: John Benajmins.

Robinson, Peter. 1995. Attention, memory, and the "noticing" hypothesis. *Language Learning* 45(2). 283–331.
Rouhshad, Amir, Gillian Wigglesworth & Neomy Storch. 2015. The nature of negotiations in face-to-face versus computer-mediated communication in pair interactions. *Language Teaching Research* 20(4). 514–534.
Russell, Jane & Nina Spada. 2006. The effectiveness of corrective feedback for the acquisition of L2 grammar. In John Norris & Lourdes Ortega (eds.), *Synthesizing research on language learning and teaching*, 133–164. Amsterdam/Philadelphia, PA: John Benjamins.
Sacks, Harvey, Emanuel A. Schegloff, & Gail Jefferson. 1974. A simplest systematics for the organization of turn-taking conversation. *Language* 50(4). 696–735.
Sauro, Shannon. 2007. *A comparative study of recasts and metalinguistic feedback through computer mediated communication on the development of L2 knowledge and production accuracy*. Philadelphia, PA: University of Pennsylvania dissertation.
Sauro, Shannon. 2009. Computer-mediated corrective feedback and the development of L2 grammar. *Language Learning & Technology* 13(1). 96–120.
Schmidt, Richard. 1990. The role of consciousness in second language learning. *Applied Linguistics* 11(2). 129–158.
Schmidt, Richard. 1995. Consciousness and foreign language learning: A tutorial on the role of attention and awareness in learning. In Richard Schmidt (ed.), *Attention and Awareness in Foreign Language Learning*, 1–64. Manoa, HI: University of Hawaii.
Schmidt, Richard. 2001. Attention. In Peter Robinson (ed.), *Cognition and second language instruction*, 3–32. Mahwah, NJ: Lawrence Erlbaum.
Sheen, Younghee. 2008. Recasts, language anxiety, modified output, and L2 learning. *Language Learning* 58. 835–74.
Sim, Tam Shu, Kan Ngat Har, & Ng Lee Luan. 2010. Low proficiency learners in synchronous computer-assisted and face-to-face interactions. *The Turkish Online Journal of Educational Technology* 9. 61–75.
Skehan, Peter. 1998. *A cognitive approach to language learning*. New York, NY: Oxford University Press.
Storch, Neomy. 2008. Metatalk in a pair work activity: Level of engagement and implications for language development. *Language Awareness* 17(2). 95–114.
Swain, Merrill. 1995. Three functions of output in second language learning. In Guy Cook & Barbara Seidlhofer (eds.), *Principles and practice in applied linguistics: Studies in honour of H.G. Widdowson*, 125–144. New York, NY: Oxford University Press.
Swain, Merrill & Sharon Lapkin. 2001. Focus on form through collaborative dialogue: Exploring task effects. In Martin Bygate, Peter Skehan & Merrill Swain (eds.), *Researching pedagogic tasks: Second language learning, teaching and testing*, 99–118. Harlow, Essex: Longman.
Yanguas, Íñigo. 2010. Oral computer-mediated interaction between L2 learners: It's about time. *Language Learning & Technology* 15. 72–93.
Yilmaz, Yucel & Dogan Yuksel. 2011. Effects of communication mode and salience on recasts: A first exposure study. *Language Teaching Research* 15(4). 457–477.

Appendix A

Modified output type and timing operationalizations

Modified Output	Operationalization	Example from the dataset
Opportunity for immediate modified output	Learners were given time and space to produce modified output in the turn immediately following the interlocutor's feedback.	Learner: *Baja-debajo um **es** el lavaplatos.* Interlocutor: ***Está** el lavaplatos.* Learner: 'Low-below um **is** [wrong copula] the dishwasher.' Interlocutor: '**Is** [correct copula] the dishwasher.'
No opportunity for immediate modified output	Learners were not given time and space to produce modified output in the turn immediately following the interlocutor's feedback.	Learner: *Uh hay una um ... ¿sofá pequeña?* Interlocutor: *Un ¿un sofá pequeño? Muy bien ¿dónde?* Learner: 'Uh there is a um **small** sofa. [feminine adjective].' Interlocutor: 'Uh, a **small** sofa? Very good, where?'
Full modified output	Learners' accurate use of all feedback provided by the interlocutor in the turn immediately following feedback or a later turn.	Learner: ***Debajo** la mesa.* Interlocutor: ***Encima** de la mesa.* Learner: ***Encima** de la mesa.* Learner: '**Under** the table'. Interlocutor: '**On** the table'. Learner: '**On** the table.'
Partial modified output	Learners (in a turn immediately following the feedback or a later turn) isolated and repeated only the element that had been corrected in feedback.	Learner: *... y **es** en frente.* Interlocutor: ***Está** en frente.* Learner: ***Está**.* Learner: '... and **it's** [wrong copula] in front.' Interlocutor: '**It's** [correct copula] in front.' Learner: '**It's**'

No modified output	Learners do not produce any modified output after receiving feedback when they had an opportunity to do so. Learner acknowledgements such as *sí*, *ok* or *yeah* were also coded as no modified output, as were repetitions of their original errors.	Learner: *Un foto.* Interlocutor: *¿Una foto?* Learner: *Sí.* Learner: 'A [masculine] photo' Interlocutor: 'A [corrects to feminine] photo?' Learner: 'Yes.'
Timing of modified output	**Operationalization**	**Example from the dataset**
Immediate modified output	Learners produce modified output in the turn immediately following the interlocutor's feedback.	Learner: *Uh **es** um a la derecha donde dos paredes se uh conjuntan.* Interlocutor: *Ah ok el sofá pequeño **está** en la esquina.* Learner: *¡Esquina!* Learner: 'Uh **it's** [wrong copula] um to the right where two walls join.' Interlocutor: 'Ah ok the small sofa **is** [corrects copula] in the corner.' Learner: 'Corner!'
Delayed modified output	Learners produce modified output following interlocutor's feedback on a linguistic item during any turn proceeding the immediate turn after the feedback.	Learner: *Está en **el** mismo pared del horno.* Interlocutor: ***La** misma pared.* Learner: (96 turns after error): *En **la** misma pared e izquierda del librero...* Learner: "It's on **the** masculine] same wall of the oven." Interlocutor: "**The** [corrects to feminine] same wall." Learner: (96 turns after error) 'On the same wall and left of the bookcase.'

II **Sociocultural Theory Perspective**

Rémi A. van Compernolle
4 Dynamic Strategic Interaction Scenarios: A Vygotskian Approach to Focusing on Meaning and Form

1 Introduction

Task-based language teaching (TBLT) has received a great deal of attention in second language (L2) pedagogical research and practice, as evidenced by the proliferation of books and edited volumes dedicated to the topic in the last few years (e.g., Baralt, Gilabert, & Robinson 2014; Byrnes & Manchón 2014; Gónzalez-Lloret & Ortega 2014; Long 2015; Shehadeh & Coombe 2012). Generally speaking, TBLT focuses on creating pedagogical tasks that are meaning focused and relevant to real-word (i.e., beyond the classroom) activities. A useful, concise definition of a pedagogical task is provided by Nunan (2004):

> a pedagogical task is a piece of classroom work that involves learners in comprehending, manipulating, producing or interacting in the target language while their attention is focused on mobilizing their grammatical knowledge in order to express meaning, and in which the intention is to convey meaning rather than to manipulate form. (p. 4)

It should be noted, of course, that most tasks target specific lexicogrammatical patterns (i.e., forms) by design. For instance, students might be asked to retell a past experience as a way of eliciting the use of past tense forms in hopes that their ability to use such forms in communication will improve. In other words, while the overt focus is on meaning, there is typically an implicit focus on form.

In this chapter, I describe and illustrate an approach to TBLT that involves overt focus on meaning and form (FonMF) simultaneously – dynamic strategic interaction scenarios, or DSIS (van Compernolle 2013, 2014a, 2014b). The approach draws on two Vygotskian pedagogical applications, *strategic interaction scenarios* (DiPietro 1987) and *dynamic assessment* (Poehner 2008), which promote the internalization of patterns of meaning and patterns of language. The goal of DSIS is to promote FonFM in order to develop learners' conscious knowledge of L2 forms and meanings and to "speed up" (Paradis 2009), or "accelerate" (van Compernolle 2014a), their access to that knowledge during online language use. Specific examples are drawn from previous work involving US university

---

Rémi A. van Compernolle, Carnegie Mellon University

DOI 10.1515/9781501503399-005

learners of French who were engaged in a concept-based enrichment program focused on sociolinguistic and pragmatic variation. D-SISs can be considered tasks because 1) they focus primarily on meaning created during communication and 2) the contexts involve real-world situations that learners would be expected to encounter outside of a classroom context. As discussed later, the D-SISs were part of a larger extracurricular program that included additional, complementary metalinguistic tasks. In this way, D-SISs can be seen as part of a task-supported curriculum.

A few preliminaries are in order. From a Vygotskian perspective, meaning and form are inseparable.[1] This is because meaning is not restricted to the content of one's message. Rather, choices between forms communicate different perspectival, social-indexical, pragmatic, metaphorical, etc. meanings. A simple example is the social-indexical difference between the greetings *Hey, what's up?* and *Hello, how are you?*, both of which effectively communicate the same thing. However, the first option may point to such social-indexical meanings as informality, social closeness, youth, etc., whereas the second may be considered more standard, appropriate for use in more formal situations and between people who are socially distant. Understood this way, pedagogical tasks need to incorporate the purposeful manipulation of form, but not for form's sake; instead, form should be intentionally manipulated precisely because the choice between two or more possible forms is what makes meanings possible during communicative activity. The overarching goal of DSIS tasks is, therefore, to link learners' intended meanings with relevant forms and to support control over those forms during communication.

2 Background

2.1 Mediation and internalization

Mediation refers to Vygotsky's (1978) observation that higher forms of psychological functioning are accomplished through the integration of external stimuli that reorganize biologically endowed capacities. For example, neurological memory systems are reorganized by language so that we engage in the act of remembering things, events, people, and so on (Wertsch 1985). Similarly, other people in a child's or a learner's environment (e.g., parents, teachers) can mediate mental functioning. Examples include parents helping their children to assemble a puzzle

---

[1] Similar views are also espoused by cognitive linguistics (Tyler 2012), systemic-functional linguistics (Halliday 1978), and integrational linguistics (Harris 1998).

through prompts or modeling and teachers assisting their students in solving a mathematics problem. We can think of such external stimuli as language[2] as psychological mediators or tools while assistance from other people can be thought of as human mediation aiming to support the integration of psychological mediators into a child's or a learner's psychological functioning, that is, internalization.

Here, I would like to emphasize the distinction between assistance and mediation by other people (e.g., parents, teachers). Assistance can be seen as the broader concept, which refers to any kind of help, support, etc. provided in carrying out a task. In some cases, such assistance can be considered human mediation – as alluded to above – when the result is the development of new or modified psychological functioning. As noted in van Compernolle (2015), human mediation differs from assistance on a specific task because it involves "the construction of opportunities for mental development through the internalization of psychological tools" (p. 41). Thus, as we will see below, helping a learner to control a particular language form in a single instance is assistance, but helping the learner to understand how and when to control a particular language form for meaning-making activity across contexts (i.e., internalizing pragmatic concepts) is mediation.

It is important to note that internalization does not coequate with acquisition. Rather, as Zinchenko (2002) points out, it is about growth and transformation on the one hand and, on the other, it is bidirectional in that it involves inward and outward growth and transformation. This is to say that the internalization of a psychological mediator entails making it one's own (inward growth and transformation). In turn, the tool may be transformed in social-material activity (outward growth and transformation). A consequence of this conception of internalization is that development is operationalized as the qualitative transformation of mental capacities, as evidenced by the way mental functioning changes as new psychological mediators are integrated into our behaviors or as existing ones are modified for use in new contexts. Internalizing new, or modifying existing, psychological mediators is what allows us to plan and monitor our actions on the internal (psychological) and external (social) planes.

2.2 Formation of mental actions

One of Vygotsky's collaborators, Piotr Gal'perin (e.g., Gal'perin 1989, 1992), developed a theory of the formation of mental actions that involved three stages:

---

[2] Language has a dual mediational role. On the one hand, it is internalized to mediate internal mental activity. On the other hand, humans can mediate each other through the artifact of language. Thanks are due to an anonymous reviewer for helping to clarify this nuance.

orientation, execution, and control. *Orientation* refers to the way humans go about planning their actions, which may occur at any number of timeframes. We make split-second decisions every day that have immediate consequences (e.g., guiding the steering wheel and operating the accelerator and brake while driving), but we also make long-term plans in which the consequences of our actions are rather far in the future (e.g., when an architect begins to sketch out plans for a new building). This entails recognizing the resources that one can use and are available in the social world. *Execution* is the actual performance of the orientation, and *control* refers to our ability to monitor the execution of the orientation and adjust our actions as needed. It is important to note here that human mediators (e.g., teachers) help learners to plan, execute, and monitor and control actions.

Gal'perin's research showed that the quality of the orientation was key since it was involved in planning and controlling one's behavior (see Stetsenko and Arievitch 2010). Orientations that are based on limited information built up from specific empirical experiences (i.e., abstractions) are useful only in contexts with which learners are already familiar. By contrast, orientations derived from holistic theoretical or scientific concepts that are taught explicitly can be recontextualized or generalized to any context, including those with which learners have no experience. For example, Davydov (2004: 84) cites Spinoza's (1955: 35) scientific definition of a circle: "The figure described by any line whereof one end is fixed and the other free." As Davydov notes, the definition is superior to abstractions derived from empirical experience (i.e., familiarity with round objects) because it "gives a method for obtaining any circle – an infinite variety of circles" (p. 84). In other words, focus is on the process of generating a circle (i.e., its essence) and not simply on the characteristics of the finished product.

2.3 Metacommunicative knowledge as orientation

We can extend Gal'perin's and Davydov's arguments regarding the importance of the quality of one's orientation to L2 instruction with reference to metacommunicative knowledge. The term *metacommunicative knowledge* here is used in contrast to the more common term *metalinguistic knowledge* because it allows me to shift focus away from the form of language and toward the role that language and other semiotic means (e.g., paralinguistics, gesture) play in mediating interpersonal communication. While this includes knowledge of language forms, it also entails knowledge of the social and cultural meaning potential of discursive practices that may vary from one context to the next. Metacommunicative knowledge serves as the orienting basis for using language in communication.

As outlined in van Compernolle (2014a), high-quality knowledge of the ways in which variable forms of speech can index (Silverstein 2003) potential categories of meaning can develop in learners the ability to plan and execute interpersonal communication in sociolinguistically meaningful ways. In the study, the pedagogical focus on concepts such as self-presentation, social distance, and power, and how these concepts are instantiated in communication through the use of particular forms, afforded learners the ability to appropriate sociolinguistic and pragmatic variation as a personalized meaning-making resource. Thus, rather than relying on so-called rules of thumb to make sociolinguistic choices (e.g., form X is typically used in informal contexts), learners were able to orient their use of language according the meanings they wanted to create. In a number of cases, learners flouted sociolinguistic conventions because the expected, or conventional, sociolinguistic practices were at odds with the way in which learners wanted to present themselves to their interlocutors and/or construct social distance/closeness and power/equality in the relationship.

The reader will note that meaningful communication in this instance refers not simply to success in communicating the content of one's message but more importantly in indexing desirable social meanings relevant to one's identity and the qualities of the social relationship one has, or is establishing, with an interlocutor. This is why a focus on meaning and form must be done simultaneously: while a change in the form may not result in a different literal meaning, it can index a social meaning that is not the speaker's intended one.

2.4 Dynamic strategic interaction scenarios

Drawing on the work of DiPietro (1987), DSISs push learners to negotiate interactions in which two or more interlocutors have agendas that are in some way in conflict. For example, in one scenario used in the van Compernolle (2014a) study, students and their tutor adopted the roles of future roommates looking for an apartment to rent. The individual agendas of the interlocutors were in conflict due to different budgets, preferences for neighborhood/distance from the university campus, and so on. The stated goal of the scenario was to attempt to arrive at a compromise that suited both participants, but it was also possible for one participant to overcome the other or for no agreement to be reached.

Scenarios are carried out in a three-stage process. A rehearsal stage involves planning language use and understanding the context and one's role (cf. Gal'perin's concept of orientation). The scenario is then performed in the second stage (execution and control). The third stage involves a debriefing where the tutor and the student evaluate the performance and may revisit sources of difficulty. The point of this sequencing of task components is to raise learners' awareness of appropriate language use, which they can then deploy during communicative performance and reflect on afterwards as a means of promoting further growth. As discussed later, first exposure to explicit knowledge of meaning and language is provided in other complementary tasks, and the role of DSISs is to help learners to recontextualize their knowledge in performance contexts.

The "D" in DSIS refers to the adoption of a dynamic assessment (DA) of learner performance, namely their ability to execute and control (or modify) their plan/orientation. Since DA integrates teaching into the assessment exercise (Poehner 2008), learner difficulties can be probed and remediated within the context of the performance. In other words, the control function may be distributed between the learner and another person with whom the learner is interacting, known as the mediator (e.g., a tutor or teacher). It should be noted here that the "D" part of DSIS is where focus on meaning *and* form come together: the mediator is not simply interested in correcting a linguistic form, as is the case in traditional approaches to form-focused feedback (e.g., recasts, prompts), but in resolving performance issues as they relate to learners' control over the forms that communicate their intended social and pragmatic meanings.

3 Developing sociolinguistic and pragmatic abilities through DSIS

3.1 The orientation stage

As noted, the first stage of DSIS involved creating a plan of action, or *orientation*. This consisted of discussing with the learner the context of the scenario, the learner's role and agenda, and his or her judgments of the appropriateness of sociolinguistic and pragmatic features of language. The main goal was to link learners' developing conceptually mediated knowledge of pragmatic meaning potential to their language choices. As described elsewhere (e.g., van Compernolle 2014a), the concepts of self-presentation, social distance, and power were being appropriated by the learners in other awareness-raising and problem-solving tasks. These concepts were materialized in the forms of pedagogical diagrams depicting the relevant categories of meaning in relation to illustrative sociolinguistic and pragmatic forms. Learners were given a scenario card describing the context and their role, as well as three questions intended to have them reflect on the sociolinguistic and pragmatic meanings they wanted to create and which forms were relevant:

1. What do you think about the relationship between each person in this scenario?
2. In your opinion, what's an appropriate or desired way to present yourself in this scenario?
3. How can the language you use help to show the relationship between the two people in this scenario and how you want to present yourself?

An example is provided in excerpt 1. The student, Laurie, was planning to perform a scenario in which she would be speaking with a professor. The reader will note that she mentioned a "suit-and-tie situation" (lines 2–3), which is a reference to the materialization of the self-presentation concept, depicted as the choice between being more "t-shirt-and-jeans" (indexing an informal personality) versus more "suit-and-tie" (indexing a formal personality). This orientation to *meaning* then led her to choose particular relevant *forms* that tend to be associated with more formal registers (line 7): the second-person pronoun *vous* (as opposed to *tu*), use of *ne* in negation (as opposed to its omission), and the first-person plural pronoun *nous* (as opposed to *on*).[3]

Excerpt 1. Laurie's orientation to an office hours scenario (van Compernolle 2014a: 174)

```
1  Laurie:  ((reads scenario)) um + with the professor
2           I woul- it's a suit-and-tie situa?=I would want to
3           come off as a suit-and-tie situation?
4  Tutor:   okay
5  Laurie:  um + to show respect + and just + um yeah.
6  Tutor:   okay
7  Laurie:  so I would use vous, ne pas, and + nous. I guess.
8  Tutor:   okay.
```

Therefore, from the outset, DSIS tasks link meaning to form. However, and this should be emphasized, orientation to meaning is given priority. As noted earlier, the task is structured such that learners are prompted first to consider the meanings they want to create and second to choose the forms that correspond to those meanings.

---

3 Negation in French can be accomplished with a standard, formal construction involving preverbal *ne* and a postverbal second negative particle, such as *pas* 'not' (e.g., *il **ne** veut **pas** aller* 'he doesn't want to go'), or with the second negative alone (e.g., *il veut **pas** aller* 'he doesn't want to go'). First-person plural reference can be accomplished with the standard, formal pronoun *nous* 'we' (e.g., ***nous** avons déjà mangé* 'we have already eaten'), or as is most frequent in everyday speech, with the third-person singular pronoun *on* 'we' or 'one' (e.g., ***on** a déjà mangé* 'we have already eaten').

A second example is provided in excerpt 2. Here, the learner, Stephanie, was considering a telephone job interview scenario (the positions available were as a waitress or front desk staff at a hotel in France).

Excerpt 2. Stephanie's orientation to a job interview scenario (van Compernolle 2014a: 174–175)

1	Steph:	I don- cuz at the same time I would want to show
2		my personality?=cuz like it's a + it's a program +
3		it's like a waitress and a or a front desk?
4		so you're gonna need to be like + welcoming?
5	Tutor:	okay.
6	Steph:	so I wouldn- I wouldn't wanna necessarily use
7		*nous* and *ne pas*.=cuz that would be like + too stiff.
8		and like for me. if I were + (xxx) in this role. I
9		wouldn't wanna be like + I would wanna show that
10		I'm more laid back, I'm not like + uppity or whatever.
11		so prob- so I would probably use *on* and *pas*.
12	Tutor:	okay. + so *vous* for the + relationship. [distance.]
13	Steph:	[mhm]
14		and then *on* and *pas* to show like + my personality.

As we see, Stephanie oriented to social expectations of formality and social distance in the context of an interview, but also to her desire to present herself as a relaxed individual, a trait she considered important for the kind of job she was interviewing for (lines 6–11). As a result, rather than apply an invariable rule (e.g., use formal language in a job interview), Stephanie mixed registers, opting to use *vous* as a means of showing social distance in the relationship with the interviewer (lines 12–14, and discussed in preceding lines not shown here) but at the same time the more informal pronoun *on* (as opposed to *nous*) and negation without *ne* (i.e., *pas* alone).

Together, the two preceding excerpts provide an important basis for understanding orientation as FonMF in DSIS. In this stage of the task, learners consider the sociolinguistic and pragmatic meanings they want to create and then link those intended meanings to available linguistic resources. Meaning does not simply refer to the content of one's message, but to the indexical properties that linguistic forms acquire in the activity of communication. Accordingly, while successful communication and meaning are foregrounded, there has to be a concomitant focus on the forms that produce one's intended meanings.

3.2 Seeing FonMF in action: Execution and control

Whereas the orientation stage emphasized the plan of action in relation to intended meanings, the performance stage of DSISs focus on the execution and control of the plan (i.e., using appropriate forms). Note, however, that in both stages focus is on both meaning and form. The difference is simply one of emphasis.

Communicative performance in DSIS is intended to serve two developmental functions. The first is that use of the forms one intends to use can support learners in speeding up (Paradis 2009), or accelerating (van Compernolle 2014a), access to metacommunicative knowledge[4] during performance. Second, the performance involves control over the execution (which involving monitoring the execution), including opportunities for monitoring and controlling performance to be distributed between the learner and his or her interlocutor (e.g., a tutor). This creates opportunities for learners to be supported in recognizing difficulties and gaining control over the execution of their communicative actions. Excerpt 3 shows an example.

Excerpt 3. Mary's mediated control over negative constructions (van Compernolle 2013: 356)

01	Tutor:	tu veux pas? ou=
		do you not want to or
02	Mary:	=um ++ **je ne suis pas** + umm
		um I am not umm
03	Tutor:	hm? ((with raised eyebrow))
04	Mary:	++ ((nods head)) **je suis pas** um I don- I'm not + against?
		I'm not um
05	Tutor:	contre?
		against
		I'm not
06	Mary:	**je suis pas** contre, + um trouver + uh
		I'm not against um finding uh
07		un autre camarade de chambre,
		another roommate
08		mais ++ **je sais pas**. + uh quelqu'un.
		but I don't know uh someone

---

[4] As discussed earlier, metacommunicative knowledge involves understanding how language and other communicative resources can be deployed for meaning-making activity. This does not necessarily require specific linguistic terminology, memorization of grammar rules, etc., and it is therefore not the same as explicit metalinguistic knowledge. Instead, it is about the internalization of categories of meaning and functional knowledge of when and for what purposes one would want to use one's resources in particular ways. It should also be noted that this serves the orientation function and is therefore inextricably linked to performance. In other words, metacommunicative knowledge is *part of* one's performance abilities.

In her orientation, Mary had opted to use negation without the negative particle *ne* as a means of presenting herself as more "t-shirt-and-jeans" in this scenario (speaking with a roommate). However, her control over the appropriate form faltered at line 2, where she produced a negative construction with *ne*.[5] A short *hm?* with rising intonation (line 3) from the tutor (a very implicit form of mediation) drew her attention to this, and she subsequently self-corrected (line 4) and used *ne*-absent constructions two additional times (line 6, 8). In short, although Mary was not initially in control of her performance, the tutor's intervention supported her in regaining control over it so that her use of the available linguistic resources matched her intended sociolinguistic meaning.

Another example is shown in excerpt 4. Here, however, the focus on meaning is made explicit because of the student's, Stephanie ("St" in the transcript), rejection of her tutor's attempt to mediate her performance. Although Stephanie had planned to omit *ne* from negation, in this case she was attempting to use it as a marker of emphasis. Note that the first instance of *ne* occurred at line 8, after which the tutor drew Stephanie's attention to it (lines 9–10).

Excerpt 4. Focus on emphasis in negation (van Compernolle 2015: 35)

7	St:	#↓cher.# (.) ok↑ay. (0.4) il est très cher.
		expensive okay it is very expensive
8		e :t (.) >je n'ai pas< l'argent pour ça.
		and I [neg] have not the money for that
9	T:	{.h (h)↑m, ((tilts head down to the right
10		with left eyebrow raised))}
11		(0.8)
12	St:	#pour le::s a(h):[:#]
		for the ah
13	T:	{[wh]a↑t did y- ((makes
14		"rewind" gesture))}
15		<wha↑t did you want to say,
16	St:	#I don:'t have the mone:y for it.#
17	T:	okay, (.) do you {wanna: ((makes rewind gesture))}
18		(0.4)
19	St :	<j :e : ne ::: °pl-° n'ai : pa ::s l'argent,>=
		I [neg] (pl) [neg] have not the money
20		=>because I'm stressing that like<

---

5 It is important to note that the standard, or formal, *ne*-present construction was the most familiar to learners. Therefore, learner development was marked in part by *ne* becoming less habituated.

```
21          I d↓o:n't #have the# °mone[y for the apartment°]
22   T:                          [   o k ↑ a: y. s o    ]
23          <je ↑n'ai: p↓a:s=
            I [neg] have not
24   St:    =#ye:ah.
25   T:     you wanna stress that w[ith  yo]ur voice als↑o,
26   St:                            [ok↑ay.]
27   T:     <say it like (0.8) je ↑N'AI p↓a:s
                                 I [neg] have not
28   St :   #yeah.#
29   T :    l'argent pour [ça.  ]
            the money for that
30   St:                  [okay.] (I w-) je n'ai : pa :s
                                         I [neg] have not
31          ((laughs)) l'argent. (.) pour #uh# (ce :)
                      the money for uh this
32          appartement.
            apartment
```

We can note here that Stephanie's second attempt at her negative utterance (line 19) is elongated, suggesting that she was unsure why the tutor was trying to correct her performance. At line 20, she then made her intended meaning explicit: "because I'm stressing that like." Here, the tutor understood that it was not a mistake (i.e., using *ne* as a marker of formality), and he moved to resolve the problem by modeling an emphatic utterance with more appropriate prosodic stress accompanying *ne* as well as explaining this aspect of the form-meaning connection explicitly (lines 22–27).[6] Stephanie subsequently took up the model and continued the scenario using the appropriate forms (i.e., *ne* + prosodic stress) that communicated her intended pragmatic meaning. Thus, while their focus was certainly on form, it was in the service of creating a particular meaning.

3.3 Finding evidence of development

Development in DSIS is evidenced by shifts in the degree to which learners are capable of controlling the execution of their orientation in communicative

---

[6] The concept of emphasis had been taught through the example of using *ne* in contexts in which its absence would be expected typically (e.g., everyday conversation with friends).

performance.[7] We can think of this heuristically as a change in the locus of control from between the learner and the tutor (as in excerpts 3 and 4, discussed earlier) to within the learner (i.e., the learner is able to control his or her performance without external assistance). Note that this focus is not about the use of particular forms, but the use of forms in relation to the learners' intended meaning.

In van Compernolle (2014a), a control score was proposed as one way of tracking such development, calculated as a simple ratio:

$$\text{Score} = \frac{n \text{ occurrences of planned form}}{n \text{ possible contexts}}$$

The intent was to quantify learners' ability to execute their plans in a straightforward way that did not rely on external judgments of correctness or appropriateness. In other words, since different learners may orient to scenarios in different ways, and hence orient to different forms as appropriate, scoring of this sort should adopt an emic, or participant-relevant, approach. As Figure 1 shows, overall control in the van Compernolle (2014a) study increased from session 1 (prior to any instruction) to session 3 (following the beginning of instruction), and it remained rather stable, even after assistance was withdrawn (session 6). In essence, the data reflect the learners' maturing ability to orient to particular sociolinguistic and pragmatic meanings, and to execute these meanings in communicative performance via the use of relevant forms.

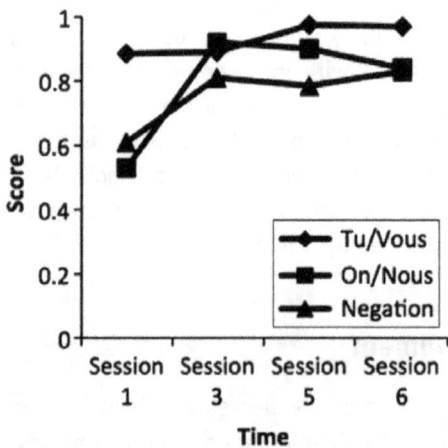

Figure 1: Overall control scores from van Compernolle (2014a: 180)

---

[7] Development may also be marked by the ability to evaluate performance, which can be part of the control process or part of separate tasks focused on interpreting one's own performance and/or the performances of others.

A more qualitative approach was used in van Compernolle (2014b), which illustrated a way of profiling individual learners across time. Simply put, a qualitative analysis of interactions was conducted in order to reveal the extent to which a learner, in this case, Laurie, was able to deploy her intended forms. The analysis is summarized in Table 1, which was presented in the study as a shorthand device for profiling Laurie's developing control over *ne* in informal scenarios (where she planned to omit the form). Note that Laurie was one of the individuals in the van Compernolle (2014a) study, and so her performance is included in the overall control scores represented in Figure 1.

Table 1: Laurie's developmental profile (van Compernolle 2014b: 96)

Time	Example	Extent of Support
Preenrichment	Two instances of *ne*-present negation	No support offered during preenrichment.
Enrichment 1	First instance: *L'autobus n'est pas loin* 'the bus is not far'	Extensive support required in (i) noticing and identifying the problem and (ii) remembering to include a verb.
	Second instance: *tu ne peux pas er- / tu marches pas* 'you cannot er- / you don't walk'	No support required. Laurie was able to notice her error and self-correct.
Enrichment 2	First instance: *je n'aimes pas manger / je ne s- / je ne veux pas manger* 'I do not like to eat / I NEG s- / I do not want to eat'	Minimal support required after her performance faltered. Corrected to *je veux pas manger* 'I don't want to eat'.
	Second instance: *j'ai pas* 'I don't have'	No support required. Laurie hesitated at first, but produced a *ne*-absent structure without assistance on the first attempt (cf. enrichment 1 where she used *ne* and then self-corrected).
Postenrichment	Four instances of *ne*-absent negation	No support required. Laurie's performance did not falter.

As we see, the qualitative profile shows a decreasing reliance on support from the tutor in controlling negative constructions. During enrichment 1, Laurie needed extensive assistance one time, and then was able to perform independently. However, she continued to need some help during enrichment 2, though this time the assistance provided was minimal. Ultimately, Laurie gained independent control over her use of the relevant forms and no longer needed the tutor's support (postenrichment). It is important to emphasize that Laurie's performance was evaluated in relation to her orientation, so the focus on using negation without *ne* emerged because of her own choice to present herself in a particular way (i.e., a social meaning), and the omission of *ne* was one linguistic resource appropriate for doing so.

4 Discussion and conclusion

Let us return to part of Nunan's (2004) definition of a task that was cited at the beginning of this chapter, where he writes that in task interaction "the intention is to convey meaning rather than to manipulate form" (p. 4). While the emphasis on meaning in communication has been a welcome alternative to strictly form-focused, and often decontextualized, grammar practice since at least the 1980s with the popularization of communicative language teaching (e.g., Canale and Swain 1980), it risks creating an unnecessary separation between meaning and form. In addition, overemphasizing "getting one's message across" (i.e., the content or literal meaning of an utterance) may be detrimental to developing learners' abilities to manipulate form in the pursuit of meaning making. Conceptualizing L2 tasks as either focusing on form or focusing on meaning creates a false dichotomy that we need to overcome because meaning and form are dialectically united in communication.

DSIS tasks are one way of bringing meaning and form together in a deliberate way. As noted, meaning is given primacy, but it is also clear that developing control over the forms that communicate one's intended meaning. Thus, far from focusing on form for form's sake, the objective of form-focused interaction (i.e., mediated performance) in DSIS tasks is to forge a link between L2 meaning potential and appropriate linguistic resources in communicative performance. The orientation stage of DSIS tasks encourages learners to reflect on the meanings they want to create and then to match intended meanings to relevant linguistic resources prior to communicative performance. Thus, from the outset, meaning is the central focus of such tasks. Subsequently, meanings are communicated during the execution stage (i.e., performance of the scenario), where the goal is to improve control over relevant forms, with assistance if needed.

4.1 DSIS in pedagogical sequence

An important aspect of DSIS tasks, at least as discussed here and in previous publications (e.g., van Compernolle 2013, 2014a, 2014b), is that they are integrated into a larger pedagogical program focused on promoting the internalization of conceptual meaning potentials as a way of mediating L2 communicative development. This is to say that the pedagogical arrangements were not DSIS based; rather, DSISs were one of several different kinds of tasks used in instruction that together developed learners' pragmatic and sociolinguistic competencies. Other tasks included explicit instruction centered on the concepts of social indexicality, self-presentation, social distance, and power and awareness-raising problem-solving tasks. The point is that while the goal of instruction was certainly to promote L2 communicative development – conceptualized as controlled use of L2 forms for meaning making – the pedagogical approach did not center exclusively, or even primarily, around so-called communicative L2 tasks. Rather, DSISs put learners' developing abilities into practice, and they provided opportunities for further support from a tutor.

In an extension of this work, van Compernolle and Henery (2014) discussed the relationship between the various tasks in terms of a dynamic expansion of knowledge and performance abilities. While explicit instruction emphasizing concepts and relevant forms serves as the point of departure, problem-solving and communicative tasks expand on, and feed into, conceptual development. Engeström's (1987) concept of learning by expanding is helpful in this regard. We can conceive of development as an iterative process in which learning tasks build on, and transform, each other, as illustrated in Figure 2.

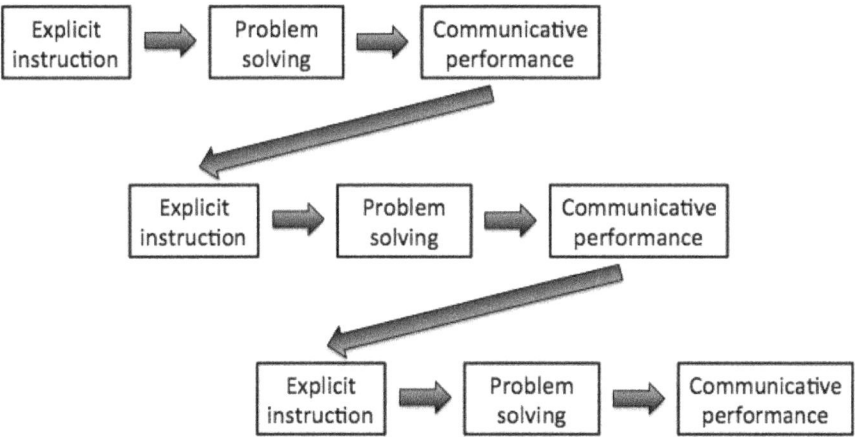

Figure 2: Expansive learning (based on Engeström 1987; van Compernolle 2014a; van Compernolle and Henery 2014)

The sequencing of the various tasks (or rather task categories) is represented by movement from left to right in figure 2. First, conceptual knowledge is forged through explicit instruction (i.e., developing conceptual knowledge of meaning potentials). Second, this knowledge is applied in problem-solving tasks (i.e., using concepts to solve language-related problems). Third, communicative tasks – such as DSIS – are used in order to link learners' conceptual knowledge and problem-solving abilities to the use of language in communication. Importantly, this is not the end of the sequence. As the movement downward suggests, communicative performance is in turn linked to a reiteration of explicit instruction, which starts the cycle again. The movement down is meant to not simply imply a repetition of the tasks, but added depth. Note also that the cycles in figure 2 are staggered such that each round of explicit instruction begins ahead of the previous one. In other words, each cycle builds on and expands the previous one, pushing learners ever forward in their development. As we see, the role of DSIS is not solely to apply conceptual knowledge and problem-solving abilities to communication but more importantly to set the stage for the further growth in subsequent cycles of instruction.

4.2 Challenges for the classroom

The overall approach to teaching sociolinguistic and pragmatic competencies discussed above has been successfully extended to classroom contexts (e.g., van Compernolle and Henery 2014; van Compernolle, Gomez-Laich, and Weber 2016). However, the use of DSIS tasks has only been used in one-on-one tutoring sessions, as discussed in this chapter and elsewhere (van Compernolle 2014a, 2014b). There are two main reasons for this.

First, learners at beginning levels of instruction may not yet have enough language to perform extended scenarios. Consequently, as discussed by van Compernolle et al. (2016), other communicative tasks may be more appropriate (e.g., written or spoken discourse completion tasks). The second reason is that the "dynamic" part of DSISs as illustrated in this chapter may not always be feasible in a classroom with 15, 20, or even more students. For instance, van Compernolle and Henery (2014) opted to use non-dynamic strategic interaction mediated by Google Chat (i.e., real-time computer-mediated communication) because all students could simultaneously perform scenarios in pairs or groups of three outside of the classroom. It would not have been possible to have all students perform scenarios in the classroom on the same day. Of course, this meant that it was not possible for the teacher to intervene to support her students' performance in real time because there were six to seven groups performing scenarios at the same time.

Although it may not be possible to implement DSIS as described in this chapter (i.e., one-on-one, teacher-student interaction) in a whole-classroom context, there are possible adaptations. One possibility involves short scenarios (e.g., intended to less than five minutes) in which 3–4 students participate at a time, taking turns. The orientation and execution stages could be carried out in front of the class, with other students providing feedback in addition to the teacher. In other words, while only a few students would be performing at a time, the others would be observing and potentially benefitting from their observation of the scenario, including any support provided to the performers during the performance or especially during the debriefing. Groups of students could take turns so that each student would then be able to perform a role in the scenario, and each group could build on the mediation provided to previous groups. It should be noted that in this format, instructional support could come from student observers as well as the teacher, thereby enhancing the collaborative nature of scenario performance. Indeed, Poehner (2009) has discussed some of these issues in relation to group dynamic assessment. The interested reader is referred to that study for more information about mediating whole classrooms using DA-inspired interaction.

A second possibility is to teach students how to provide instructional support in pair or small group work (see, e.g., Guk and Kellogg 2007). This would allow multiple groups to perform scenarios simultaneously in the classroom. Each student would be tasked with paying attention to his or her partner's performance in relation to the orientation. A simple way to train students in providing mediating support would be to adopt prescribed graduated prompts, as is done in interventionist approaches to DA (e.g., Davin 2013). In fact, the following script was proposed in van Compernolle (2014b), based on Davin's (2013) classroom DA work:

> (i) a *hmm*? with rising intonation; (ii) a repetition of the entire utterance with rising intonation (e.g., *l'autobus n'est pas loin?* 'the bus is not far'); (iii) a repetition of the locus of trouble (e.g., *n'est pas?* 'is not'); (iv) forced choice (e.g., *n'est pas or est pas?* 'is not'); and (v) overt correction with explanation. (van Compernolle 2014b: 97)

This kind of graduated prompt list should be relatively easy to teach to students and implement in the classroom. Likewise, it may have the potential to enhance collaborative interaction and peer scaffolding (Donato 1994; Swain 2000) by providing students with a principled and focused approach to supporting each other's performance during tasks.

4.3 Final comments

DSIS tasks unite *focus on meaning* and *focus on form* because of the emphasis on orienting to meaning first and then to relevant linguistic resources for communicating intended meaning second. The dynamic part of DSIS tasks refers to the integration of instructional support in regaining and maintaining control over the forms a learner has oriented to as appropriate for creating his or her intended meanings. Focus on meaning and form, or *FonMF*, eschews the traditional separation of meaning and form, usually conceptualized as the content of one's message as opposed to the means by which the message is communicated because meaning is not restricted to an utterance's locutionary force (i.e., content). Rather, since language form indexes social-relational and contextual meaning in addition to "content" (or literal meaning),[8] a focus on meaning – which is advocated in task-based language teaching – must involve a concomitant focus on form. It is my hope that the discussion of DSIS tasks offered in this chapter will serve as an opening to an extended conversation focused on the ways in which pedagogical tasks may be designed with FonMF processes in mind.

References

Byrnes, Heidi & Rosa M. Manchón (eds.). 2014. *Task-based language learning – Insights from and for L2 writing*. Amsterdam: John Benjamins.
Baralt, Mellisa, Roger Gilabert, Peter Robinson (eds.). 2014. *Task sequencing and instructed second language learning*. New York: Bloomsbury.
Canale, Michael & Merrill Swain. 1980. Theoretical bases of communicative approaches to second language teaching and testing. *Applied Linguistics* 1. 1–47.
Davin, Kristin J. 2013. Integration of dynamic assessment and instructional conversations to promote development and improve assessment in the language classroom. *Language Teaching Research* 17. 303–322.
Davydov, Vasily V. 2004. *Problems of developmental instruction: A theoretical and experimental psychological study* (Trans. P. Moxay). Moscow: Akademyia Press.
Di Pietro, Robert J. 1987. *Strategic interaction: Learning languages through scenarios*. Cambridge: Cambridge University Press.
Donato, Richard. 1994. Collective scaffolding in second language learning. In James P. Lantolf & Gabriele Appel (eds.), *Vygotskian approaches to second language research*, 33–56. Norwood, NJ: Albex.
Engeström, Yyjö. 1987. *Learning by expanding: An activity-theoretical approach to developmental research*. Helsinki, Finland: Orienta-Konsultit Oy.
Gal'perin, Piotr I. 1989. Organization of mental activity and the effectiveness of learning. *Soviet Psychology* 27(3). 65–82.
Gal'perin, Piotr I. 1992. Stage-by-stage formation as a method of psychological investigation. *Journal of Russian and East European Psychology* 30(4). 60–80.
González-Lloret, Marta & Lourdes Ortega (eds.). 2014. *Technology-mediated TBLT: Researching technology and tasks*. Amsterdam: John Benjamins.
Guk, Iju & David Kellogg. 2007. The ZPD and whole class teaching: Teacher-led and student-led interactional mediation of tasks. *Language Teaching Research* 11. 281–299.

---

8 Note, for example, how systemic-functional linguistics (e.g., Halliday 1978) conceptualizes the relationship between meaning, form, and context through the notions of ideational, interpersonal, and textual metafunctions.

Halliday, Michael A. K. 1978. *Language as social semiotic. The social interpretation of language and meaning*. London: Edward Arnold.
Harris, Roy. 1998. *Introduction to integrational linguistics*. Oxford: Pergamon.
Long, Michael. 2015. *Second language acquisition and task-based language teaching*. Oxford, England: Wiley.
Nunan, David. 2004. *Task-based language teaching*. Cambridge: Cambridge University Press.
Paradis, Michel. 2009. *Declarative and procedural determinants of second languages*. Amsterdam: John Benjamins.
Poehner, Matthew E. 2008. *Dynamic assessment: A Vygotskian approach to understanding and promoting second language development*. Berlin: Springer Publishing.
Poehner, Matthew E. 2009. Group dynamic assessment: Mediation for the L2 classroom. *TESOL Quarterly* 43. 471–491.
Shehadeh, Ali & Christine A. Coombe (eds.). 2012. *Task-based language teaching in foreign language contexts: Research and implementation*. Amsterdam: John Benjamins.
Silverstein, Michael. 2003. Indexical order and the dialectics of sociolinguistic life. *Language and Communication* 23. 193–229.
Spinoza, Benedict de. 1955. *On the improvement of the understanding*. New York: Dover.
Stetsenko, Anna & Igor M. Arievitch. 2010. Cultural-historical activity theory: Foundational worldview, major principles, and the relevance of sociocultural context. In Suzanne R. Kirschner & Jack Martin (eds.), *The sociocultural turn in psychology: The contextual emergence of mind and self*, 231–252. New York: Columbia University Press.
Swain, Merrill. 2000. The output hypothesis and beyond: Mediating acquisition through collaborative dialogue. In James P. Lantolf (ed.), *Sociocultural theory and second language learning*, 97–114. Oxford: Oxford University Press.
Tyler, Andrea. 2012. *Cognitive linguistics and second language learning: Theoretical basics and experimental evidence*. New York: Routledge.
van Compernolle, Rémi A. 2013. Interactional competence and the dynamic assessment of L2 pragmatic abilities. In Steven J. Ross & Gabriele Kasper (eds.), *Assessing second language pragmatics*, 327–353. Basingstoke, UK: Palgrave/Macmillan.
van Compernolle, Rémi A. 2014a. *Sociocultural theory and L2 instructional pragmatics*. Bristol: Multilingual Matters.
van Compernolle, Rémi A. 2014b. Profiling second language sociolinguistic development through dynamically administered strategic interaction scenarios. *Language and Communication* 37. 86–99.
van Compernolle, Rémi A. 2015. *Interaction and second language development: A Vygotskian perspective*. Amsterdam: John Benjamins.
van Compernolle, Rémi A. & Ashlie Henery. 2014. Instructed concept appropriation and L2 pragmatic development in the classroom. *Language Learning* 64. 549–578.
van Compernolle, Rémi A., María Pía Gomez-Laich & Ashley Weber. 2016. Teaching L2 Spanish sociopragmatics through concepts: A classroom-based study. *Modern Language Journal* 100. 341–361.
Vygotsky, Lev S. 1978. *Mind in society: The development of higher mental processes*. Cambridge, MA: Harvard University Press.
Wertsch, James V. 1985. *Vygotsky and the social formation of mind*. Cambridge, MA: Harvard University Press.
Zinchenko, Vladimir P. 2002. From classical to organic psychology. *Journal of Russian and East European Psychology* 39. 32–77.

Caroline Payant
5 Effects of L3 Learner Proficiency and Task Types on Language Mediation: A Sociocultural Perspective

1 Introduction

Task-based language teaching (TBLT) pedagogy is an approach to language education that views functional uses of language as the vehicle for language learning. It is through the implementation and completion of tasks that language develops as learners must use language to meet their immediate, authentic communicative needs. Through task-based interaction, learners draw on multiple skills simultaneously, thus mirroring real-world expectations (Richards and Rodgers 2014). From a sociocultural theory (SCT) perspective, language is an important tool for learners during collaborative tasks since learners draw on their linguistic repertoire to resolve gaps in their interlanguage (Lantolf, Thorne, and Poehner 2015). These collaborative dialogues can lead to the co-construction of more complex linguistic structures (Swain and Watanabe 2013). Since collaborative dialogue engages learners cognitively in the process of solving a linguistic problem, they have been found to create opportunities for learners to expand their second language (L2) knowledge (Swain and Lapkin 1998, 2001; Swain, Brooks, and Tocalli-Beller 2002).

Task-based language studies have shown that collaborative dialogue is subject to task types (Swain and Lapkin 2001), task modality (Adams and Ross-Feldman 2008; Azkarai and García Mayo 2015; Niu 2009), group size (Edstrom 2015; Fernández Dobao 2014; Kim 2008; Lasito and Storch 2013), pair dynamics (Kim and McDonough 2011; Storch 2001, 2002a, 2002b; Storch and Aldosari 2013), and learner proficiency (Kim and McDonough 2008; Leeser 2004; Storch and Aldosari 2013; Watanabe and Swain 2007; Williams 1999, 2001). Moreover, the benefits of interaction during task-based pedagogy have been reported across instructional settings (i.e., second language, foreign language, content-based language instruction, and immersion contexts); however, these have been limited to learners acquiring an L2. As of late, discussions pertaining to third language (L3) acquisition are on the rise and there is a growing interest in understanding the acquisition processes underlying L2s and L3s (de Bot and Jaensch 2015;

Caroline Payant, Université du Québec à Montréal

Slabakova and García Mayo 2015). In this article, I examine how two types of pedagogical tasks create opportunities for collaborative dialogue between learners of French as an L3 when paired with more and less proficient peers. I further investigate how learners use their linguistic tool kit (first language (L1), L2, and L3) during dyadic interaction to complete task-based lessons. To situate the paper, I begin by examining research on L3 learners and move to discuss how proficiency mediates collaborative dialogue during task completion.

1.1 Language learning beyond an L2

Plurilingualism is on the rise (Grosjean 2008; Hammarberg 2010); nevertheless, L3 theorizing and research are still in their infant stages compared to the field of second language acquisition (SLA) (Falk and Bardel 2010). A plurilingual speaker's ability to alternate between two or more linguistic systems with fluency and accuracy generates curiosity (Cabrelli Amaro, Flynn, and Rothman 2012; García Mayo and González Alonso 2015). Research has demonstrated that plurilingual speakers may alternate between languages because each language serves unique mediating functions during interaction (Payant 2015; Payant and Kim 2015). Further, there is undeniable evidence that multiple languages are activated and accessed during L3 output (Lindqvist 2010; Lindqvist and Bardel 2014). The variables hypothesized to impact cross-linguistic influence (CLI[1]) include: age of acquisition, order of acquisition, context of use and acquisition, language typology, recency and frequency of use (Aronin and Hufeisen 2009; De Angelis and Dewaele 2011).

Within the CLI literature, research examining which languages are the sources of influence has identified that both the L1 and the L2 are possible candidates. Williams and Hammarberg (1998) and Hammarberg (2001) collected longitudinal data from one English (L1) learner of Swedish (L3), who had three L2s (German, French, Italian) and coded for language switches produced during spontaneous conversations. Both the L1 and the dominant L2 (German) were found to be sources of influence in the L3. Specifically, English (L1) played a more important role for editing output, producing metalinguistic comments/questions, and generating lexical inserts. German (L2) was, to a lesser extent, identified for these functions but it was also coded as having no identified pragmatic purpose. Jessner (2005) examined instances of metatalk with German/Italian balanced

---

[1] Following De Angelis (2007), the terms cross-linguistic influence and transfer are used interchangeably and should be understood as the influence knowledge of languages have on other languages.

bilinguals learning English (L3). To qualify for the study, the participants had to come from bilingual families and be upper intermediate learners of English. To identify the source languages during metatalk, participants completed writing tasks which were accompanied by think-aloud protocols. The findings indicated that both German and Italian were utilized for metalinguistic comments and questions. However, German switches slightly outnumbered Italian switches. The author posits that this may be due to the context of use: during the study, participants were in a German speaking country. Recently, Giancaspro, Halloran and Iverson (2015) examined morphosyntactic transfer with 43 Spanish (L1) – English (L2) or English (L1) – Spanish (L2) learners of Brazilian Portuguese (L3). All the participants completed a grammaticality judgement task which targeted differential object marking. They found that Spanish was a source of influence – an indication that native and non-native languages are sources of CLI. In sum, we have evidence that multiple languages may be active in the processing of an L3.

To examine the impact of language proficiency in the target language and the L2 on CLI, Bardel and Lindqvist (2007) used semi-guided conversations to examine CLIs with a learner of Italian (L3) who had Swedish as an L1 and three L2s (French, English, Spanish). Results suggest that Spanish, the least developed L2, played an important role, especially during the early stages of Italian development. Nonetheless, when making conscious attempts to resolve lexical gaps, the learner turned more frequently to French (the dominant L2). Lindqvist and Bardel (2014) later examined a Swedish/Italian L1 speaker learning Spanish (L3), with English and French as L2s. Unlike their 2007 findings, the L2 did not play a decisive role in L3 production; rather, they found more evidence for Italian (L1) influence.

Attention to lexis has also become a focus of empirical studies. For instance, Lindqvist (2009) focused on lexical development with 30 learners of French (L3) from various L1 and L2 backgrounds. In addition, she conducted a case study analysis, which included four beginner French students and two advanced learners from the group. Evidence of code-switching and word construction attempts were mostly based on the L1, regardless of L3 proficiency. However, instances of L2 output were more frequently identified for the less proficient L3 learners. These findings suggest that although the L2 played a minor role in L3 output, the least proficient learners of French tended to activate the L2 at a higher rate. In a subsequent study, Lindqvist (2010) identified lexical inter- and intralingual influences within advanced learners of French (L3). The 14 participants completed a one-on-one interview with the researcher who analyzed lexical deviances in terms of form and meaning. Overall, meaning deviances only marginally outnumbered form deviances with the advanced learners, and there was minimal evidence of L2 influence. These findings may provide support that with more advanced target language proficiency, CLI at the lexical level, evidence declines. In sum, CLI is a pervasive phenomenon and appears to be subject to L2, target language proficiency, and typology and language distance.

1.2 Mediating variables on collaborative dialogue during interaction

From a SCT perspective, language is an important symbolic tool (Lantolf, Thorne and Poehner 2015). During task-based interaction, learners use language as a mediating tool for meaning making purposes and for completing real-world tasks. In this process, learners build on each other's expertise to scaffold learning (Richards and Rodgers 2014). TBLT researchers have examined the functions the L1 serves during interaction as well as the construction of collaborative dialogue. Operationalized as Language-Related Episodes (LREs), Swain and Lapkin (1998) define collaborative dialogue as moments during the interactions where learners may interrupt communication to explicitly discuss or question their language use. The focus of collaborative dialogue covers meaning, form, and pragmatics (Swain and Watanabe 2013; Taguchi and Kim 2016). The occurrence of collaborative dialogue is mediated by task design and implementation (e.g., task type, task modality, task repetition) as well as learner factors (e.g., pair dynamics and proficiency). Keeping in line with the goals of the present study, namely the investigation of learner proficiency and collaborative dialogue as they unfold during task completion, the following section emphasizes studies that have examined proficiency effects in collaborative dialogue.

Research which has considered differences across learner levels as well as within dyads shows that collaborative dialogue is more frequent with higher target language proficiency. For instance, Williams (1999) examined collaborative dialogue across four English as a Second Language (ESL) levels (beginner to advanced)[2]. She found that in the more proficient groups there were greater instances of LREs and learners tended to discuss a wider range of form-based LREs during their interactions. Leeser (2004) investigated how learner proficiency mediated the production and resolution of LREs in four content-based Spanish classrooms using a dictogloss task (Wajnryb 1990). Each learner was assigned to one of three proficiency dyads (High-High, High-Low, Low-Low). Leeser found that High-High proficiency dyads produced more LREs than the other proficiency dyads. In addition, the High-High dyads tended to focus more on form than on

---

2 In Williams (1999), the data originated from tasks as well as traditional form-oriented activities.

meaning whereas the Low-Low dyads had a greater percentage of lexis-based LREs. In terms of resolution rate, High-High proficiency dyads had a high rate of correct resolutions (84%) compared to the Low-Low dyads (58.3%). Storch and Aldosari (2013) examined collaborative dialogue with Arabic learners of English (L2) who completed a joint writing task. In this setting, learners were most accustomed to teacher-centered pedagogy; however, to examine the role of proficiency during task completion, 60 learners were recruited and participated in task-based activities outside their regular scheduled class time. Based on proficiency levels, learners were assigned to three types of dyads (High-High; High-Low; Low-Low). The High-High dyads produced more LREs (N = 67) compared to the High-Low (N = 47) and to the Low-Low (N = 24). Overall, the success rate in resolving the LREs was similar across the three proficiency groupings. Kim and McDonough (2008) conducted a similar study with Korean learners of English from one intensive Korean language program at an intermediate level of proficiency using a dictogloss task. Eight participants completed a dictogloss task twice. On one occasion, they were paired with an intermediate proficiency peer (I-I) and on the other, with a higher proficiency peer (I-H). The researchers found a proficiency effect in the resolution of form-based LREs, as I-H dyads correctly resolved 78% compared to I-I dyads correctly resolving 56%. As for lexis-based LREs, again I-H had more correctly resolved LREs (70%) compared to I-I (58%). Overall, findings show that proficiency in the target language, and within dyads, mediates the production and resolution of LREs as learners engage in a variety of tasks.

Proficiency, as a mediating variable, has been examined in various instructional settings and with different task types. This line of research has identified that a learner working with a more proficient peer benefits as they construct a collective scaffold and, consequently, perform at higher levels than when working individually. This level of potential development is captured by the concept of Zone of Proximal Development (ZPD) (Vygotsky 1978). During pair and group work, learners may outperform their actual level of development when interacting with an expert interlocutor(s) as they successfully negotiate a ZPD (Donato 1994; van Compernolle and Williams 2013; Storch and Aldosari 2010). With learners, this expert status is prone to change in the microgenetic domain, as each learner may have expert knowledge on a given topic or during different types of interaction (Donato 1994; Ohta 1995; 2000). Since L3 researchers have identified that proficiency in the L2 and target language are important variables for CLI, and also, L2 researchers have found that proficiency is an important variable in collaborative dialogue, it is important that we examine how L3 proficiency may impact collaborative dialogue in forming a ZPD in a task-based classroom. Further, it is important to examine how proficiency may play a role as learners complete a series of tasks within a task-supported learning environment over a sustained period of time.

2 The current study

The number of studies that examine L3 learners is on the rise (García Mayo and González Alonso 2015). Many of these studies, concerned with CLI, have been small scale studies and have drawn primarily on interview data or researcher-participant led dialogues or have approached the acquisition of an L3 from the generative perspective. Within the discipline of instructed SLA, researchers are concerned with identifying optimal conditions that promote L2 development (Loewen 2014) and research on L3 development has not been the object of primary investigation. In fact, within the realm of learner-learner task-based interaction, with a focus on proficiency effects, research has focused uniquely on learners of an L2. The role of L3 proficiency in multiple languages during collaborative dialogue has not been explicitly investigated. As instructed SLA researchers search for variables that impact language development during pedagogical tasks, it is important to examine whether L3 learners in different proficiency groupings draw on multiple languages to meet task demands during interaction. The goal of the present study is to examine how the proficiency in an L3 mediates collaborative dialogue with learners of an L3 in a task-based language learning environment.

The three research questions that guided the present study are the following:
1. To what extent do adult, L3 learners of French engage in collaborative dialogue during two pedagogical tasks (story completion and text reconstruction tasks)?
    a. If so, what is the focus and resolution of the collaborative dialogue?
2. How does the proficiency grouping in the L3 mediate the occurrence and resolution of language-related episodes (LREs)?
3. What is the relationship between L3 proficiency grouping and language use (L1, L2, and L3) of language-related episodes (LREs)?

2.1 Methodology

2.1.1 Instructional setting

This study is part of a larger study that was conducted at a private university in central Mexico. At this university, all students are required to study English as a foreign language and obtain a minimum score of 500 on the paper-based TOEFL examination. Students may study an additional language, if they meet this minimum, or they may continue with their English training. In this setting, the Language Department offers six courses of French as a foreign language and follows the Common European Framework of Reference for Languages. The data collection took place in one A2 intact French class with learners of French (L3). The teacher followed a task-supported curriculum and implemented tasks regularly.

Participants

The participants included in this study were 15 L1 Spanish speakers, had satisfied the English (L2) requirement, and were studying French (L3). Their average age was 20.2 (min: 18 and max: 24). Their average time of French language study was 2.0 years (min: 6 months and max: 3 years) while the average time of English language study was 12.1 years (min: 6 years and max: 16 years). All the participants were registered in the same French class; however, their French and English language proficiencies differed. These differences were measured via in-house tests (French: modified version of the Diploma in French Studies (DELF) exam; English: modified version of the TOEFL exam). To ensure reliability of the test scores, oral and written tests were individually rated by two different French and English speakers for each language test. Any score differences were resolved

Table 1: Learner proficiency scores

Learner	L3 – French	French	L2 – English	L2 – Other
Tania	2.1		4.4 (–)	
Julia	2.3		5.2	
Alexa	2.3	Lower	6.5	
Mari	3.3		7.4 (+)	
Pedro	4.5		8.1 (+)	
Marimar	5.0		7.4	
Tulio	5.0		5.4	
Ismael	5.4	Intermediate	6.0	German
Alicia	6.3		3.4 (–)	
Jasmine	6.5		2.2 (–)	
Alicia G.	8.1		6.4	
Fausto	8.1		6.4	
Daril	8.8	Higher	8.7 (+)	German; Japanese
Anita	8.8		6.4	
Aurora	9.4		3.9 (–)	

Note: For the English proficiency, the symbol '–' designates low; '+' designates high; blank designates intermediate proficiency by a third rater. To capture proficiency differences, the raters were instructed to use the entire 10-point scale to show range among the students within a single intermediate level. The participants' final comprehensive scores, on a 10-point scale for English (L2) and French (L3), are listed in Table 1. These are further divided into three French proficiency groupings: low (min: 2.1 and max: 4.5), intermediate (min: 5.0 and max: 6.5), and high (min: 8.1 and max: 9.4).

Instructional tasks
Within TBLT, it is of paramount importance that emphasis be placed on meaningful language output. Also, to foster language intake, learners must notice how meaning is encoded in linguistic forms. Thus, to provide ample opportunities for learners to focus on meaning and notice linguistic forms, the participants completed a total of twelve pedagogical tasks over a 16-week period. The data for this study focuses on the learner-learner interactions produced during two task types, namely two collaborative story completion tasks and two collaborative text reconstruction tasks. The selection of these task types was guided by their contrastive features. Specifically, the story completion relied uniquely on images (no written input) whereas the text reconstruction task included written input. Each task was completed during 50 minute classes and interactions between the dyads were audio-recorded. Story completion tasks #1 and #2 were implemented during Week 5 and Week 11, respectively, and the text reconstruction tasks #1 and #2 during Week 7 and Week 13, respectively. Given the context of implementation, namely an intact classroom, learners collaborated with a different, randomly assigned, partner on each occasion.

The story completion tasks were two-way information gap tasks, included visual input alone, and required oral and written output. During the oral output phase, each learner had an equal number of pictures and was instructed to elicit descriptions from their peer who kept their pictures hidden. These interactions encouraged the production of language output that resembled language used in authentic contexts. Once the pictures were described, learners negotiated a logical sequence. Then, the participants engaged in a collaborative writing task. This step encouraged the production of written output; however, this component required that learners discuss propositional content and come to an agreed upon story via collaboration and negotiation. The second type, the text reconstruction task, provided learners with written input. Specifically, for this task, each dyad was provided with a 160-word passage that contained 40 omissions, thereby obscuring the meaning of the text. Collaboratively, learners were to reconstruct their text in writing. This type of pedagogical task again required that learners work in collaboration to discuss the meaning of the text and this process promoted the production of authentic linguistic output. Although multiple solutions are conceivable, learners were subsequently provided with a proposed reconstructed version, created by the teacher, and were asked to compare and discuss the two versions of the text. To promote collaboration, learners shared a single printed text. Time on task ranged between 29 to 44 minutes for the story completion task and from 28 to 39 minutes for the text reconstruction task.

To examine if proficiency differences within dyads may influence the quantity and quality of collaborative dialogue, only data from learners, who were paired in one of three following configurations, were included in the study: Low-High (L-H), Low-Intermediate (L-I), and Intermediate-High (I-H). To ensure a balance between the number of proficiency dyads per configuration and task type, data from 16 dyads were included for analysis (eight from each task type) (See Table 2.)[3].

Table 2: Proficiency groupings across three configurations

	Story completion task (N)	Reconstruction task (N)
Low-High (L-H)	2	2
Low-Intermediate (L-I)	2	2
Intermediate-High (I-H)	4	4
Total	8	8

Data coding and analysis

The task interaction data was transcribed verbatim. The data was coded for types of LREs, namely, lexis-based LREs and form-based LREs. Lexis-based LREs include instances where learners discuss aspects of meaning, spelling, and phonology. In Example 1, Julia explicitly asks Daril for the meaning of the word *étroit* 'narrow'. In this example, Daril and Julia engaged in a meaning-oriented LRE.

Example 1. *Learner-learner correctly resolved lexis-based LRE*

(1) Julia: Qu'est-ce que c'est étroit? [What is narrow]

    Daril: estrechos [*narrow*]

    Julia: Ah, sí cierto. [*Ah, of course*]

    Daril: Je crois que c'est ça, étroits [I think that it's that, narrow].

---

[3] Although all 15 participants completed the four tasks, the post-hoc analysis of learner proficiency precluded me from including all learners in the study. Only dyads with the target proficiency pairings were included in the analysis.

Form-based LREs include instances where learners discuss aspects of morphology and/or syntax. In Example 2, Mari questions the use of the auxiliary verb and Alicia repeats the incorrect auxiliary verb *sommes*. Interestingly, Mari has some doubts but Alicia argues that the verb *to visit* requires the auxiliary verb *to be*. Their discussion then focuses on applying the rules of agreement between the subject and the participle for the simple past tense (i.e., gender and number).

Example 2. *Learner-learner incorrectly resolved form-based LRE*

(2) Mari: Ensuite nous sommes visité, sommes, así?
            [After we are visited, are like this?]

    Alicia: nous sommes [we are]

    Mari: Non, verdad [no, right]

    Alicia: Creo que sí, nous sommes visité pero aca va –s porque somos, sí
            [I think so, we are visited but here put –s because are, yes]

    Mari: Sí, doble –e? [yes, double –e]

    Alicia: Sí, porque son mujeres [yes, because they are women]

In addition to types, four resolution patterns were identified, namely, learner-learner correctly resolved, learner-teacher correctly resolved, incorrectly resolved, and unresolved. Learner-learner correctly resolved LREs are instances where learners collaboratively arrive at a correct resolution (see Example 1). In this example Daril provides the accurate translation equivalent. Learner-teacher correctly resolved LREs are similar with the exception that learners initiated the LREs and requested their teacher's help for resolution (see Example 3). Here, Ismael asks the teacher for the definition of the word *allées* 'alley' and the teacher, after prompting them further in turn 2, provides a definition helping Anita in providing the equivalent meaning.

Example 3. *Teacher-learner correctly resolved lexis-based LRE (meaning)*

(3) Ismael: Ensuite nous... qu'est-ce que allées... [Then we... what is alley]

    Teacher: C'est quoi des allées [What are alleys]

    Ismael: Corredor [corredor]

    Teacher: C'est des petits chemin... comme dans les villes... Guanajuato, San Miguel... [It's a small path... like in the cities... Guanajuato, San Miguel...]

    Anita: Callejones [alleys].

Incorrectly resolved LREs are those where learners collaboratively arrive at an incorrect solution (see Example 2). In Example 2, the learners adopted the incorrect auxiliary verb. And finally, unresolved LREs are instances in which learners question their language use but do not provide a resolution and subsequently continue the task. In Example 4, Anita asks for the translation equivalent of the word *caja* 'box'; unfortunately, her partner could not provide the French equivalent and so Anita repeats her sentences and inserts the Spanish word and they move on with the interaction.

Example 4. *Learner-learner unresolved lexis-based LRE (meaning)*
(4) Anita: La femme qui porte les, como se dice caja [The woman who carries the, how do you say box]
 Ismael: Je ne sais pas [I don't know]
 Anita: La femme qui porte des cajas [The woman who carries some boxes]

The data coding also focused on which language participants depended on in the process of resolving LREs. Three language categories were established for each LRE: L1-dominant (more than half of words in a given LRE were mediated via Spanish), L2-dominant (more than half via English), and L3-dominant (more than half via French). Example 3 is an example of an L3-dominant LRE and Example 2 is an example of an L1-dominant LRE.

Intercoder reliability was established by a second rater coding 10% of the LREs and 20% of the language patterns. The agreement was 93% for the LREs and 100% for language patterns. Disagreements in coding were resolved through discussion. Due to a small sample size, no inferential statistical analyses were conducted.

3 Results

The first research question examined whether learners of French as an L3 engage in collaborative dialogue during task-based interaction. A total of 595 LREs were identified with a mean of 37.2 LREs per dyad. Of these, 346 form-based LREs (58.1%) and 249 lexis-based LREs (41.8%) were identified during the completion of the two task types (See Table 3). Although correct resolution patterns were similar for both LRE types (67.3%: form-based and 62.2%: lexis-based), differences in erroneous resolutions were identified. Specifically, incorrectly resolved form-based LREs were higher (23.7%) than incorrectly resolved lexis-based LREs

(14.5%). Also, unresolved LREs were much higher for lexical items (12.0%) compared to form (2.0%). Finally, the teacher contributed to the resolution of lexis-based LREs (14.5%) more frequently than form-based LREs (5.5%).

Table 3: LREs: Production and resolution patterns of LREs

	Correct	Incorrect	Unresolved	Teacher resolved	Total
Form-based LREs	235 (67.3)	84 (23.7)	6 (2.0)	21 (5.5)	346
Lexis-based LREs	152 (62.2)	34 (14.5)	28 (12.0)	35 (14.5)	249
Total LREs	387	118	34	56	595

Note: Percentages are based on total number of LRE by resolution pattern divided by type

The second research question examined whether the L3 proficiency groupings mediated the occurrence and resolution of LREs (Table 4.). The findings indicate that the Low-High group produced the smallest mean number of LREs (M = 31.0), followed by Low-Intermediate (M = 36.3). Intermediate-High produced the greatest number of LREs (M = 40.8).

With respect to the resolution patterns of form-based LREs, Intermediate-High dyads had the highest mean number of correct learner-learner resolution (M = 16.8), followed by Low-Intermediate dyads (M = 13.0), and by Low-High (M = 12.3). For lexis-based LREs, both the Low-Intermediate and Intermediate-High dyads fared similarly (M = 10.0 and 10.6, respectively). Low-High dyads had the smallest mean number of correctly resolved LREs (M = 6.8)

The third question examined the language drawn on in the production and resolution of LREs. For each proficiency grouping, the percentages of dominant language patterns associated with each LRE (type and resolution) was tabulated (see coding section). Salient differences across the three groups were identified for form-based LREs (See Figure 1). The Intermediate-High group had the highest percentage of L3-dominant correctly resolved LREs (62%) followed by Low-High (51%). The Low-Intermediate group had limited evidence of correctly resolving LREs via the L3 (24%) and tended to favor the L1 (41%). Incorrect resolutions via the L3 were highest for the Low-High (23%) and Low-Intermediate (20%) groups. Finally, for form-based LREs, there was no evidence of L2-dominant mediation by any proficiency groupings.

Figure 2 illustrates the role of the learners' L1, L2, and L3 for resolving lexis-based LREs. Both Low-High (53%) and Intermediate-High (43%) groups mediated the resolution of lexis-based LREs via the target language more often than the Low-Intermediate (20%). Low-Intermediate groups had the highest percentage of correctly resolved LREs via the L1 (40%). There was minimal evidence, 2% of all LREs for Low-Intermediate groups, of L2 mediation for the resolution of lexis-based LREs.

Table 4: Proficiency dyads and the production and resolution of LREs

	Low-High (N = 4)				Low-Intermediate (N = 4)				Intermediate-High (N = 8)			
	Form-based LREs		Lexis-based LREs		Form-based LREs		Lexis-based LREs		Form-based LREs		Lexis-based LREs	
	n	Mean	n	Mean	n	Mean	n	Mean	n	Mean	n	Mean
Correct	49	12.3	27	6.8	52	13.0	40	10.0	134	16.8	85	10.6
Incorrect	21	5.3	9	2.3	25	6.3	8	2.0	38	4.8	17	2.1
Unresolved	3	0.8	3	0.8	0	0.0	8	2.0	3	0.4	14	2.1
Teacher resolved	6	1.5	6	1.5	3	0.8	9	2.3	12	1.5	20	2.5
Total	79	19.8	45	11.3	80	20	65	16.3	187	23.4	139	17.4
Total combined	M = 31.0				M = 36.3				M = 40.8			

Note: The findings reflect LREs produced during the four tasks

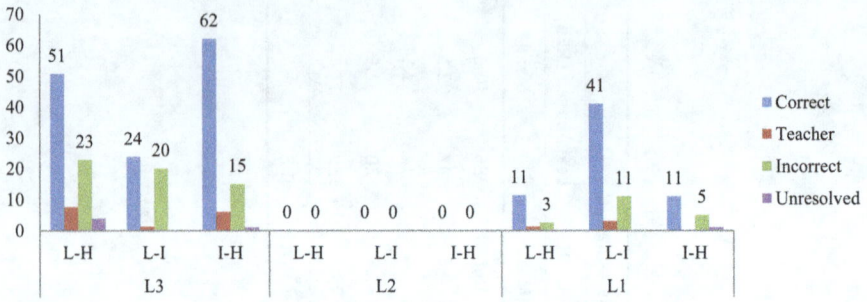

Figure 1: Percentages of form-based LREs by language and proficiency groupings

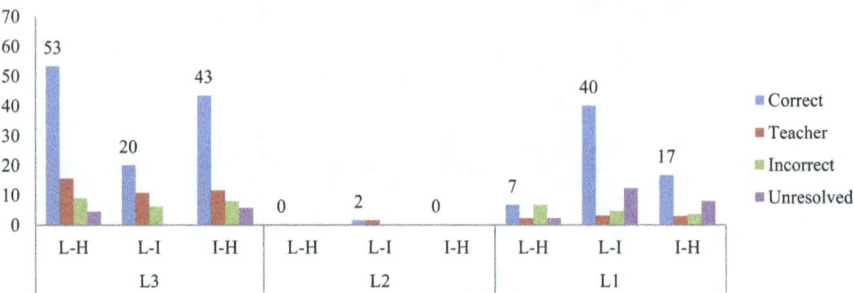

Figure 2: Percentages of lexis-based LREs by language and proficiency groupings

4 Discussion

Within the field of SLA, empirical evidence indicates that L2s develop through interaction, which is facilitated through task completion (Gass and Mackey 2015). During these interactions, language development is guided by internal acquisition processes and learner proficiency is an important variable to examine. Thus, the present study examined the role of learner proficiency on collaborative dialogue during task-based interaction and expanded this line of research to L3 learners. Within this learning environment, there was an indication that L3 learners engage in collaborative dialogue while jointly completing story completion gap tasks and text reconstruction tasks. Furthermore, proficiency was an important mediating variable. Overall, the implementation of these tasks created authentic opportunities for learners to discuss the language that they needed to successfully communicate with their peers and integrate various skills (speaking, listening, reading, and writing), which mirrors real-world expectations.

The use of tasks in classroom contexts not only provides an avenue for learners to use a new language for meaningful and authentic purposes, but also creates opportunities for learners to discuss the language (i.e., LREs). Merely producing LREs, however, may not be sufficient. For language development to occur, correct outcomes are desirable. To date, learners have shown their ability to correctly resolve LREs (Basterrechea and García Mayo 2013; Kim 2008; Lasito and Storch 2013; Lesser 2004; McDonough and Sunitham 2009). The present findings further support this observation such that foreign language learners can draw on their collective knowledge to correctly resolve LREs and create a ZPD. However, at times, learners produce erroneous solutions or leave LREs unresolved. While these LREs did not lead to immediate changes, or development in the microgenetic domain (Vygotsky 1978), the process of discussing the language may be an important precursor to development. Through these discussions, learners may notice gaps in their interlanguage and noticing is an important condition for development (Schmidt 1995). The question persists, nonetheless, as to why learners arrive at these incomplete conclusions.

For lexis-based LREs, we can provide a partial explanation to the occurrence of incorrect and unresolved LREs by examining the setting. Specifically, in this classroom environment, learners drew on their shared L1 to provide lexical information to ensure comprehension (see Example 5).

Example 5: *Unresolved lexis-based LRE*

(5) Alicia: Enseñando. ¿Cómo se dirá? [Showing. How would you say that?]

　　Alexa:　Enseignement o no sé. [Teaching or I don't know]

　　Alicia:　O mostrando. [Or showing]

　　Alexa:　Elle a... mostrando, o no sé [She has shown, or I don't know]

In this example, Alicia begins her request by providing the Spanish word *enseñando* 'teaching' and while they brainstorm a possible translation, they end up using the Spanish term and continue with the task. Thus, there was no pressing need for them to engage in prolonged discussions about the target words. This observation provides support for Ellis' (2003) suggestion that task-based classes should commence with a heavy vocabulary focus to provide the necessary building blocks for communication. For form-based LREs, learners were sometimes found to seek their teacher's help. Resolving form-based LREs requires declarative knowledge which learners sometimes did not possess and, thus, cannot be resolved via L1 solutions (or the L3). Therefore, teachers may play a more important role in task-based language classroom in the resolution of form-based LREs.

One of the primary goals of this study was to examine L3 learner proficiency effects on collaborative dialogue during the completion of collaborative tasks. Results showed that a higher proficiency learner engaged in more LREs when paired with an intermediate learner than when paired with a lower proficiency learner, a finding that echoes previous research (Kim and McDonough 2008; Leeser 2004; Williams 2001). Metatalk may require a certain level of proficiency from both participants. It was interesting to note, however, that form-based LREs outnumbered lexis-based LREs, regardless of proficiency. Kim and McDonough (2008) and Watanabe and Swain (2007) also found similar patterns. Leeser (2004), however, observed that while higher proficiency dyads produced more form-based LREs than lexis, low proficiency dyads had a higher percentage of lexis-based LREs. These findings may have some implications for pairing learners during group work. For scaffolded learning to occur, it may be important to create dyads where proficiency differences are minimal. In sum, while there seems to be growing evidence that greater proficiency leads to more LREs that focus on linguistic forms, additional work in this area is warranted especially in terms of identifying optimal grouping strategies.

Building on findings from previous studies from cognitive orientations with plurilingual speakers, the present study also sought to uncover a link between L3 proficiency and the languages used to create a collective scaffold during tasks. It was hypothesized that learners with lower L3 proficiency would access their L1 and their L2 during collaborative dialogue to form a ZPD in order to complete the tasks. However, only two instances in the entire data set were L2-dominant. The limited evidence of LREs via the L2 prompted a post hoc, qualitative analysis of all L2 output. In total, 27 LREs (4.5%) included some L2 and were produced primarily during the story completion task (N = 24). The limited evidence of L2 was identified almost equally across the learners' L3 proficiencies (Low: N = 7; Intermediate: N = 10; High: N = 10). Even with the limited evidence of L2 mediation, it is worth noting that of the 27 instances, 17 were produced by the High L2 proficiency learners compared to 4 by the Intermediate L2 learners, and 6 by the Low L2 learners. Future work should compare lower and higher L2 proficiency learners of an L3 to determine whether higher L2 proficiency learners draw more frequently on their non-native languages than lower L2 proficiency learners during task-based interaction.

A perhaps more interesting finding was the specific functions these L2 words served during collaborative dialogue. Namely, the learners' L2 was only used for lexical functions: 7 were explicit lexical requests and 16 instances were identified as L2 lexical inserts (See Examples 6 and 7). The remaining three instances of L2 output were identified as social play. Example 6 illustrates an explicit request produced by one of the higher proficiency learners of French. In this example,

Daril makes the request for the L3 word *propre* 'clean' via the L1 (*limpio*) and the peer responded via the L2.

Example 6: *Explicit lexical requests*

(6)   Daril: Elle est très très… comment dire ça… limpio. Elle est très…
                 [She is very very… how do you say that… clean. She is very…]
      Mari: No sé [I don't know]
      Daril: clean
      Mari: clean.

Example 7 shows an instance of a lexical insert, produced during the stage of describing the pictures.

Example 7: *L2 lexical insert*

(7)   Marimar: de la main et ils sont in love je je je se enamoran
                     [by the hand and they are in love he he he they fall in love]
      Pedro: je je je en amour [he he he in love]
      Marimar: en amour [in love]

Since these L2 words emerged during the story completion task, we can hypothesize that task type may have increased the need for mediation and learners may have turned to their entire linguistic repertoire to do so. Unlike the text reconstruction task, learners did not have access to any written input during the story completion. Rather, they were prompted to create a story orally, based on a series of images. In searching for L3 words, the participants sometimes turned to English. The tendency of turning to the L2 for lexical functions has been identified previously in CLI research (Bardel and Lindqvist 2007; Hammarberg 2001; Lindqvist 2010; Williams and Hammarberg 1998). Thus, for material development within task-based programs, limiting the quantity of written input may lead learners into searching their entire linguistic repertoires to ensure successful communication.

     The limitations of the study should be taken into account. This small scale classroom-based research provides a small glimpse into the relationship between language proficiency and collaborative dialogue. Nevertheless, these findings may not be generalizable to other instructional settings. Building on the current study, future research is warranted to examine the role of proficiency during task-based instruction. Also, the study did not include same proficiency dyads, which might have induced unique patterns of collaborative dialogue. Thus, future studies should counterbalance the number of dyads across same and different proficiency groupings. Finally, the specific role of task type was not considered in this analysis and it would be worthwhile to examine more closely if the task type mediates the occurrence of L2-dominant and L3-dominant LREs.

5 Future directions

The study of L3 development is a burgeoning area of research. In studying the development and use of an L3, it is important to consider learner proficiency as well as the nature of the oral/written tasks, the settings in which interactions unfold, the relationships between the interlocutors, and the languages under study. The finding that L2 output was limited to the story completion tasks suggests an important role for task design: The provision of written input may lessen the need to implicitly or explicitly turn to an additional L2 as it provided additional amounts of L3 input. The context may also have mitigating effects on L2 output (Jessner 2005). In formal language classrooms, where students go to learn an L3, learners may de-activate additional languages and operate in a monolingual or bilingual mode (Grosjean 2008). Finally, intermediate learners may already have a rich lexical repertoire in the target language to draw on while producing output. Implementing pedagogical tasks with learners in their earlier stages of L3 development may uncover new insights about the L2 as a cognitive tool for aiding language development. Despite having modest evidence for L3 proficiency and L2 mediation, this line of research warrants additional attention. I hope that my interest will generate additional research with L3 learners in classroom, learner-learner interaction settings.

References

Abadikhah, Shirin. 2011. Investigating language-related episodes during mechanical and meaningful output activities. *International Journal of English Linguistics*. 1(2). 281–294.
Adams, Rebecca & Lauren Ross-Feldman. 2008. Does writing influence learner attention to form? In Diane. D. Belcher & Alan Hirvela (eds.), *The oral-literate connection: Perspectives on L2 speaking, writing, and other media interactions*, 243–266. Ann Arbor: The University of Michigan Press.
Alegría de la Colina, Ana & María del Pilar García Mayo. 2007. Attention to form across collaborative tasks by low-proficiency learners in an EFL setting. In María del Pilar García Mayo (ed.), *Investigating tasks in formal language learning*, 91–116. Clevedon, UK: Multilingual Matters.
Aronin, Larissa & Britta Hufeisen (eds.). 2009. *The exploration of multilingualism*. Amsterdam: John Benjamins Publishing Company.

Azkarai, Agurtzane & María del Pilar García Mayo. 2015. Task-modality and L1 use in EFL oral interaction. *Language Teaching Research*. 19(5). 1–22.
Bardel, Camilla & Christina Lindqvist. 2007. The role of proficiency and psychotypology in lexical cross-linguistic influence. A study of a multilingual learner of Italian L3. In Marina Chini, Paola Desideri, Maria Elena Favilla & Gabriele Pallotti (eds), *Atti del VI congresso di studi dell'associazione Italiana di linguistica applicata*, Napoli, 9–10 febbraio 2006, 123–145. Perugia: Guerra Editore.
Basterrechea, María & María del Pilar García Mayo. 2013. Language-related episodes during collaborative tasks: A comparison of CLIL and EFL learners. In Kim McDonough & Alison Mackey (eds.), *Second language interaction in diverse educational contexts*, 25–43. Amsterdam: Publishing Company.
Cabrelli Amaro, Jennifer, Suzanne Flynn & Jason Rothman (eds). 2012. *Third language acquisition in adulthood*. Philadelphia/Amsterdam: Publishing Company.
De Angelis, Gessica. 2007. *Third or additional language acquisition*. Clevedon, UK: Multilingual Matters.
De Angelis, Gessica & Jean-Marc Dewaele (eds.). 2011. *New trends in crosslinguistic influence and multilingualism research*. Bristol, UK: Multilingual Matters.
De Bot, Kees & Carol Jaensch. 2015. What is special about L3 processing? *Bilingualism: Language and Cognition*. 18(2). 130–144.
Donato, Richard. 1994. Collective scaffolding in second language learning. In James. P. Lantolf & Gabriel Appel (eds.), *Vygotskian approaches to second language research*, 33–56. Norwood, New Jersey: Ablex Publishing Corporation.
Edstrom, Anne. 2015. Triads in the L2 classroom: Interaction patterns and engagement during a collaborative task. *System* 52. 26–37.
Ellis, Rod. 2003. *Task-based language learning and teaching*. Oxford: Oxford University Press.
Falk, Ylva & Camilla Bardel. 2010. The study of the role of the background languages in third language acquisition. The state of the art. *IRAL: International Review of Applied Linguistics in Language Teaching* 48. 185–219.
Fernández Dobao, Ana. 2014. Attention to form in collaborative writing tasks: Comparing pair and small group interaction. *Canadian Modern Language Review* 70(2). 158–187.
García Mayo, María del Pilar & Jorge González Alonso. 2015. Introduction. L3 acquisition: A focus on cognitive approaches. [Special issue]. *Bilingualism: Language and Cognition* 18(2).
Gass, Susan, M. & Alison Mackey. 2015. Input, interaction, and output in second language acquisition. In Bill VanPatten & Jessica Williams (eds.), *Theories in second language acquisition. An introduction*, 180–206. London: Routledge.
Giancaspro, David, Becky Halloran and Michael Iverson. 2015. Transfer at the initial stages of L3 Brazilian Portuguese: A look at three groups of English/Spanish bilinguals. *Bilingualism: Language and Cognition* 18(2). 191–207.
Grosjean, Francois. 2008. *Studying bilinguals*. Oxford: Oxford University Press.
Hammarberg, Bjorn. 2001. Roles of L1 and L2 in L3 production and acquisition. In Jasone Cenoz, Britta Hufeisen & Ulrike Jessner (eds.), *Cross-linguistic influence in third language acquisition*, 21–41. Clevedon, UK: Multilingual Matters.
Hammarberg, Bjorn. 2010. The languages of the multilingual: Some conceptual and terminological issues. *International Review of Applied Linguistics in Language Teaching* 48(2/3). 91–104.

Jessner, Ulrike. 2005. Multilingual metalanguage, or the way multilinguals talk about their languages. *Language Awareness* 14(1). 56–68.

Kim, YouJin. 2008. The contribution of collaborative and individual tasks to the acquisition of L2 vocabulary. *The Modern Language Journal* 92(1). 114–130.

Kim, YouJin. 2013. Promoting attention to form through task repetition in a Korean EFL context. In Kim McDonough & Alison Mackey (eds.), *Second language interaction in diverse educational settings*, 3–24. Philadelphia, PA: John Benjamins.

Kim, YouJin & Kim McDonough. 2008. The effect of interlocutor proficiency on the collaborative dialogue between Korean as a second language learners. *Language Teaching Research* 12(2). 211–234.

Kim, YouJin & Kim McDonough. 2011. Using pretask modeling to encourage collaborative learning opportunities. *Language Teaching Research* 15(2). 183–199.

Lantolf, James P., Steven L. Thorne & Matthew E. Poehner. 2015. Sociocultural theory and second language development. In Bill VanPatten & Jessica Williams (eds.), *Theories in second language acquisition. An introduction*, 207–226. London: Routledge.

Lasito & Neomy Storch. 2013. Comparing pair and small group interactions on oral tasks. *RELC Journal* 44(3). 361–375.

Leeser, Michael J. 2004. Learner proficiency and focus on form during collaborative dialogue. *Language Teaching Research* 8(1). 55–81.

Lindqvist, Christina. 2009. The use of the L1 and the L2 in French L3: examining cross-linguistic lexemes in multilingual learners' oral production. *International Journal of Multilingualism* 6(3). 281–297.

Lindqvist, Christina. 2010. Inter- and intralingual lexical influences in advanced learners' French L3 oral production. *IRAL: International Review of Applied Linguistics in Language Teaching* 48(2/3). 131–157.

Lindqvist, Christina & Camilla Bardel. 2014. Exploring the impact of the proficiency and typology factors: Two cases of multilingual learners' L3 learning. In Mirosław Pawlak & Larissa Aronin (eds.), *Essential topics in applied linguistics and multilingualism, second language learning and teaching*, 253–266. Switzerland: Springer International Publishing.

Loewen, Shawn. 2014. *Introduction to instructed second language acquisition*. New York: Routledge.

McDonough, Kim & Wichian Sunitham. 2009. Collaborative dialogue between Thai EFL learners during self-access computer activities. *TESOL Quarterly* 43. 231–254.

Niu, Ruiying. 2009. Effect of task-inherent production modes on EFL learners' focus on form. *Language Awareness* 18(3–4). 384–402.

Ohta, Amy. S. 1995. Applying sociocultural theory to an analysis of learner discourse: Learner-learner collaborative interaction in the zone of proximal development. *Issues in Applied Linguistics* 6(2). 93–121.

Ohta, Amy. S. 2000. Rethinking interaction in SLA: Developmentally appropriate assistance in the zone of proximal development and the acquisition of L2 grammar. In James. P. Lantolf (ed.), *Sociocultural theory and second language learning*, 51–78. Oxford: Oxford University Press.

Payant, Caroline. 2015. Plurilingual learners' beliefs and practices toward native and nonnative language mediation during learner-learner interaction. *The Canadian Modern Language Review* 71(2). 1–25.

Payant, Caroline & YouJin Kim. 2015. Language mediation in an L3 classroom: The role of task modalities and task types. *Foreign Language Annals* 48(4). 706–729.

Richards, Jack. C. & Theodore S. Rodgers. 2014. *Approaches and methods in language teaching* (3rd Ed). Cambridge: Cambridge University Press.

Schmidt, Richard. 1995. Consciousness and foreing language learning: A tutorial on the role of attention and awareness in learning. In Richard Schmidt (ed.), *Attention and awareness in foreing language learning and teaching*, 1–64. Honolulu, HI: University of Hawaii Press.

Slabakova, Roumyana & María del Pilar García Mayo. 2015. The L3 syntax–discourse interface. *Bilingualism: Language and Cognition* 18(2). 208–226.

Storch, Neomy. 2001. How collaborative is pair work? ESL tertiary students composing in pairs. *Language Teaching Research* 5(1). 29–53.

Storch, Neomy. 2002a. Patterns of interaction in ESL pair work. *Language Learning* 52(1). 119–158.

Storch, Neomy. 2002b. Relationships formed in dyadic interaction and opportunity for learning. *International Journal of Educational Research* 37(3–4). 305–322.

Storch, Neomy & Ali Aldosari. 2010. Learners' use of first language (Arabic) in pair work in an EFL class. *Language Teaching Research* 14(4). 355–375.

Storch, Neomy & Ali Aldosari. 2013. Pairing learners in pair work activity. *Language Teaching Research* 17(1). 31–48.

Swain, Merrill & Sharon Lapkin. 1998. Interaction and second language learning: Two adolescent French immersion students working together. *Modern Language Journal* 82(3). 320–337.

Swain, Merrill & Sharon Lapkin. 2001. Focus on form through collaborative dialogue: Exploring task effects. In Martin Bygate, Peter Skehan & Merrill Swain (eds.), *Researching pedagogic tasks: Second language learning, teaching and testing*, 99–118. Harlow, Essex: Longman.

Swain, Merrill & Yuko Watanabe. 2013. Language: Collaborative dialogue as a source of second language learning. In Carol A. Chapelle (ed.), *The encyclopedia of applied linguistics*, 3218–3225. Hoboken, NJ: Wiley-Blackwell.

Swain, Merrill, Lindsay Brooks & Agustina Tocalli-Beller. 2002. Peer-peer dialogue as means of second language learning. *Annual Review of Applied Linguistics* 22. 171–185.

Taguchi, Nayoko & YouJin Kim. 2016. Collaborative dialogue in learning pragmatics: Pragmatic-related episodes as an opportunity for learning request-making. *Applied Linguistics* 37(3). 416–437.

van Compernolle, Rémi A. & Lawrence Williams. 2013. Group dynamics in the language classroom: embodied participation as active reception in the collective Zone of Proximal Development. *Classroom Discourse* 4(1). 42–62.

Vygotsky, Lev. 1978. *Mind in society: The development of higher psychological processes*. Cambridge: Harvard University Press.

Watanabe, Yuko & Merrill Swain. 2007. Effects of proficiency differences and patterns of pair interaction on second language learning: Collaborative dialogue between adult ESL learners. *Language Teaching Research* 11(2). 121–142.

Williams, Jessica. 1999. Learner-generated attention to form. *Language Learning* 51. 303–346.

Williams, Jessica. 2001. The effectiveness of spontaneous attention to form. *System* 29(3). 325–340.

Williams, Sarah & Bjorn Hammarberg. 1998. Language switches in L3 production: Implications for a polyglot speaking model. *Applied Linguistics* 19(3). 295–333.

Wajnryb, Ruth. 1990. *Grammar dictation*. Oxford: Oxford University Press.

Lawrence Williams
6 Task-Based Language Teaching and Concept-Based Instruction

1 Introduction

This chapter proposes the integration of Concept-Based Instruction (CBI)[1] into Task-Based Language Teaching (TBLT) within a multiliteracies framework (New London Group, 1996). CBI "is predicated on the Vygotskian principle that schooled instruction is about developing control over theoretical concepts that are explicitly and coherently presented to learners as they are guided through a sequence of activities designed to prompt the necessary internalization of the relevant concepts" (Negueruela and Lantolf 2006: 80). The present study examines the implementation of CBI within a model for TBLT used in the context of the French curriculum at a large, public university in the U.S. In addition to demonstrating the ways in which CBI is compatible with and can enhance TBLT, a secondary objective is to advance the notion that SLA and pedagogy are interdependent (Ellis 2003; van Lier 1994).

Although various models of TBLT have become quite popular over the past few decades (see Ellis 2003; González-Lloret and Ortega 2014; Nunan 2004; Shehadeh and Coombe 2012; Van den Branden, Bygate, and Norris 2009; Willis 1996; Willis and Willis 2007), one dimension of TBLT that arguably deserves more attention is the stage of TBLT that provides opportunities for "language focus" (Willis 1996: 36) or a "focus on linguistic elements" (Nunan 2004: 34), especially when difficult grammar points or sociolinguistic and pragmatic dimensions of language are incompletely or inaccurately depicted and explained in textbooks (Negueruela and Lantolf 2006; Williams 2016).

2 Concept-based instruction

The motivation for adopting a concept-based approach for part of the learning module reported in this study stems from a lack of comprehensive and effective

---
[1] CBI is also referred to as Systemic-Theoretical Instruction.

Lawrence Williams, University of North Texas

explanations of French auxiliary verb choice in textbooks for beginning and intermediate learners published in the U.S. One of the key components of a concept-based approach to teaching is the use of scientific concepts (see Galperin 1979; Lantolf and Thorne 2006) instead of everyday concepts. In the case of the current study, an everyday concept (i.e., a rule of thumb) for explaining French auxiliary verb choice would be to say that the French verbs that require *être* 'to be' as their auxiliary are "verbs of motion" (see Williams 2016). This type of explantion, which is found in most textbooks, represents an incomplete view of French auxiliary verb choice in two ways. First, there are dozens of "motion verbs" that also happen to require *avoir* 'to have' as their auxiliary. Second, the list of verbs that require *être* 'to be' as their auxiliary also typically includes verbs that can take either *avoir* 'to have' or *être* 'to be' as their auxiliary, and the only way to distinguish when *avoir* vs. *être* is required is to understand the concept of transitivity (as shown below in Table 1), yet the concept of transitivity is glaringly absent in most French textbooks (published in the U.S.).

Within a CBI framework, this means that transitivity (for the present study) is the scientific concept that must be materialized, for example, in the form of a diagram, flowchart, or some other type of representation of the concept, which is used as an "Orienting Basis of an Action (or OBA) as a means of mediating [the learners'] performance of an activity" (Lantolf and Thorne 2006: 305). As Lantolf and Thorne also point out, "it is not sufficient to provide the concepts in the form of a verbal explanation, since in spoken form they are ephemeral; even in written form they are often too complex and therefore not easily assigned psychological status" (p. 305). The other key component of CBI is verbalization, which forces students to express their thought process in oral or written form. For the present study, students were required to display their thought process in a live, online chat setting so that the author could provide feedback to individuals and groups with the goal of helping them to improve their understanding of the concept and their ability to engage more effectively in verbalization. Table 1 indicates how the three principles of CBI are related to Galperin's "general theory of human mental functioning" (Lantolf and Thorne 2006: 304).

Table 1: CBI and Human Mental Functioning

Principles of CBI	Theory of Human Mental Functioning (Galperin 1979)
Concept as unit of instruction	Orientation function (of an activity)
Materialization of relevant concepts	Execution function (of an activity)
Verbalization for fostering internalization of concepts	Control function (of an activity)

In sum, for any CBI lesson "the expectation is that through [CBI] learners will develop a deeper understanding of and control over the object of study" (Lantolf and Thorne 2006: 306). Negueruela and Lantolf (2006) offer the following clear summary of the primary concerns that teachers should keep in mind when developing a CBI lesson: "The concept that is the object of instruction and learning [transitivity, in the case of the present study] must be organized into a coherent pedagogical unit of instruction. This unit must have two fundamental properties: It must retain the full meaning of the relevant concept and be organized to promote learning, understanding, control, and internalization (Negueruela 2003)" (82).

For the present study, the analysis of verbalizations in the form of chat transcripts was used to seek answers to the following questions:
- To what extent was each student/group able to determine the correct answer (or, depending on the case, an appropriate answer)?
- To what extent did students understand or misunderstand the representation of the scientific concept (e.g., diagram, flowchart)?
- To what extent did each student's/group's answer correspond to an understanding of the concept?
- To what extent did each student/group apply a concept-based approach to learning as indicated through explicit discussion of the concept during the verbalization task?

3 A multiliteracies approach to pedagogy

For the present study, the multiliteracies approach to pedagogy proposed by the New London Group (1996) was used to shape the content into components of a project aimed at fostering the internalization of the concept of transitivity as a main objective. The framework by the New London Group is centered on four components that provide students with different learning opportunities: situated practice, overt instruction, critical framing, and transformed practice. This model for organizing learning opportunities offers flexibility (as do other models of TBLT) because there is no prescribed order in which the different components must be organized. Moreover, any single component can be used more than once, depending on the expected learning outcomes. When using a multiliteracies approach to pedagogy for TBLT, the components (all of which are explained below) situated practice and transformed practice are considered tasks (see Ellis 2009: 223 for criteria), while overt instruction and critical framing are supporting activities that can be separate lessons used to prepare learners for the tasks, review problems encountered during the tasks, or provide supplemental information or practice after the tasks have been completed (i.e., missed learning opportunities).

3.1 Situated practice

In the framework proposed by the New London Group (1996), situated practice "is constituted by immersion in meaningful practices within a community of learners who are capable of playing multiple and different roles based on their backgrounds and experiences" (85). For a grammar-centered segment of a class meeting, one of the most efficient types of situated practice is to ask students (as individuals, in small groups, or as part of a whole-class participation structure) to identify the targeted concept or feature in an existing text or perhaps texts that the students have already produced themselves.

3.2 Overt instruction

According to the New London Group (1996), overt instruction is not necessarily providing students with facts and explaining rules. Instead, "it includes all those active interventions on the part of the teacher and other experts that scaffold learning activities, that focus the learner on the important features of their experiences and activities within the community of learners, and that allow the learner to gain explicit information at times when it can most usefully organize and guide practice, building on and recruiting what the learner already knows and has accomplished" (86). In other words, overt instruction is more about drawing learners' attention to whatever they have overlooked, possibly misunderstood, or dismissed as unimportant. Overt instruction should involve leading students in the right direction instead of quickly providing them with knowledge or information that they could eventually discover on their own.

3.3 Critical framing

According to the New London Group (1996), "the goal of Critical Framing is to help learners frame their growing mastery in practice (from Situated Practice) and conscious control and understanding (from Overt Instruction) in relation to the historical, social, cultural, political, ideological, and value-centered relations of particular systems of knowledge and social practice" (86). This component of a learning module is often used to make connections to other disciplines or to highlight various issues related to culture, language, and pedagogy as intertwined elements of foreign language education.

3.4 Transformed practice

When learners engage in transformed practice, "they should be able to show that they can implement understandings acquired through Overt Instruction and Critical Framing in practices that help them simultaneously to apply and revise what they have learned" (New London Group 1996: 87). For the present study, learners had two opportunities to engage in transformed practice. First, they completed the worksheet (see Appendix) on French auxiliary verb choice, then they completed a written essay based on an important historical figure from the francophone world from a first-person perspective.

4 Method

4.1 Participants

The present study was conducted with an intact class of learners (age range of 19–23) in their third semester (i.e., first semester of the second year) of French at a large, public university in the U.S. The 15 students present for the lesson focused on French auxiliary verbs were divided into 6 groups of 2 and 1 group of 3 using random group generator software. Data from Group 4 were not used because one of the students in this group did not sign and submit the Informed Consent document at the beginning of the session. The list of participants (i.e., those who had given written consent) was not shared with the instructor.

4.2 The learning module

The learning module designed for the study reported here included a series of lessons that led learners toward a culminating task that required them to "become" a famous (or infamous) francophone artist, explorer, politician, or some other important historical figure from the francophone world. Table 2 displays some basic details about each lesson.

Table 2: List of Lessons

Lesson	Class Period	Multiliteracies Component
1	1 (80 minutes)	Situated Practice (Task 1 – Writing)
2	2 (20 minutes)	Critical Framing (Supporting Activity)
3	2 (60 minutes)	Overt Instruction (Supporting Activity) – Explanation of Transitivity – Small-Group Chat Sessions – Worksheet
4	3 (80 minutes)	Transformed Practice (Task 2 – Writing)

The writing assignments (Task 1 and Task 2) used for this learning module were developed according to the criteria proposed by Ellis (2009: 223) for defining a task within a TBLT framework:

1. The primary focus should be on 'meaning' (by which is meant that learners should be mainly concerned with processing the semantic and pragmatic meaning of utterances).
2. There should be some kind of 'gap' (i.e. a need to convey information, to express an opinion or to infer meaning).
3. Learners should largely have to rely on their own resources (linguistic and non-linguistic) in order to complete the activity.
4. There is a clearly defined outcome other than the use of language (i.e. the language serves as the means for achieving the outcome, not as an end in its own right).

The CBI component of this learning module supports students' progress as they move from Task 1 (beginning of the module) to Task 2 (end of the module). Consequently, this type of learning module is part of a task-supported curriculum since explicit or overt instruction is provided. For a recent study comparing task-based and task-supported language instruction, see Li, Ellis, and Zhu (2016).

The source material for the situated practice component (Task 1) of this learning module was an excerpt from *L'histoire de ma vie* 'The Story of My Life' (2007) by Théophile Dujardin (born in northern France). Using this source material allowed students to examine and analyze what might be considered a typical autobiographical text. This gave them opportunities to explore the structure of such narratives, commonly used verb structures, recurring vocabulary, common turns of phrase, and so forth. Even though most U.S. university students have likely read some type of autobiography at some point during their previous studies, an entire class period was dedicated to Task 1 in order to acclimate students to this type of writing in an L2.

For the critical framing component of the learning module, the instructor and the author led a whole-class review of what the students had learned previously about French auxiliary verbs, relying primarily on the mnemonic device *DR & MRS VANDERTRAMP(P)* and the visual aid *la maison d'être* 'the house of être'. Many different instantiations of these learning aids are widely available in textbooks and on line, and all participants reported having used them at some point in the past. This lesson was conducted in the form of a metalinguistic discussion, with the main objective being to raise the students' awareness of different ways to explain principles or rules of grammar and some of the limitations of written explanations in textbooks and in other sources. Due to time constraints, critical framing was the shortest lesson in this learning module; however, this component of a multiliteracies approach to pedagogy could be expanded and made more motivating, strategic, and differentiated, among other things (Candlin 2009: 25) by asking students to compare different resources in order to establish the lists of verbs associated with questions 2, 3, and 4 on the French auxiliary verb flowchart (see Table 3) since these groups of verbs are often inconsistently represented or largely ignored in textbooks (at least those published in the U.S.) for learners of French (Williams 2016). For the present study, the students were given the lists of lexical verbs needed to use the flowchart, but asking students to identify these verbs would certainly expand opportunities for critical framing.

For the overt instruction component, a CBI-inspired flowchart (see Table 3) was used as a way to present auxiliary verb choice. While the learners engage in the verbalization activity in small-group chat sessions, they simultaneously complete the worksheet (see Appendix) as a way to record their work. Incidentally, having this written record of their answers allows them to consult previous items in order to compare and contrast structures that appear to be similar. One advantage of using a flowchart as a didactic device (following the model proposed by Galperin 1979) is being able to avoid overly simplistic rules-of-thumb or incomplete lists that only match whichever structures happen to appear in the exercises in a given textbook. The main advantage of using a CBI-inspired didactic device is, of course, the ability to focus on a concept as the foundation for overt instruction since learners will later be able to apply their knowledge of the concept (e.g., transitivity) to structures and communicative activities beyond the context in which they learned it (in this case, French auxiliary verb choice).

Table 3: French auxiliary verb choice flowchart

Question	Action
1) Pronominal use of verb?	Yes > Use *être*.
	No > Continue to the next question.
2) Group of verbs that always use *être* as auxiliary?	Yes > Use *être*.
	No > Continue to the next question.
3) *Paraître* or a prefixed form of this verb?	Yes > Either *avoir* or *être* can be used. Choice depends on a semantic nuance. Consult a grammar guide for details.
	No > Continue to the next question.
4) Group of verbs that can use *avoir* or *être* as auxiliary?	Yes > Continue to the next question.
	No > Use *avoir*.
5) Transitive use of this verb?	Yes > Use *avoir*.
	No > Use *être*.

For the present study, learners had an opportunity to engage in transformed practice by writing and sharing an essay (Task 2) based on an important historical figure from the francophone world from a first-person perspective. As second-year university-level language learners, they all had experience writing more than one autobiographical essay in the second language. Therefore, they were being challenged to write in the first person based on the perceived or imagined experiences of someone else in order to view the human experience from a different perspective. For this task, they were able to meld fact and fiction. For example, any paragraph of the essay could begin with a true (i.e., reported in reliable sources) premise or statement, but subsequent parts of the paragraph could introduce anecdotal, unproven, or humorous statements that would make the text seem more like a contemporary personal (written or digital) diary than formal memoirs. While it is unlikely that learners would engage in this type of task outside a structured learning environment, this task was "designed to instigate the same kind of interactional processes ... that arise in naturally occurring language use" (Ellis 2009: 227). The results and analysis provided later in this chapter do not cover the writing task since the aim of the present study is to explain and examine the integration of CBI into a (French) curriculum.

5 Results and analysis

In this section, different types of results are provided in order to illustrate various aspects of the students' understanding of the concept (i.e., transitivity) and their understanding of the importance of verbalizations as a pedagogical and developmental tool. The first time a flowchart (or some other type of representation of a scientific concept) is used, and the first time that students encounter a CBI lesson, it is especially important to focus on the quality of the materials and the quality of the verbalizations. This means that although it is certainly important for students to provide correct or appropriate answers, the focus should remain on the students' development of the understanding of the concept and, eventually, its internalization, which will not likely occur immediately, in most cases.

In tables that display results, each group is indicated with their original number (e.g., Group 1 = G1). Results for Group 4 are not provided since one member of this group did not submit a signed Informed Consent document.

The results from each group's worksheet (see Appendix) are provided in Table 4, with incorrect answers shaded in gray. It is clear that Groups 2 and 7 encountered more difficulties than the other groups, and overall, Items E and F seemed to be the most problematic; however, at this point in the learners' developmental trajectory, the number of correct answers is not a primary concern. Instead, the emphasis is on determining the extent to which the flowchart is an effective didactic device across most groups so that even learners with slower cognitive development will be able to use the flowchart to understand the concept over time.

Table 4: French Auxiliary Choice Worksheet Results

Group	A	B	C	D	E	F	G	I	J	K
1	e	a	a	a	e	e	a	a	e	a
2	a	a	e	a	e	a	e	a	e	a
3	e	a	a	a	a	a	a	a	e	a
5	e	a	a	a	a	a	a	a	e	a
6	e	a	a	a	a	e	a	a	e	a
7	a	a	a	a	e	a	a	a	e	a

In order to determine the extent to which the participants used the verbalization activity as a way to develop and reinforce their understanding of transitivity, a rubric (see Table 5) was created so that feedback to the learners would allow them to identify some best practices that should be incorporated into subsequent CBI lessons in order to foster better understanding of concepts and their internalization. As mentioned above, the worksheet was completed while the learners were engaged in the verbalization activity during the small-group chat sessions.

Table 5: Rubric for Coding Written Verbalizations

Level	Description
0-No Explanation	Learners agreed on an auxiliary verb (*avoir* or *être*), but did not explain their choice.
1-Partial Explanation	Learners agreed on an auxiliary verb (*avoir* or *être*) and mentioned a part of speech or the meaning/translation of one or more words; however, they did not explicitly indicate how transitivity was related to their choice of *avoir* or *être*.
2-Complete Explanation	Learners agreed on an auxiliary verb (*avoir* or *être*), and they explicitly indicated how transitivity was related to their choice of *avoir* or *être*.

Table 6 offers an overview of the extent to which the participants applied a concept-based approach to learning by engaging in explicit discussion of the concept of transitivity during the verbalization task. Ideally, as students become more familiar with the expectations of CBI lessons, the ratings of Level 0 will disappear. The results in Table 6 should eventually demonstrate a pattern with the lowest frequencies for Level 0 ratings and the highest frequencies for Level 2 ratings. Only the results for Group 6 produced this ideal pattern, which means that the other participants might need more specific instructions regarding the expectations associated with this type of activity.

Table 6: Summary of the Application of Concept-Based Instruction

Group	Level 0 Frequency	Level 1 Frequency	Level 2 Frequency	Total
1	3	6	1	10
2	4	5	1	10
3	1	5	4	10
5	5	1	4	10
6	2	3	5	10
7	7	2	1	10
Total	22	22	16	—

In Table 7, the level of application of CBI (see Table 6) is indicated in the CBI column. In the Answer (ANS) column, an *X* is used to indicate the incorrect choice of a French auxiliary verb.

Table 7: Application of Concept-Based Instruction and Answers

Item	G1 CBI	G1 ANS	G2 CBI	G2 ANS	G3 CBI	G3 ANS	G5 CBI	G5 ANS	G6 CBI	G6 ANS	G7 CBI	G7 ANS
A	2		0	X	2		2		2		0	X
B	0		0		2		2		2		1	
C	1		0	X	2		2		2		2	
D	1		2		2		0		2		0	
E	1	X	1	X	1		0		1		1	X
F	0		1	X	1	X	0	X	2		0	X
G	1		0	X	1		0		1		0	
I	1		1		0		0		1		0	
J	0		1		1		1		0		0	
K	1		1		1		2		0		0	

In the case of Item A (dealing with the pronominal use of a verb), there is a clear positive correlation between an explicit discussion of the flowchart – as a tool for understanding the concept of transitivity – and determining the correct answer. In fact, this item only required consulting the first line of the flowchart, which even included an example, in case students had forgotten the examples presented during their review of French auxiliary verb choice at the beginning of the class meeting. This item was not a distractor in the typical meaning of the term (as used in survey research); it was simply intended to give students a very easy item at the beginning of the task in order to ease them into using the flowchart.

There is also an obvious positive correlation between ratings at Level 2 and correct answers; even Groups 2 and 7, which had the most incorrect answers, were able to determine the correct answers for items that involved explicit indications of the concept while they were working toward agreeing on an answer.

The transcripts are the final type of evidence to examine in order to understand how students did not meet the expectations of the verbalization activity. The verbalizations (in the form of chat transcripts) of Group 2 – and selected excerpts from other transcripts – are provided below. Although Group 2 had the highest error rate (5/10, 50%), they did not have the greatest frequency of Level 0 ratings. Unfortunately, they began their chat (i.e., verbalization) session by adopting practices that did not indicate the application of a concept-based approach to developing a better understanding of French auxiliary verb choice, as shown in Excerpt G2-1.

Excerpt G2-1. Group 2, 10:12 am–10:29 am

Chris joined the chat
Chris: Hello
Chris: I think 1 is avoir. Confirm?
Jay joined the chat
Chris: Hi Jaye
Jay: Hey…
Chris: I got avoir for the first 2. Confirm?
Jay: I think that is right.
Jay: and you add an s to the 2nd verb
Chris: what are your thoughts on the rest?
Jay: I'm still working on them … Gimme a sec
Chris: kk
Jay: I think that C is etre
Chris: Confirmed.
Jay: k

Nonetheless, they did actually engage in an explicit discussion of transitivity when some uncertainty about the correct answer for Item D was expressed by Jay, as shown in Excerpt G2-2. In fact, Chris is responsible for guiding the group toward the correct answer by taking the time to explain the concept, based on the flowchart, and it really seems as if Chris himself is reasoning through the problem while he is explaining it to Jay.

Excerpt G2-2. Group 2, 10:30 am–10:33 am

Jay: What do you think D is?
Chris: etre
Jay: I'm leaning more towards avior
Chris: Because tomber is on the list
Jay: Really? Ok.
Chris: So then we see if it's transitive.
Jay: Gotcha … I overlooked that
Chris: And "Son adversaire" is "your _____"
Chris: Sorry it's "it
Chris: anyway, son is 3rd person singular
Jay: ok
Chris: Which makes me think it's a noun phrase
Chris: And yeah
Jay: True …

Chris: Avoir
Chris: I confirm with you.
Jay: Oh ... lol
Jay: Ooops.
Chris: yeah

Chris and Jay (Group 2) then abandoned their application of using the representation of the concept (i.e., the flowchart) to think through Items E, F, and G, and, consequently, they did not produce the correct answers (see Excerpt G2-3). If Chris, for example, had not simply accepted Jay's incorrect answer for Item G and initiated a discussion of this item, one or both members of this group might have realized that Item D (which had been discussed thoroughly) was almost identical in many ways to Item G. This type of excerpt was, therefore, identified as an important part of the feedback for this group as a way to demonstrate how ignoring the concept does not promote development.

Excerpt G2-3. Group 2, 10:33 am–10:36 am

Chris: Ok for E I have etre
Jay: Yea, me too
Chris: because it has "de un homme"
Chris: Ok
Chris: F I have avoir
Jay: MmmHmm!
Chris: because it's just "lieutenant"
Chris: lol
Jay: Yea, yea ... lol
Chris: etre, avoir, etre, avoir
Jay: I got etre for G
Chris: same here
Jay: K
Chris: avoir etre avoir
Chris: Confirm?
Jay: I put the exact opposite ... smh. Hold on ...
Chris: Ok

After skipping the discussion part of the instructions for the previous items, this group eventually returned to thinking through Items I and J (even though they only took a few seconds to agree on Item K) with the help of the flowchart representing the concept of transitivity, as shown in Excerpt G2-5.

Excerpt G2-5. Group 2, 10:36 am–10:49 am

Chris: I is monter which means 4th box which means noun phrase which means avoir, no?
Jay: That's right.
Jay: So then avior would be used.
Chris: Ok
Chris: Ok I just looked up jusqu'au and that means "until the" and that would make it a prepositional phrase, yes?
Jay: Yes
Chris: and that gets etre, right?
Jay: I think so. What was the word he wrote on the board that started with a "P"
Chris: Prepositional Phrase
Chris: Plage
Chris: Passer
Chris: Politique
Jay: Lol … The french word that meant Prepositional Phrase
Chris: He didn't give us a french translation
Chris: He just wrote Prepositional Phrase
Jay: I thought he did … Oh well
Chris: Yep
Chris: So what do we put for J?
Jay: Oh, it's actually in english … lol. It was transitive.
Chris: Oh ok
Jay: I honestly think it's avior … simply because jusqu'au means "until the"
Chris: Right
Chris: but "until" is a preposition
Jay: I'm looking at that. It's etre
Chris: right
Chris: And since monter is followed by a noun phrase "la lente" I think it's avoir.
Jay: Ok. so we have A) avior B) avior C) etre D) avior
Jay: right
Chris: Yes
Jay: E) etre
Jay: F) avior
Jay: G) etre
Jay: I) avior
Jay: J) etre

Jay: K) avior
Chris: Yes
Chris: I confirm with all of that.
Jay: Yay! lol.\
Jay: ok
Chris: Have a good weekend!

Group 5 demonstrated a different pattern that fully embraced practices associated with a concept-based approach to learning French auxiliary verb choice, as shown in Excerpt G5-1. Even though this group did not mention the terms *transitive* or *transitivity* during their discussion of Item C, they were using structural features of the sentence in order to determine whether or not the sentence included a transitive use of the verb *retourner* 'turn around/over'.

Excerpt G5-1. 10:24 am–10:32 am
Heather joined the chat
Cal joined the chat
Cal: Bonjour!
Heather: Bonjour!
Cal: I think A is etre because it is pronominal, what do you think
Heather: I agree. I think B is avoir because it's got a transitive phrase/noun phrase.
Cal: That is also what I got!
Heather: Did you get the same one for C also?
Cal: I think C is also avoir for the same reason
Cal: Oh wait, I changed my mind. Haha
Heather: So you think C uses etre?
Cal: Etre because of "sur la question" which is a prepositional phrase. Is that right?
Heather: I'm not sure. I'm going to look up what "sa veste" means
Cal: Ok
Heather: The phrase "retourner sa veste" means to change sides. So the sentence says that the government changed their minds on the question of neutrality. I think it would be avoir.
Cal: Oh ok. That seeme like it makes sense. Especially if "sa veste" is what we look at for the phrase. Avoir it is.

After agreeing on answers for Items D, E, and G, Group 5 seems to have accidentally skipped the discussion of Item I, which is why the rating for the level of the application of CBI was 0; however, the group submitted a correct answer for Item I on their worksheet. This type of example was also identified as a priority for the feedback to these learners since they had clearly forgotten the importance of the verbalization activity (i.e., as a way to allow the teacher to know if they were developing a better understanding of the concept of transitivity).

In Excerpt G5-3, the group appears to have once again realized the importance of developing a better of understanding of transitivity through explicit discussion of the concept. Heather's second turn in this excerpt was actually identified as one of the best examples of helping someone else to think through the concept of transitivity, and this excerpt was included in the feedback given to each student.

Excerpt G5-3. 10:38 am–10:47 am

Cal:	I'm not completely sure on the last two
Cal:	On the last one "sur des cailloux" makes me think it is etre.
Heather:	In J, jusqu'au is "up" and I think that's prepositional, so it would be etre. And in K, the verb is directly followed by a noun, so I think that's what would make it avoir.
Cal:	Haha man I'm bad at this! I saw the noun but just figured because it was followed with the sur des cailloux that it would be a prepositional phrase in the end.
Heather:	I'm not completely sure, but I think it depends on what directly comes after the verb. If the verb is before a noun, then the noun modifies that verb; If the verb is before a preposition, then the preposition modifies that verb. And in the cases where the noun after the verb comes before a preposition, like in "la tente sur des cailloux", then the preposition modifies that noun. I hope that kind of makes sense?
Cal:	Thanks, that actually does make sense, and helps!
Heather:	Haha ok, good. I'm normally not very good at explaining things. Hopefully we got them right! 10:47
Cal:	Hopefully! Thanks! Have a good day!

The verbalization transcript from Group 6 showed a high level of engagement in the explicit discussion of the concept of transitivity, a practice that was adopted by the group at the very beginning of the task. Although they did not engage in any explicit discussion of transitivity for the last two items, it seems that they felt confident enough – at this point in the task – to agree on answers proposed by one of the group's members.

The verbalization activity of Group 7 is especially remarkable because this group produced the highest frequency of Level 0 ratings (7 out of 10 items), yet they did not have a relatively high error rate (3/10). Consequently, their transcript was only about one printed page of dialog since they simply agreed to everything that anyone proposed as an answer. Given the type of verbalizations that Group 7 produced, they were asked to repeat (i.e., extend) this verbalization activity during individual tutoring sessions with the author at the request of their teacher, who wanted to be sure that they had indeed begun developing an understanding of the concept of transitivity since they could have simply agreed on several correct answers by chance.

Although space limitations do not allow for a detailed analysis of the transcript of each group's verbalization activity, this section has provided a model, with examples, for teachers who want to implement CBI and follow the longterm development of learners. When preparing lessons or curricular innovations that rely on CBI, it is important to keep in mind that, "as Vygotsky reminds us, development is a revolutionary rather than an evolutionary process that can follow unexpected twists and turns" (Lantolf and Thorne 2006, p. 306).

6 Conclusion

While it seems that learners (and teachers) are often impressed with low error rates, focusing on grades and scores would be missing the point of verbalization and CBI, which is to understand the extent to which (and ways in which) development follows instruction.

> Although the use of flow charts is not unique to CBI approaches to teaching grammar (see, for example, Massey 2001), in a CBI approach they are not primarily aimed at ensuring that students get the right answer to teacher questions, as often happens in encapsulated education (Engestrom 1996). Rather, they are but one component in an integrated approach to instruction whose purpose is to help learners develop new meaning-making resources, a different thinking for speaking framework, as Slobin (1996) might put it. (Negueruela and Lantolf 2006: 84–85)

For the present study, CBI was used primarily for the overt instruction component of the learning module as a way to introduce students to the concept of transitivity, an awareness of which has the potential to help them understand and control much more than just French auxiliary verb choice. In this case, a didactic device to promote cognitive development and language learning was developed by the author and reviewed several times with instructors, which follows one of the principles that should guide TBLT, according to Ellis (2009): "Ideally, the teachers involved in teaching a task-based course must be involved in the development of the task materials" (241). This line of thinking has been reinforced and expanded more recently by Van den Branden (2016). Ellis also emphasizes that "tasks need to be trialled to ensure that they result in appropriate L2 use and revised in the light of experience" (241), which is why the primary concern of the present study was the general application of the flowchart and additional focus would be placed on development in subsequent learning modules. Perhaps the most important recommendation for TBLT (Ellis 2009: 241) is to be sure that teachers and students are "aware of the purpose and rationale for performing tasks (e.g. they need to understand that tasks cater to incidental learning of the kind that will facilitate their communicative skills)." Although a substantial amount of time was spent consulting with the instructor before undertaking this study, future research could certainly benefit from spending more time explaining the purpose and rationale to learners as a possible way to increase their agency and motivation in their own learning experience.

References

Candlin, Christopher N. 2009. Towards task-based language learning. In Kris Van den Branden, Martin Bygate & John M. Norris (eds.), *Task-based language teaching: A reader*, 21–40. Amsterdam: Benjamins.
Dujardin, Théophile. 2007. *L'histoire de ma vie* [The story of my life]. Paris: Société des Écrivains.
Ellis, Rod. 2003. *Task-based language learning and teaching*. Oxford: Oxford University Press.
Ellis, Rod. 2009. Task-based language teaching: Sorting out the misunderstandings. *International Journal of Applied Linguistics* 19. 221–246.
Engeström, Yrjö. 1996. *Non scolae sed vitae discimus:* Toward overcoming the encapsulation of school learning. In Harry Daniels (ed.), *An introduction to Vygotsky*, 151–170. New York: Routledge.
Galperin, Piotr. 1979. The role of orientation in thought. *Soviet Psychology* 18. 19–45.
González-Lloret, Marta & Lourdes Ortega (eds.). 2014. *Technology-mediated TBLT: Researching technology and tasks*. Amsterdam: Benjamins.
Lantolf, James P. & Steven L. Thorne. 2006. *Sociocultural theory and the genesis of second language development*. Oxford: Oxford University Press.
Li, Shaofeng, Rod Ellis & Yan Zhu. 2016. Task-based versus task-supported language instruction: An experimental study. *Annual Review of Applied Linguistics* 36. 205–229.
Massey, Anne. 2001. In pursuit of preterit: A flow-chart of conjugations. *Hispania* 84. 550–552.
Negueruela, Eduardo. 2003. *A sociocultural approach to the teaching and learning of second languages: Systemic-theoretical instruction and L2 development*. University Park, PA: Pennsylvania State University dissertation.
Negueruela, Eduardo & James P. Lantolf. 2006. Concept-Based Instruction and the acquisition of L2 Spanish. In Rafael Salaberry & Barbara A. Lafford (eds.), *The art of teaching Spanish: Second language acquisition from research to praxis*, 79–102. Washington, DC: Georgetown University Press.

New London Group. 1996. A pedagogy of multiliteracies: Designing social futures. *Harvard Educational Review* 66. 60–92.
Nunan, David. 2004. *Task-based language teaching*. Cambridge: Cambridge University Press.
Shehadeh, Ali & Christine A. Coombe (eds.). 2012. *Task-based language teaching in foreign language contexts: Research and implementation*. Amsterdam: Benjamins.
Slobin, Dan. I. 1996. Two ways to travel: Verbs of motion in English and Spanish. In Masayoshi Shibatani & Sandra A. Thompson (eds.), *Grammatical constructions: Their form and meaning*, 195–219. Oxford: Clarendon Press.
Van den Branden, Kris. 2016. The role of teachers in task-based language education. *Annual Review of Applied Linguistics* 36. 164–181.
Van den Branden, Kris, Martin Bygate & John M. Norris (eds.). 2009. *Task-based language teaching: A reader*. Amsterdam: Benjamins.
van Lier, Leo. 1994. Forks and hope: Pursuing understanding in different ways. *Applied Linguistics* 15. 328–347.
Williams, Lawrence. 2016. Authenticity and pedagogical grammar: A concept-based approach to teaching French auxiliary verbs. In Rémi A. van Compernolle & Janice McGregor (eds.), *Authenticity, language, and interaction in second language contexts*, 35–60. Bristol: Multilingual Matters.
Willis, Jane. 1996. *A framework for task-based learning*. Harlow: Longman.
Willis, Dave & Jane Willis. 2007. *Doing task-based teaching*. Oxford: Oxford University Press.

Appendix

French Auxiliary Choice Worksheet Instructions
1) Choose the appropriate auxiliary verb (*avoir* or *être*) for each sentence below.
2) Here are the past participles you will need: *fracturé, retourné, tombé, passé, monté*.
3) In some cases, you may need an extra –e or –s, but don't worry about that too much right now.
4) Work with a chat partner to discuss why you **both** agree on the auxiliary verb that should be used, according to the flowchart provided in class. Use your assigned Chatzy room.
5) After you have decided why you agree on each auxiliary verb, rate your level of confidence for each sentence according to the following choices:

1-Not at all confident   2-Not really confident   3-Neutral
4-Somewhat confident   5-Very confident

French Auxiliary Choice Worksheet Items and Comments

Note: The answers (*avoir* or *être*) and the comments in brackets were not on the worksheet given to the participants. Due to an oversight, the letter H was skipped when the labels (A, B, C, etc.) were added to the list, but the participants were reassured that nothing was missing.

Item A
L'ex-premier ministre François Fillon __être__ (se fracturer) une cheville dans un accident de scooter sur l'île de Capri.

[A pronominal verb was used as the first item in order to acclimate students to the flowchart, which indicates the correct auxiliary for pronominal verbs on the first line.]

Item B
Les cambrioleurs ___avoir___ (retourner) l'appartement.

[Since sentence B has a transitive-direct structure (*l'appartement* 'the apartment' is a direct object), *avoir* is required.]

Item C
Le gouvernement ___avoir___ (retourner) sa veste sur la question de la neutralité de l'Internet.

[Since sentence C has a transitive-direct structure (*sa veste* 'its vest/jacket'), *avoir* is required.]

Item D
Le lutteur favori ___avoir___ (tomber) son adversaire très tôt dans l'affrontement.

[Since sentence D has a transitive-direct structure (*son adversaire* 'his opponent'), *avoir* is required.]

Item E
Notre cousine ___avoir___ (tomber) plus d'un homme.

[Since sentence E has a transitive-direct structure (*plus d'un homme* 'more than one man' is a direct object), *avoir* is required.]

Item F
Pierre Lissou ___être___ (passer) lieutenant avec la mention *très bien*.

[Since sentence F does not have a transitive-direct structure (even though *lieutenant* 'lieutenant' is a noun, when *passer* means *promoted*, the noun phrase that follows the verb is an *attribut du sujet* 'predicate nominative' in this case), which means that *être* is required; a copula verb does not allow a transitive-direct structure.]

Item G
En 2001, il ___avoir___ (passer) son permis de conduire.

[Since sentence G has a transitive-direct structure (*son permis de conduire* 'his driver license' is a direct object), *avoir* is required.]

Item I

Il ___avoir___ (monter) un site Web sur un serveur gratuit.

[Since sentence I has a transitive-direct structure (*un site Web* 'a website' is a direct object), avoir is required.]

Item J

Il ___être___ (monter) jusqu'au sommet de la colline.

[Since sentence J does not have a transitive-direct structure (*jusqu'au sommet de la colline* 'until/up to the summit of the hill' is a prepositional phrase, not a direct object), *être* is required.]

Item K

Il ___avoir___ (monter) la tente sur des cailloux.

[Since sentence K has a transitive-direct structure (*la tente* 'the tent' is a direct object), *avoir* is required.]

III Complexity Theory Perspective

Martin Bygate
7 Dynamic Systems Theory and the Issue of Predictability in Task-Based Language: Some Implications for Research and Practice in TBLT[1]

1 Introduction

Language is by definition a form of socio-cognitive action. So too is learning. The social dimension derives from the fact that in both language and learning meanings, patterns and values are not absolute and unvarying, but emerge from, and are shaped and ratified, by social practices, which differ from one era to another, and between social groups. At the same time, the cognitive dimension is also essential since the meanings, patterns and values cannot be apprehended or activated without the involvement of individual mental processes. This starting point means that any language teaching approach has to engage with both the social and the cognitive (see Batstone 2010). This however is not enough: a language teaching approach also has to engage with the professional responsibilities of the teacher (e.g. planning, managing, advising and assessing learning), in a way that is answerable to the various stakeholders – the learner and his/her sponsors, and the institution and wider society in which the teacher works.

Task-based language teaching (TBLT) is an approach which aims to integrate these three facets of second/foreign language education – the social, the cognitive and the professional – around the selection and use of a range of tasks. Language learning tasks require learners to select and interpret language relevant to completing the task in hand, in light of their own intentions and those of their interlocutors. At the same time, the use of tasks enables teachers to engage pedagogically with learners' actual language use, rather than limiting their intervention to essentially hypothetical 'form-focused' uses of language. That is, TBLT enables teaching to be grounded in what might be called 'learners' language-in-action'.

---

[1] This chapter is a revised version of an invited plenary given to the 5th Biennial International TBLT Conference, at Banff, October 2013.

Martin Bygate, Lancaster University

DOI 10.1515/9781501503399-008

However, within TBLT, there is disagreement about the use of tasks to engage learners with particular areas of language. Some (e.g. Long 2015) see language pedagogy as less effective when teachers proactively set an agenda for learners' learning. In this view, SL learning is most effective when learner-directed, and so for teaching to be effective it needs to intervene reactively to learners' current focus of attention. In this view, tasks are an ideal context for enabling learners to set the agenda, with the teacher following behind, a perspective which is consistent with a dynamic systems (DST) view of language learning that prioritises the learner's autonomy. DST however also accepts that patterning emerges, and in this chapter I wish to argue that because tasks create discourse demands, which in turn imply patterning, they can be used productively to orientate students' language learning, proactively as well as retroactively. In what follows I first discuss the notion of predictability, and then introduce a DST perspective, adopting the notion of 'useful trajectory' to understand how students might negotiate their way through a task. Following a study of sample data, I conclude by suggesting that seeing tasks in terms of likely 'useful trajectories' can improve our understanding of tasks, of what learners might learn on tasks, and on how tasks might be designed and used.

2 Background

TBLT is grounded in the educational principle of 'learning-by-doing'. However this principle is not unique to TBLT. For example the teaching of wood, metal or textile work revolves around learners' engagement in hands-on tasks with wood, metal or textiles, but hands-on tasks are just as important in subjects such as biology or zoology, maths, sports education, music, and in the human sciences. In these various disciplines, tasks are a central site for engagement with the matter of the discipline. They provide learners with the opportunity to better understand the discipline by engaging with it materially, helping to relate it to the real world. For instance, wood is transformed into real world objects such as stools, chairs, and bowls and in the process learners' knowledge and skills take shape. At the same time, the learner's engagement with the task becomes a real world site for the teacher to appraise and feed into the learners' emerging knowledge and skills. Learning takes the form of the development of functional knowledge and skills, and teaching can then orientate to that emerging functional development. This implies that the cognitive, the social and the pedagogical are all interrelated through tasks. Learners' knowledge and skills, and the teacher's intervention are all grounded in learner action rather than being unhinged from the real world.

Choice and use of tasks then needs to relate not only to the needs of the learner but also to the roles and responsibilities of the teacher, such as the commitment to facilitate, support and advise learners on their learning; and the need to be accountable to the teaching institution, to other stakeholders (such as parents and relatives, future course providers, and potential employers) and the wider society. If tasks are to be used, this implies among other things an understanding of the language development that different tasks can be expected to mediate. Within TBLT, the content of tasks must be a potential key connection point between classroom activities and the language curriculum. For this connection to function, however, course designers and teachers need a degree of predictability in how learners will handle them so as to be able to select and use tasks professionally. In what follows I first consider arguments for and against predictability in task-based language, and then outline ways in which DST might shed light on the issue.

2.1 Some arguments against predictability in task-based language

As Ellis (2009) has noted, the concept of predictability has tended to be side-lined in discussions of task-based-language teaching. One reason is the belief, derived from second language acquisition (SLA) research (see for instance Long 2015: 4–10) that teaching should follow learners' development rather than attempt to lead it down pre-defined pathways. Since no two learners can be expected to be at the same point of development at the same time, and since the initiative for learning depends on the learner, predicting what might be appropriate language focus for any learner at any one time becomes problematic. Rather the merit of tasks is to provide a context where learners can establish their own level in relation to the needs of the task and negotiate new language into their proficiency as and when they are ready for it. Thus key moments of interpersonal communication difficulty arising during a task are seen as optimum opportunities for language learning, since they offer the possibility of what might be called 'learning at the point of need'. Hence not only is predicting seen as impossible; trying to do so is seen as undermining the freedom of the individual learner to say and learn what is appropriate to them. Further, prediction on the part of the teacher would have the effect of blocking and possibly even derailing natural acquisition processes.

This perspective is in some ways similar to that of socio-cultural (neo-Vygotskian) theory (SCT) (see for example Lantolf 2000). SCT starts from the assumption that learning is materially co-constructed by the learner and by those they interact with, so that learning derives from the content and interactive influences arising in specific encounters. Inevitably different learners and their interactants will talk about different things, and will do so in different ways, resulting in differences not just in what learners learn, but in the manner in which they learn. Wells' (1981, 1985) extensive study of child L1 acquisition provides good empirical support for this perspective. In similar vein, Coughlan and Duff (1994) among others have argued that the discourse generated in a task with different students contains significant linguistic differences. This leads them to the conclusion that prediction of task-based language behaviour is impossible.

While there is no doubt that learners do follow different learning paths, do it in their own time, and do co-construct their learning experiences (and hence their learning) in individually different ways I nevertheless want to argue that even so predictability is a matter of degree, that there is no such thing as total unpredictability, and that indeed there is enough predictability in language and learning to enable reasonable and useful predictions to be made about the language and learning that is likely to arise on given tasks without sacrificing the learners' personal agenda. The next section considers some reasons why this might be so.

2.2 Some reasons for predictability in task-based language

Instead of thinking about tasks as essentially open-ended and unpredictable, I would like to suggest approaching them as discourse events. Seeing tasks as 'discourse events' implies that although interaction on a totally new type of task might at first be hesitant and unpredictable, it can quickly be expected to pattern in characteristic ways, just like real world discourse events. Examples of such events include doctor-patient interviews (e.g. Ranney 1992), job interviews, news interviews, sales encounters, talks and presentations, guided tours, meetings (for a number of these discourse types see for instance Carter and McCarthy 1997), or family talk (e.g. Ochs and Taylor 1992), or even small talk (Coupland 2014). Study of discourse events shows them to be typically bounded purposeful activities mediated through language, motivated by participants' purposes, and structured according to socially accepted pragmatic principles. Structuring is helpful both psychologically and interpersonally, reducing workload while also reducing uncertainty.

Discourse analysts are not alone in acknowledging structure in discourse. Emergentist approaches, including DST, also see patterning as fundamental language use, language learning, and language change. Although complexity is seen as pervasive in language and its use, some argue that:

> despite its lack of overt government, instead of anarchy and chaos, there are patterns everywhere. Linguistic patterns are not preordained by God, genes, school curriculum, or other human policy. Instead, they are emergent – synchronic patterns of linguistic organization at numerous levels (phonology, lexis, syntax, semantics, pragmatics, discourse, genre, etc.), dynamic patterns of usage, diachronic patterns of language change (linguistic cycles of grammaticalization, pidginization, creolization, etc.), ontogenetic developmental patterns in child language acquisition, global geopolitical patterns of language growth and decline, dominance and loss, and so forth.' (The "Five Graces Group", 2009: 18)

Patterning then is not imposed from without, but instead emerges naturally through language use.

This would apply to the language of classroom tasks, which are just one type of 'discourse event'. For example, an activity requiring students to use some apparatus to work out why water and air behave in a certain way (see Barnes 1976: 38–74) leads students to explore what the apparatus does, observe what happens, and then consider why. The actual design of the activity focuses the discourse in predictable ways. Similarly, even a simple 'picture differences' activity is likely to focus the discourse, for instance leading students to name and describe features in the pictures, to formulate differences, to check, and then prepare to report. As discourse event, the purposes or functions of the discourse, the stages they go through, and the actual choice of language are to some extent predictable. And the implications sit well with the assumption (e.g. Long and Crookes, 1992) that 'task' is a relevant unit for structuring the language curriculum.

In their seminal paper, Long and Crookes propose organising programmes around tasks rather than around lists of language features. This shifts the focus of learning and teaching from decontextualized features of the target language to the task as a whole. One implication of their proposal (which Long and Crookes do not dwell on) is that performance on the task itself becomes a focus of learning and assessment. For example, Van den Branden (2015) reported a lesson in which students were accompanied on visits to local businesses to carry out everyday tasks. Each encounter involved predictable discourse moves, implicating language. Hence on such a task learners learn relevant discourse moves. This implies learning ways of negotiating pragmatically relevant stages of the event, whether a visit to the doctor (e.g. Ranney 1992), a meeting with a school teacher or a social services interview (e.g. Tarone and Kuehn 2000), or a more pedagogic task, such as some kind of problem solving task. Task-based learning therefore involves becoming proficient in chunking events into relevant phases, and mobilising appropriate language to mediate those phases. All this implies some degree of pragmatic predictability.

As Ellis 2009 argues, some degree of predictability is important for both teacher and learner. It is valuable for the teacher to be able to anticipate some of the key meanings that learners will need to express, and some of the language which is likely to be helpful. This helps the teacher to select tasks, and anticipate phases of the task worth monitoring and focusing on for formative assessment. From the learner's perspective too, predictability is valuable. Not that the learner needs to know precisely what specific meanings or particular language forms will be activated. But knowing that learners and teacher all share a thematic discourse focus, that negotiating the task as a whole is valuable, and that there are thematic connections between tasks, and between tasks, associated practice activities, and assessment is likely to be significant for learners' commitment. Hence the rationale for seeking a degree of predictability in task-based language.

Empirically, however, we need to know whether there is predictability in learners' task-based language. Some evidence is available. For instance, in an early study, Ellis 1987 found that simple past forms occurred in the context of picture story tasks. In a later series of studies (Ellis 2001) Ellis showed that vocabulary features embedded in a task could be acquired as a result of engagement in the task. Mackey (1999) showed that use of four types of task – a story completion task, a picture sequencing task, a picture differences task, and picture drawing ('describe and draw') – resulted in occurrence and acquisition of question structures (Mackey, 1999: 567–8). Samuda (2001) has shown that a task designed to engage learners in speculating about who might own a collection of objects generally lead them to express meanings involving epistemic modality (expressing degrees of probability). Bygate and Samuda (2005) found that repeating narrations led speakers to include more elaboration about the place, manner and motivations of characters' actions. That is, in all these studies learners tended to generate predictable features of language. This patterning implied similarities in negotiating the tasks, and similar discourse strategies. These layers of engagement, and the patterning that they suggest, seem explicable from the perspective of dynamic systems theory (DST).

2.3 A DST perspective: tasks in terms of 'trajectory'

Some proponents of a DST perspective (e.g. Larsen-Freeman 2006, Verspoor, Chan, and de Bot personal communication) argue that it is impossible to predict language behaviour. Learning is seen as a self-regulating system simultaneously shaped by many influences (Larsen-Freeman and Cameron, 2008), including internal influences such as learners' internal motivations, orientations, existing knowledge structures, skills and intentions, and external influences such as other individuals in the classroom, classroom practices and activities, prior and future encounters with aspects of the language, relationships inside and outside the classroom, and other stakeholders in society (e.g. family, school management, and future employers). These influences vary in their relative strengths and consequently in their impact on learners' activity and learning. Thus the language learning space is a complex one, which it can reasonably be argued makes it impossible to predict learning. Yet, DST also allows that behaviours pattern. A lesson for example is its own naturally emerging 'system', which will evolve as a function of the nature and strength of the factors that typically influence it.

In order to understand systems of behaviour, Van Geert (2008) offers the metaphor of somebody observing the movements of Alice in Wonderland in order to infer the the logic of her behaviour and the nature of the strange terrain in which she finds herself. Alice's sequence of movements forms a 'trajectory' providing useful clues about that terrain. The trajectory is 'emergent' in the sense that it is not predestined or pre-scripted, but arises from the interaction between Alice's intentions and the environment. Some movements might appear random, but can be explained by the presence in the terrain of unexpected features. Initial trajectories might seem relatively disorganised, but as Alice becomes more familiar with the terrain trajectories may stabilise in the interests of economy and efficiency. Leech (1983) suggested a similar metaphor – that of an animal using trial and error to create a path through the jungle in search for water – to explain the way pragmatic patterns become conventionalised within a language. Where a stable patterning arises, DST explains this in terms of 'attractors' which make a pattern seem preferable (motivations such as efficiency or attractiveness that shape strategic choices). 'Strange attractors' (Larsen-Freeman and Cameron, 2008, p. 57) can cause periods of chaotic behaviour. However stable behaviour emerges as the system 'self-organizes' (op cit, pp. 58–60). The implication is that to understand phenomena (such as tasks) we need to observe behaviours and seek patterns to infer the nature of the system.

Many applied linguists have used DST to understand trajectories of interlanguage development However in this paper, rather than consider development, I would like to use the metaphor of trajectory to consider how learners use discourse to negotiate their way through classroom tasks, arguably the starting point for task-based learning.

2.4 Trajectory and task

Let us take as a simple non-linguistic example, Long and Crookes' (1992) task of 'painting a fence', well known in TBLT circles. Although a task like this seems

fairly straightforward, it clearly involves a number of distinct identifiable 'things to do', including:
- Preparing the materials – such as getting an appropriate paint, reading the instructions on the tin, cleaning down the fence, preparing one or more paintbrushes and the paint, maybe finding something to mix it with, and a cloth to wipe away unwanted drips
- Painting the slats of the fence – from top to bottom (or bottom to top), and the upper, lower and side edges
- Moving the pot, and cleaning drips as you go
- Cleaning up afterwards – the pot, the brush, your hands...

This activity is not 'pre-designed' – even for a simple task like this we will not think through all the various steps involved. Rather the activity arises mainly in response to an overall objective ('get the fence painted'), which breaks down into a number of subordinate objectives, improvised as we go. Further, each person will evolve an individual way of performing the activity by trial and error – the manner of carrying it out will be influenced by experience: some will get into relatively more successful patterns of performance while others will not. As people become more familiar with the task, they will settle into routines, with the various skills – both lower order skills, such as the control of brush and paint, and higher order skills, such as calculating times and quantities needed to complete the job – initially consciously controlled, but gradually becoming second nature. However, although contextually shaped (by the nature of the fence for instance), the activity will structure similarly in other contexts, however big or complex the painting task. Skills will therefore transfer. Finally, as DST would suggest, this task has indeterminate boundaries – many of the elements of the task will be enacted in other quite different types of activity.

A central point in this account is that the task 'painting a fence' has content, with a structure that emerges, in the form of the kinds of phases listed above. The phases create a trajectory by which we negotiate such tasks. It is impossible to complete the task without doing some of the things on this list, and a preferred order will also emerge. Some elements might recur (such as moving the pot), some might not, and in any case the phases are not simply linear. The actual task of course is certainly not the same thing as a list: the actual task can only be reflected in the trajectories that people follow in completing it. My overall argument then is that we cannot understand the nature of the task – what is being learnt through the task, and the kinds of learning the task might be used to promote – without first understanding the trajectories by which real people complete it. Yet although this might seem obvious, little of the TBLT literature has studied it.

There are potentially interesting implications for teaching, learning and testing, since if this view of tasks is correct, TBLT would need to develop a picture of how learners' task performance changes and improves over time. For instance, we might anticipate a lack of experience resulting in variability in first encounters with a particular type of task, but speculate that over time people would settle on a trajectory they find satisfactory in terms of effort and desired outcomes, reflecting in DST terms a possible 'attractor state'. Notice that this account of the task assumes some element of predictability, both about initial and subsequent encounters. On this basis, anyone teaching a task to someone would need to have some kind understanding of what the task involves and how it can be mastered.

Of course painting a fence is a task that is not obviously crucially mediated by language. But if language learning tasks are discourse events, then we can assume that learners will transform a task into a 'space' which they have to cross in order to achieve the intended outcome (solve a problem, meet a challenge, create a physical product, produce a linguistic product such as a set of recommendations or a report). A trajectory of some sort is then inevitable. And we can assume that the ways the learners work together will reflect their intelligence, their social relations including what they know about each other, the tools they have available within the task or provided by the teacher, their language knowledge, and their previous experience of working on similar tasks. Nonetheless, the 'things' they would need to do, and the ways they go about doing them, and eventually do them 'better', can be expected to have some predictability in terms of pragmatic options.

This chapter then sees tasks, like other discourse events and forms of learning, in terms of pragmatic trajectories that students trace in order to complete them, exhibiting a degree of predictability. The next section investigates this view of predictability in terms of the trajectories students pursue on a simple task. The central question is, given that the students were not told how to go about performing the task, do they follow similar or different trajectories? Any similarities or patterning would suggest predictability in the ways students handle the task, supporting the suggestion of that the task has predictable content features. A lack of similarity would suggest a lack of predictability.

3 A simple case study

In order to investigate predictability in task performance, the study explores how five groups of students carried out the same picture story task.

Five groups of six international students carried out a picture story task, 'The Dog and the Crow' (adapted from Dechert 1983). The students were all in their first year of full time study at a university in the UK, and although they had been previously enrolled on an English language programme, for this study they were volunteer participants and the activity itself – which had originally been designed for research purposes – was not part of a language programme. The task itself however is not unlike many supplementary oral language materials (e.g. Ur 1982). And its relevance for language teaching is illustrated by the fact that the author has often used it on teacher education courses as a basis for discussing the nature, complexity and use of picture sequencing story tasks for the language classroom.

The picture story consisted of six pictures involving just two characters – a crow, a dog attached to a lead which was tied to a post, and a bowl of food in front of the dog. Each student could only see one of the pictures, and together they had to work out the story so as to be able to retell it.

As can be seen (see Appendix), although the elements of the story are simple, there are a number of challenges for the students to resolve. Firstly, the fact that there are few elements means that there are few differences between the six pictures, making it hard to sequence them without seeing them all together. Secondly, the fact that the students could only see one picture rather than all six likely made it harder to interpret the individual pictures. Having sight of only one picture can make it harder to recognise what the pictures show, and to understand the relevance of features in the picture. For instance the precise position of the bird and the dog could affect the interpretation (in particular, in different pictures the crow was in different positions, which taken together showed that it was hopping around the dog); and a useful clue to the story, but not evident on one picture, was that across several the length of the lead got shorter and shorter, until the dog was bound up to the post. A third challenge is that the more pictures that are involved, the greater the likely memory load for the students as they attempt to interrelate them. These kinds of issues (rarely if ever mentioned in TBLT studies) could have a significant impact on how the task unfolds.

The five groups were each recorded, and the recordings then transcribed. The focus of the analysis is on whether and how far the five groups independently went through similar or different phases in performing the task. As noted above, there was no prior instruction to the groups on how to go about it – they were simply told to talk to each other without seeing each others' pictures, in order to work out and then retell the story. A lack of predictability would be demonstrated if groups worked through the tasks in different ways, focusing the discourse in different ways. On the other hand, finding similarities across the approaches of the five groups would provide support for the view that the task sets similar demands to different people, and that groups will tend to use similar strategies for handling the task.

3.1 Data analysis

The transcripts were analysed in terms of 'discourse phase'. A phase was defined in terms of the pragmatic coherence of a stretch of discourse which while not in itself achieving the overall task goal, likely contributed to achieving a useful enabling sub-goal. For instance, descriptions of the individual pictures in random order would contribute to the sub-goal of sharing information about the pictures, but would not themselves achieve the overall goal of sorting out the sequence and telling the story (even if by chance the students did actually provide the descriptions in the exact sequence of the narrative). Similarly, discourse during which students exchanged information about what they thought was going on in their respective pictures could not be interpreted as 'telling the story' either. Where students spent time suggesting potential sequencing of the pictures (still without seeing them), possibly accompanied by brief justifications, this kind of talk too contributes to a potentially useful subgoal, but still does not constitute the 'telling of the story'. Hence the macro-purposes of the different discourse phases were inferred in relation to the pragmatic criterion: what are the speakers jointly trying to do at this point? Identification of phases enabled an assessment of the trajectories that the groups followed.

3.2 Findings

3.2.1 Potential phases

Analysis of the data suggested that sequences of discourse occurred that reflected five distinct 'phases' of the task. These were labelled as follows:
  i. Description
  ii. Comparison
  iii. Interpreting gist
  iv. Sequencing
  v. Narrative

The phases are described and illustrated in the following extracts.

Description

In this first extract the speaker is describing an aspect of the content of the picture, particularly the appearance of the dog. The reader should bear in mind that the speaker does not yet know the content of the other pictures, and so has no idea what is unique and so especially relevant, and what is common to other pictures. Both unique content and common content are likely to be useful information to share.

> G: My dog look not surprised, but kind of, no, yes surprised. He's surprised by something. But I don't know what the bird did. But the dog is surprised by, by something, you know kind of, not surprised in the sense that you know when you kind of you are surprised but scared by something, you know the first reaction you have. And it's kind of, he's kind of reacting like that.

Part of the difficulty for the speaker is conveying the attitude of the dog, and for this s/he uses the strategy of exemplification, use of near synonyms ('surprised' – 'scared'), explicitly marking approximation by using the phrase 'kind of' four times, and at the same time also appealing to listeners' real world experience of typical contexts from which they might imagine the dog's appearance, using the phrase 'you know' twice.

Comparison

In the next extract, four of the speakers are comparing and contrasting their pictures.

Ap:	But er, in my picture is pretty much the same thing.
Yas:	Mine too
Ap:	Yeh, but erm the; so we all get the same? ... Ok and err. <<Laughter>>
Ap:	Oh so you have the bird, the bird eating the food.
Am:	Yeah
Ap:	What do you have?
Yan:	There is no food in my picture.
Yas:	My dog looks happy, and excited, and bird is on the left side and the food is on the right side.
Several:	Yeah

Here the speakers' purpose has shifted from the precise content of their own pictures, to its relationship to others. Although not mentioned in the instructions to the task, this phase could have a central function in this kind of task: reconstructing a story from elements depends partly on finding the similarities, which provide the continuity between one picture and another, and partly on discovering the differences, which are likely to relate to narrative development. Listeners endorse similarities (as in the final 'Yeah'), or note potentially significant differences (such as 'Oh so you have the bird, the bird eating the food').

Interpreting the gist
Arriving at a plausible sequence needs more than a list of similarities and differences: it also depends on identifying potential meaningful links between the pictures, which may in addition require attributing intentions and/or consequences to the actions. For the purposes of the analysis, I label this 'interpreting the gist'. The following extract shows the students trying out a possible interpretation, in particular motivations of the bird, and possibly of the dog

Am: He is very very angry, there, it looks like smoke
Ap: so the bird could tie the dog up and that would be a nice idea but
G: Mmm, no. I don't think so. Just the bird wanted to eat something so and then maybe the dog
Yan: I think maybe the bird eat the leader of the dog
Ap: Leader?
Yan: Lead

The motivations of the bird and the dog provide a stepping stone to identifying a potential resolution to the story. Note that in speculating, the students are going beyond what they can see and what they have heard from their colleagues so as to project an overall logic onto the available information. Worth also noting here once again that students were not instructed to do this – the fact that they do it simply emerges from their interaction with the task.

Sequencing
Once they have agreed an overall gist for the story, it remains for them to sequence the pictures according to that schema. The difficulty here is partly a function of the number of pictures, and the potential for alternative coherent sequences. The extract makes clear however that even for such a simple task, none of these students knows for sure what the optimum sequence is.

Ap: So what's the sequence?
G: I don't know xxx
Ap: It starts, it either starts with hers and ends with hers or ends with h, um begins with her and ends with hers

Am: I think for me my picture is the last
Ap: Ok, so then it begins
Yan: I think my picture maybe in the middle... not er start

Here student Ap offers two possible pairs of beginnings and endings to the narrative, while two other students suggest potential sequential positions for their individual pictures. This type of episode can often lead to some trial runs through to see whether they can find a sense to a sequence, suggesting that at this point students can still be uncertain about the actual final sequence.

Narrative
At this point, students can be in a position to re-tell the narrative, possibly on a trial-and-error basis. In this extract, the students recite the narrative on the basis of a hypothetical sequence of pictures that they have set up, and the transcript (particularly Yan's turn) shows that at some points they are still unsure of whether they have cracked it.

G: and then the bird I mean arrive next to the food and the dog is surprised and the dog is kin(d) of not so happy that the bird is xxx the food at him. And the dog wants to get rid of the bird but kind of scared at the same time so ... that it
Yan: I have maybe the wrong sequence. Just the dog just come from another place and then and then went to the bird and the bird flying to a branch not on a not on ground and maybe the black stuff everyone see is food and I think also it's food <<Laughter>> on the right side. I can see a high, maybe it's like tree, a high on .. in the middle, so this all the information.
Am: in my picture the dog is ... is connected to the tree and it is very very angry, and the bird is on the ground close to the food and it is eating the food ... from the dishes

The telling of the narrative can be a straight demonstration of achievement. But equally it can function as a further trial, which might help confirm or disconfirm the sequence they have generated.

Having illustrated the five types of phase that occurred in the data, the next section reports the results.

3.2.2 Distribution of phases across groups

The results of the analysis of the data set for the five groups are shown in table 1.

Table 1: Use of different task phases by different groups

	Group K	Group O	Group V	Group H	Group S
Description	✓	✓	✓	✓	✓
Comparison	✓	✓	✓	✓	–
Getting gist	✓	✓	✓	–	✓
Sequencing	✓	✓	✓	✓	–
Narrating	(✓)	–	(✓)	(✓)	✓

Firstly in terms of frequency of use of the five phases, one – description – was used by all five groups. The other four phases were each used by four of the groups. Taken together this suggests that the five phases have a high degree of probability of occurrence on this type of task. It is worth noting that the narrating phase was carried out more or less thoroughly by the various groups, as indicated by the use of parentheses.

Looking at the result in terms of group patterns, two groups used all five phases. Two used four of the five phases – one group not producing any kind of final narrative, and the other doing little in terms of 'getting the gist'. The data from the fifth group were somewhat anomalous. Group S made no use of comparison or sequencing phases. This anomaly however is itself interesting: the speed with which this group completed the task, and the lack of any attempt at comparing the pictures or at exploring alternative sequences suggests that they may well have looked at each others' cards (flouting one of the instructions they had been given).

Although these data are fairly simple, they are rarely documented in studies of tasks or task performance. The next section suggests some interpretations and possible implications.

4 Discussion

First of all, the analysis shows patterning in the use of the different types of discourse phase, which can be interpreted as an index of predictability: although not all groups used all the types of phase, all five phases were widely used. Since the phases are defined pragmatically, that is, in terms of their overall purpose, it is reasonable to conclude that the reason they occur is because they are pragmatically useful in completing the task. Secondly, it is significant that the phases occurred spontaneously, and not because of any explicit instruction or training. It seems reasonable to infer therefore that their occurrence is emergent, in response to the task. Thirdly, it is important to note that the phases do not imply total predictability. For one thing, the phases sometimes occur more than once in a single transcript, with students going backwards and forwards between, say, finding the gist and trying out a sequence. Also, groups can complete the task without using all the phases. Furthermore, it is self-evident that the occurrence of pragmatically useful phases does not determine the use of a specific linguistic formulation: different groups will use different lexico-grammatical tools to do the job. It seems though that we *can* predict the likely usefulness of particular linguistic *domains*. In this case, the language for expressing impressions, inferences and approximations; the language of description and for identifying similarities and differences; the language for expressing motivations and consequences; the language for sequencing; and the language used for checking understandings.

Secondly in analysing performance in terms of phases which reflect the students' trajectories through the tasks, the table provides an insight into what the task involved for the five groups (and the 30 students who took part), something that is untouched by the commonly used measures such as overall fluency, accuracy, complexity and vocabulary richness, for instance. It also provides a window on the kinds of things learners can be expected to gain from doing the task, in terms of discourse domains that students are likely to find useful. This also opens up potential connections between this activity and other classroom work, and can provide a reference point for the teacher and learners to appraise their performance, to target their attention to language domains and to ways of verbalising them.

The picture this analysis provides is also helpful because it helps to remind us that task-based work involves students in a socio-cognitive dynamic, in which they take decisions and perform purposeful situated verbal actions. Adopting a DST perspective enables us to see students' performance as contingent on the task conditions and purposes, but subject to attractor states which could bring about change in future task encounters in the interests of effectiveness or economy.

Further, a DST approach seems to steer a middle course between the traditional deterministic uses of activities (i.e. insisting on knowing the specific language forms an activity is supposed to help learners to master), and a more radical approach in which learners follow their own internal syllabus. At the same time, this approach to studying tasks uses DST to analyse the trajectories of performance as a gateway to development, rather than for plotting interlanguage development (see for instance Larsen-Freeman 2006).

There are also potentially important practical implications from this analysis for teachers and learners. One is that it centres attention on the *content* of tasks, making it easier to justify their selection and use. At the same time because it is non-deterministic, seeing the content in terms of broad strategic domains of action (that is, the pragmatic phases contributing to task completion), the language used becomes open to the judgement of learners and teachers, rather than being inflexibly oriented to norms specified by the curriculum. For example, if the task involves working with modality (cf. Samuda 2001), it is left open to teacher and learners to explore options rather than impose a straitjacket on the forms to be highlighted. This perspective can help to resolve the problem of whether teachers and learners should be able to reflect on the language used for handling a given task, and of how a given task can contribute to the overall language curriculum. Tasks continue to have value as tasks in their own right, but in addition, can be understood for what they bring to the language programme in terms of discourse domains (see Bygate and Samuda 2009 for a further exploration of this issue). Further, this approach also contributes to improving the basis for understanding and appraising performance, since knowing what the learners are trying to do with the language is bound to help assessment. As with classroom tasks, the test tasks cannot be understood without a grasp of what they involve.

There are limitations to my argument. Clearly, the data set is small, but even a larger data set would not be able to account for all possible responses to the task, and space precludes discussion of other data sets. Examples of other tasks would be needed (see for instance Bygate 1988 for a study of the processes involved in 'picture differences', '20 questions' or 'map' tasks, and their different pragmatic challenges). Further, as noted above, the phases proposed are not always self-contained: comparison between pictures can be inter-spliced with gist comments, or with sequencing suggestions. This makes the analysis open to dispute. However the pervasive use of all five phases by at least four of the groups suggests a significant degree of predictability in the ways students handle the tasks. Furthermore, the anomalous pattern of Group S provides a degree of 'negative confirmation' of the logic that underlies the occurrence of the five phases. A group *can* complete the task without attempts at comparison or sequencing – for instance, it isn't outlawed – but considering the circumstances is instructive. To achieve the task without using those phases implies unproblematic interpretation and communication of the content of the pictures, a set of pictures that can be easily held in memory by the participants, enabling easy inference of a narrative 'script', and the immediate re-telling of the story. Such a rapid reconstruction of the story might well constitute a valuable TBLT task. However the analysis proposed here at least helps us to narrow our focus on the purpose the task design is intended to serve, and in particular in this case the justification for using sets of pictures some of which are more problematic for sequencing, and some of which are less so. Finally, the data set does not make development accessible. However, identification of the phases of the task does enable appraisal of how effectively students complete those phases. A longitudinal data set would then permit analysis of whether and if so in what ways learners adjust their handling of tasks as they become more familiar with them, more familiar with the ways of managing the challenges (through trial-and-error or meta-reflection), and as they perhaps converge towards more long term 'attractor states' in the ways of performing the tasks. Thus SLA concepts, such as 'U-shaped' development, could well turn out to apply not just to language acquisition, but to evolving patterns of performance.

More generally, this analysis suggests that the design of tasks can, and probably inevitably does, contribute to a degree of predictability in the trajectories students uncover for completing them. This has applications beyond TBLT to tasks in general education (see Barnes' 1976 monograph). That predictability is not total. It does not enable us to say how a task should be done or will be done. Nor does it tell us precisely what meanings students will choose to use, how they will sequence them, or how they will express them. Nevertheless, seeing predictability as a matter of degree offers a window on task design, task selection, and on how teachers might orientate towards the way the task is used.

5 Conclusion

In this chapter I have argued that communicative language learning tasks enable the engagement of cognition, social involvement, and pedagogic action. While there are reasons for agreeing that learners' engagement with tasks is bound to be to some degree unpredictable, nonetheless there are general empirical grounds, practical reasons, and drawing on DST, theoretical reasons for expecting there to be some degree of predictability in learner discourse. In particular this is supported by the study of the trajectories students improvise in order to get through a task from beginning to end. These trajectories arise for common sense pragmatic reasons, and tend to come from a relatively limited range of options in terms of potentially effective discourse strategies. As the data from group S suggests, the selection and omission of trajectories may reflect the extent to which the students take seriously the intended design and purpose of the task. Predictability goes further than the discourse strategies, since these also motivate the selection of relatively predictable meanings to be shared, and of a relatively predictable range of formulations of those meanings.

So although it is clear that students' task-based discourse is not entirely predictable, and indeed that there can be surprises in how students complete a task, when we select a task for students to do, what we are doing is not just selecting a broad topic area, but a task with its own internal challenges which we hope that, by doing them, students will get better at handling. Understanding the likely phases and moves that learners could find useful on a given task, and consequently that they would be likely to use, can then provide pedagogically useful insights into the nature of the task, and into how abilities developed on one task can be developed through subsequent work, whether through teacher-student talk, further student-student talk, or the use of written media. Studying the nature of students' on-task trajectories can also give insights into how its design can be improved and exploited, and inform our thinking about what it is about the task that students might be learning. Task-based language learning is concerned both with the learning of language and with learning how to handle useful, relevant and hopefully interesting tasks.

There is however a more fundamental theoretical reason for hoping for a degree of predictability. Popper consistently argued (e.g. 1977) that human development has always depended on our ability to learn by testing out our predictions:

> we may consider that natural selection will favor those organisms that try out, by some method or other, the possible movements that might be adopted *before they are executed*. In this way, *real* trial-and-error behavior may be replaced, or preceded, by imagined or vicarious trial-and-error behaviour [...] On every level, making [i.e. creating options] comes before matching; that is, before selecting [a preferred option]. The creation of an expectation, of an anticipation, of a perception (which is a hypothesis) precedes its being put to the test.

I suggest that teachers, teacher educators, materials and course designers cannot function and cannot develop without expectations of what learning will occur on different tasks. If there is little that is predictable in students' language on tasks, there is little we can do to improve the design or use of the tasks. If true, this would likely spell the demise of TBLT.

Since the beginnings of TBLT over 35 years ago, the perspective I have been suggesting has received little if any attention. It seems to me attending to this aspect of language learning tasks is crucial. If my argument is correct, it could enable the pedagogic potential of TBLT to become far more central to the project, more transparent for teachers and learners, more amenable to studies of instructed discourse development, and ultimately for tasks to become an essential resource for the language classroom.

References

Barnes, Douglas. 1976. *From communication to curriculum*. Harmondsworth: Penguin.
Batstone, Rob (ed.). 2010. *Sociocognitive perspectives on language use and language learning*. Oxford: Oxford University Press.
Bygate, Martin. 1988. *Linguistic and strategic features of the language of learners working in oral communication exercises*. Unpublished doctoral thesis, Institute of Education, University of London.
Bygate, Martin & Virginia Samuda. 2005. Integrative planning through the use of task repetition. In Rod Ellis (ed.), *Planning and task performance in a second language*, 37–74. Amsterdam/New York: John Benjamins Publishers.
Bygate, Martin & Virginia Samuda. 2009. Creating pressure in task pedagogy: The joint roles of field, purpose and engagement within the interactional approach. In Alison Mackey & Charlene Polio (eds.), *Multiple perspectives on interaction*, 90–116. New York: Routledge.
Carter, Ronald & Michael McCarthy. 1997. *Exploring spoken English*. Cambridge: Cambridge University Press.
Coughlan, Peter & Patricia A. Duff. 1994. Same task, different activities: Analysis of SLA from an activity theory perspective. In James Lantolf & Gabriela Appel (eds.), *Vygotskian approaches to second language research*, 173–194. Oxford: Oxford University Press.
Coupland, Justine (ed.). 2014. *Small talk*. Abingdon, Oxford: Routledge.
Dechert, Hans. 1983. How a story is done in a second language. In Claus Faerch & Gabriele Kasper (eds.), *Strategies in interlanguage communication*, 175–195. Harlow: Longman.
Ellis, Rod. 1987. Interlanguage variability in narrative discourse: Style shifting in the use of the past tense. *SSLA*. 9. 1–20.
Ellis, Rod. 2001. Non-reciprocal tasks, comprehension and second language acquisition. In Martin Bygate, Peter Skehan & Merrill Swain (eds.), *Researching pedagogic tasks: second language learning, teaching and testing*. Harlow: Pearson Education Ltd.
Ellis, Rod. 2009. Task-based language teaching: Sorting out the misunderstandings. *International Journal of Applied Linguistics* 19(3). 221–246.
Larsen-Freeman, Diane. 2006. The emergence of complexity, fluency, and accuracy in the oral and written production of five Chinese learners of English. *Applied Linguistics* 27. 590–619.
Larsen-Freeman, Diane & Lynne J. Cameron. 2008. *Complex systems and applied linguistics*. Oxford: Oxford University Press.
Leech, Geoffrey. 1983. *Principles of pragmatics*. Harlow: Longman
Lantolf, James. 2000. *Sociocultural theory and second language learning*. Oxford: Oxford University Press.
Long, Michael H. 2015. Building the road as we travel. In Martin Bygate (ed.), *Domains and directions in the development of TBLT: A decade of plenaries from the international conference*, 1–26. Amsterdam: John Benjamins Publishing.
Long, Michael H. & Graham Crookes. 1992. Three approaches to task-based syllabus design. *TESOL Quarterly* 26. 27–56
Mackey, Alison. 1999. Input, interaction, and second language development. *SSLA* 21. 557–587.
Mackey, Alison (ed.). 2007. *Conversational interaction in SLA*. Oxford: Oxford University Press.
Ochs, Elinor & C. Taylor. 1992. Family narrative as political activity. *Discourse and Society* 3(3). 301–340

Popper, Karl. 1977. Natural selection and the emergence of mind. First Darwin Lecture, Darwin College, Cambridge, 8 November 1977. http://www.informationphilosopher.com/solutions/philosophers/popper/natural_selection_and_the_emergence_of_mind.html

Ranney, Susan. 1992. Learning a new script: An exploration of sociolinguistic competence. *Applied Linguistics* 13/1. 25–50.

Samuda, Virginia. 2001. Guiding relationships between form and meaning during task performance. In Martin Bygate, Peter Skehan, & Merrill Swain (eds.), *Researching pedagogic tasks: Second language learning, teaching and testing*, 119–140. Harlow: Longman.

Sinclair, John McH. & R. Malcolm Coulthard. 1975. *Towards an analysis of discourse*. Oxford: Oxford University Press.

Tarone, Elaine & Kimberley Kuehn. 2000. Negotiating the social services oral intake interview: communicative needs of non-native speakers of English. *TESOL Quarterly* 34(1). 99–126.

The "Five Graces Group". 2009. Language is a complex adaptive system: Position paper. *Language Learning* 59, Suppl. 1. 1–26.

Ur, Penny. 1982. *Discussions that work*. Cambridge: Cambridge University Press.

Van den Branden, Kris. 2015. Tasks for real. Hold on, how real is 'real'? 6th Biennial International Conference on TBLT 'Tasks for real'. Leuven, 16–18 September 2015.

Van Geert, Paul. 2008. The dynamic systems approach in the study of L1 and L2 acquisition: An introduction. *Modern Language Journal* 92 ii. 179–199.

Wells, Gordon. 1981. *Learning through interaction*. Cambridge: Cambridge University Press.

Wells, Gordon. 1985. *Language development in the pre-school years*. Cambridge: Cambridge University Press.

Appendix

Dog and Crow picture story (after Dechert, 1983)

Hoa Nguyen and Diane Larsen-Freeman
8 Using Tasks to Teach Formulaic Sequences: Interindividual and Intraindividual Variation

1 Introduction

Task-based language teaching (TBLT) has received a great deal of attention from both researchers and teachers (e.g., Long 1985; Nunan 1989). Other research (e.g., Pawley and Syder 1983; Wray 2002) has shown that speakers make substantial use of multi-word units or formulaic sequences in language production. In addition, research has demonstrated that instruction in such sequences yields positive results (e.g. Bishop 2004; Boers et al. 2006; Jones and Haywood 2004; Rott 2009). Therefore, it is natural to seek an answer to the question of whether using tasks to teach formulaic sequences makes sense. This is what we propose to do in this chapter.

However, there is an additional consideration in our attempt. Most findings on the value of TBLT are based on statistical testing using group means. While group data provide one measure of the success of an intervention, advocates of a complex dynamic systems approach to second language development contend that interindividual variation and intraindividual fluctuation are important characteristics of language learning as well (Larsen-Freeman 2006; Larsen-Freeman and Cameron 2008; van Geert and Steenbeek 2005; Verspoor, Lowie, and van Dyck, 2008).

Accordingly, this study investigates the developmental paths of 30 high intermediate ESL learners in instructed contexts, focusing on the interindividual variability of their performance as well as identifying patterns in their intraindividual process of acquiring 30 target English formulaic sequences (phrasal verbs, idioms, collocations). The learners were divided into 3 groups. Two of the groups were instructed; the third was a comparison group. One of the instructed groups was taught using collaborative gap-fill tasks (Gapfill, $n = 10$). The second instructed group was taught with spot-the difference tasks (SpotDif, $n = 10$). The instruction took place over 3 sessions. Instruction effectiveness was measured by immediate and delayed post-tests, comprising a cued gap-fill test followed

---

Hoa Nguyen, Teachers College, Columbia University
Diane Larsen-Freeman, University of Michigan and University of Pennsylvania

DOI 10.1515/9781501503399-009

by a multiple-choice question test. Data obtained from ANOVAs and correlation analysis revealed that learners' performance varied depending on the type of formulaic sequences being taught and the type of instruction they received. Findings also showed that even though mixed between-within subjects ANOVAs conducted using average group scores showed that both groups improved at a statistically significant level as opposed to a comparison group ($n = 10$), some learners were more responsive to instruction than others. In addition, a disaggregation of group data revealed relatively significant interindividual and intraindividual variation.

2 Literature review

Formulaic language has now become more acknowledged by researchers as an important part of language (Moon 1998; Nattinger and DeCarrio 1992; Pawley and Syder 1983; Schmitt and Carter 2008; Sinclair 1991). In this study, the term *formulaic sequences* (henceforth FSs), instances of formulaic language, will be used to indicate any multiword sequences, including phrasal verbs (e.g. *mull over, wind down*), collocations (e.g. *firmly entrenched*), idioms (e.g. *drop the ball, at the mercy of*) – expressions that are mostly prefabricated but also allow the insertion or deletion of certain items. These expressions comprise a large proportion of any type of discourse, both spoken and written. Researchers have reported different percentages, depending on their methodologies and definitions of formulaic language, but they all fall within the range of 30–50% of a given text.

Many consider FSs part of the lexicon (e.g. Nattinger and DeCarrio 1992; Schmitt and Carter 2008), but these sequences should not be considered strictly lexical units. The formation and ubiquity of these sequences as a type of linguistic construction are accounted for in a usage-based approach to first and second language acquisition. The claim is that formulaic sequences are, in fact, the result of a common cognitive process, chunking, which is in turn the result of repeated use (Bybee and Beckner 2010; N. Ellis and Simpson-Vlach 2009; Tomasello 2003; Wulff 2008). Each use of such sequences contributes to the entrenchment of the form-meaning link, which reduces the semantic autonomy of the individual components (N. Ellis 2001, 2003; Wulff 2008). This claim challenges the lexis-syntax dichotomy, placing FSs at the intersection of vocabulary and grammar. Following Schmitt and Carter (2004), we examined FSs with regard to students' productive and receptive knowledge. From a usage-based perspective, we also looked at FSs' corpus-informed characteristics, such as frequency, mutual information score (henceforth MI score, the indicator of the strength of association among individual words in a FS) and how they might or might not influence the effectiveness of instruction.

FSs serve some important functions in the storage and retrieval of language in the minds of native speakers; yet L2 learners, including those who have reached advanced levels of proficiency, continue to experience difficulty when processing (Gerald 2007) or producing FSs in both speech and writing. Many studies address the difficulty of EFL learners, but others also present strong evidence that even in an ESL setting, where learners are immersed in the second language, learners continue to struggle with using FSs appropriately. Learners are found to overuse certain FSs, and not to employ as wide a range of FSs as native speakers do (Erman 2009a, 2009b; Qi and Ding, 2011; Foster 2001; Laufer and Waldman 2011; Liao and Fukuya 2004). Understandably, how second language learners acquire these sequences is a newly emergent research area. In the past few years there has been research about the acquisition, processing and use of formulaic sequences among ESL learners, which has started to yield some results.

While research on the matter has been preliminary, the nature of acquiring FSs in L2 promises important implications for selecting pedagogical materials and designing interventions (Schmitt and Carter 2004). Various types of classroom activities have been put to the test: gap-fill exercises, encouraging learners to highlight FSs (Boers et al 2006; Jones and Haywood 2004), a pre-writing brainstorming task (Rott 2009), discussion (Hsu 2010), input enhancement (Bishop 2004; Jones and Haywood 2004), raising students' awareness of phonological or FSs' etymological features (Boers et al. 2004; Lindstromberg and Boers 2008), and communicative tasks (Wood 2009). All these instructional types aim to retune learners' selective attention through form-focused instruction or consciousness raising (N. Ellis 2008). However, since much of this research is limited to techniques such as input enhancement, explicit instruction that encourages learners to look up certain sequences, and explaining semantic aspects of FSs, there is a pressing need for research on intervention types that fit better into a communicative classroom, such as those employed by Wood (2009), but more specifically tailored to the instruction of FSs.

Many researchers in the field of instructed second language acquisition (dealing mostly with L2 grammar) concur that the optimal classroom activities should be primarily meaning-focused and at the same time allow for learners to focus on L2 form. Long (1991) introduces the concept of *focus on form* as a type of instruction that "overtly draws students' attention to linguistic elements as they arise incidentally in lessons whose overriding focus is on meaning or communication" (1991: 45–46). Tasks are usually implemented as form-focused classroom activities to provide learners with the opportunities to notice low-saliency forms, modify input, interact with each other, modify output, negotiate and give corrective feedback to each other (see for example Doughty and Pica 1986; Long 1981; Nunan 1989; Pica, Kang and Sauro 2006).

Even though focus on form is generally discussed in second language acquisition as related to grammar, Laufer (2005) argues that 'form' could be lexical items as well. In this study, we use "focus on form" to refer to any kind of instruction that draws learners' attention to FSs, considered lexicogrammatical items in nature, whether it be in a meaning-based context or in a decontextualized activity, following Laufer's (2005) definition.

However, despite the demonstrated effectiveness of communicative tasks in the L2 classroom, not much research has examined the use of such tasks in teaching vocabulary. There have been a few studies that have lent evidentiary support to the usefulness of communicative tasks for this purpose, such as R. Ellis, Tanaka and Yamazaki (1994), R. Ellis and He (1999), Gass and Torres (2005), Kim (2008), Kowal and Swain (1994), and Loewen and Philp (2006). These studies have found that communicative tasks such as jigsaw, dictogloss (both individual and interactive), opinion gap, story narration, and match/label tasks are useful in a number of ways. First, tasks encourage learners to modify their input and to help each other with figuring out the meaning of unknown vocabulary, even when the task's main aim is not to teach vocabulary (Kowal and Swain 1994; Loewen and Philp 2006). Second, tasks lead to better vocabulary acquisition, both at receptive and productive levels (R. Ellis and He 1999; Gass and Torres 2005). Third, tasks benefit learners even when they do not actively participate in the interaction (R. Ellis et al. 1994). An important finding by Kim (2008) is that a collaborative dictogloss is more effective than the individual dictogloss. These studies suggest that interaction between learners benefits vocabulary learning in general.

Little research, however, has been done on the possible contribution of interactive tasks to the acquisition of L2 formulaic sequences, or on their effectiveness in comparison to other types of instruction. The study by Wood (2009) attempts to do so among other objectives, but obtained very limited data from only one participant. Additionally, the tasks used in Wood's study were not specifically designed to facilitate the participant's acquisition of FSs.

This gap in research justifies the need for designing and conducting a study that aims at testing the possible effectiveness of communicative tasks for learning the use of FSs, which is what we propose to do in this study. As Robinson (2011) contends, experimental research in task-based language teaching and learning has been helpful in exploring "connections between pedagogical practice and the second language acquisition processes they may stimulate" (2011: 5). Tasks provide a useful way of engaging students in "meaningful interaction because engaging them so provides the optimal way for learners to benefit from frequency and saliency" of target structures (Larsen-Freeman 2002: 283). Tasks thus can create conditions not otherwise available to learners due to the lack of target language exposure. Tasks can be designed to allow learners to attend to FSs, which would be obscured by other language levels, such as individual words or grammatical structures. Since FSs are, in essence, form-meaning pairings, tasks need to be created to facilitate learners' attention to both form and meaning. In the two types of tasks used as interventions for this study, one is more geared towards the meaning (and use) of the FSs (Gap-fill), and the other directs learners' attentional resources more to the form (SpotDif). Thus, these interactive tasks aim at optimizing the L2 input by increasing the saliency of the target FSs and by engaging learners. Both tasks require learners to interact with each other to achieve a mutual goal, relying on their own linguistic resources to understand the input and solving the problem at hand. During task implementation, learners have plenty of opportunities to interact while still attending to the meaning of the passages. Additionally, these form-focused tasks are designed to maximize learners' attention to the target FSs through output. For example, the interactive gap fill task facilitates learner-learner interaction, pushing them to comprehend thoroughly the meaning of the passage as well as the meaning of the FSs in order to reach a successful task outcome. Through this meaningful goal-oriented interaction, learners will likely notice forms that have otherwise low-saliency, have opportunities to produce ample output, and potentially enhance their metalinguistic awareness with regard to the FSs.

These interactive tasks are likely to induce either or both of learners' productive and receptive knowledge of the target FSs. It has been widely accepted in vocabulary research that there exists a discrepancy between language users' receptive and productive knowledge (Nation 2001), with receptive vocabulary size 19–25% smaller than productive vocabulary (Schmitt and Meara 1997). While productive vocabulary knowledge might be more sophisticated than receptive knowledge, learners have a better chance of using a lexical item productively when the receptive knowledge of that particular item is already in place (Webb 2008).

3 The study

3.1 Participants and materials

Participants in the study are students enrolled in graduate programs at a large research university in the Northeast United States, who have a TOEFL iBT score ranging from 90–110 (or an equivalent test score) and have studied in the United States for 1–2 years. They all use Mandarin-Chinese with native-like proficiency.

A total of 30 students (25 females, 5 males) were randomly assigned to 3 groups, one control group and two experimental groups (n = 10 in each group).

The study is designed as a quasi-experiment with independent variables and dependent variables. The independent variables are (i) type of instruction (no FS-focused instruction, collaborative Gap-fill and collaborative Spot-the-Difference tasks) and (ii) corpus-derived properties of the FSs (n-gram length, frequency and MI score). The dependent variables are (i) receptive knowledge of FSs in multiple-choice tests and (ii) productive knowledge of FSs in c-tests.

Each of three texts used in the three treatment sessions are approximately 400 words in length. All texts share a common theme: information and communication technology and its influence on people's lives. Each passage presents 10 target FSs.

As Read and Nation (2004) note, validity in measuring FSs is one of the most prominent challenges in this research area. The primary criterion of a FS relates to its holistic storage and retrieval (Wray 2002, 2008), which is "a difficult one to operationalize" (Read and Nation, 2004: 35). Thus to ensure internal validity of FS research, Read and Nation argue that a triangulation of methods is necessary. This study follows Underwood et al. (2004) and Schmitt and Underwood's (2004) methodological triangulation. Three methods are used to identify FSs in the text: intuition, corpus analysis, and a cloze test. After target FSs were intuitively selected, they were tested in Corpus of Contemporary American English (CoCA) for two criteria: a MI score of at least 3, as N. Ellis et al. (2008) recommend, but with a minimal raw frequency of 50 – a lower frequency threshold than that used in N. Ellis's study. This is because N. Ellis et al. (2008) aim at formulating a list of most popular and useful FSs that should be included in the English for Academic Purpose classroom, such as *at the beginning of, it should be noted that*. These FSs are probably too frequent and are likely already a part of our participants' lexicon, hence a lower frequency threshold is necessary for our study. Finally, all the FSs were included in a cloze test, which provided initial, sometimes middle, letters of content words in the FSs. FSs were put in short contexts. The cloze tests were then administered to native speakers, whose feedback led to revision of the test. This test was later used as the Productive Knowledge post-test for learners.

3.2 Pre-tests and post-tests

Figure 1 below summarizes the tests used in this study.

Pre-test
- 3-level Vocabulary Knowledge Scale (both Productive & Receptive)

Immediate Post-test
- Productive Knowledge test: cued gap-fill
- Receptive Knowledge test: multiple choice, 2 sections (Form & Meaning)

Delayed Post-test (2 weeks post-treatment)
- Productive Knowledge test: cued gap-fill
- Receptive Knowledge test: multiple choice, 2 sections (Form & Meaning)

Figure 1: Pre and post-tests

The pre-test is a modified version of the 5-point Vocabulary Knowledge Scale proposed by Paribakht and Wesche (1997). This test shows whether learners have (1) neither receptive knowledge nor productive knowledge of the item (2) receptive knowledge only or (3) both receptive and productive knowledge. For each lexical item in the pretest, which includes 30 individual words as distractors and the 30 target FSs, participants were instructed to choose one of the 3 following levels:
1. I don't know this word/phrase.
2. I know the meaning of this word/phrase, but I never use it in my writing/speaking.
3. I use this word/phrase quite often in my writing/speaking.

Following Paribakht and Wesche's model, learners were asked to write down the meaning of the word/phrase in question if they chose level 2 or 3. They could explain the word using as many words as they wish, or using a sentence that contained the word. If they chose level (1), no point was given. 1 point was given each time level (2) was chosen, and 3 points for each answer at level (3) with the correct meaning of the FSs provided. If learners provided an incorrect meaning for both options 2 and 3, they were considered to be at level 1 and received no point.

3.3 Treatment

The instructor and materials for instruction were identical across the three groups. All groups met once a week for 3 weeks. Lessons for all groups started with a warm-up activity to introduce the topic of the reading passage. Then learners read the passage for the first time in order to answer a few comprehension questions (main idea and specific details). In order to answer these comprehension questions, learners may or may not have used FSs – none of the questions require that FSs be used. They then read the passage for the second time, this time with different activities.

The control group spent the entire lesson reading and discussing several comprehension questions with no FS-focused instruction. The collaborative Gap-fill group completed the collaborative Gap-fill tasks following regular reading comprehension activities. They were, in pairs, given a gap-filling exercise based on the reading passage. Students read the original passage again with target FSs deleted. They were given a word bank from which to choose and were asked to complete the exercise collaboratively. Only one word bank was given to each pair/group of students. In the Spot-the-Difference group, after reading the passage for the first time and answering comprehension questions, learners worked in pairs. Each pair was given a version of the original passage, with the target FSs modified in one version. Each version of the passage contained both target FSs and modified FSs. The learners collaboratively compared the two passages, identified the differences and negotiated which FS provided was target-like.

At the end of each class, all reading passages given as handouts to learners during class time were collected. Participants' underlinings and notes served as additional qualitative data and were examined to determine if learners in the control group noticed the target FSs in the absence of form-focused instruction.

The procedures of these two types of tasks presumably focus learners' attention on FSs and allow for negotiation of meaning between learners. The assumed potential of these two communicative tasks is also based on a vocabulary acquisition hypothesis advanced by Laufer and Hulstijn (2001), the "Involvement Load Hypothesis" (see also Laufer and Girsai 2008). This hypothesis posits that a classroom task requiring higher involvement load will be more effective than tasks with lower involvement load. Involvement load is determined by three factors: *need*, which is the motivational dimension of involvement, *search*, the attempt to find the meaning of an unknown word or trying to find a word in an L2 to express a certain concept, and *evaluation*, which is the process of comparing between meanings of the same words, or different words to make a task-essential decision. Even though Laufer and Hustijn's hypothesis is concerned with the acquisition of individual words, their hypothesis seems applicable to the acquisition of FSs.

Gap-fill and SpotDif both entail opportunities for learners to engage in a crucial cognitive process: evaluation, which helps increase their involvement load. In Gap-fill, in order to fill in the gaps, learners will likely feel a strong *need* to know the meaning of all FSs in the word bank we have given them, then *search* for their meaning and *evaluate* between different options made available to them. In this task, learners have to evaluate the meaning of the FSs in the word bank in relation to the meaning of a particular sentence (or that of several sentences) in the original passage. However, once learners figure out the meaning of the FSs in the word bank, they probably have no reason to attend more to the form of these FSs, because they do not have to evaluate between different forms of the same FS, as in the SpotDif task.

In completing the SpotDif, learners have to work with two versions of the passage, where FSs differ. For example, when the target FS is *on the books* (being part of the law), the altered version will be *in the book*. Learners will have to evaluate the appropriateness of the form of these two alternatives and choose one that fits the context. In the process of evaluating in SpotDif, learners likely will have the motivation, or *need*, to learn the meaning of this sequence, and this will encourage them to *search* for its meaning, or to ask the instructor about it. However, the intensity of *search* in SpotDif is probably not as high as in the Gap-fill exercise because they do not have to choose from different FSs. Laufer and Hustijn believe that *need* is moderate when learners are asked by the teacher to use a word in a sentence, and *need* is strong when the learners themselves deem it necessary to know a certain word. SpotDif involves a moderate level of *evaluation* where learners have to evaluate the correct form of the target FSs.

3.4 Research questions

The study aims to find answers to the following research questions:
1. Do Gap-fill and SpotDif tasks help learners acquire higher levels of productive knowledge of FSs? If yes, which type of treatment is more effective?
2. Do Gap-fill and SpotDif tasks help learners acquire higher levels of receptive knowledge of FSs? If yes, which type of treatment is more effective?
3. Are the frequency, MI-score, and *n*-gram length of FSs related to learners' acquisition of receptive and productive knowledge of FSs?

While questions (1) and (2) directly address the issue of pedagogical intervention, question (3) looks at characteristics of the FSs that might mediate their acquisition, which in turn has important implications for selecting pedagogical materials and intervention (Schmitt and Carter 2004).

3.5 Data analysis

Mixed between-within subjects ANOVAs were conducted to determine whether learners' performance showed statistically significant improvement between pre-test, immediate post-test and delayed post-test. The timing of the pre-tests, post-tests and delayed post-tests is the within-subject (repeated measures) factor. The treatment type is the between-subject factor. Post hoc analyses were conducted to determine if there were statistically significant differences between test score means across control and treatment conditions. Besides statistical significance testing, effect sizes using Cohen's *d* were also calculated in order to serve as indicators of educational significance. Finally, correlations between frequency, *n*-gram length and MI Score were calculated.

3.6 Post-tests

Two tests were used as both immediate and delayed post-tests: the Productive Knowledge test and the Receptive Knowledge test.

The Productive Knowledge test, with a maximum score of 90, is a c-test following Schmitt et al.'s (2004) study. In this test, the initial letter(s), at times middle letters, of the target FSs are provided in the same sentences as in the Receptive Knowledge test, with the meaning of the target FSs provided in parentheses at the end of each sentence. A scale of 0 to 3 was used to evaluate participants' response on the c-test.

> 3 = Correct phrase (even with incorrect inflectional morphemes, e.g., *saddle with* when the correct form is *saddled with*, *touch off* when the correct form is *touching off*)
>
> 2 = Correct phrase but problems with spelling, or correct key words but incorrect preposition or article (e.g., *at a mercy of*)
>
> 1 = Some idea of phraseology but could not produce the correct phrase, e.g. *at the merit of* instead of *at the mercy of*
>
> 0 = No idea of phraseology, i.e. when no answer is provided

Learners' performance on the c-tests was evaluated by two raters. An interrater reliability analysis using the Kappa statistic was performed to determine consistency among raters. The Kappa interrater reliability for the raters was found to be 0.84 ($p < .001$).

The Receptive Knowledge test is a two-part multiple choice question test tapping learners' knowledge of the form and meaning of the target FSs, with a maximum score of 30 for each section. (Previous research (e.g., Schmitt et al 2004) did not attend to learners' receptive knowledge of the meaning of the target FSs.) Learners chose from 4 possible answers, in addition to the 5th choice of "I don't know" for each part of a multiple choice question. What follows is an example:

1. *Many students in the United States are* _____ *student loan debt. In a little more than 10 years, the total amount of student loan debt in this country has doubled to more than $1 trillion.*
   a. saddled with
   b. saddlen with
   c. saddled by
   d. saddlen by
   c. I don't know
   This phrase means:
   a. burdened with
   b. disappointed with
   c. saddened by
   d. frustrated by
   e. I don't know

Cronbach's alpha for all 60 items in the Receptive Knowledge test was .904, and the Receptive Knowledge test was piloted with 20 native speakers of English. These same Productive Knowledge and Receptive Knowledge tests were administered 2 weeks after the last treatment session as delayed post-tests.

4 Results

4.1 Productive Knowledge

Mixed between-within subjects ANOVAs conducted on the Productive Knowledge pre-tests, immediate, and delayed post-tests revealed statistically significant improvement among learners of all groups from pre-tests to post-tests. Results also showed that the two TBLT groups outperformed the control group, with the Gap-fill group achieving higher scores than the SpotDif group. In the immediate post-test, both treatment groups outperformed the control group at a significant level. In the delayed post-test, statistically significant difference was found only between the Gap-fill group and control group. Effect sizes using Cohen's d were large for all treatment groups in both immediate and delayed post-tests.

Table 1: Mean scores of three groups on the Productive Knowledge pre-tests, immediate and delayed post-tests (Max. score = 90)

Timing	Pre-test			Immediate Post-test			Delayed Post-test		
	Control group	Gap-fill	SpotDif	Control group	Gap-fill	SpotDif	Control group	Gap-fill	SpotDif
Mean	0.30	0.30	0.60	34	80	72	25	46	35
SD*	0.95	0.95	1.3	18	8.1	11	12	15	12

*Most learners received a 0 on the pre-tests. In the control and Gap-fill groups, 9 learners scored 0, 1 scored 3 point, thus the SD is 0.95. In the SpotDif group, 2 learners scored 3 points, which brought the SD to 1.3

Normality, independence and sphericity assumptions were met for a mixed between-within subjects ANOVA to be conducted. Mauchly's test of sphericity yielded $p > .05$. The homogeneity of variance assumption was violated, with Levene's test of homogeneity of variance showing significant unequivalent variances in the pre-test, but not the immediate and delayed post-tests. Thus ANOVA was conducted with Games-Howell post hoc analyses ($\alpha = .05$), which does not assume equal variance.

Results revealed significant differences between the control group and both TBLT groups, and no statistically significant difference between the two experimental groups. There were a significant effect for Time across the pre-test, the immediate and delayed post-test, $F(2,72) = 574$, $p < .001$, $\eta_p^2 = .94$, a significant interaction effect between Group and Time $F(6, 72) = 17$, $p < .001$, $\eta_p^2 = .58$, and a significant effect for Group $F(3,36) = 16$, $p < .001$, $\eta_p^2 = .58$. Games-Howell post hoc analyses with $\alpha = .05$, revealed two important findings: (1) The two experimental groups outperformed the control group in the immediate and delayed post-test at a statistically significant level; and (2) There were no statistically significant differences between the two types of treatment, possibly because of the small group size ($n = 10$).

The effect sizes using Cohen's d for the analysis of the immediate posttests, respectively for the Gap-fill group ($d = 3.38$), and SpotDif group ($d = 2.64$), as compared to the control group, were found to considerably exceed Cohen's convention for a large effect ($d = .80$), suggesting a large magnitude of instructional effect. The magnitude of instructional effect on the Productive delayed test scores of both the Gap-fill group ($d = 1.53$) and SpotDif group ($d = 0.87$), as compared to the control group, exceeded Cohen's convention for a large effect ($d = .80$), suggesting a large magnitude of instructional effect for both treatment conditions even 2 weeks after treatment ended.

4.2 Receptive Knowledge

Immediate and delayed post-tests revealed statistically significant improvement among learners of all groups from pre-tests to post-tests. Overall results revealed significant differences between the control group and the SpotDif group. In the immediate post-test, all treatment groups outperformed the control group at a significant level. Effect sizes for all treatment groups as compared to the control group far exceeded Cohen's convention for a large effect. On the delayed post-test, no statistically significant difference was found across groups, but effect sizes using Cohen's d remain above the large level for both treatment groups as compared to the control group.

Table 2: Mean scores of the three groups on the Receptive Knowledge pre-tests, immediate and delayed post-tests (Max. score = 60)

Timing	Pre-test			Immediate Post-test			Delayed Post-test		
	Control group	Gap-fill	SpotDif	Control group	Gap-fill	SpotDif	Control group	Gap-fill	SpotDif
Mean	3	0.80	2.3	44	56	55	41	48	50
SD	2.2	1	2.7	9.3	3.4	2.6	8.8	9.2	7.7

Normality, independence and sphericity assumptions were met for a mixed between-within subjects ANOVA to be conducted. Mauchly's test of sphericity yielded $p > .05$. The homogeneity of variance assumption was violated, with Levene's test of homogeneity of variance showing significant unequivalent variances in the pre-test and immediate post-tests, but not the delayed post-tests. Thus ANOVA was conducted with Games-Howell, analyses ($\alpha = .05$) which do not assume equal variance. Similar procedures will apply in the rest of this study.

A mixed between-within subjects ANOVA was conducted to compare the mean scores of the three groups in order to examine whether the scores improved significantly from pre-test to immediate and delayed post-test and if there were significant differences across groups.

There were a significant effect for Time across the pre-test, the immediate and delayed post-test, $F(2, 72) = 1513$, $p < .001$, $\eta_p^2 = .98$, a significant interaction effect between Group and Time $F(6, 72) = 126$, $p < .001$, $\eta_p^2 = .34$, and a significant effect for Group $F(3, 36) = 5.2$, $p < .005$, $\eta_p^2 = .30$.

All three groups displayed significant improvement from the pre-test to the immediate post-test; however, the significant interaction for group and time suggested that the gain in scores differed across groups. Games-Howell post hoc analyses (α = .05) were also conducted. Results revealed significant differences between the control group and the SpotDif group. There was no statistically significant difference between experimental groups, probably because of the small sample size (n = 10).

When examining more closely learners' performance in the Form and Meaning sections of the Receptive Knowledge post-tests (see Table 3), we find that (1) in the Form section of the immediate post-test, the SpotDif groups obtained better scores than the control group at a statistically significant level, and effect sizes for all treatment groups as compared to the control group still exceeded Cohen's convention for large effect sizes (2) in the Meaning section of the immediate post-test, a statistically significant difference existed between the control group and the Gap-fill group yet effect sizes remained large for both experimental groups (3) in the Form section of the delayed post-test, only the Gap-fill group outperformed the control group at a statistically significant level, but effect sizes continued to exceed the large level using Cohen's convention (4) in the Meaning section of the delayed post-test, there were no statistically significant differences across groups.

Table 3: Mean scores of by the three groups on the Form and Meaning sections of the Receptive Knowledge immediate and delayed post-test (Max. score = 30)

		Immediate Post-test			Delayed Post-test		
		Control group	Gap-fill	SpotDif	Control group	Gap-fill	SpotDif
Form	Mean	19	27	27	16	22	19
	SD	5.9	2.3	1.7	5.1	5.2	2.2
Meaning	Mean	25	29	28	25	26	26
	SD	3.9	1.4	1.9	4.5	4.7	2.5

4.3 *n*-gram, frequency and MI-score

FREQ and participants' test scores on the immediate Productive Knowledge post-test were correlated at a significant level, $r(28)$ = .37, p < .05. FREQ and learners' performance on the delayed Productive Knowledge post-tests were somewhat correlated at a level close to significant, $r(28)$ = .34, p = .069. As can be seen from Table 4, there was little correlation between FREQ and all Receptive Productive tests. *n*-gram length was not correlated at a significant level with any test scores, even though the correlation between n-gram length and the Productive Knowledge immediate post-tests was close to significant, $r(28) = .36$, $p = .054$.

MI Score, on the other hand, was inversely correlated with participants' performance on the Meaning section of the immediate Receptive Knowledge test. This correlation did not endure to the delayed post-test. No correlation was found between MI Score and all Productive Knowledge post-tests, nor between MI Score and the Form section of the Receptive Knowledge post-tests.

Table 4: Correlations between FREQ, *n*-gram length, MI Score and test scores

		Productive Knowledge Immediate post-test	Productive Knowledge Delayed post-test	Receptive Knowledge – Immediate post-test – Form section	Receptive Knowledge – Immediate post-test – Meaning section	Receptive Knowledge – Delayed post-test – Form section	Receptive Knowledge – Delayed post-test – Meaning section
FREQ	Pearson Correlation	.368*	.336	.105	.185	−.019	.059
	Sig. (2-tailed)	.046	.069	.581	.329	.922	.756
	N	30	30	30	30	30	30
n-gram length	Pearson Correlation	−.355	−.297	−.236	−.229	−.072	.129
	Sig. (2-tailed)	.054	.111	.210	.224	.706	.497
	N	30	30	30	30	30	30
MI Score	Pearson Correlation	.026	.053	.131	−.401*	.110	−.151
	Sig. (2-tailed)	.892	.779	.489	.028	.563	.426
	N	30	30	30	30	30	30

* Correlation is significant at the 0.05 level (2-tailed)

5 Discussion

5.1 TBLT and the acquisition of FSs

Overall, findings from the study support the effectiveness of using interactive tasks in the classroom to facilitate learners' acquisition of FSs. In comparison with the control group where learners meaningfully engaged with the input for an equal period of time with no form-focused instruction, the task-based groups retained the target FSs better at both the receptive and the productive level. Gains made by the learners in the task-based groups were statistically significant with medium to large effect sizes as measured by Cohen's *d* convention, especially from the pre-test to the immediate post-tests. This finding accords with published research on TBLT, and confirms the usefulness of using tasks in the language classroom to encourage focus on form. In what follows, we will discuss in the light of complexity theory caveats to this understanding by disaggregating these results from group levels.

5.2 Differential effectiveness of instruction

It can be seen from the results reported in the previous section that using tasks about the target FSs had an overall positive effect on improving learners' performance at both the productive and receptive levels. However, the common practice in the field of calculating effects based on the mean scores and arriving at group-level conclusions yields statistical findings that might not be meaningful to individual learners (Larsen-Freeman 2006; Molenaar 2008; van Geert 2011). Group data tends to cloud meaningful findings at the individual learners' level in ways that might inhibit a complete understanding of the acquisition process.

For instance, in the Control group, there were 3 students (S1, S2, S3) who were particularly sensitive to the target FSs. Without the teacher's instruction, these students noticed target FSs in the input, evidenced by their underlining in the reading passages that were collected at the end of all treatment sessions, and as a result, scored high in the both the Productive and Receptive Knowledge tests. Unlike the other 7 students in the Control group, these students were able to focus on form despite the lack of focused instruction. As a result, their delayed Productive Knowledge test scores equalled or exceeded the SpotDif group's mean score (M = 35).

In contrast, there were 3 learners in the experimental groups (S18, S26, S29) who did not seem to have benefited from instruction or interaction with the materials. They scored significantly below the group mean level of even the control group in the delayed post-tests, although their scores on the immediate post-test were higher than the control group's mean score. This shows that despite the immediate effect of instruction on their learning, other variables came into play that weaken that effect over time. Interestingly, the same 3 students displayed an upward pattern in their Receptive Knowledge development over time, different from all other students. Their receptive knowledge of the target FSs increased significantly from pre-test to immediate post-test, and continued slightly increasing from immediate to delayed post-test. This pattern contrasts with all other students participating in the study, whose scores reflected an attrition of knowledge from immediate to delayed post-tests.

Table 5: Individual learners' scores in the Productive Knowledge and Receptive Knowledge tests

	S1	S2	S3	S4	S5	S6	S7	S8	S9	S10	S11	S12	S13	S14	S15
PK Pre	4	2	4	2	2	0	2	0	6	4	2	2	0	2	0
PK Im	51	68	70	37	37	31	33	43	20	43	69	83	87	73	80
PK Del	35	44	44	18	18	22	13	20	11	21	33	46	48	32	36
RK Pre	0	0	0	0	0	0	0	0	3	0	3	0	0	0	0
RK Im	48	56	52	52	40	31	50	36	30	42	55	56	59	53	58
RK Del	39	52	48	41	38	21	48	40	35	46	46	54	48	46	50
	S16	S17	S18	S19	S20	S21	S22	S23	S24	S25	S26	S27	S28	S29	S30
PK Pre	2	0	0	0	2	0	2	6	0	0	0	4	5	0	6
PK Im	86	88	61	81	84	78	87	72	55	71	61	82	78	60	81
PK Del	53	37	24	78	44	58	45	47	31	34	19	43	41	10	32
RK Pre	0	0	0	0	0	3	0	0	0	0	0	3	0	0	0
RK Im	56	48	57	57	57	58	56	53	58	56	55	60	52	54	54
RK Del	47	25	60	54	51	54	53	35	51	50	56	56	39	56	46

(S1–S10: Control group; S11–S20: Gap-fill Group; S21–S30: SpotDif group)

5.3 Differential rate of progress/regress over time

Less extreme but also noticeable is the differential rate at which students' receptive or productive knowledge develops or attrites over time, especially from the immediate post-test to the delayed post-test.

Figure 2 illustrates the retention rate over a course of 2 weeks' time from the immediate post-test to the delayed post-test. The retention rate is the learners' score in the delayed post-test divided by that in the immediate post-test.

Learners tend to retain receptive knowledge better than productive knowledge, shown in the higher mean retention rate. The mean retention rate for Receptive Knowledge is .90 in comparison with a mean of 0.5 for Productive Knowledge. How Receptive Knowledge, instruction and learners' retention interact with each other over time scales is evidently different from how Productive Knowledge and other factors change learners' ability to produce target FSs in a cued context.

A closer examination of learners' individual performance reveals that with regard to productive knowledge, one learner in the SpotDif group (S29) only retained 17% of the knowledge he had on the immediate post-test, which means this learner only managed to retain a minimal proportion of the initial productive knowledge acquired through instruction. A related finding is that this same

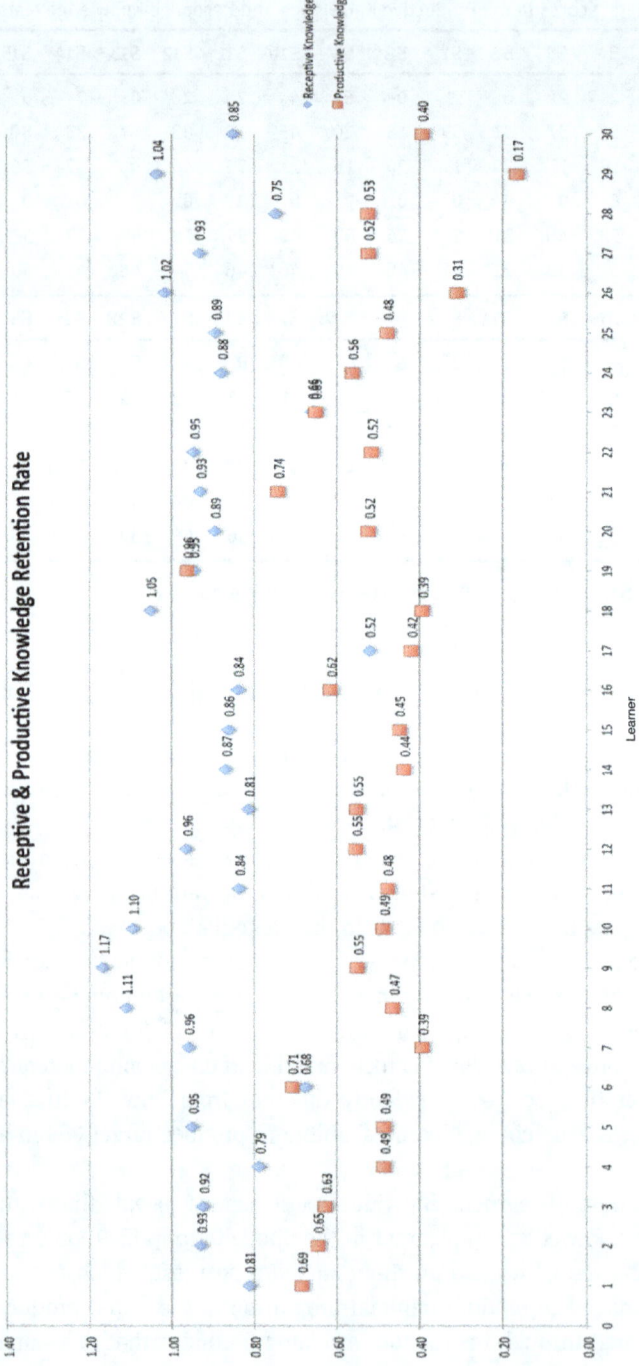

Figure 2: Productive and Receptive Knowledge retention rate Horizontal axis: 1–10: learners in the control group; 11–20: Gap-fill; 21–30: SpotDif (Retention rate = delayed post-test score/immediate post-test score)

learner, who had difficulty with retaining knowledge, did not attrite any of the receptive knowledge 2 weeks after the last treatment session, with the retention rate of 1.04, i.e. the score in the delayed RK post-test was slightly higher. Similar to S29, other students (S8, S9, S10, S18, S26) exhibit a difference in their retention of Productive Knowledge and Receptive Knowledge over time.

Another group of learners (S1, S6, S17, S19, S23) display a minimal difference in retention rate over time across the two tests, suggesting that other variables impact how they retain both levels of lexical knowledge in somewhat similar ways. The rest of the participants, constituting a larger group, seem to display a moderate difference in their retention rate of Productive and Receptive knowledge (~20–40% difference).

This examination shows that TBLT was not the only variable influencing how learners develop or attrite their lexical knowledge over time. Both the TBLT and the control groups have participants who can be categorized as members of all groups (minimal difference, moderate difference and large difference). This also adds to the finding by Caspi (2010), who compared the raw score regarding four learners' receptive-productive gap and found interindividual differences even though the gap was evident across all learners. Based on our study's results, it can be argued that not only the receptive-productive gaps differ from one learner to another, the rate of retaining different types of knowledge also displays individuated patterns.

5.4 Patterns suggested by low correlation between corpus-derived variables and test scores suggests complex interaction between variables and learners as well as instruction types

Another finding that might be obscured by group data is how FSs with different properties are acquired across groups receiving different types of instruction.

This section will examine how the FSs' corpus-related and semantic properties, as well as the structural nonequivalence in L1, add to the complexity of how they are acquired.

5.5 Receptive Knowledge level

With regards to Receptive Knowledge, phrasal verbs tend to pose more difficulty for learners in that they are more susceptible to attrition over a period of only 2 weeks. *Touch off* and *bank on* are such examples. While the learners' score on the immediate post-tests reached 7–9 (out of 10), on the delayed post-tests, learners in all groups only scored from 2 to 4 points out of 10. Learners seem to do better with *mull over* and *beef up*, but the scores on the Receptive Knowledge test regarding these items are on the lower end of the spectrum when compared with other FSs. Learners in the SpotDif group did quite well on the delayed posttest question on *beef up and mull over*. As can be inferred from the results of the tests, learners seem not to have much difficulty with the recognizing the meaning of the phrasal verbs, but struggled with recognizing the correct form.

This resonates with Nation's (2001) argument that memorizing the form of new lexical items, even at the receptive knowledge level, is not an easy task for L2 learners. The finding complements that in Verspoor, Schmid and Xu (2012), which shows that the productive use of phrasal verbs is a strong discriminator at levels 4 and 5, the two most advanced levels in their study. Additionally, phrasal verbs do not exist in Mandarin Chinese, i.e., there is no structural equivalence between the learners' L1 and L2, and these verbs are characterized by semantic opaqueness or non-compositionality, i.e., learners cannot derive the meaning of the multiword lexical unit by combining the meaning of individual words. While idioms are also characterized as semantically opaque, their etymology can be explained to students (e.g. *jump the gun, all the rage, short end of the stick*) or can be somewhat predictable based on conceptual near-equivalence between the two languages (e.g. *a pretty penny, have a lock on*). However, there are ambiguous cases with two phrasal verbs of high frequency, *dawn on* and *wind down*, which learners did not have much difficulty with. These two phrasal verbs both have high frequency of more than 1,200 occurrences in CoCA, while the other phrasal verbs occur with less than half of this frequency. It is likely that these learners had encountered these phrasal verbs elsewhere but never had the motivation or need to focus on form. Another reason is that they could have learned the literal meaning of *dawn* (to begin to grow light as the sun rises) and *wind* (as in *wind the clock*), thus could establish a link between form and meaning. In contrast, the prototypical meaning of *touch* and *bank* is unrelated to *touch off* and *bank on*. *Mull* is an extremely infrequent verb (FREQ = 315) and *beef* is much more commonly used as a noun whose denotation has little to do with that of *beef up* (FREQ = 540).

This finding suggests that many phrasal verbs with the main verbs being used with a non-prototypical meaning or an infrequently occurring verb may challenge the durability of instructional effectiveness. In addition to phrasal verbs, *on the books* and *over a barrel* are the two other target FSs learners whose form (but not meaning) struggled with acquiring. Similar to *touch off* and *bank on*, *over a barrel* is characterized by semantic opaqueness, a lack of etymological elaboration during instruction, and a low frequency of both the entire idiom

(FREQ = 81) as well as the key word *barrel* (FREQ = ~7000). *Short end of the stick*, in comparison, while having a lower frequency (FREQ = 69) and lack of semantic transparency, did not pose as much difficulty for learners because the individual words in the idiom are of higher frequency (*short* (FREQ = ~72,000) , *end* (FREQ = ~142,000), *stick* (FREQ = ~21,000), and it was presented to learners in the two TBLT groups with etymological explanation, which has been proven by Boers and his colleagues to be an effective way of teaching idioms (Boers et al. 2004; Lindstromberg and Boers, 2008). Because of this, for these FSs, the effect on students' retention might be less because of TBLT, and more likely the result of cognitive linguistic explanations, or a combination of both. However, it should be noted that the effect is no more significant than other FSs, which were not taught with etymological explanation. *Gloom and doom* (FREQ = 85) was also of the same frequency range with *over the barrel*, but the former is semantically transparent and the rhyming of the key words was probably more conducive to learning.

5.6 Productive Knowledge level

Most target FSs seem not to be as responsive to instruction at the Productive Knowledge level, as opposed to the Receptive Knowledge level, proving that the acquisition of FSs exhibits the same characteristics as that of other lexical items, e.g. as can be seen in Schmitt and Meara (1997) and Webb (2008). Scores for many FSs on the delayed Productive Knowledge post-test fall below 10 out of 30. Such FSs include *at her beck and call, goof off, push the envelope, step up to the plate, touch off, short shrift, over a barrel, mull over, all the rage*, and *bode well*. *Touch off* is the only FS with which no learner scored any points on the delayed post-test. This is in tandem with the finding from the Receptive Knowledge test, where *touch off* is the FS with the lowest score. Similarly, *over a barrel* was successfully recalled by only 3 learners in the Gap-fill group, while the other 27 learners were not able to recall it at all on the delayed post-test. The markedness of *touch off* and *over a barrel* was discussed above. In contrast, learners acquired *at odds with* quite effortlessly, with all learners in all groups scoring close to the highest score possible. Semantic transparency seems to be at play in this case, together with the high frequency of the key word *odd* (FREQ = ~13,000). In addition, *at odds with* speaks to humans' proclivity for dualism or thinking in binary concepts. The finding challenges to some extent that in Verspoor, Schmid and Xu (2012), which renders phrasal verbs and particles, nouns or verbs that receive prepositions or particles, one of the strong discriminators between level 4 and level 5 essays, the two highest levels. It suggests that not all phrasal verbs or particles are equal, and learners may struggle more with some than others because of the semantic characteristics of the chunks, not merely because of the presence of prepositions or particles.

Table 6: Learners' performance in the Productive Knowledge post-tests

	go haywire	have a lock on	at the mercy of	wind down	at her beck and call	saddled with	gloom and doom	short end of the stick	beef up	bank on
PK Im Control	13	2	14	15	6	15	8	9	9	9
PK Im Gapfill	30	23	28	27	22	30	24	24	24	28
PK Im SpotDif	24	20	24	30	15	30	30	18	22	21
PK Del Control	8	2	11	12	4	19	6	3	6	3
PK Del Gapfill	8	10	0	19	8	7	22	9	14	25
PK Del SPotDif	11	6	14	19	7	25	17	15	12	6

	step up to the plate	all the rage	touching off	dawned on	short shrift	push the envelope	old hat	goof off	dig in their heels	drop the ball
PK Im Control	11	7	3	17	13	9	15	13	10	21
PK Im Gapfill	25	27	27	30	28	27	29	30	26	30
PK Im SpotDif	24	25	14	23	23	28	30	18	21	27
PK Del Control	2	3	0	13	3	3	11	5	3	17
PK Del Gapfill	8	11	0	19	8	7	21	9	14	25
PK Del SPotDif	2	5	0	14	3	6	16	5	10	21

	at odds with	in droves	over a barrel	firmly entrenched	muddle through	pretty penny	on the books	mull over	bode well	jump the gun
PK Im Control	26	15	4	11	21	7	2	6	4	21
PK Im Gapfill	28	26	21	30	23	29	29	18	28	30
PK Im SpotDif	27	25	17	26	26	30	28	24	24	27
PK Del Control	26	8	0	18	14	14	3	3	4	9
PK Del Gapfill	23	14	8	11	24	28	23	8	12	27
PK Del SPotDif	20	10	0	11	13	25	19	9	6	21

6 Conclusion

While there has been much research within the realms of SLA on the topic of TBLT, and despite solid theoretical and empirical findings on this topic, not much research has been done on TBLT in classroom contexts (Bygate 2015). This study, therefore, brought SLA and language teaching together in a unique setting of the classroom. It also provides additional evidence of the versatility of TBLT pertaining to the instruction of a less commonly taught and largely neglected linguistic form: formulaic sequences. Such links between the language classroom and the field of SLA, is important as the need for putting theories to use in language teaching is increasing, as well as the need for improving the relevance of instructed SLA theories to teaching practices (Long 2014). The findings from this study lend evidence to the overall effectiveness of TBLT in directing learners' attentional resources to language forms that are not otherwise noticed, and suggest potential facilitating effects of TBLT on acquisition of these multi-word lexical chunks. The study provides evidence supporting the use of TBLT not only with grammatical structures and individual words, but also with formulaic sequences. Both task-based groups outperformed the control group at a statistically significant level, and the Gap-fill group performed best in the Productive Knowledge test and in the Form section of the Receptive Knowledge test.

However, while this study was not designed with complexity theory in mind, one insight from the theory proved important to this study. That insight was the importance of examining results at different levels of granularity, individual-level as well as group-level. In the case of this study, an analysis of individuals' performance demonstrated that the process of developing one's knowledge or and retaining one's knowledge is unique in that different individuals retain, attrite or develop their receptive knowledge and productive knowledge in different ways.

Second language learners have already developed a first language system, which shapes their neural attunement (N. Ellis and Larsen-Freeman 2006). The history of individuals' learning experience, their individual learning styles, and idiosyncratic processing mechanism of external information in the context (i.e. what is provided through instruction) interact with each other to yield different possibilities in learners' developmental paths (Larsen-Freeman 2006). From a complexity theory view, what already exists in the interlanguage system of a learner acts as a resource or retards further development. This explains the difficulty of our participants' learning phrasal verbs, when the structural non-equivalence (first language influence) is combined with semantic opaqueness, non-prototypical meaning of the key word, and low frequency (features of language forms and meaning).

The complexity and interindividual variability of the data when we disaggregate them shows that learning FSs, like the learning of other skills or knowledge system, is not a one-size-fits-all situation. Not only did we find interindividual variability in the data, we also found intraindividual differences in the sense that both levels of knowledge (receptive vs. productive) did not develop within learners in the same way. While one type of knowledge regressed, the other type of knowledge may be retained or even advanced. From a complexity theory perspective, difference and variation must be the center of SLA research, not a universal learner (Larsen-Freeman and Cameron 2008: 156).

An implication drawn from this study is to make more complex the causality between instruction and acquisition (used in the sense of "development"). At the group level, instruction and acquisition seem to be in a unidirectional relationship, with instruction being the key variable leading to the success in acquisition. However, when data are disaggregated and the messy little details are revealed, findings suggest that the effectiveness of instruction is mediated by other variables, such as the semantic and structural properties of the target FSs, and variables related to learners' experiential histories and cognitive capacities.

References

Bishop, Hugh. 2004. The effect of typographical salience on the lookup and comprehension of unknown formulaic sequences. In Norbert Schmitt, *Formulaic sequences: Acquisition, processing and use*, 227–248. Amsterdam/Philadelphia: John Benjamins.

Boers, Frank, Murielle Demecheleer & June Eyckmans. 2004. Etymological elaboration as a strategy for learning figurative idioms. In Paul Bogaards & Batia Laufer (eds.), *Vocabulary in a second language: Selection, acquisition and testing*, 53–78. Amsterdam/Philadelphia: John Benjamins.

Boers, Frank, June Eyckmans, Jenny Kappel, Hélène Stengers & Murielle Demecheleer. 2006. Formulaic sequences and perceived oral proficiency: Putting a lexical approach to the test. *Language Teaching Research* 10(3). 245–261.

Bybee, Joan. L. & Clay Beckner. 2010. Usage-based theory. In Bernd Heine and Heiko Narrog (eds.), *The Oxford handbook of linguistic analysis*, 827–856. Oxford: Oxford University Press.

Bygate, Martin. 2015. Sources, developments and directions of task-based language teaching. *The Language Learning Journal*. 1–20.

Doughty, Catherine & Teresa Pica. 1986. Information gap tasks: An aid to second language acquisition? *TESOL Quarterly* 20. 305–325.

Ellis, Nick C. 2008. Usage-based and form-focused language acquisition: The associative learning of constructions, learned-attention, and the limited L2 endstate. In Peter Robinson and Nick Ellis (eds.), *Handbook of cognitive linguistics and second language acquisition*, 372–405. London/New York: Routledge

Ellis, Nick C. & Diane Larsen-Freeman. 2006. Language emergence: Implications for applied linguistics. Introduction to the special issue. *Applied Linguistics* 27(4). 558–589.

Ellis, Nick C., Rita Simpson-Vlach & Carson Maynard. 2008. Formulaic language in native and second language speakers: Psycholinguistics, corpus linguistics, and TESOL. *TESOL Quarterly* 42(3). 375–396.

Ellis, Nick C. 2001. Memory for language. In Peter Robinson (ed.), *Cognition and second language instruction*, 33–68. Cambridge: Cambridge University Press.

Ellis, Nick C. 2003. Constructions, chunking, and connectionism: The emergence of second language structure. In Catherine J. Doughty & Michael H. Long (eds.), *The handbook of second language acquisition*, 63–103. Oxford: Blackwell.

Ellis, Rod & Xien He. 1999. The roles of modified input and output in the incidental acquisition of word meanings. *Studies in Second Language Acquisition* 21. 285–301.

Ellis, Rod, Yoshihiro Tanaka & Asako Yamazaki. 1994. Classroom interaction, comprehension and the acquisition of L2 word meanings. *Language Learning* 44(3). 449–491.

Erman, Britt. 2009a. Beyond the single word: Collocations in the writings of native speakers and first-term university students of English. *Gothenburg Studies in English* 96. 23–36.

Erman, Britt. 2009b. Formulaic language from a learner perspective: What the learner needs to know. In Roberta Corrigan, Edith A. Moravcsik, Hamid Ouali, & Kathleen M. Wheatley (eds.), *Formulaic language Vol 2. – Acquisition, loss, psychological reality and functional explanations*, 323–346. Philadelphia/Amsterdam: John Benjamins.

Foster, Pauline. 2001. Rules and routines: A consideration of their role in the task-based language production of native and non-native speakers. In Martin Bygate, Peter Skehan & Merrill Swain (eds.), *Researching pedagogic tasks: Second language learning, teaching and testing*, 75–94. Harlow: Longman

Gass, Susan M. & María José Alvarez Torres. 2005. Attention when? An investigation of the ordering effect of input and interaction. *Studies in Second Language Acquisition* 27(1). 1–31.

Gerard, Jessica E. 2007. *The reading of formulaic sequences in a native and non-native language: An eye movement analysis*. Tucson, AZ: The University of Arizona dissertation.

Hsu, Jeng-yih T. 2010. The effects of collocation instruction on the reading comprehension and vocabulary learning of college English majors. *Asian EFL Journal* 12(1). 47–87.

Jones, Martha & Sandra Haywood. 2004. Facilitating the acquisition of formulaic sequences. In Norbert Schmitt (ed.), *Formulaic sequences*, 269–300. Amsterdam/Philadelphia: John Benjamins.

Kim, Youjin. 2008. The contribution of collaborative and individual tasks to the acquisition of L2 vocabulary. *The Modern Language Journal* 92(1). 114–130.

Kowal, Maria & Merrill Swain. 1994. Using collaborative language production tasks to promote students' language awareness. *Language Awareness* 3. 73–93.

Larsen-Freeman, Diane. 2002. Making sense of frequency. *Studies in Second Language Acquisition* 24(2). 275–285.

Larsen-Freeman, Diane. 2006. The emergence of complexity, fluency and accuracy in the oral and written production of five Chinese learners of English. *Applied Linguistics* 27(4). 590–619.

Larsen-Freeman, Diane & Lynne Cameron. 2008. *Complex systems and applied linguistics*. Oxford: Oxford University Press.

Laufer, Batia. 2005. Instructed second language vocabulary learning: The fault in the 'default hypothesis'. In Alex Housen & Michel Pierrard (eds.), *Investigations in instructed second language acquisition*, 311–329. Berlin & New York: Mouton de Gruyter.

Laufer, Batia & Nany Girsai. 2008. The use of native language for improving second language vocabulary: An exploratory study. In Anat Stavans & Irit Kupferberg (eds.), *Studies in language and language education*, 261–275. Jerusalem: The Hebrew University Magnes Press.

Laufer, Batia & Jan Hustijn. 2001. Incidental vocabulary acquisition in the second language: The construct of task-induced involvement. *Applied Linguistics* 22(1). 1–36.

Laufer, Batia & Tina Waldman. 2011. Verb-noun collocations in second language writing: A corpus analysis of learners' English. *Language Learning* 61(2). 647–672.

Liao, Yan & Yoshinori J. Fukuta. 2004. Avoidance of phrasal verbs: The case of Chinese learners of English. *Language Learning* 54(2). 193–226.

Lindstromberg, Seth & Frank Boers. 2008. The mnemonic effect of noticing alliteration in lexical chunks. *Applied Linguistics* 29(2). 200–222.

Loewen, Shawn & Jenefer Philp. 2006. Recasts in the adult English L2 classroom: Characteristics, explicitness, and effectiveness. *The Modern Language Journal* 90. 536–556.

Long, Michael H. 1981. Input, interaction, and second language acquisition. *Annals of the New York Academy of Sciences* 379. 259–278.

Long, Michael H. 1985. A role for instruction in second language acquisition: Task-based language teaching. In Kenneth Hyltenstam & Manfred Pienemann (eds.), *Modeling and assessing second language development*, 77–99. Clevedon, UK: Multilingual Matters.

Long, Michael H. 1991. Focus on form: A design feature in language teaching methodology. In Kees de Bot, Ralph B. Ginsberg & Claire Kramsch (eds.), *Foreign language research in cross-cultural perspective*, 39–52. Amsterdam/Philadelphia: John Benjamins.

Long, Michael H. 2014. *Second language acquisition and task-based language teaching*. West Sussex, UK: Wiley-Blackwell.

Molenaar, Peter C. M. 2008. On the implications of the classical ergodic theorems: Analysis of developmental processes has to focus on intra-individual variation. *Developmental Psychobiology* 50. 60–69.

Moon, Rosamund. 1998. *Fixed expressions and idioms in English: A corpus-based approach*. Oxford: Clarendon Press.

Nation, Paul. 2001. *Learning vocabulary in another language*. Cambridge: Cambridge University Press.

Nattinger, James R. & Jeanette S. DeCarrico. 1992. *Lexical phrases and language teaching*. Oxford: Oxford University Press.

Nunan, David. 1989. *Designing tasks for the communicative classroom*. Cambridge: Cambridge University Press.

Paribakht, Sima T. & Marjorie Wesche. 1997. Vocabulary enhancement activities and reading for meaning in second language vocabulary acquisition. In James Coady & Thomas Huckin (eds.), *Second language vocabulary acquisition: A rationale for pedagogy*, 174–199. Cambridge: Cambridge University Press.

Pawley, Andrew and Frances Hodgetts Syder. 1983. Two puzzles for linguistic theory: Nativelike selection and nativelike fluency. In Jack C. Richards & R. W. Schmidt (Ees.) *Language and communication*, 191–226. New York: Longman.

Pica, Teresa, Hyun-Sook Kang & Shannon Sauro. 2006. Information gap tasks: Their multiple roles and contributions to interaction research methodology. *Studies in Second Language Acquisition* 28. 301–338.

Qi, Yan & Yanren Ding. 2011. Use of formulaic sequences in monologues of Chinese EFL learners. *System* 39(2). 164–174.

Read, John & Paul Nation. 2004. Measurement of formulaic sequences. In Norbert Schmitt (ed.), *Formulaic sequences: Acquisition, processing, and use*, 23–35. Amsterdam/Philadelphia: John Benjamins.

Robinson, Peter. 2011. Task-based language learning: A review of issues. *Language Learning*, 61(Suppl.1). 1–36.

Rott, Susanne. 2009. The effect of awareness-raising on the use of formulaic constructions. In Roberta Corrigan, Edith A. Moravcsik, Hamid Ouali, & Kathleen M. Wheatley (eds.), 405–422. Philadelphia/Amsterdam: John Benjamins.
Schmitt, Norbert & Ronald Carter. 2004. Formulaic sequences in action: An introduction. In Norbert Schmitt (ed.). *Formulaic sequences: Acquisition, processing and use*, 1–22. Amsterdam/Philadelphia: John Benjamins.
Schmitt, Norbert & Paul Meara. 1997. Researching vocabulary through a word knowledge framework. *Studies in Second Language Acquisition* 19. 17–36
Schmitt, Norbert & Geoffrey Underwood. 2004. Exploring the processing of formulaic sequences through a self-paced reading task. In Norbert Schmitt (ed.), *Formulaic sequences: Acquisition, processing, and use*, 173–189. Philadelphia: John Benjamins.
Sinclair, John M. 1991. *Corpus, concordance, collocations*. Oxford: Oxford University Press.
Tomasello, Michael. 2003. *Constructing a language: A usage-based theory of language acquisition*. Cambridge, MA: Harvard University Press.
Underwood, Geoffrey, Norbert Schmitt & Adam Galpin. 2004. The eyes have it: An eye-movement study into the processing of formulaic sequences. In Norbert Schmitt (ed.), *Formulaic sequences: Acquisition, processing, and use*, 153–172. Philadelphia: John Benjamins.
van Geert, Paul. 2011. The contribution of complex dynamic systems to development. *Child Development Perspectives* 5. 273–278.
van Geert, Paul & Henderien Steenbeek. 2005. Explaining after by before: Basic aspects of a dynamic systems approach to the study of development. *Developmental Review* 25(3–4), 408–442.
Verspoor, Marjolijn, Wander Lowie & Marijn Van Dijk. 2008. Variability in second language development from a dynamic systems perspective. *The Modern Language Journal* 92(2). 214–231.
Verspoor, Marjolijn, Monica S. Schmid & Xiaoyan Xu. 2012. A dynamic usage based perspective on L2 writing. *Journal of Second Language Writing* 21(3). 239–263
Webb, Stuart. 2008. Receptive and productive vocabulary sizes of L2 learners. *Studies in Second Language Acquisition* 30. 79–95.
Wood, David. 2009. Effects of focused instruction of formulaic sequences on fluent expression in second language narratives: A case study. *Canadian Journal of Applied Linguistics* 12(1). 39–57.
Wray, Alison. 2002. *Formulaic language and the lexicon*. Cambridge: Cambridge University Press.
Wray, Alison. 2008. *Formulaic language: Pushing the boundaries*. Oxford: Oxford University Press.
Wulff, Stefanie. 2008. *Rethinking idiomaticity: A usage-based approach*. London/New York: Continuum.

Claire Kramsch and Jean-Paul Narcy-Combes
9 From Social Tasks to Language Development: Coping with Historicity and Subjectivity

1 Introduction

The initial rationale of Task Based Language Teaching (TBLT) was to provide language learners not with decontextualized assignments to practice the rules of grammar and vocabulary, but real-world tasks that would require them to abide by the norms of use enacted by native speakers and native institutions like schools, families and workplaces. "Task-based" also applies to other fields of research, as exemplified by the concept of task-based organization (Garicano and Wu 2010). Their dominant ideologies are clearly very different if some of the psycho-social tenets are identical. Indeed, Prabhu (1987) had noticed that his students could learn language just as easily with a non-linguistic problem as when they were concentrating on linguistic questions. So tasks were meant to be neither based on linguistic problems, nor on school-like assignments since: "... by 'task' is meant the hundred and one things people *do* in everyday life, at work, at play, and in between. 'Tasks' are the things people will tell you they do if you ask them and they are not applied linguists" (Long 1985: 89)". In addition to that, we were reminded that:
1. "classroom learning should be connected with students' personal experiences, or classroom teaching should be authentic." (Samuda and Bygate 2008: 20).
2. "If task-based teaching is to make the shift from theory to practice it will be necessary to go beyond the psycholinguistic rationale (...) and to address the contextual factors that ultimately determine what materials and procedures teachers choose." (Ellis 2003: 337).

Clearly, this was an ambitious rationale, and we may wonder if the theoretical and teaching background was propitious to reaching such goals. In this chapter, we first review the original and the subsequent theoretical underpinnings of TBLT, we then examine on one concrete example what an ecologically conceived task-based pedagogy would look like.

Claire Kramsch, University of California at Berkeley
Jean-Paul Narcy-Combes, Sorbonne nouvelle

2 Theoretical background: Towards an ecological approach to TBLT

TBLT started in the 1980s when scholars like Breen and Candlin (1980) argued that communicative language teaching should focus on both grammar and meaning and that communication was about the expression, interpretation and negotiation of intended meanings. Since the 1990s, TBLT has moved from an emphasis on negotiation of meaning to an investigation of a number of issues related to form-focused instruction (Long 1991). It relies on a myriad of learning theories, as exemplified in Shehadeh and Coombe (2012) covering cognitive theory (noticing, focus on form, error correction, explicit teaching), theories of information (input) processing, neo-Vygotskian sociocultural theory and interactionist Second Language Acquisition (SLA), among others. TBLT is both the result of soundly based research in applied linguistics theory and an approach to teaching practice in which focus on form exemplifies a rule-based view of language production and assessment which is mainly normative (ibidem).

In the last twenty years, some of these positions have been questioned. Advances in neuropsychology (Damasio 1994; Pavlenko 2005; Schumann 1997), cognitive science (Lakoff and Johnson 2003; Varela 1993), and the study of bi- and multilingualism (Gonzalez-Lloret and Ortega 2014; Herdina and Jessner 2006; Ortega 2009, 2011; Ortega et al. 2013) have shown that the mind:
- is embodied, not just embrained (Damasio 1994);
- operates in a non-linear, complex way (de Bot et al. 2013);
- thinks relationally – analogically and metaphorically (Hofstadter and Sander 2013; Lakoff and Johnson 2003).

The interplay of emotions, perception and cognition makes it impossible to ignore affects and subjectivity. Perceptions are conditioned by past experiences: an individual's history and that of their environment cannot be overlooked as they may lead to misconstruction of what is understood : *"Every act in every moment is the emergent product of context and history, and no component has causal priority"* (Thelen 2005: 271).

In terms of language, humans use translanguaging (Williams and Hammarberg 1998) (both as code-switching and as a switching of modes and modalities, i.e., genres, registers, styles, and voices) (Canagarajah 2012; Cenoz and Gorter 2011) to construct and convey meaning.

As a consequence, it is now understood that:

- cognitive development is necessarily cultural (Troadec 2007) and discourse-based (Gavins 2007), and knowledge has been described as resulting from a social construction (Berger and Luckmann 1966);
- action and thought, and/or action and discourse cannot be separated (Schurmans 2001);
- expectations need to be destabilized (de Bot et al. 2013) if learners need to alter their habitus (Bourdieu 1980) and to engage in a process of accommodation after initial assimilation (Piaget 1970);
- becoming conscious of an activity is the result of the interaction between individuals and their environment. It emerges from the pooling of their interpretations (Gibbs 2001);
- learning is performing (Fisher 2012), adapting one's ways of doing things as the activity unfolds in order to integrate what is new. It is not made possible by a pre-organized course of action, such as pre-programmed tasks.

So, living in society implies becoming familiar with the ways social activities are performed and with the tools used by members of that society. Learning cannot be restricted to the classroom, learners have to encounter « real » people in all their moral and social complexities (see the example below).

As far as SLA is concerned:
- Connectionism, exemplified in Dynamic systems theory (de Bot et al 2013) and emergentism, which takes a processual approach to linguistic and cognitive phenomena, holds that discourse is more than the simple sum of its lexical, syntactic and morphological components (Ellis, N.C. 1998; O'Grady 2010). Syntax, lexis, and phonology are parallel processes that work in such a way that information can be dealt with effectively, quickly and economically and that communication is facilitated.
- The emergence of language is non-linear, not totally predictable among individuals, and regression is likely. Training can facilitate development (De Bot et al. 2013) but it cannot program it. This may put into question pre-organized course sequences.
- Socioeconomic and identity issues have to be factored in. Multilingualism is an asset in higher income families and a drawback in lower income families and also depending on whether the languages involved are highly valued or not (Bündgens Kosten and Elsner 2014; Genesee 2007). Loyalty to their group may cause some children to refuse institutional education (Meirieu 2000).

This section clearly stresses the fact that teaching will be effective only if 'freedom to learn' and learner reflexivity and responsibility go hand in hand with respect of who the learners are, where they come from and where they would like to go, and if a compromise is found between institutional demands and the learners' personal objectives and values. Furthermore, if we apply the construct of transductive (indissociable) relation (Simondon 1989) to applied linguistics, we may postulate that there is such a link between discourse, content(s) and culture(s). As a consequence teaching "language" means designing courses in which, discourse, "content(s)" and culture(s) are taken in consideration in a way which may put into question the more traditional interpretations of TBLT.

3 A controversial episode

After having staked out the theoretical foundations of an ecological approach to TBLT which takes care of the relationships between individuals and their environments, we now turn to a particularly controversial episode in a content-based class in order to measure the principles outlined above against the hard realities of the academic world.

The following recent case of academic literacy caused quite a bit of debate on the "teach-net" listserv of the teaching faculty at a large research university in the Western United States. The instructor of Econ 1, a required beginning course for some 720 undergraduate students majoring in economics, had given her students as their first assignment of the semester to write a short essay about some "growth-enhancing strategy" employed in any country, in any time period. The point was for them to think about the applicability of one economic growth-enhancing strategy to a very poor country today and to cite their sources. The essay, which combined discourse, content and culture, was to be maximum one page or 400 words, whichever came first. We have little information on the learning environment, however this was an individual assignment, turned in by students to their teaching assistants, who gave it an individual grade.

One Chinese-American student, who had arrived in the U.S. from China at age 17, searched the internet and wrote an essay about Adolf Hitler's economic policies, i.e., how Hitler's growth-enhancing strategies helped Germany effectively deal with unemployment during the Great Depression through the development of the road/transportation system and through wage and price controls (see full text of student's essay in the Appendix). The student specifically added:

> Hitler was ... clear with his intention and announced his plans to reorganize the nation with his National Socialist principles, thus uplifting spirits and ensuring positive thoughts and less resistance to his plans. As long as prices remained stable and there were more jobs created to ensure efficiency in production, the economics could continue to grow

The teaching assistant felt uneasy about this essay and contacted the instructor who posted the following note on the teach-net listserv of the university, hoping to get advice from other faculty members:

> [The student] cites her source and does a fine job on the essay. But it struck me as odd that someone would write about Hitler, Nazi Germany, and how Hitler's National Socialist principles "uplifted spirits and ensured positive thoughts." It's all written as if Hitler was a great leader who did great things, with no mention of anything negative. The source she cites is from the "institute for historical review" which, according to Wikipedia (https://en.wikipedia.org/wiki/Institute_for_Historical_Review), is a center of the holocaust-denial movement. According to Wikipedia "The Institute for Historical Review (IHR), founded in 1978, is an organization primarily devoted to publishing and promoting pseudo-historical books and essays that deny established facts concerning the Nazi genocide of Jews".
>
> Choices.
>
> [1] Let it go. It's 3 points out of 500, she's 1 of 720 students. Perhaps she is simply naive and googled "transportation growth-enhancing" and grabbed this hit.
>
> [2] Write her an email. And say what? Not the first thing that came to my mind, clearly. I haven't a clue whether she tripped on this and thought it looked legit, or if she is a holocaust-denier. I don't want to approach this as if she knew what she was doing. If she did, I can only imagine the arsenal she could deploy (starting with a publicity machine funded elsewhere) in response to what I say.
>
> [3] Is there a third choice?

The Econ 1 instructor admitted that "there is nothing on the site, aside from the content, that signals 'oooh, not a real history site!', and that she had to google "Institute for Historical Review" to figure it out". But what did she actually figure out? Were there any norms the student had to discover? Which is the legitimate version of History regarding Hitler's economic policies? The instructor sensed that she owes this student a one-on-one chat, but she is not sure of what the student's expectations are, nor whether she can really fault the student for not meeting the expectations of American readers. After all, she might feel that Econ 1 is about economics, not politics, and in that respect the student has fulfilled the task. Is it her responsibility to alert the student that even if Hitler's economic policies were successful, they are not a "legitimate" example of "growth-enhancing strategies" because of their national socialist origin? Or because of Hitler's later anti-semitic policies? Isn't this going beyond the assigned task?

There are many intriguing aspects to this case. On the face of it, students were to consult real-world sources on the Internet, check their sources by cross-examining them (and in this assignment it was OK to have only one source given the brevity of the essay), and cite their source according to the expectations of an academic research paper. In all this, one could say that this non-native English speaking Chinese student conformed to the Econ 1 discourse required. The essay is written in grammatically and lexically correct and idiomatic English and it shows mastery of the genre. The author does not plagiarize and she responds to the prompt accurately and comprehensively. In many ways, TBLT would call the task outcome "successful". But was it legitimate? The reactions of some of the respondents are instructive in this regard.

The first, from a university librarian, points out that "this is a good opportunity to teach this student, and others about evaluating sources according to academic standard. Yes, it's only one student. And yes, it's not many points. But if we can't graduate students who can critically evaluate the sources of the information they use, what are we doing?"

The second is from a professor of Public Policy, who suggests reminding the student that using such controversial sources is likely to be viewed "with hostility and resentment by many... and that she might want to dissociate herself from them so people don't get the wrong idea". The third is from a Japanese foreign language instructor who strongly feels it is the "obligation for university faculty to educate youth to contribute to world peace" and thus to enlighten this student as to who started WWII.

The response of the librarian is professional and scientific: Students should check their sources ! But the sources cited in the article (Weber 2011; 2012) are bona fide sources, such as this one by eminent Harvard economist Galbraith who wrote in *Money*: *Whence it came, where it went* (1975):

> "The elimination of unemployment in Germany during the Great Depression without inflation – and with initial reliance on essentially civilian activities – was a signal accomplishment. It has rarely been praised and not much remarked. The notion that Hitler could do no good extends to his economics as it does, more plausibly, to all else." (p. 237)

The problem doesn't seem to lie in the sources, but in the expectations/perceptions of legitimacy of any source associated in some way with an organization (the Institute for Historical Review) that is said by Wikipedia to promote anti-semitic sentiments. So even if the facts reported are accurate, was it OK for the student to report them without any mention of their political origin, namely socialism and nationalism? Was it the moral duty of the student to mention in a one-page essay that economics are inseparable from ideology?

The Public Policy professor seems to believe that some facts are ideologically and politically motivated such as national socialist economic policies while others are not. He seems to suggest that the former have to be bracketed by some distancing device such as quotation marks or disclaimer clauses, whereas the latter can be stated in direct speech through the voice of the author. But in this case the author is a Chinese student for whom Adolf Hitler might be just another historical figure with a nationalist and socialist agenda that she doesn't feel the need to put in quotation marks.

The response by the Japanese instructor shows yet another facet of the conflicted reception of this essay in an American context. For her, this period of history is painfully connected to WWII. She reacts viscerally to a war that destroyed her country and that has become as demonized in Japan as the Holocaust has become demonized in the U.S. And she immediately sees here a teachable moment of urgent moral and political importance. But how far does an economic problem-set have to take into consideration its moral and political context if it was not required by the task?

For applied linguists this example, although not taken from a language class but from a content-based introductory economics course, is a dramatic illustration of why TBLT needs to go beyond its original mandate to design tasks that approximate the real-world and take an ecological stance that engages students with larger issues of time, space and ethical responsibility (Kramsch 2002). First, an ecologically valid TBLT needs to factor in the temporal dimension of discourse. The student did not pick up on the fact that many of the sources cited in the original were written at a time when the later Nazi policies and crimes committed during the Holocaust were not yet perpetrated or not widely known. Some discourses that were (politically) appropriate in the early thirties have become totally inappropriate since then. Second, TBLT needs to factor in the spatial dimension of discourse. The same essay written today in Chinese for a Chinese professor at a Chinese university might get a different response, as Hitler is just another historical figure, not the demonized dictator he has become in the American moral imagination. Finally, an ecologically oriented TBLT has to deal with the issue of moral responsibility. The fact that this essay was titled "Problem set 1" and that this Econ 1 course saw it as its mission to help students solve real-world economic problems made it particularly difficult for students to imagine that economic tasks might have a moral and political dimension. Even more difficult to imagine was that perfect English grammar and vocabulary were no guarantee of social and moral acceptability at an American university. Nor, we might add, is it reducible to merely "evaluating your sources."

Perhaps the student lacked the historical and political consciousness necessary to meet the expectations of her American readers. Indeed, her language was correct, but her discourse did not correspond to the subjectivity and history of her Jewish-American teaching assistant, who alerted the professor to the student's unorthodox essay. The professor in turn, like the other faculty who responded on the teach-net listserv, shared the American taboo on Hitler and his policies. However, while the student needed to know how to shape her discourse to meet American expectations, her instructor too needed to know how to

read a student discourse that was factually correct, but politically incorrect. For this, both instructor and student needed to become aware of:
- The historical taboo on anything related to the Third Reich at U.S. institutions
- The Wikipedia information that the IHR is discredited because of its anti-semitic stance
- The fact that not all the sources cited in this article are *ipso facto* discredited and that Wikipedia, too, is fallible.
- The fact that scientific evidence is sometimes tainted by politics
- It was important to check each one of the sources cited in the article as to its date of publication and its "discursive voice".
- Both instructor and student had to reflect on their respective subject positions as raised and educated in countries with potentially different views on History.

4 Re-framing the pedagogic challenge

One would be tempted to say that the Econ 1 course is not a language course. However for the student involved, if we refer to the construct of transductive relation mentioned above, we would say that it is a Content and Language Integrated Learning (CLIL) course at an advanced level (B2/C1 of European Framework of Reference for Languages) since she is not a native user of English. The controversy is definitely connected to history, subjectivity and culture(s). This apparently is not taken in consideration, so who the students are and how they work is not deemed important, and apparently only the product matters. Though the student involved seems to be able to write very adequate English, no trace is probably available of how she actually wrote her assignment.

One may wonder whether some of the problems that have just been described would have been avoided in another type of learning environment and in a different approach to the task.

In the following, after exchanging our views in a dialogue reverberating our different positions, we attempt to reframe the pedagogic challenge presented by the Chinese student's essay by discussing (1) a learner-centered approach to Content and Language Learning Environments, and (2) a flexible approach to TBLT.

4.1 A learner-centred approach to language and content learning environments

Computer Mediated Communication (CMC) (see Lamy and Hampel 2007 for instance) has been shown to lead to creating virtual/physical learning communities. Learners can collect and organize their learning materials following their teachers' instructions while relying on peer mediation, feedback and collaboration as well as on teacher instruction. Research shows that interactions with native speakers, peers and tutors are more effective than teacher instruction in finding collocations and terms that are sociolinguistically appropriate in a given context (DuFon 2010). All this was not implemented in the Econ 1 course: there was no tutor feedback during the writing of the task, nor any collaborative substitute that can be just as effective. The effectiveness of peer mediation and feedback is exemplified in O'Brien (2004), or Storch (2013). Problem-solving, meaning and form negotiation can be more effective in collaborative tasks than in traditional classroom interactions (Pica, Kang and Sauro 2006). CMC learning environments are now directly connected to the real world and learners may « meet » real users of the language and specialists of the disciplinary content they learn, whereas in the economics course, students apparently wrote their assignments in isolation. Transmission of knowledge is replaced by flexible and adaptive, collaborative, situated and distributed co-construction of knowledge (Hutchins 1995; Vygotsky 1962), and this was not the case in the course. These numerical environments can either complement or replace physical environments.

The organization of all learning environments is context-dependent (ideologies, cultural habits, expectations, needs and of course means will be taken into account), and learners coming from other contexts may find it difficult to adapt (as shown in our example). Research results show that:

Digital identity and socialization develop without any specific difficulty and roles/postures and self-esteem do not pose any particular problem (Lamy and Hampel 2007). Misunderstanding and cultural problems are less risky as they can be decoded and analyzed easily (Catroux 2006; Chi and Derivry-Plard 2009; Lamy and Hampel 2007) which might have sensitized participants in Econ 1 to the arising problem sooner and reduced the resulting perplexity. Empowerment and responsibility for learning result from different mutual expectations between learners and tutors (ibidem).

In the controversial episode, learners were isolated. Their apparent autonomy did not help to make them responsible since they had no say in the evaluation process. The discussion of the problematic issues raised was carried out between academics in the absence of exchanges with the students. The tutor may have met with the student to discuss the issues, but only once the paper had been turned in. The work was clearly product-oriented while the issues were connected to the process of writing such a paper.

One may object that most instructors at American institutions make use of electronic forums, blackboards, chatrooms and the like to encourage their students to discuss the readings or their lecture notes. They often even make such postings a formal feature of the course and the students can get credit for writing and responding to others' postings online. In smaller classes, these postings are to be read and responded to before a given class each week and they are then further discussed in small groups in class. Participation in these forums generally accounts for 10% of the final grade. However such use of forums is one form of mediation which falls short of what CMC and TBLT would like to offer, as exchanges on specific spaces for collaborative work should be more precisely connected to actually negotiating the construction of the tasks.

There is no denying that peer and/or tutor mediation becomes a real challenge when ethical values (plagiarism for instance) and cultural values (contributions reflecting either the learner's habitus or stereotypical views) are concerned or when pragmatic difficulties arise. These problems require a deeper dialogical reflection (Bakhtin 1981) which collaborative work may provide, especially if the community is culturally diverse (see also Lamy and Hampel 2007), and teacher or tutor mediation will prove necessary, and consequently they will need to be trained to do so. Indeed in our example, the Chinese student's peers might have been able to point out a problem, but not in terms that would really help the student who would have had to turn to the tutor. Such a way of working seems more effective than the direct or post-task teacher intervention of our example; it can indeed lead to the critique and reconstruction of values and expectations. In our controversial episode, one may postulate that peer mediation would have sensitized the writer to what was controversial in her position and made students and teacher aware that economic facts are also historical facts that can be interpreted from many different perspectives indeed, it is sometimes impossible (and unethical) to separate epistemological and moral values, even in courses that seem to be teaching only objective, factual knowledge.

The problem of large number of students in class can be raised: what to do in an ideological learning environment where economics is presented as having nothing to do with politics and where with some 720 students in a freshman introductory course in Econ 1 the instructor may have neither the time nor the resources to discuss ethical questions in online forums? An ethically-minded professor of chemistry discussed in a class of 500 students the Bhopal disaster of 1984 in India, in which 3800 people died of a gas leak at the pesticide plant of the Union Carbide Corporation. The instructor had each student at the end of the class turn to his/her neighbor to discuss the ethical question he had written up on the blackboard: "Was Union Carbide responsible for the gas leak and what should it have done to compensate the families?" and then calling on individual students to voice their opinion or tallying students' responses through their clickers. Though this made the class more interactive and actually established a dialogue between the professor and the students, ethical questions rarely have yes/no answers and such a pedagogic task might not have been suitable for such a complex issue as the one exemplified in section 3. One may also add that this communicative approach technique may improve the situation, but it remains a pedagogic activity, not a task with a clear measurable social outcome for each student.

Other solutions to some of the above-mentioned problems have been researched. Learning conditions may be radically changed to adapt to the varying origins and needs of the learners.

Such a course could certainly have a different organization. The 720 students could be divided into small work groups who could collaboratively work together and produce either group assignments, or part collective and part personal assignments, and have regular meetings with the tutors (see McAllister et al 2012 for a similar TBLT organization). The collaboration would make it possible to highlight likely content, discourse/language or cultural problems and sensitize each learner to whether they need or not the mediation of the tutor to overcome their difficulties. Resource centres could be made available to help students who need some support both in terms of contents and/or of discourse/language (see Brudermann 2010). If all the assignments were published on, say, a blog, the controversial ones would certainly raise a debate among students, that would have to be mediated by the course tutor who would then have to admit that history, philosophy, social sciences and language studies are all linked!

4.2 A flexible approach to CLIL-oriented TBLT

The organization of the course does not need to be rigidly pre-planned nor linear but to be constantly adapted to emerging demands and the constraints of the curriculum. In a flexible conception of a task-based approach (Bertin et al. 2010; McAllister et al. 2012), the tutor-learner relationship is at the centre of the learning environment. The theme and content of the sequences are determined by the curriculum and justified to the students, but preferably negotiated with them: in some university courses, the students actually determine what the contents of the course should be and confront their views with the course tutor and then a scientifically viable compromise is reached (Narcy-Combes and Narcy-Combes 2014).

A macro task, initially social if possible but often realistic in the more traditional school settings, can be proposed to the learners. A social task has a real effect in the outside world or actually affects the group or the individual learner, a realistic task pretends to have one, as a consequence, an academic content task may be considered a social task. Collaborative tasks are preferable especially if the outcome can bear traces of each participant's activity. (1) If this initial task is validated, i.e., has reached its goal, then another social/realistic task follows suit; (2) when difficulties arise, micro (training) tasks are suggested until the macro task can be performed. Micro tasks will vary according to the specific needs of each learner as revealed by the social tasks. They can take place at any time during the course of a given social/macro task and a virtual resource centre can be implemented, which will help cater to individual needs (see Brudermann 2010 and http://www.taskbasedenglish.eu/useful-links/ for the actual online resource centre). This approach can be applied to the learning of disciplinary content.

Follow-up and assessment of the various tasks are carried out at different levels (the learners themselves and outside participants, the course tutor and the institution), in order to maintain the social value of the tasks and to restrict avoidance strategies linked to simulations that have no true social outcome (Narcy-Combes 2005). In our controversial episode, as far as assessment is concerned, power remained with the instructors.

All TBLT features and phases mentioned in Ellis (2003) or in Park (2012), for instance, are observable in such learning environments but in a random order. Research results (Bozhinova et al. 2016; McAllister et al. 2012; Brudermann 2010) show this type of work leads to developments that (1) satisfactorily meet institutional demands, (2) compensate for the unspecific objectives of some courses, and (3) can be adapted to the different learning cultures.

Belonging to a « real » community of discourse seems to have a positive influence on the motivation to participate in the task and negotiate the norms expected. School-like tasks or tasks confined to the school environment do not seem to trigger the same implication when social needs are not immediate (Catroux 2006; Chi and Derivry-Plard 2009; Lamy and Hampel 2007; Narcy-Combes and Narcy-Combes 2014). Such tasks have positive effects on how individuals face what is new or different and reduce teacher interference. Critical episodes like the one we have discussed reflect the social and subjective construction of knowledge (see section 1). They offer a vital challenge involving the students, the faculty and their relation to the dominant ideology, and, as said above, no clear cut ethical solution can be envisaged. The learning environments and tasks we advocate give more responsibility to the learners in their construction of knowledge and may help maintain the complexity and the potentially damaging relational effects of such episodes at a more manageable level.

5 Discussion: The ecology of task in moral and political practice

In this chapter, we have attempted to revisit and broaden the notion of task and TBLT. Instead of focusing exclusively on linguistic, social and institutional behaviors, TBLT should be embedded into an ecology of learning whose "social space" is also a "symbolic space", i.e., a space of symbolic struggle to impose a definition of the real world of tasks and behaviors in a relational economy of space and time (Bourdieu 1994:14–29). It is in that respect that TBLT should start with the expectations of learners based on their past experiences of interaction with various fields. They have "memorized" these experiences in their habitus, they (re)construct them at each interaction and give meaning to their lives by a constant search for relationality between people and events. The historicity of the learners' experiences is constituted by a congruence or divergence between their subjective memories/ projections and the symbolic order of institutions. But it is also constituted by their interaction with the expectations of their teachers who may have different subjectivities and historicities.

Concretely speaking, we have seen that both learners and teachers need to engage with different kinds of expectations:

1. The teacher's and learners' expectations of their roles and power. Teachers would no longer see their role as transmitting factual knowledge that can be assessed through (psychometric) testing techniques, but as occupying a subject position within an institution and a society that allow certain forms of knowledge and disallow others. Learners would no longer be accountable to computers or disembodied instructors, but to historical and ideological subjects, e.g., faculty at an American institution in the 21st century.
2. The teacher's and learners' expectations of what learning language and content actually implies, namely, occupying a given subject position (e.g., as a Chinese student), addressing a given reader (e.g., an American teacher), at a given location (e.g., an American West Coast university). Such a postmodern view of learning goes against neoliberal claims about the globalized or universal nature of knowledge.
3. The expectations of the source texts (blogs, wikis, online resources) towards their readers, namely that these readers should not only be proficient in English but that they should share the universal assumptions and presuppositions of these texts' authors regarding historical events.
4. The learners' expectations of what the world is like, which may lead to misunderstandings, and of how they are expected to behave, which may not correspond to what others expect. For example, teachers should not assume

that Chinese youngsters studying in the U.S. have ever heard of the Holocaust, nor that many American youngsters know about it through more than *Schindler's List*.
5. The teacher's expectations of learner's language production. For example, teachers might be alerted to the fact that the demonization of historical figures like Adolf Hitler is not universal.
6. The learner's expectations of the addressees (peers and teacher) both as individual interlocutors/readers and as members of a historical collectivity. For example, awareness of such expectations might have led the Chinese student to add a disclaimer addressed to the reader, such as: "Many American readers will be surprised//shocked to read that …". Peer mediation might have suggested that she do so, but discussion groups online or in the classroom may shy away from confronting or even challenging each other's views in some cultural environments. Adequate mediation will necessitate a tutor aware of how to deal with such episodes.

All this requires a radical change in the way we view the transmission of knowledge (see sections 1 and 3). Starting with the expectations of the learners necessarily entails situating these expectations in an individual habitus that might have been socialized differently from that of the teacher and the institution. It means awareness on the part of the teachers of their own collective habitus and of the growing generational gap between them and their students. Indeed, the term "expectation" might be ill-suited for thoughts and behaviors that are increasingly unexpected and unexpectable, given the increasing diversity of classrooms under global learning conditions. The classroom mentioned above is an extreme case of the growing fragmentation of knowledge, that cannot assume anything known except for what is on that semester's syllabus, and that can be tested through multiple choice tests.

6 Conclusion

In this ocean of uncertainty, what kind of ethical universe does TBLT belong to? Its pragmatic morality is based, as we saw above, on the value of diversity, contact, and negotiation. In a sense, if the focus is on the task and its accomplishment, and if hybrid outcomes are valued, empathy is needed to understand and negotiate diverse approaches to accomplishing the task. But empathy with whom or what?

The present system of values based on shared cultural traditions, spatially-bounded community and behavioral norms, could/should be reframed into a system of values based on cultural diversity, spatial contact and negotiation of norms. In an ecological perspective (Kramsch 2002), we need to reinstate empathy into TBLT, by bringing back the focus on the learners, their memory and imagination, their capacity to conceive of a world that is different from the one they are living in and to interact discursively in it in a way that respects who they are, how they work and that suits their aims. Focusing on the learner may also mean letting go of "pedagogic" control.

Ultimately, TBLT might be at its most meaningful when it ceases to propose tasks focused on answering questions about real world problems and turns to tasks generating questions about possible worlds in collaboration with others.

References

Bakhtin, Mikhail. 1981. *The dialogic imagination. Four essays by M. M. Bakhtin*. Michael Holquist (ed). Translated by. Emerson Caryl and Michael Holquist. Austin and London: University of Texas Press.
Berger, Peter L. & Thomas Luckmann. 1966. *The social construction of reality: A treatise in the sociology of knowledge*. New York: Anchor.
Bertin, Jean-Claude, Patrick Gravé & Jean-Paul Narcy-Combes. 2010. *Second language distance learning. Theoretical perspectives and didactic ergonomics*. Hershley, PA: IGI Global.
Bourdieu, Pierre. 1980. *Le sens pratique*. Paris : Ed. de Minuit.
Bourdieu, Pierre. 1994. Espace social et espace symbolique. In *Raisons pratiques*, 15–29. Paris: Seuil.
Bozhinova, Krastanka, Jean-Paul Narcy-Combes & Sonia Zaouali. 2016. La production écrite vue comme un processus bilingue : dans quelle mesure les TIC peuvent-elles aider ? . *Pratiques, le Déjà là*, no. 169–170.
Breen, Michael & Christopher Candlin. 1980. The essentials of a communicative curriculum in language teaching. *Applied Linguistics* 1(2). 89–112.
Brudermann, Cédric. 2010. From action research to the implementation of ICT pedagogical tools: taking into account student's needs to propose adjusted online tutorial practice. *ReCall* 22(2). 172–190.
Bündgens-Kosten, Judith & Daniela Elsner. 2014. Rezeptives Code-Switching ein- und mehrsprachiger Lerner/innen in multilingualen Settings. *Fremdsprachen lehren und lernen* (*FLUL* 2/2014). 56–73.
Canagarajah, Suresh. 2012. *Translingual practice: Global Englishes and cosmopolitan relations*. New York: Routledge.
Canagarajah, Suresh. 2013. From intercultural rhetoric to cosmopolitan practice: Addressing new challenges in Lingua Franca English. In Diane Belcher and Gayle Nelson (eds.), *Critical and corpus-based approaches to intercultural rhetoric*, 381–401. Ann Arbor: University of Michigan Press.

Catroux, Michèle. 2006. L'apprentissage collaboratif médiatisé par Internet: conditions de mise en œuvre chez de jeunes apprenants d'anglais. *Les Cahiers de l'Acedle* 2. 52–73.

Cenoz, Jasone & Dick Gorter (eds.). 2011. A holistic approach in multilingual education: Introduction. Special issue: Toward a multilingual approach in the study of multilingualism in school contexts. *The Modern Language Journal* 95(3). 339–343.

Chi, Hsinping & Martine Derivry-Plard. 2010. Médiations culturelles à travers une expérience d'e-twinning franco-taïwanaise. *Recherches en didactique des langues – les langues tout au long de la vie*. Dec. 2009. 39–54.

Damasio, Antonio, R. 1994. *Descartes' error: Emotion, reason, and the human brain*. New York: Putnam Books.

De Bot, Kees, Wander Lowie, Stephen L. Thorne & Marjolijn Verspoor. 2013. DST as a comprehensive theory of second language development. In María del Pilar García Mayo Junkal Gutierrez Mangado & María Martínez Adrián (eds*.)*. *Contemporary approaches to second language acquisition*, 199–220. Amsterdam: John Benjamins.

DuFon, Margaret A. 2010. The acquisition of terms of address in a second language. In Anna Trosborg (ed.), *Pragmatics across languages and cultures (Handbooks of pragmatics)*, 309–332. Berlin: Walter de Gruyter.

Ellis, Nick C. 1998. Emergentism, connectionism and language learning. *Language Learning* 48(4). 631–664.

Ellis, Rod. 2003. *Task-based language learning and teaching*. Oxford: Oxford University Press.

Fisher, G. 2012. Effectuation, causation, and bricolage: A behavioral comparison of emerging theories in entrepreneurship research. *Entrepreneurship Theory and Practice* 36(5). 1019–1051.

Galbraith, John K. 1975. *Money. Whence it came, where it went.* Boston: Houghton Mifflin.

Garicano, Luis. & Yanhui Wu. 2010. *A task-based approach to organization: Knowledge, communication and structure*. London: Centre for Economic Performance.

Gavins, Joanne. 2007. *Text world theory: An introduction*. Edinburgh: Edinburgh University Press.

Genesee, Fred. 2007. The suitability of French immersion for students who are at risk: A review of research evidence. *Canadian Modern Language Review*. 63(5). 655–687.

Gibbs, Raymond W. 2001. Intentions as emergent products of social interactions. In Bertram F. Malle, Louis J. Moses and Dare A. Baldwin (eds.), *Intentions and intentionality: Foundations of social cognition*, 105–122. Cambridge, MA: The MIT Press.

Gonzàlez-Lloret, Marta & Lourdes Ortega. 2014. *Technology-mediated TBLT: Researching technology and tasks*. Amsterdam: John Benjamins

Herdina, Philip & Ulrike Jessner. 2006. *A dynamic model of multilingualism, perspectives of change in psycholinguistics*. Clevedon, UK: Multilingual Matters.

Hofstadter, Douglas & Emmanuel Sander. 2013. *Surfaces and essences: Analogy as the fuel and fire of thinking*. New York: Basic Books.

Hutchins, Edwin. 1995. *Cognition in the wild*. Cambridge, MA: MIT Press.

Kramsch, Claire. 2002. Introduction. How can we tell the dancer from the dance? In Claire Kramsch (ed.), *Language acquisition and language socialization. Ecological perspectives*, 1–30. London: Continuum.

Lakoff, George & Mark Johnson. 2003. *Metaphors we live by*. Chicago: University of Chicago Press.

Lamy, Marie-Noëlle & Regina Hampel. 2007. *Online communication in language learning and teaching*. Basingstoke: Palgrave McMillan.

Long, Michael. 1985. A role for instruction in second language acquisition: Task-based language teaching. In Kenneth Hylstenstam & Manfred Pienemann (eds.), *Modelling and assessing second language acquisition*, 77–99. Clevedon, UK: Multilingual Matters.

Long, Michael. 1991. Focus on form: A design feature in language teaching. In Kees de Bot, Ralph Ginsberg & Claire Kramsch (eds.), *Foreign language research in cross-cultural perspective*, 39–52. Amsterdam: John Benjamins.

McAllister, Julie, Marie-Françoise Narcy-Combes & Rebecca Starkey-Perret. 2012. Language teachers' perceptions of their roles, self-identity and teaching practices in a large-scale task based blended learning programme in a French University. In Ali Shehadeh & Christine A. Coombe (eds.), *Task-based language teaching in foreign language contexts: Research and implementation*, 313–342. Amsterdam: John Benjamins.

Meirieu, Philippe (ed.). 2000. *L'école et les parents. La grande explication*. Paris : Plon.

Narcy-Combes, Jean-Paul. 2005. *Didactique des langues et TIC, vers une recherche-action responsable*. Paris : Ophrys.

Narcy-Combes, Jean-Paul & Marie-Françoise Narcy-Combes. 2014. Formations hybrides en milieu pluriculturel : comment concilier théories, pratiques et contraintes. In Dagmar Abendroth-Timmer and Eva-Maria Hennig (eds.), *Plurilingualism and multiliteracies: International research on identity construction in language education*, 211–227. Frankfurt: Peter Lang.

O'Brien, Teresa. 2004. Writing in a foreign language: Teaching and learning. *Language Teaching* 37(1). 1–28.

O'Grady, William. 2010. Emergentism. In Patrick C. Hogan (ed.), *The Cambridge encyclopedia of the language sciences*, 274–76. Cambridge: Cambridge University Press.

Ortega, Lourdes. 2009. *Understanding second language acquisition*. London: Routledge.

Ortega, Lourdes. 2011. SLA after the social turn. Where cognitivism and its alternatives stand. In Dwight Atkinson (ed.), *Alternative approaches to second language acquisition*, 167–180. London: Routledge.

Ortega, Lourdes, Alastair Cummins & Nick C. Ellis. 2013. Agendas for language learning research. *Currents in Language Learning 1, Language Learning* 63: Suppl 1. 25–51.

Park, Moonyoung. 2012. Implementing computer-assisted task-based language teaching in the Korean context. In Ali Shehadeh & Christine A. Coombe (eds.), *Task-based language teaching in foreign language contexts. Research and implementation*, 215–241. Amsterdam: John Benjamins.

Pavlenko, Aneta. 2005. *Emotions and multilingualism*. Cambridge: Cambridge University Press.

Piaget, Jean. 1970. *Psychologie et épistémologie: pour une théorie de la connaissance*. Paris: Gonthier-Denoël.

Pica, Teresa, Hyun-Sook Kang & Shannon Sauro. 2006. Information gap tasks: Their multiple roles and contributions to interaction research methodology. *Studies in Second Language Acquisition* 28(2). 301–338.

Prabhu, N. S. 1987. *Second language pedagogy*. Oxford: Oxford University Press.

Samuda, Virginia & Martin Bygate. 2008. *Tasks in second language learning*. New York: Palgrave MacMillan.

Schumann, John H. 1997. *The neurobiology of affect in language learning*. Oxford: Wiley-Blackwell.

Schurmans, Marie-Noëlle. 2001. *La construction sociale de la connaissance comme action*. Brussels: De Boeck Supérieur.

Shehadeh, Ali & Christine A. Coombe (eds.). 2012. *Task-based language teaching in foreign language contexts. Research and implementation*. Amsterdam: John Benjamins.

Simondon, Gilbert. 1989. *L'individuation psychique et collective*. Paris: Aubier.

Storch, Neomy. 2013. *Collaborative writing in L2 classrooms*. Clevedon, UK: Multilingual Matters.
Thelen, Esther. 2005. Dynamic systems theory and the complexity of change. *Psychoanalytic Dialogues* 15. 255–283.
Troadec, Bertrand. 2007. *Psychologie culturelle. Le développement cognitif est-il culturel ?* Paris: Belin Sup.
Varela, Francisco. 1993. *L'Inscription corporelle de l'esprit*. Paris: Seuil.
Vygotsky, Lev S. 1962. *Thought and language*. Edited and translated by Eugenia Hanfmann & Gertrude Vakar. Cambridge: MIT Press
Weber, Mark. 2011/2012. How Hitler tackled unemployment and revived Germany's economics. www.ihr.org/other/economicshitler2011.html (Accessed 10 October 2015).
Williams, Sarah & Bjorn Hammarberg. 1998. Language switches in L3 production: Implications for a polyglot speaking model. *Applied Linguistics* 19(3). 295–333.

Appendix: The student's essay

Problem set 1

A development in Nazi Germany that enhanced growth was the development of a new road/transportation system. Within three years, Hitler managed to decrease unemployment and grow the German economics. He implemented large scale borrowing for public expenditures such as building railroad canals, and highways. It helped unemployment more than focusing on any other industry (Weber par.14). High income and stable prices were the results of these actions, as well as full employment. Hitler recognized that full employment was only possible when placed with wage and price control (Weber par.4). Hitler was also clear with his intention and announced his plans to reorganize the nation with his National Socialist principles, thus uplifting spirits and ensuring positive thoughts and less resistance to his plans. As long as prices remained stable and there were more jobs created to ensure efficiency in production, the economics could continue to grow.

The gross taxable income increased by 148%, overall tax volume increased by 23.2%, there was almost no unemployment, prices were stable, and taxation was progressive (Weber par.24). New highways and more efficient methods of transportation were built to increase productivity, crime rates fell, diseases were noticeably diminished, and the psychological-emotional well-being of Germans were improved (Weber par.28). Industries like housing construction, investment, consumer spending, and tourism rose rapidly as did the standard of living. These conditions led to "sharp increase in birth rate" (Weber par.29).

If there is another poor country like Burundi, I would recommend a similar development. They would first need to increase building methods of travel and transportation, as that is where jobs are created and unemployment slashed. This in turn will create a rise in economics. This should be feasible as underdeveloped countries will not have more sophisticated structures. This will help create jobs and raise standards of living as that one implementation creates a domino effect on the other industries.

IV Pedagogic and Educational Perspective

Martin East
10 "If It Is All About Tasks, Will They Learn Anything?" Teachers' Perspectives on Grammar Instruction in the Task-Oriented Classroom

1 Introduction

How grammatical accuracy should be attended to within a Task-Based Language Teaching (TBLT) approach to language pedagogy is a source of concern to language teachers. Teachers are often uncertain about the relationship between learner-centred tasks and explicit grammar teaching. This is particularly so in school settings, where the target language and the language of instruction are distinct, and where time and exposure to the target language are limited. The aim of this chapter is to explore the interface between tasks and grammar teaching from the perspective of teachers of additional languages in schools, and to draw some conclusions that will help to answer some questions that arise from the debates around instruction and use in the task-oriented classroom. The context I draw on is New Zealand, where approaches such as TBLT are being encouraged as means to enhance the communicative proficiency of school students who are studying an additional language other than the language of instruction (e.g., French, Japanese). The issues I raise have relevance for attention to grammar, whatever the target language.

It is important at the outset to establish why grammar teaching is such a controversial issue for TBLT, both in theory and in practice. Essentially, TBLT is conceptualised as a learner-centred and experiential pedagogical approach whereby learners' active language use through tasks is seen as a crucial element in promoting language acquisition (Nunan 2004). On this basis, at least as far as the strong form of TBLT is concerned, the task and the negotiation of meaning promoted through task completion are the all-important components (Skehan 1996). Strong TBLT is therefore principally a 'zero grammar' approach in which it is believed that there is effectively no need for teachers to teach the students anything about the rules. The students will pick these up and assimilate them by themselves.

Martin East, The University of Auckland

DOI 10.1515/9781501503399-011

Weaker forms of TBLT concede that some level of explicit instruction may be required for students to master the grammatical rules more proficiently. From this perspective, the acquisition of grammatical knowledge is essentially theorised as being through a focus on form approach (Long 1991, 2000). Focus on form is predicated on the assumption that attention to form arises from students' noticing of grammatical patterns as they engage in task completion (Schmidt 1990, 2001). Unlike in the traditional communicative classroom, where overt attention to grammatical form would most likely precede any kind of communicative activity, the grammar focus would generally proceed from the noticing that has already occurred during language in actual use. However, so-called task-*supported* language teaching is a weak form of TBLT that more closely resembles the traditional communicative classroom. In this model, tasks become vehicles to "complement or support ... existing structure-based programmes," providing opportunities for "additional communicative language use" in an "existing language-focused syllabus" (Bygate 2016: 387).

Given the range of means of attending to grammar that find expression in task-based approaches (whether zero grammar, post-task exploitation of noticing, or more overt instruction), it is perhaps not surprising that teachers who wish to embrace innovative practices such as TBLT struggle with understanding if and how explicit grammar teaching should become part of the task-based classroom, leading to teacher uncertainty about how to reconcile task-based with formal knowledge. In Littlewood's words (2004: 319–320), "[c]an teaching and learning grammar be described as a task, and if not, should teachers feel guilty when they teach grammar?"

How, then, do teachers reconcile grammar instruction with the task-oriented classroom? And what are the implications of their thinking and practices for TBLT? East (2012) presented an account of a research project arising from a context of curriculum reform in New Zealand in which TBLT was being encouraged in instructed foreign language (L2) school classrooms. The project investigated participants' emerging understanding of the reforms, as seen from a task-based perspective. This chapter revisits the original data and re-interrogates the data for what they reveal about teachers' beliefs and practices related to grammar instruction. What is presented here is an exposition of the themes emerging from this re-interrogation which add to those already reported in East (2012).[1] After this re-interrogation, the implications for TBLT are explored.

---

[1] The findings presented here draw on some data reported in East (2012), Chapter 5. However, most data presented here have not been previously published.

2 Background

2.1 Approaches to grammar and TBLT

Long (1991, 2000) proposes three concepts which have become archetypal to our framing of approaches to acquisition of grammatical competence: focus on forms; focus on meaning; and focus on form.

A focus on forms approach has traditionally informed teacher-centred behaviourist pedagogical models such as grammar translation. However, its use has been apparent in more traditional communicative language teaching classrooms and operationalised through what Klapper (2003) refers to as the 'classic lesson structure' of present/practice/produce or PPP. In this approach, the grammar is first *presented* in an explicit expository way. Then it is *practised* in some way, perhaps through different grammar exercises. Then it is *proceduralised* or *produced* in some kind of communicative activity. The problem with focus on forms, according to Long (2000: 182), is that "[d]espite the best efforts even of highly skilled teachers and textbook writers," the approach "tends to produce boring lessons, with resulting declines in motivation, attention, and student enrollments." As a consequence, instruction and acquisition are less effective, and communicative automaticity – the ability of students to communicate in the target language spontaneously and fluently – is hampered (DeKeyser 2001; Segalowitz 2003).

Focus on meaning, by contrast, eschews any need to teach grammar in any formal way, based on an understanding that acquisition and learning are quite distinct (Krashen 1981, 1982), and that learners' own internal processing of the input is sufficient to derive functional rules from the data. The problem with focus on meaning, however, is that it became what Savignon (1983: 1) describes as an "'anything-goes-as-long-as-you-get-the-message-across' approach to second language teaching." Grammatical accuracy no longer appeared to have any direct role to play, thereby hindering effective (i.e., accurate) communicative automaticity.

Focus on form essentially aims to reconcile the limitations of a focus on either forms or meaning. It effectively reverses the PPP model on the basis that input, output and interaction come first, and that forms encountered in the input and attempted in the output and interaction (i.e., the language *production* stage) should subsequently be attended to more explicitly. In Long's words (2000: 185), focus on form "involves briefly drawing students' attention to linguistic elements … as they arise *incidentally* in lessons whose *overriding* focus is on meaning, or communication" (my emphases). This attention is "triggered by students' problems with comprehension or production." It is therefore "learner-centered" and "under learner control" because the focus occurs "just when he or she has a communication problem and so is likely already at least partially to understand the meaning or function of the new form and when he or she is attending to the input." In essence, having first encountered a problem in communication, or having first noticed a particular pattern, students' overt attention is subsequently drawn to the solution or pattern.

Focus on form fits comfortably with a learner-centred and experiential TBLT approach (Long and Norris 2000). Theoretically at least, focus on form enables learners to attend to both meaning and form, leading to a more rounded experience and enhanced potential for ultimate communicative automaticity. However, the notion of 'noticing' as put forward by Schmidt (1990, 2001), and which informs a focus on form approach, has been subject to considerable critique and differences in understanding (Schmidt 2010). There are also genuine challenges to putting TBLT (and focus on form) into practice in the instructed L2 context.

2.2 Focus on form and the instructed context

Courses in instructed contexts, in contrast to naturalistic or 'immersion' environments, are constrained both by the time available for instruction and by limited opportunities for students to use the L2 outside the classroom. In these so-called acquisition-poor environments it has been proposed that TBLT, at least in its strong form, is inadequate and ineffective (Bruton, 2005; Ellis, 2009; Klapper, 2003; Swan, 2005). Also, bearing in mind Mitchell's (2000: 296) argument that "much remains to be done before the most 'effective' mixes and sequences of instruction and use can be identified," in the instructed context a counter-argument to the efficacy of focus on form is essentially that students simply do not have sufficient opportunities to notice, and require pre-planned instruction and careful practice.

According to Swan (2005: 394), even beginners in a language need to be provided with "a simple grammatical repertoire." Swan thus argues for "planned approaches involving, among other elements, careful selection and prioritizing, proactive syllabus design, and concentrated engagement with a limited range of high-priority language elements, so as to establish a core linguistic repertoire which can be deployed easily and confidently."

Furthermore, findings of studies into TBLT from the teachers' perspective have highlighted the reality that teachers interpret TBLT in a variety of ways and that, when it comes to grammar instruction, they adhere to a range of practices that span the complete focus on forms-meaning-form trichotomy (Andon and Eckerth 2009; Carless 2003, 2007, 2009; East 2012; Van den Branden 2009b; Van den Branden, Van Gorp and Verhelst, 2007; Xiongyong and Samuel, 2011).

Andon and Eckerth (2009: 305), for example, note that teachers' pedagogical decisions are "made on a lesson-by-lesson assessment as to whether or not to draw on [a range of] principles and techniques." These decisions are influenced by limited time and student demands, leading teachers to "adapt TBLT, omit stages in the task cycle, or combine TBLT with more direct language-focused activities."

Teachers' choices are also inevitably influenced by their own beliefs and understandings about effective pedagogy, shaped by their own prior learning experiences (Nunan 2004; Shehadeh 2012). These beliefs become a filter through which new information and experiences are interpreted (Borg 2003; Pajares 1993; Phipps and Borg 2007) and it is often challenging to move teachers away from the 'tried, tested and familiar' onto new ways of thinking, being and acting (Van den Branden 2009a).

Seen in the above light, it is not surprising that teachers struggle when confronted with TBLT and its departure from more established norms of language teaching and learning. Problematic here is that, potentially, this sees teachers, with the best of intentions, continuing to resort to a focus on forms approach and a PPP model that negate the apparent benefits of TBLT (East 2015). In turn, this raises questions about what TBLT is, or ought to be, in the instructed context. The study that is the focus of this chapter explores these issues.

3 The study

In 2007, a completely revised curriculum for New Zealand's schools was published, and fully mandated from 2010 (Ministry of Education 2007). The revised document encouraged, across all curriculum areas, a learner-centred experiential pedagogical approach. For L2 programmes, detailed and prescriptive curriculum guidelines for teachers which had contained a strong grammatical element and which had advocated to teachers what they should teach, and when they should teach it, were officially withdrawn. In their place, a more open-ended, non-prescriptive and generic statement presented, on a single page in the new curriculum document, three interwoven strands of learning: *communication*, *language knowledge*, and *cultural knowledge*.

The *communication* strand was characterised as 'core'. In other words, principally, and across a range of language skills, "students learn to use the language to make meaning ... and ... become more effective communicators" (Ministry of Education, 2007: 24). Language knowledge (i.e., grammatical competence) is constructed as important, but only insofar as it *supports* these communicative aims. Although not explicitly stated in the curriculum document, there was an implicit impetus (made more explicit in a range of support documents) to encourage TBLT as a key means of operationalising communication as core and language knowledge as supporting in learner-centred experiential ways (e.g., Ministry of Education 2011, 2012).

East (2012) explored the reform from a task-based perspective. The study drew on a series of individual in-depth interviews. It focused on curriculum implementers' (i.e., practising teachers') struggles with coming to terms with the revised curriculum for schools (n = 19), and curriculum leaders' (i.e., advisory support workers') understandings of TBLT and task (n = 8). One finding emerging from the data was that, despite the attention being drawn to concepts such as TBLT and task in the New Zealand context, these concepts represented something new and unfamiliar for many. This is because these teachers were more accustomed to a more traditional PPP approach, predicated on the published curriculum guidelines which, as stated above, had officially been withdrawn.

East (2012: 197–198) presented the perspective of one curriculum leader (Alison) who asserted that a learner-centred approach to grammatical knowledge was perceptually challenging for many teachers. Alison explained, "I mean, I think that teachers say that they're communicative but they are probably still feeling that they've got to spend a long time still talking and discussing and explaining and showing things." Teachers, in her view, struggled with "that idea of just giving it over to the children, giving them a few patterns, letting them work with them, standing back, letting the kids get on with it," as well as "the fact that you may just focus on form at the end rather than having a big focus on form at the beginning." She concluded that, for teachers, "I think really letting go is probably the biggest challenge," fuelled by an anxiety that the students were "not going to learn." East argued on this basis, "[t]hat teachers 'feel' this [need to spend a long time instructing] suggests that they hold a core belief that it is beneficial for the students if the teachers stay in charge."

In what follows, I present findings emerging from a re-examination of the original data that uncover teachers' thinking and beliefs about effective language teaching in light of the recent curriculum reforms, and teachers' thinking, beliefs and practices about effective grammar teaching in this reform context. Two questions are addressed:

1. How do languages teachers conceptualise effective language learning?
2. How do languages teachers (a) conceptualise and (b) enact attention to grammar?

4 Findings

4.1 How do languages teachers conceptualise effective language learning?

Participants were asked initially about their perceptions of what made a 'good' language lesson in the context of the core *communication* strand. There was clear evidence that participants held core beliefs that a 'good' (i.e., effective) language lesson was one in which opportunities for learner-focused communicative interaction were maximised. A good language lesson would be "child-centred" (Anna-Frances), a lesson in which the students are "the main actors" (Françoise), "active" (Cuifen, Changying), "involved" (Faye, Sophie, Changying) and "engaged" (Sophie). This interactive environment would be one where "the students are using the language as much as possible" (Andrew) and there are "a lot of opportunities to communicate" (Gretta) or "to use the language for a real purpose and to interact meaningfully" (Annette).

Several participants clearly articulated an understanding that a principal focus within the core *communication* strand should be on spoken interaction, and that this stood in contradistinction to grammar learning. Janice noted, "that communication strand is there [to promote] a lot of speaking activities going on in the classroom *rather than* sit there and then learn the grammar, I think" (my emphasis). Anna-Frances argued that the emphasis on communication would ideally eliminate the rote-learnt aspects of language learning, that is, it would "get rid of the tedious vocabulary lists ... and ... verb tables." In this regard, Gretta and Annette argued that 'getting the message across' was the priority. Stressing that her students "have to communicate," Gretta asserted, "it doesn't even matter whether the accuracy is there at the start because that will come [in] time." In practice, the students "have to get over that kind of threshold" to "open their mouth" and be "confident even if not everything is perfect." After all, perfection "does not matter. Native speakers are not perfect. Communication is achieved when you actually can get your message across." Annette similarly argued, "the word 'communication', I suppose, says it all. Language is for use and we need to learn how to use language, how to use it to interact with people and get messages across."

An allied message was that a focus on learner-centred interactive communication was motivating for the learners. In other words, "enthusiasm, passion and a lot of talking" (Jennifer) created a situation in which "students will be interested ... and get motivated" (Jin) and be "engaged and on task" (Alison). As Sandra put it, "if they're enjoying it, they're engaged in it and they're ... experiencing success in it." Sandra went on to argue, "being able to produce language by themselves ... you kind of see them enjoying all the success that they enjoy when they're able to do it by themselves."

4.2 How do languages teachers conceptualise attention to grammar?

When, however, questions turned to the *language knowledge* strand of the curriculum, a discourse began to emerge that suggested that students' ability to 'do it by themselves', the ultimate goal of automaticity, was predicated on the requirement for structured teacher input. Andrew noted, "so you've got communication as the core strand, and in order to communicate you need to have the language knowledge," where language knowledge is "the vocabulary and the structures and those sort of nuts and bolts of the language." For Andrew, "the knowledge of vocab and pronunciation and grammar and all that, you *combine* that ... *that's* how you communicate" (my emphases). Learners therefore "need to have the tools" (Sandra) if they are to communicate effectively. Thus, "the language strand *supports* communication because if you don't have the building blocks, you can't actually construct communication" (Grace, my emphasis).

In essence, and in practice, the grammar has "always been a sort of *parallel* thing in our teaching [and] we've always *taught* that alongside communication, and I think probably we'll just *continue to do that*" (Gillian, my emphases). Faye argued that a "good language lesson" would be "a lesson that gets the students to be involved in the work that they're doing *but is also controlled* ... so that your objectives are being met" (my emphasis). In this regard, Grace presented the view that it was important to begin with the teacher, and to move the lesson "from more teacher led ... towards more student led, so you're working *towards* communication and *towards* unsupported communication if at all possible ... that's pretty much the kind of build-up that I'd want to see" (my emphases). As Anna-Frances put it, the focus ideally needed to be "more centred on [students] using and producing language than the teacher standing at the board." Nevertheless, there also needed to be "plenty of opportunity to use the language *after* they've learnt it" in order to "give them as much opportunity to *learn* and use the language" (my emphases).

It became apparent that, as teachers struggled to reconcile the primary emphasis on communication with the supporting requirement to develop language knowledge, a tension was emerging between top-down teacher-led and bottom-up learner-focused. This tension appeared to create an uncertain environment in which teachers were making a range of choices around how to exploit grammar within the principle of the communication-focused classroom with which they clearly agreed.

Gillian and Sophie bring out two opposite sides of the debate, but appear to reach similar conclusions. For these two teachers, the bottom line was that grammatical accuracy "does have a bearing on the communication" (Gillian) and is there "to back up the communication" (Sophie). Gillian, reflecting on the limitations of an essentially meaning focused or 'zero grammar' approach, mused, "you do wonder sometimes whether we haven't neglected it rather." She commented, "have we gone too far away from that? Should we be doing more understanding of language and how does it fit together, and so on?" Sophie by contrast tussled with her own prior experiences of learning a language in an apparently deductive focus on forms way. She acknowledged that a de-emphasis on grammar was "kind of a different approach to what I was educated with where you had to get everything right otherwise you were slammed for it." Nevertheless, "at the same time you need to aim for a good level of accuracy, otherwise communication isn't really achieved." As a consequence of wrestling with these apparently conflicting notions, Sophie accepted a mixed model in which "sometimes I do [grammar], sometimes I don't." For Gillian it was a question of "I usually try and find a way that sort of fits into the topic that we're doing." She also conceded, "I've made up a little grammar booklet which I work through with them."

4.3 How do languages teachers enact attention to grammar?

The principle of 'sometimes I do, sometimes I don't' was in evidence among several teachers. Frances argued, "I don't think there's a best approach [to grammar teaching], but there is just the approach that you do on the day and depending on the grammar point." Françoise similarly conceded, "it's hard to say 'best approach'. I think there are so many different things that do play a part ... depending on how much they know from before." Grace noted that the approach "very much depends on what you are actually trying to teach at the time."

Comments by Frances, Anna-Frances and Anita are illustrative of a struggle to reconcile *forms* with *form*. On the one hand, these respondents conceded that "some things, in my opinion, just need to be taught in an explicit direct approach" (Frances); "there are times where, in response to your students, you may need to take the time and teach it explicitly" (Anna-Frances); "I don't think that there's anything wrong with explicit teaching of form ... I think there is need for chunks of time, kind of as the need arises, to be spent on explicit teaching of form" (Anita). Nevertheless, "there are some [grammar points] where it's really easy to get them to elicit the grammar point ... themselves" (Frances), and "I don't think that you have to always explicitly teach the structures ... by exposure to implicit grammatical structures, students are starting to see those patterns" (Anna-Frances). Therefore a direct and rule-based approach "probably shouldn't be in very *big* chunks" (Anita, my emphasis). When the grammar is "completely decontextualised" and "you give them a series of exercises which are basically the same sentence with different vocab in it, sort of 10 or 15 times," then "you wonder why they're bored."

The above findings illustrate conceptualisations of grammar instruction that include both explicit attention to forms and implicit noticing of form within an overarching understanding that, although communication may be central, language knowledge is an important supporting component – that is, an approach to grammar that is "part of every single lesson but ... hopefully not the focus" (Giselle) and "more interwoven with what we're doing" (Sophie).

East (2012) reported the approaches adopted by Jennifer and Faye. Jennifer is illustrative of a teacher whose classroom practices appeared to reflect a conscious decision to emphasise a learner-centred rather than teacher-led approach. Jennifer described herself as "not a 'talk and chalk' teacher" but "just the conductor" of an orchestra that "has to want to play in tune." On that basis, she asserted, "I want them to discover [for] themselves" (p. 125).

Jennifer went on to explain that "[y]ou can get them to be inquisitive about the sentence ... And if they've got that attitude already ... that it's not just words on a piece of paper, but there's some sort of a pattern, and if ... they've got that skill [to work it out themselves] when it becomes more difficult ... they can make deductions themselves."

Faye was more eclectic in her approach, nevertheless conceding the importance of her choices for communication. On the one hand, she acknowledged a clear focus on "the mechanics" in a taught grammar class, even though her goal was to "get it into communicating, communication stuff as much as possible, as quickly as possible." On the other hand, she might begin with the communication but would then say to her students "well, look at the structure you've been using, what's the structure in this?" (East 2012: 123–124).

As other teachers attempted to reconcile teacher-led and learner-centred in actual practice, several other examples emerged of what might be called a 'directed noticing' principle in which it is not entirely left up to the students to notice, but noticing is co-constructed ('look at the structure; what's the structure?') – or, as Schmidt (1990) would put it, instruction is having "a priming effect, increasing the likelihood of noticing features in input through the establishment of expectations" (p. 143). The following four cases illustrate this principle at work, and a subtle flow between direct exposition and indirect noticing.

Susan chose a simple junior level example of reflexive verbs in Spanish. She noted that, through language in actual use, her students, "know how to say 'my name is …' (*me llamo*)." However, "I don't tell them that it's a reflexive … I don't let them know. That's just the way that it's said." As she began to introduce different parts of the verb, there would again be no explicit instruction, "but what we're concentrating on is 'so what do these all end in?' and 'what does that mean?' It means that I'm talking about myself." Through exposure to examples, "they've been able to follow the patterns." However, "I don't *explicitly* teach those patterns." Rather, Susan would "provide them with the opportunity to *notice* the patterns *as we do it together*" (my emphases).

Frances outlined a similar approach, this time for senior level students. She explained:

> If I take a typical kind of grammar point like Year 12 'conditional' … I would write up a whole lot of conditional sentences or conditional structures like *je voudrais* or whatever and ask the students 'what do you think is happening here? What similarities, what patterns can you see?' So I might [include] *je voudrais / tu voudrais / je mangerais, tu mangerais* and so they're getting the sense of the endings and everything. And hopefully someone would say "*ais*' is happening a lot' or … 'I think I've seen that before' or 'that means *I would like*'.

Having thus elicited the students' understanding through co-constructed noticing, Frances noted that "then you just start talking them through it … 'so this is the conditional. This is 'would', and let's look at how it's formed'." This more explicit instruction would be followed "by doing some drill, I think … and then just some really great activities to back it up."

Andrew and Sally both drew on the future tense to illustrate their approaches. Andrew's approach appeared to be more indirect. That is, "[i]nstead of saying 'today we're going to talk about, learn the future tense' or whatever, I'd try to relate it to something that they wanted to talk about and say 'well, how would we do that?' And give some examples and then … try to get the students to recognise the pattern."

Sally's apparently more guided approach reflected that adopted by Frances. When introducing the future tense:

> I start by giving them a very short sentence [in Spanish] about … *I will travel* and *I will go*, and I draw an aeroplane on the blackboard and I draw an island or something, 'I will go to a tropical island' or something. And then I'll say 'now what have I said?' and I make them translate that. And some of them get the 'will'. They realise they haven't done that tense and they realise it's in the future because I will put in *in two weeks' time* or something … and then I show them how to do it and then we repeat…

Sally concluded that, through this process, "they've got it, supposedly. It works … it works."

5 Discussion and conclusions

In the context of recent curriculum reform in New Zealand which is encouraging TBLT as a realisation of learner-centred and experiential pedagogical approaches, East (2012) reported the viewpoint of Alison. Alison acknowledged the perceptual challenges for teachers of a learner-centred approach to grammatical knowledge, summed up in the title of this chapter, "if it is all about tasks, will they learn anything?"

The data presented above reveal teachers' understandings of, and commitment to, central emphases on communication and interaction for which TBLT has a clear role to play. The data also reveal struggles as teachers aim to reconcile these emphases with a perceptual need to impart grammatical knowledge. In other words, a strong approach to TBLT, where the task is everything, is clearly not favoured. However, a weak approach to TBLT that is predicated on noticing and post-task focus on form is also to some extent brought into question. Teachers, it seems, are not, as Alison put it, able to 'stand back' and give the thinking entirely over to the learners. The teachers argue a need for explicit grammar instruction, not as an exclusive approach, but as one that sits alongside implicit inductive approaches. As a consequence, a 'directed noticing' appears to emerge, where a clear focus is on the learners and their ability to process the language for themselves, but where, alongside that, there is a place for co-construction with the teacher.

As to the extent to which co-construction relies on explicit exposition and practice, teachers appear to differ in their emphases. Teachers therefore tap into different dimensions of the forms-meaning-form trichotomy, and appear to do so in response to what they see as their students' needs at the time. This eclecticism in practice is commensurate with findings from other studies into TBLT from the teachers' perspective (Andon and Eckerth 2009; Carless 2003, 2007, 2009; Van den Branden 2009b; Van den Branden et al. 2007; Xiongyong and Samuel 2011).

Where do these findings leave TBLT? In particular, do they really point to a PPP form of instruction under a different guise? Yes and no. Yes, in the sense that explicit exposition is not eschewed. No, in the sense that the 'directed noticing' model, as exemplified by several practitioners in this study, attempts to reconcile explicit grammar teaching with a learner-centred noticing principle and reflection on language in actual use.

A fundamental question to ask is this: Are these teachers' beliefs and practices at odds with what a task-based pedagogy actually is? Put another way, are eclectic choices with regard to grammar instruction and, more particularly, more formal grammar instruction, compatible with an open-ended learner-centred and experiential TBLT approach?

This fundamental question raises a limitation to the study that must be acknowledged. As East (2012) explained, in the light of very recent curriculum innovation, the participants were at an early stage in emerging from more grammar-focused PPP approaches and considering what TBLT might mean for them. They also exhibited a range of understandings of TBLT and task, from quite well developed to not developed. It may well be that, as TBLT, supported by different professional development initiatives, becomes more established and 'mainstream' for these teachers, teachers' understandings and practices will shift towards a more strongly articulated learner-centred post-task focus on form approach. Future studies to investigate this potential shift, and its impact on learning, would be valuable.

That said, it would be wrong to conclude that learner-centred post-task focus on form is the only approach to grammar available to TBLT. This has implications for our understanding of TBLT going forward. Ellis (2009: 233) notes that, within TBLT, "[a]ttention to form can occur in a variety of ways – not just through 'focus on form' as defined by Long." In response to Swan (2005), East (2012: 204) asserts that a task-based approach "does not preclude elements such as 'planned approaches,' 'careful selection and prioritising,' and 'proactive syllabus design'." Mitchell (2000: 296) argues that, whilst in theory TBLT "would seem to have little to do with grammar pedagogy, but to promote an experiential approach to classroom learning," in practice TBLT "can offer a balanced approach in which grammar pedagogy and focus on form are linked with communicative experience."

Certainly, the data I have presented in this chapter indicate that teachers who are *beginning* to think about what TBLT might look like in their classrooms are making clear links between communicative experience and a grammar pedagogy that contains several explicit and directly taught elements. At least at this stage in these teachers' understanding and development, it seems that teachers' practices are most aligned with a task-supported form of TBLT. Bygate (2016) suggests that such an approach has validity as an adoption of TBLT in language education.

As we continue to investigate TBLT as operationalised in classrooms, the interface, balance and relationship between a learner-centred and experiential task-based approach and teacher-directed didactic grammar explanation will no doubt become clearer. Provided that this does not see a return to (or continuation of) overtly teacher-led practices that hinder the development of communicative proficiency – or, in the words of the revised New Zealand curriculum, communication is *core*, and language knowledge is *supporting* – there is arguably nothing wrong with exploring that interface.

References

Andon, Nick & Johannes Eckerth. 2009. Chacun à son goût? Task-based L2 pedagogy from the teacher's point of view. *International Journal of Applied Linguistics* 19(3). 286–310.

Borg, Simon. 2003. Teacher cognition in language teaching: A review of research on what language teachers think, know, believe, and do. *Language Teaching* 36. 81–109.

Bruton, Anthony. 2005. Task-based language teaching: For the state secondary FL classroom? *The Language Learning Journal* 31(1). 55–68.

Bygate, Martin. 2016. Sources, developments and directions of task-based language teaching. *The Language Learning Journal* 44(4). 381–400.

Carless, David. 2003. Factors in the implementation of task-based teaching in primary schools. *System* 31(4). 485–500.

Carless, David. 2007. The suitability of task-based approaches for secondary schools: Perspectives from Hong Kong. *System* 35(4). 595–608.

Carless, David. 2009. Revisiting the TBLT versus P-P-P debate: Voices from Hong Kong. *Asian Journal of English Language Teaching* 19. 49–66.

DeKeyser, Robert. 2001. Automaticity and automatization. In Peter Robinson (ed.), *Cognition and second language instruction*, 125–151. Cambridge: Cambridge University Press.

East, Martin. 2012. *Task-based language teaching from the teachers' perspective: Insights from New Zealand*. Amsterdam/Philadelphia: John Benjamins.

East, Martin. 2015. Taking communication to task – again: What difference does a decade make? *The Language Learning Journal* 43(1), 6–19.

Ellis, Rod. 2009. Task-based language teaching: Sorting out the misunderstandings. *International Journal of Applied Linguistics* 19(3). 221–246.

Klapper, John. 2003. Taking communication to task? A critical review of recent trends in language teaching. *The Language Learning Journal* 27. 33–42.

Krashen, Stephen. 1981. *Second language acquisition and second language learning*. Oxford: Pergamon Press.

Krashen, Stephen. 1982. *Principles and practice in second language acquisition*. Oxford: Pergamon Press.

Littlewood, William. 2004. The task-based approach: Some questions and suggestions. *ELT Journal* 58(4). 319–326.

Long, Michael. 1991. Focus on form: A design feature in language teaching methodology. In Kees de Bot, Ralph Ginsberg & Claire Kramsch (eds.), *Foreign language research in cross-cultural perspective*, 39–52. Amsterdam/Philadephia: John Benjamins.

Long, Michael. 2000. Focus on form in task-based language teaching. In Richard D. Lambert & Elana Shohamy (eds.), *Language policy and pedagogy: Essays in honor of A. Ronald Walton*, 179–192. Amsterdam/Philadelphia: John Benjamins.

Long, Michael & John Norris. 2000. Task-based teaching and assessment. In Michael Byram (ed.), *Routledge encyclopedia of language teaching and learning*, 597–603. London: Routledge.

Ministry of Education. 2007. *The New Zealand curriculum*. Wellington: Learning Media.

Ministry of Education. 2011. *New Zealand Curriculum Guides Senior Secondary: Learning Languages*. http://seniorsecondary.tki.org.nz/Learning-languages (accessed 8 April 2011).

Ministry of Education. 2012. *What's new or different?* (updated 28 August, 2012). http://seniorsecondary.tki.org.nz/Learning-languages/What-s-new-or-different (accessed 22 January 2014).

Mitchell, Rosamond. 2000. Applied linguistics and evidence-based classroom practice: The case of foreign language grammar pedagogy. *Applied Linguistics* 21(3). 281–303.
Nunan, David. 2004. *Task-based language teaching*. Cambridge: Cambridge University Press.
Pajares, Frank. 1993. Teachers' beliefs and educational research: Cleaning up a messy construct. *Review of Educational Research* 62. 307–332.
Phipps, Simon & Simon Borg. 2007. Exploring the relationship between teachers' beliefs and their classroom practice. *The Teacher Trainer* 21(3). 17–19.
Savignon, Sandra. 1983. *Communicative competence*. Reading, MA: Addison-Wesley.
Schmidt, Richard. 1990. The role of consciousness in second language learning. *Applied Linguistics* 11(2). 129–158.
Schmidt, Richard. 2001. Attention. In Peter Robinson (ed.), *Cognition and second language instruction*, 3–32. Cambridge: Cambridge University Press.
Schmidt, Richard. 2010. Attention, awareness, and individual differences in language learning. In Wai Meng Chan, Seo Won Chi, Kwee Nyet Chin, Johanna Istanto, Masanori Nagami, Jyh Wee Sew, Titima Suthiwan & Izumi Walker (eds.), *Proceedings of CLaSIC 2010*, Singapore, December 2–4 (721–737). Singapore: National University of Singapore, Centre for Language Studies.
Segalowitz, Norman. 2003. Automaticity and second languages. In Catherine Doughty & Michael Long (eds.), *The handbook of second language acquisition*, 381–408. Oxford: Blackwell.
Shehadeh, Ali. 2012. Broadening the perspective of task-based language teaching scholarship: The contribution of research in foreign language contexts. In Ali Shehadeh & Christine Coombe (eds.), *Task-based language teaching in foreign language contexts: Research and implementation*, 1–20. Amsterdam/Philadelphia: John Benjamins.
Skehan, Peter. 1996. Second language acquisition research and task-based instruction. In Jane Willis & David Willis (eds.), *Challenge and change in language teaching*, 17–30. Oxford: Heinemann.
Swan, Michael. 2005. Legislation by hypothesis: The case of task-based instruction. *Applied Linguistics*, 26(3). 376–401.
Van den Branden, Kris. 2009a. Diffusion and implementation of innovations. In Michael Long & Catherine Doughty (eds.), *The handbook of language teaching*, 659–672. Oxford: Wiley Blackwell.
Van den Branden, Kris. 2009b. Mediating between predetermined order and chaos: The role of the teacher in task-based language education. *International Journal of Applied Linguistics*, 19(3). 264–285.
Van den Branden, Kris, Koen Van Gorp & Machteld Verhelst (eds.). 2007. *Tasks in action: Task-based language education from a classroom-based perspective*. Newcastle-upon-Tyne: Cambridge Scholars Publishing.
Xiongyong, Cheng & Samuel Moses. 2011. Perceptions and implementation of task-based language teaching among secondary school EFL teachers in China. *International Journal of Business and Social Science* 2(24). 292–302.

Andreas Müller-Hartmann and Marita Schocker

11 The Challenge of Thinking Task-Based Teaching from the Learners' Perspectives – Developing Teaching Competences Through an Action Research Approach to Teacher Education

1 Introduction

Developing teachers' task-based teaching competence has been shown to be a challenging endeavour (East 2012; Van den Branden 2006). While there are different reasons depending on the respective educational context, teachers often seem to lack an understanding of task concepts. Implementation studies of task-based teaching have shown that in opposition to one-shot in-service training sessions that focus on theoretical input, long-term programs that facilitate teachers' reflective capacity when integrating tasks into their local teaching practice are much more conducive to developing teachers' task-based teaching competence (Van den Branden 2006). One area that has been especially challenging when developing task-based teaching competence is the focus on intercultural communicative competence (ICC), an area which has been largely neglected in task-based research (East 2012).

This paper draws on findings from a collaborative national research project in Germany. Following unsatisfactory PISA results, the *National Institute for Developing Quality in Education* (IQB[1]) had commissioned a national classroom-based research program to explore the potential of learning tasks while developing teachers' task-based teaching competences. The research was carried out in collaboration with practising *English as a Foreign Language* (EFL) secondary school teachers and their learners. Depending on their approach and the textbooks they use in their specific contexts, these teachers follow a more or less task-supported approach to language teaching (TSLL). Based on an action research oriented concept of exploratory practice (EP) we collaborated with

---

[1] The IQB is funded by the state ministries of education to implement and test standards in education.

Andreas Müller-Hartmann, University of Education Heidelberg
Marita Schocker, University of Education Freiburg

DOI 10.1515/9781501503399-012

twenty teachers for three years to develop competences in designing, implementing and researching tasks. Teachers learned how to document, reflect on and share their experiences in video-recorded case studies, which included the perspectives of their learners, participating colleagues and researchers. Data analysis showed that the question of how to develop ICC through tasks and content that is meaningful for learners is one of the central issues. In our paper we show how the approach of EP allows teachers to collaboratively develop an understanding of task-supported language teaching. We demonstrate how they negotiate principles of ICC tasks in their professional discourses when they reflect on the appropriateness of ICC tasks they design for their classrooms in groups. We illustrate the development of teachers' task-based discourse by categorizing video- and audio-recordings of teachers' group discussions by way of grounded analysis to demonstrate how developments become visible in teachers' narratives.

2 Literature review

The literature review considers relevant findings in two areas: Insights into teacher development processes when following a task-based approach through approaches of reflective practice, with a focus on establishing a community of inquiry (1) and ICC task design as a central dimension of teachers' task-based teaching competence (2).

2.1 Literature review 1: Research on the processes of second language teacher education and professional development in TBLT

The role of the teacher in TBLT has been described as guide or facilitator who tries to motivate students to engage in tasks (Samuda 2001; Van den Branden 2006; Willis 1996). As Van den Branden has explained,

> rather than providing all the course content, delivering elaborate and explicit monologues on the structure of the language or the meaning of isolated words, the teacher tries to act as a true interactional partner, negotiating meaning and content with the students, eliciting and encouraging their output, focusing on form when appropriate and offering them a rich, relevant and communicative input (Van den Branden 2006: 217).

But research has found that developing these task-based teaching competences is a challenging task for teachers. In a long-term implementation program in

Flanders, Belgium, Van den Branden and his team have shown that TBLT is a complex approach to be implemented in schools (Van den Branden 2006; Van den Branden et al. 2007). In Hong Kong Carless (2007) has found that teachers were concerned about the time factor and losing control in the classroom. East has pointed out that the wide range of different understandings and interpretations of what a task is leads to "considerable teacher uncertainty about what a task-based approach actually means" (East 2012: 6). Other studies concur that this is the major challenge for teachers who need to try make sense of an innovation and then develop experiential knowledge in the constraints of their local classrooms (Chan 2012; Van den Branden 2006).

When it comes to traditional forms of in-service training where teacher trainers impart theoretical knowledge, expecting teachers to make the transfer to concrete practice in their classrooms, Van den Branden (2006) has rightly claimed that teachers consider it as too theoretical and that the topic selection is dominated by the trainers and not the participants.

From our own experience with organising and researching teacher education processes at the pre- and in-service level and from research done in other contexts, we know that we need to focus on the person who teaches and on the activity of teaching in the diverse contexts of practice if we wish to make an impact (Freeman and Johnson 1998; Johnson 2009; Schocker-v. Ditfurth 2001) – an insight that Van den Branden has confirmed:

> (I)t is not so much the educational training enjoyed by teachers or the academic wisdom they are offered in in-service training or in educational journals, but what they have done and do in the classroom itself, and the meaning that they attach to these experiences, that constitute the backbone of what they think and believe about education (Van den Branden 2006: 222).

Focus on the person who teaches: Learning-to-teach studies (Appel 1995; Johnson 1994; Schocker 2001) have demonstrated that, unless student teachers encounter practice situations that allow them to experience convincing alternative practices and to experiment with new ideas, the imprints from their 'apprenticeship of observation' (Lortie 1975) are extremely resistant to change. The same is true for in-service teachers who may find readings on innovative approaches persuasive but not credible or too demanding to be a do-able option for their context of practice. Another powerful argument to support the integration of teachers' perspectives is that teaching is fundamentally a person-centred activity based on relationships: patterns of teacher role in research have repeatedly revealed that success in motivating and involving learners depends on teachers' attitudes to learners (for a summary of research into teacher role and tasks see Müller-Hartmann and Schocker-v. Ditfurth 2011: chapter 7; see also Hattie 2012).

We therefore favour approaches of professional development that do not reduce teachers to linguists capable of mediating language only.

Focus on the activity of teaching: Schön's (1983) publication on the nature of professional action in dynamic situations of practice has demonstrated that teachers have to cope with situations of uncertainty, complexity, uniqueness, instability, and value conflict. Managing processes in a task-based classroom appropriately means "working out the relationships among the participating persons and their positions and identities, their stance towards topics, processes, roles, values and ideologies which (... are) to be negotiated through a process of constant, creative, and useful exploratory struggle" (Candlin 2003: 41). Classrooms are not just backgrounds to teaching, but define the very nature of teaching and learning (Breen 1985). The interpretive paradigm of the sociocultural turn defines human learning as a dynamic social activity that is situated in the contexts within which teachers work (Johnson 2009). These contexts shape how and why teachers do what they do. Knowledge does not just develop by accumulating information, but is shared, negotiated and co-constructed through experience in the communities of practice in which the individual participates (see Wells and Chang-Wells 1992). In Flanders Van den Branden (2006) has shown that when trainers went to the schools to work with a local team of teachers, and coaching started from concrete classroom actions training was especially effective. While trainers need "to help the teachers to discover their own truths" (Van den Branden 2006: 240), it is also the teacher colleagues who provide feedback and support, "because they had similar experiences, worries or problems" (ibid: 242). The importance of group dynamics and teamwork have also been found in other TBLT studies "to play a key role in developing a common culture in terms of their approach to language teaching" (MacAllister et al 2012; see also Andon and Eckert 2009; and Jackson 2012).

An important part in this process are the so-called "small stories" (Vasquez 2011) or teachers' short personal narratives, which they exchange to generate ideas, clarify approaches, and provide support. Therefore teacher education needs to create opportunities to reflect on the appropriateness of teachers' theories of learning in their local contexts (see also Van den Branden 2006: 239–240). East comes to the conclusion that "classroom-based action research in which teachers themselves, individually and collaboratively, and working with either researchers or other practitioners" will help teachers develop TBLT competences (East 2012: 216).

From the various approaches resulting from these considerations (for a survey see Johnson 2009: 25), we decided to organize the project following the rationale of explorartory practice (see research methodology). We were convinced that both practitioners and researchers would benefit from the collaboration following our positive experience in other projects (i.e. Schart and Schocker 2013).

Tasks
1 *motivate learners to get involved:* they → *provide relevant / meaningful content* → *activate learners' resources* → *provide a clear communicative purpose and audience*
2 *are complex:* they → *provide choice, individual focus* → *provide rich resources* → *are process-oriented*
3 *integrate a focus on form*
4 *are interaction based on real-life problem-solving*
5 *are sequenced (task cycle) and balance demands and support*

The task features allow teachers to design tasks by making statements about the learning potential of a task. Breen has distinguished this task-as-workplan from the task-in-process (1987: 24–25), making us aware that a task is 'just' "a plan for learner activity.... The actual activity that results may or may not match that intended by the plan" (Ellis 2003: 9).

Teachers were introduced to both the ICC and the task features models (see below) to theoretically ground their ICC task design. Before we present the research context and methodology we describe in detail how we organized the project.

3 Resulting teacher education model

The project was organized as blended learning: face-to-face meetings (workshops) were followed by teachers' experimenting with tasks in their classrooms. During this time colleagues, participating researchers and teacher educators provided continuous support and advice, usually via e-mail.

The Workshops. The first of five three day workshops introduced teachers to the project, the basic task features as outlined above, and focused on various data collection methods that teachers could use to integrate their learners' and participating observers' (colleagues) perspectives at their schools (see Altrichter and Posch 2007). Each of the following workshops dealt with a particular aspect related to learners' competence development through tasks, i.e. how to integrate a form focus or how to design tasks that potentially develop ICC, the focus of this article.

Both teachers' experiential knowledge and published research knowledge were integrated in the collaborative development process. Each workshop started with teachers' conceptions and understandings of tasks. In our classroom contexts we follow a task-supported approach since the textbook is compulsory. Depending on the publisher, they contain tasks of varying degrees of difficulty and quality. Since teachers' ideas are closely related to textbook activities they need to be able to evaluate the learning potential of the tasks against their learners' needs and to re-write or exchange tasks if necessary (see task features above). The workshops organized teachers' development as reflected experience, following the *ERA principle* (*Experience – Reflection – Application*; see Legutke 1995). We illustrate this principle using the ICC research and development cycle as an example.

Experience: Workshops started by teachers exchanging their views on issues related to ICC tasks in teams, based on examples of tasks and the resulting learner texts they had brought along from their classrooms (phase I, see below). The presentation and discussion of the issues as seen from their perspectives in the plenary was compared to tasks that we had developed and taught in secondary EFL classrooms and to published research results such as Byram's model of ICC that we presented (see summary in Müller-Hartmann and Schocker-v. Ditfurth 2011: chapter 9) (phase II).

Reflection: This exchange of experiences resulted in a number of mutually agreed on key questions to be considered when planning ICC tasks for teachers' classrooms. These questions were based on intensive reflection of the practicability and appropriateness of research results and our task examples for the teachers' contexts (phase II). Some of these questions were:
- How to involve learners to make them curious about other cultural practices
- How to make learners aware of their own cultural practices
- How to help learners discover other cultural practices

Application: Finally teachers co-operatively planned tasks in teacher teams (phase III), a process that was continuously supported by us and participating teacher educators.

Experimentation with tasks in classrooms, support and research: During the interim period before the next workshop, teachers experimented with the tasks they had collaboratively developed in their classrooms. They documented their experiences in case studies which included the task-as-workplan, reflection of video-recorded tasks, learner feedback and participating colleagues' feedback (participant observation) and a selection of critical incidents that demonstrated both their successes and the issues which they shared at the following workshop. During this phase we provided continuous support mostly through e-mail: we commented on the first task-as-workplan version and, if appropriate, asked clarification questions or suggested alternative procedures (see Schocker-v. Ditfurth 2002). The revised task-as-workplan was then taught, video-taped and complemented by the teachers' research of their learners' perspectives and those of participating colleagues. The teacher in question, the researchers and teacher educators all received a copy of the lesson(s)' film. Independently of each other, they identified the critical incidents, which, viewed from their perspectives, highlighted the issues of ICC tasks (open retrospection). The issues resulting from the critical incidents were discussed in the following workshop and principles of appropriate design and practice of ICC tasks were commonly agreed on. The teachers documented their experiences in their case studies.

4 Participants

The participants, all EFL teachers in secondary schools, represent the different types of school in German secondary education (high school, grammar school, comprehensive school), all language learning levels (learners aged 11–16), and all levels of job experience (from novices to experts). All of the teachers are well qualified, that is, their target language competences may be classified as near-native, they have completed a 3–4 year university course in applied linguistics (involving various reflective practice phases), followed by a 1.5 year internship organized as reflected practice with teacher education support. They all subscribe to a professional idea of self which may be roughly described as learner-oriented which they expressed in the portraits we asked them to write at the beginning of the project.

Participating teachers were aware of the potential of tasks and were highly motivated to develop professionally through team and task expert support. It was the central motivation for all of the teachers to participate in the project. In this one respect participating teachers do not qualify as being representative for secondary EFL teachers in our context in general. But apart from this distinctive feature, they do. Our study was longitudinal, lasting for three years. Teachers were selected following the procedure of selective sampling (Kelle and Kluge

2010: 50, 55), which aims at getting a heterogeneous group that qualifies as being representative in a qualitative case study (if not in a statistical sense).

Teachers could reduce their teaching load through funding provided by the Ministries of Education. Professional support was provided by the two researchers, participating teacher educators and colleagues.

5 Research methodology – exploratory practice

The participation of teachers in our project was motivated by the prospect of constructing disciplinary knowledge collaboratively, and their interest in experimenting with tasks that would allow their learners to develop the competences set in the national attainment standards. In Wells and Chang-Wells (1992) words, our group of teachers and external advisors represented a "community of inquiry" engaging in action research in which "opportunities are set up for teachers and researchers to construct knowledge (...) collectively over time. Pedagogical knowledge construction thus occurs through dialectic interaction and critical exchange" (Burns 2009: 294).

The action research (AR) approach has a long tradition in classroom-based research in Europe, being low-scale in terms of size and interference in classroom processes. It is self-reflective, allowing teacher-researchers to better understand and possibly change their classroom practices by going through action research cycles (cf. Nunan and Bailey 2009: 227). Allwright and Hanks (2009) make us aware though that the focus needs to be on teachers' "particular understandings that are directly appropriate to their unique situations" prioritizing "learner understandings" (ibid: 149). Allwright and Hanks therefore call their approach of practitioner research exploratory practice (EP): "AR starts out as an intention to change in order to solve a problem, or at least to introduce an innovation. EP starts out with an intention to try to understand, rather than change" (ibid: 172–173). While the ultimate goal is a change in teaching methodology, we pointed out that research has shown that teachers mainly lack an understanding of what TBLT is and how it works in the classroom. Hence they need to have the opportunity to ask their questions and reflect about theoretical models in light of their local practices.

EP does just that by integrating teaching, learning, and research in the belief that teachers "need particular understandings that are directly appropriate to their unique situations, not high-level generalisation" (ibid: 146). By combining teaching, learning, and research we have tried to align both concerns, teachers' understanding of their practice as well as the development of their ICC task competences.

This dual perspective on understanding and change is also reflected in the role of our data collection tools. For the teachers and their learners they functioned as reflection tools.

Given the limited space, we provide one "action case study" of a community of inquiry, setting out "to learn what is happening" in our own practice as teacher educators (Nunan and Bailey 2009: 165, 158). Since case studies are about particularization and not generalization (van Lier 2005), we invite readers to establish connections from our research results to their own specific contexts and draw their own conclusions.

We addressed the following research question:

How can the teacher education project facilitate teachers' development of ICC task competences?

6 Data collection

To establish validity we combined different triangulation procedures: participants (teachers, learners, teacher researchers), researchers (two teacher researchers), and data collection. The rich data corpus included the following data sources providing etic and emic perspectives on the teachers' learning process:
A) Documentation of and reflection on participating teachers' perspectives, as recorded in their case studies, which included:
    – A description of their professional idea of self at the beginning of the EP phase
    – Commented and reflected versions of tasks-as-workplan, including perspectives of learners and their texts that resulted from doing the tasks
    – Selected critical incidents as seen from the teachers' perspectives and compared to researchers' and teacher educators' perspectives (documented through transcripts of videotaped task-in-process and of audio or video recordings made during face-to-face workshops)
B) Video documentation and transcripts of all of the discourses which took place during face-to-face workshops (discussions within teacher teams, presentations of issues based on their experiences, group discussions) and of advice and support given virtually.

In our paper we specifically focus on data from B) when teachers discussed issues in their small groups.

Data coding was done inductively in terms of the emerging ICC and task-based concepts in teachers' conversations. Two sets of codes emerged from the analysis, one pertaining to teachers' understanding of the complex cluster of ICC (i.e. references to cultural knowledge, dealing with stereotypes, facilitating a change of perspective), and the other to their increasing use of task-based discourse (i.e. involving the learners, looking for the purpose and goal of a task) and concepts in their endeavor to design ICC tasks. The two researchers compared the two sets of codes and looked for critical incidents where the two concepts intersect and influence each other (i.e. focus on task features in the ICC task design).

We are now going to show how they represent teachers' competence development.

7 Data analysis

To trace teachers' learning process we specifically look at the communities of inquiry they formed (see B above) based on the grades they usually teach (ages 11–12, 13–14, and 15–16). The group we selected is representative of their learning process and the ICC and task-based issues they raise. In this group four teachers discuss their experience, textbooks and tasks they brought to the workshop and they begin to design the task-as-workplan (ERA – phases I–III, see overview above) for a 5th or 6th grade (ages 11–12). We try to show how the teachers profit from the overall set-up of the in-service training when developing a concept of task-supported language teaching (TSLL) when designing an ICC task sequence, and how they engage in task discourse to design an ICC task sequence.

In terms of task features the focus is on the role of the teacher in stepping back and involving the learners. We also try to show how the community of inquiry ('small stories') supported this process.

In this phase of the project the teachers have already gone through two workshops, one focusing on integrating skills and the other on how and when to integrate a focus on form. They have started using task terminology such as task demand, task support, choice, and learner involvement from the beginning of the project, and in this third workshop which focuses on ICC one can see how their understanding of the task concept helps them to analyze and design ICC tasks.

We present their learning process following the different phases of the workshop.

7.1 Phase I – analyzing textbook tasks, presenting ICC tasks from local classrooms, trying to understand cultural concepts

In this first phase of the workshop the teachers analyze the ICC tasks their textbooks provide and present the ones they used in their classrooms. Like in the other groups they address two issues, the difference between area studies and ICC and the extent to which their textbooks include ICC tasks. In preparation of this workshop they read an introduction by Byram, Gribkova and Starkey (2002) on teaching ICC for language teachers which explains Byram's 'savoirs' of attitudes, knowledge, skills and critical cultural awareness. The data show that this pre-task to the workshop helped them organize their ideas about ICC.

Clarifying cultural concepts

The teachers start by trying to clarify their understanding of the concept of ICC by comparing it to the traditional concept of area studies most of them were introduced to in their pre-service teacher training. Next they address textbook analysis and methodological questions of task design. While trying to help Anneke[2] understand the differences they pool their pre-knowledge in this community of inquiry.

Anneke:	I would like to know if intercultural learning is different from area studies.
Bettina:	Area studies are part of this.
Anneke:	For me these are two different things.
Bettina:	One includes knowledge, like in this table [she refers to Byram's savoirs], but intercultural goes beyond this. Beyond factual knowledge.
Stefanie:	You should also be able to talk about it, to talk about the differences.
Bettina:	Or to reflect it critically.
Stefanie:	Right, exactly. Or to develop a certain empathy.
	(…)
Anneke:	I imagine that you can develop this without knowledge about a country.
	(…)

---

[2] All participants' names have been anonymized. Since the teachers originally talked in German the authors translated their communication.

Bettina: This is certainly possible. It depends on the topic and what you would like to achieve. That's why there are several dimensions: attitudes, knowledge, skills.
(...)
Anneke: But can intercultural learning also happen, if my neighbour is different?
Stefanie: I would say yes, it may begin like this on a small scale.
Anneke: Yes, then I am really involved, when I realize that even though we have the same cultural background, we are, however, totally different. The next step then is not difficult anymore (WS3-TA-SG5&6[3]).

While the teachers are still insecure about the precise meaning of ICC, their discussion shows that they have grasped important aspects of ICC, such as the fact that cultural knowledge (area studies) is just one dimension of ICC among others, and that the focus is not necessarily on learners' different national or ethnic backgrounds, but on cultural practices in general. At the same time they still focus on the differences between cultural practices, disregarding similarities. Later in the discussion Anneke makes them aware of this important issue:

Anneke: We have only looked at what is different. It is more difficult to look at what is similar, but this is also more productive (WS3-TA-SG5&6).

As we can see below they later take on this advice and focus on both aspects when designing tasks. In the analysis of their textbooks they quickly conclude that they have generally focused on cultural knowledge and that ICC task complexity is not considered.

Stefanie: In every story that tells something about the country, or about school, or the school system, something intercultural is considered. You can find many examples of this in the book. But they don't use the potential of this task, they say one or two sentences about it and that's it. Intercultural learning on a very minimal level (WS3-TA-SG5&6).

These exchanges show that discussing the theoretical input (Byram, Gribkova and Starkey 2002) as a group helps them clarify the ICC model to a certain

---

[3] WS3-TA-SG5&6 refers to the small group conversation of 5th and 6th teachers on textbook and task analysis in workshop 3.

extent, and also helps them analyze their textbooks since they can pool their knowledge.

From cultural concepts to personal narratives, clarifying methodological questions

When exchanging tasks they taught in their classrooms, the group quickly moves to methodological questions of how to design ICC tasks, such as how to include cultural experts in their class. Teachers conceptualise teaching from tasks, as has been reported in a study on in-service teachers' professional knowledge (2000). The following data show that they have developed an understanding of the potential of cultural diversity in their classrooms.

Stefanie: Learners already understand a lot because of the different cultures in their classroom. In my classroom there are six different cultures. And everybody shares their festivities and customs and through this they learn a lot (WS3-TA-SG5&6).

The teachers also use small stories or personal narratives to clarify issues such as the role of stereotypes which then again result in methodological considerations of how to get learners adopt a different perspective of understanding other cultural practices.

Anneke: My pen pal when I went to visit her for the first time when I was 14, expected a girl with long blond pigtails and wearing a dirndl because her grandmother had told her so.
Bettina: But these are her ideas of Germany. (...) You need to know about English people's ideas of Germans (WS3-TA-SG5&6).

Understanding cultural concepts with the help of task-based concepts

But their experience tells them that this approach is not feasible in a 5th or 6th grade since it requires too much cultural pre-knowledge of their learners. In their discussion they move from a more theoretical concept of changing perspectives (seeing your own cultures through the eyes of others) which might create stereotypical notions of what is typically German, to an understanding that they need to start the ICC process by activating their learners' experiences.

Petra: Learners can't be involved through a role play.
(...)
Stefanie: I agree, this is impossible. They are too young for that.
(...)
Stefanie: For me the task would definitely need to be more realistic. I could formulate it like this: If an exchange student came to you, how would he experience your place?
Petra: Why do I have to put him in such a situation? Why can't I just say: In our task you describe how diverse Germany is, for a students' newspaper or something.
Bettina: I still feel that this is about what is typically German, which leads in the wrong direction. (...)
Stefanie: ... there are the clichés again.
Bettina: ... I like Marita's task idea of 'Life in our Street' [learners compare what lives in their streets are like]. You and your street. It doesn't matter whether they are Germans, English or Greek (WS3-TA-SG5&6).

This process is supported by the input provided in the first workshop: teacher researchers had illustrated the task features on the basis of a task sequence on "Life in my street" that allowed learners to exchange experiences (see Müller-Hartmann, Schocker and Pant 2013: 37–62). The teachers begin to think in terms of the central task features, the need to involve one's learners, to establish a purpose for their task, and to make it as real-world as possible; making their learning process visible.

However, the teachers still do not fully understand the complex competence cluster of ICC. They need expert support to do so.

Anneke: Inter means between, this is why I am looking for the similarities. I don't really understand this about the other culture. For me this [the difference between cultures] is not really that important. That's why I am really curious what they [Anneke is referring to us, teacher researchers] are going to say in a minute [in the plenary] (WS3-TA-SG5&6).

In the following plenary phase of the workshop teacher researchers deal with these issues.

7.2 Phase II – discussing group results in plenary, developing cultural concepts

In the second phase the groups present their findings. They had arrived at some basic understanding of the role of ICC related to their local contexts (textbooks and tasks) and the group now begins to develop a better understanding of Byram's complex competence cluster. They achieve this by discussing the tasks they selected to present in the plenary phase as well as the tasks the teacher researchers presented. Some issues, such as the competence of developing critical cultural awareness, lead to lively discussions in the group. Teachers have to develop ICC themselves, for example the skill of discovery, i.e. trying to understand and read between the lines of culturally loaded texts (such as advertisements carrying hidden stereotypes) to be able to design ICC tasks for their learners. The plenary discussion highlights the learning process the teachers have gone through in their communities of inquiry.

Reflecting appropriateness of cultural concepts in textbooks

The teachers show that they are able to use a theoretical text to analyze their textbooks in light of ICC, and they have also realized that after analyzing the textbook tasks they often need to change or replace them if they want to develop their learners' ICC:

Bettina: With all the topics that are covered in our textbooks we noticed that the publisher strongly focuses on knowledge, or area studies, and that the other dimensions we read about in our [theoretical] text are not represented. At least not in detail, so we have to see for ourselves how best to integrate them (WS3-Plenary).

Clarifying cultural concepts in the light of task-based concepts

As regards teacher role they realize that they have to step back to activate their learners' ideas to be able to understand what they think, to then be able to tackle the cultural stereotypes their learners might harbor:

Stefanie: I often bring pictures, for example Winnetou [a stereotypical representation of a Native American in a famous German novel and film] which I have grown up with. My 5th or 6th graders have other ideas of Indians. I think it is important that you step back and don't start with the image you have yourself (WS3-Plenary).

Already in earlier workshops this teacher's idea of her role as a teacher had been obvious: she organized all of the input for her learners herself instead of involving them in this process to be able to learn about their associations and ideas. Here she shows that she has understood this concept of cultural learning, where any development has to begin with the learners' images, ideas or stereotypes. This also becomes obvious in the task design phase.

7.3 Phase III – designing ICC tasks as a community of inquiry

This phase shows how the teachers are now able to become independent of their textbooks as they design ICC tasks themselves, integrating the task-based discourse. At first they discuss a number of possible issues that could be interesting for their learners, by starting from topics the textbooks suggest (dialects, Guy Fawkes day, Thanksgiving, Diwali), which they then try to re-write to adapt it to a topic that is appropriate to their learners in their local contexts.

Generating task ideas – from textbook to community of inquiry

Stefanie, for example, decides to focus on festivities. But providing choice to involve learners in the beginning of a task potentially leads to insecurities since learners will react individually and produce unexpected responses. While Stefanie is insecure about her teacher role, the other teachers support her in designing the different steps of her task sequence focusing on important task features, as well as intercultural issues. They stress the positive dimensions of choice and involvement, also using arguments from the input phase in the plenary:

Stefanie: But this way I will get many different answers.
Bettina: Exactly, but that's the nice thing about it. That's what Andreas [one of the teacher researchers] said earlier that we…
Stefanie: We have this choice.
Bettina: … react flexibly.
Petra: And the involvement (WS3-TD-SG5&6[4]).

They make suggestions of how to activate learners' pre-knowledge and how to organize this:

---

[4] WS3-TD-SG5&6 refers to the small group conversation of 5th and 6th teachers on task design in workshop 3.

Stefanie: Yes, but what do I do now with all these different ideas...⁵ maybe I let them ... I could ask them to write a short text at home ... or ... we collect ideas together...?
Stefanie: Perhaps start by collecting ...
Petra: Yes, simply collecting at first ...
(...)
Petra: Or, they could think for a moment what kinds of activities they can think of, then you could give them paper slips and they write down their ideas and put them on the board.
Stefanie: I like this idea, because then everybody is involved ... then you will get 'Christmas' seven or eight times, but that it is totally ok (WS3-TD-SG5&6).

They know that a task needs to be sequenced and that there should be a target task, and her group remind her to plan task steps by considering the outcome of the task:

Petra: Maybe we should think about what the product should be.
Stefanie: Right, where do we actually want to go (...)?
(...)
Stefanie: And what actually is the final product? (WS3-TD-SG5&6).

The group also stresses the potential of intercultural learning by focusing on the existing similarities between different cultural practices in their classrooms. This is an important development, as teachers and textbooks tend to focus on what is different and neglect what different cultures have in common.

Petra: With different people ... that is nationalities ... religious affiliations ... a lot of the criteria will be the same ... a big family comes ... they eat a lot ... they drink a lot ... you give presents to each other, (...) ... they need to become aware of this. It may be called differently and may have a different background, but there are many similarities ... which would already be something.
Stefanie: Which would be great ... (WS3-TD-SG5&6).

Again the group support Stefanie on the methodological level of how to put the ICC task into practice:

---

5 ... means that the speaker pauses to think.

Petra: This is why it is very important that you – at the beginning ... list who does what, where, and when, ... so that all the learners deal with this, otherwise you won't find the similarities ... (WS3-TD-SG5&6).

In her final task-as-workplan Stefanie does just that, beginning the task sequence with a homework where students are involved by providing choice:

> Which festivals do you celebrate together with your family? Write down which festival you celebrate and why you like it. You can also stick a picture next to your text or draw something. Bring it back to class next lesson.
>
> Think of: What? When? Why? Who? Where?

As the data show, the community of inquiry is crucial in generating ideas and in providing support in the teachers' learning process.

8 Discussion

In our research question we were interested in finding out how such a long-term teacher education project can facilitate teachers' development of ICC task competences. In the case study we looked at the interface of the training's structure, its mix of small group work and plenary discussions, and teachers' desire to develop an understanding of ICC task design in their local practice.

The specific cyclical set-up of the training allowed teachers to look at ICC task design from their own experience, working with and analyzing the textbooks they have to use in their local contexts, and asking the questions they feel need to be answered to develop an understanding of the complex construct of ICC tasks. As Van den Branden stresses, "teachers will not adopt let alone integrate new practice if they do not believe in or have a clear understanding of the rationale behind these new practices" (2006: 234).

As we could see in the case study their competence development was supported by this change from small group negotiation of the ICC concepts and their representation in teachers' textbooks and the task design based on these textbooks (phase I), to a plenary discussion and reflection of the different local experiences, combined with the theoretical input and exemplary tasks as well as feedback of the teacher researchers (Phase II), back to another round of small group negotiation in a community of inquiry where teachers integrated theoretical input on the task features and Byram's model of ICC as well as practical advice of their colleagues to generate ideas for a first task-as-workplan (Phase III). When negotiating task design in their groups, teachers repeatedly made reference to suggestions the teacher researchers had made in the plenary. Teachers' competence development was further supported after they had taught the designed task sequence in their local classrooms through another round of reflection in their community of inquiry (not shown in the data here), in which the teachers presented and discussed critical incidents they had chosen from their videotaped lessons together with their colleagues and a teacher researcher.

This learning process can be seen in the developing task discourse the teachers use when they talk about involving their learners. It is interesting to note that it is the growing awareness and incorporation of the task features of involving learners and providing choice that seem to help teachers also generate ideas for ICC tasks that start from the premise that you need to design these tasks from the learners' experience.

In this process the role of the community of inquiry has been central. By pooling their knowledge and experiences teachers provided a safe learning atmosphere to each other where different ideas could be voiced and where, as we could see in Stefanie's case, the ongoing support from her peers helped her to take the risk of changing her approach to a more learner-oriented one, thinking task design from what her learners bring to the classroom. The community of inquiry is also important in helping them to make sense of Byram's ICC model in relation to their respective classroom practices. The support comes from more experienced colleagues, but it is also provided by telling each other 'small stories' about their experience of developing intercultural tasks in these reflective phases, something Vasquez (2011: 539) has also found in "post-observation meetings between novice ESL teachers and their mentors".

What starts out as a general discussion of what ICC comprises (phase I) is soon grounded in their everyday practice when teachers analyze the task in their textbooks, realizing that just cultural knowledge is insufficient. When telling stories about their local practice teachers move the learner into the foreground of task design, becoming aware of the other dimensions of Byram's model, such as how to involve learners to make them curious about other cultural practices and how to make learners aware of their own cultural practices (e.g. which festivities do you celebrate with your family?), which will help "students themselves develop an understanding of culture through a process of noticing, reflecting on and interpreting aspects of culture presented through language" (Liddicoat 2008: 284), moving a step forward on the way of becoming intercultural speakers.

By thinking tasks from their learners' perspective, involving them with their experiences, the teachers are able to turn from a theoretical discussion of cultural concepts to identifying do-able ideas of how to transfer concepts to make them manageable for their learners in their local classrooms. This process is supported by an increasing use of TSLL terminology, where teachers move from talking about the necessity to involve learners and for that reason create more real-world and with that problem-solving tasks (see task features one and four in the table above) to the question of how to structure a task sequence by thinking about the goal or target task, designing sub-tasks to reach this goal (task feature five).

The EP approach, which is based on the premise that teachers as well as teacher researchers need to understand practice, facilitates this learning process through a consistent focus on teachers' questions and their beliefs about teaching to make them aware through the community of inquiry and the support from the teacher researchers about possibilities of methodological development and change.

9 Conclusion

Our research project illustrates that, through an approach of EP, the concerns of research and practice can be aligned, as EP encourages the development of teachers' task-based discourse as well as their ability to design ICC tasks. At the same time it allows teachers and researchers alike to identify the emerging issues, results, and experiences, which may then be generalized for use in other foreign language teaching contexts.

We have tried to show how the teachers developed professionally through the specific set-up of the training. In-service education needs to be long-term, cyclical and organized as reflected experience to allow teachers to understand theoretical concepts and reflect their potential in their specific local contexts. This supports Van den Branden's conclusion that "educational innovation strategies need to address the practical and theoretical concerns that teachers have while adapting their classroom practice, preferably in an integrated way" (Van den Branden 2006: 234).

We have demonstrated that communities of inquiry are especially helpful in this regard as they provide the space teachers need to tell about their practical experience, voice their personal ideas, and to openly address the challenges they face as they provide a safe atmosphere through small group interaction where they learn from their peers in the process.

There are obvious restrictions to the findings since we only present one case study. The analysis needs to be extended to the impact of other task features such as the relationship between task demand and task support, and especially the integration of a focus on form in ICC task sequences since the focus on form has been shown as being especially challenging for teachers (see Müller-Hartmann and Schocker, forthcoming).

References

Allwright, Dick & Judith Hanks. 2009. *The developing language learner.* Houndmills: Palgrave Macmillan.

Altrichter, Herbert & Peter Posch. 2007. *Lehrerinnen und Lehrer erforschen ihren Unterricht.* Bad Heilbrunn: Klinckhardt.

Andon, Nick & Johannes Eckert. 2009. Chacun à son goût? Task-based L2 pedagogy from the teacher's point of view. *International Journal of Applied Linguistics* 19(3). 286–310.

Appel, Joachim. 1995. *Diary of a language teacher.* Oxford: Heinemann.

Appel, Joachim. 2000. *Erfahrungswissen und Fremdsprachendidaktik.* München: Langenscheidt.

Breen, Michael. 1985. The social context for language learning – a neglected situation? *Studies in Second Language Acquisition* 7. 135–158.

Breen, Michael. 1987. Learner contributions to task design. In Christopher N. Candlin & Dermot Murphy (eds.), *Language learning tasks*, 23–46. Englewood Cliffs, NJ: Prentice-Hall International.

Burns, Anne. 2009. Action research in second language teacher education. In Anne Burns & Jack C. Richards (eds.), *The Cambridge guide to second language teacher education*, 289–297. Cambridge: Cambridge University Press.

Byram, Michael. 1997. *Teaching and assessing intercultural communicative competence.* Clevedon, UK: Multilingual Matters.

Byram, Michael, Bella Gribkova & Hugh Starkey. 2002. *Developing the intercultural dimension in language.* Strasbourg: Council of Europe.

Candlin, Christopher N. 1987. Towards task-based language learning. In Christopher N. Candlin & Dermot Murphy (eds.), *Language learning tasks*, 5–22. Englewood Cliffs, NJ: Prentice-Hall International.

Candlin, Christopher N. 2003. Communicative language teaching revisited. In Michael K. Legutke & Marita Schocker-v. Ditfurth (eds.), *Kommunikativer Fremdsprachenunterricht: Rückblick nach vorn*, 41–58. Tübingen: Narr.

Carless, David. 2007. The suitability of task-based approaches for secondary schools: Perspectives from Hong Kong. *System* 35. 595–608.

Caspari, Daniela & Andrea Schinschke. 2009. Aufgaben zur Feststellung und Überprüfung interkultureller Kompetenzen im Fremdsprachenunterricht – Entwurf einer Typologie. In Adelheid Hu & Michael Byram (eds.), *Interkulturelle Kompetenz und fremdsprachliches Lernen. Modelle, Empirie, Evaluation*, 273–287. Tübingen: Narr.

Chan, Sui Ping. 2012. Qualitative differences in novice teachers' enactment of task-based language teaching in Hong Kong primary classrooms. In Ali Shehadeh & Christine A. Coombe (eds.), *Task-based language teaching in foreign language contexts. Research and implementation*, 187–213. Amsterdam: John Benjamins.

Devlieger, Mieke & Greet Goossens. 2007. An assessment tool for the evaluation of teacher practice in powerful task-based language learning environments. In Kris Van den Branden; Koen Van Gorp & Machteld Verhelst. (eds.), *Tasks in action: Task-based language education from a classroom-based perspective*, 92–130. Newcastle: Cambridge Scholars Publishing.

East, Martin. 2012. *Task-based language teaching from the teachers' perspective.* Amsterdam: John Benjamins.

Ellis, Rod. 2003. *Task-based language learning and teaching.* Oxford: Oxford University Press.

Freeman, Donald & Karen E. Johnson. 1998. Reconceptualizing the knowledge-base of language teacher education. *TESOL Quarterly* 32(3). 397–417.

Göbel, Kerstin. 2007. *Qualität im interkulturellen Englischunterricht. Eine Videostudie*. Münster: Waxmann Verlag.

Guth, Sarah & Francesca Helm. 2010. *Telecollaboration 2.0: Language, literacies and intercultural learning in the 21st century*. Bern: Lang.

Hattie, John. 2012. *Visible learning for teachers: Maximizing impact on learning*. London: Routledge.

Ishii, Eriko. 2009. The effects of task-based intercultural instruction on the intercultural competence of Japanese secondary EFL learners. *Asian Journal of English Language Teaching* 19. 159–181.

Jackson, Daniel. 2012. Task-based language teacher education in an undergraduate program in Japan. In Ali Shehadeh & Christine A. Coombe (eds.), *Task-based language teaching in foreign language contexts. Research and implementation*, 267–285. Amsterdam: John Benjamins.

Jäger, Anja. 2011. *Kultur szenisch erfahren. Interkulturelles Lernen mit Jugendliteratur und szenischen Aufgaben im Fremdsprachenunterricht*. Frankfurt: Lang.

Johnson, Karen E. 1994. The emerging beliefs and instructional practices of pre-service English as a second language teachers. *Teaching & Teacher Education* 10(4). 439–452.

Johnson, Karen E. 2009. *Second language teacher education. A sociocultural perspective*. New York: Routledge.

Kelle, Udo & Susann Kluge. 2010. *Vom Einzelfall zum Typus: Fallvergleich und Fallkontrastierung in der qualitativen Sozialforschung*, rev. edn. Wiesbaden: VS Verlag.

[KMK] Sekretariat der Ständigen Konferenz der Kultusminister der Länder in der Bundesrepublik Deutschland (eds.). 2004. *Bildungsstandards für die erste Fremdsprache (Englisch / Französisch) für den Mittleren Schulabschluss. Beschluss vom 04.12.2003*. München: Luchterhand.

Legutke, Michael K. 1995. Lehrerfortbildung: Einführung. In Michael K. Legutke (ed.), *Handbuch für Spracharbeit Teil 6: Fortbildung. Band 1*, 1–22. München: Goethe-Institut.

Liddicoat, Anthony. 2008. Pedagogical practice for integrating the intercultural in language teaching and learning. *Japanese Studies* 28(3). 277–290.

Lortie, Dan C. 1975. *Schoolteacher. A sociological study*. Chicago: Chicago University Press.

MacAllister, Julie; Marie-Francoise Narcy-Combes & Rebecca Starkey-Perret. 2012. Language teachers' perceptions of a task-based learning programme in a French university. In Ali Shehadeh & Christine A. Coombe (eds.), *Task-based language teaching in foreign language contexts. Research and implementation*, 313–342. Amsterdam: John Benjamins.

Miller, Jennifer. 2009. Teacher identity. In Anne Burns & Jack C. Richards (eds.), *The Cambridge guide to second language teacher education*, 172–181. Cambridge: Cambridge University Press.

Müller-Hartmann, Andreas. 2006. The role of tasks in promoting intercultural learning in electronic learning networks. *Language Learning & Technology* 4(2). 129–147.

Müller-Hartmann, Andreas & Marita Schocker. forthcoming. The challenges of teaching focus on form tasks: Results from a classroom research project in secondary EFL classrooms. In Michael Bygate, Virginia Samuda & Kris Van den Branden (eds.), *TBLT as a researched pedagogy*. Amsterdam: John Benjamins.

Müller-Hartmann, Andreas & Marita Schocker-v. Ditfurth. 2010. Research on the use of technology in task-based language teaching. In Michael Thomas & Hayo Reinders (eds.), *Task-based language learning and teaching with technology*, 17–40. London: Continuum.

Müller-Hartmann, Andreas & Marita Schocker-v. Ditfurth. 2011. *Task-supported language teaching*. Paderborn: Schöningh.
Müller-Hartmann, Andreas & Marita Schocker-v. Ditfurth. 2013. Developing teachers' intercultural communicative competences for task-supported language classrooms. *Fremdsprachen Lehren und Lernen* 42(2). 85–98.
Müller-Hartmann, Andreas, Marita Schocker & Hans Anand Pant. 2013. *Kompetenzentwicklung in der Sek. I. Lernaufgaben Englisch aus der Praxis*. Braunschweig: Westermann Diesterweg.
Nunan, David, & Kathleen M. Bailey. 2009. *Exploring second language classroom research. A comprehensive guide*. Boston: Heinle.
Reiman, Andrew. 2010. Task-based cultural awareness raising through learner ethnographies. In Alia Shehadeh & Christine A. Coombe (eds.), *Applications of task-based learning in TESOL*, 49–66. Baltimore: TESOL Publications.
Samuda, Virginia. 2001. Guiding relationships between form and meaning during task performance: The role of the teacher. In Michael Bygate, Peter Skehan & Merrill Swain (eds.), *Researching pedagogic tasks: Second language learning, teaching and testing*, 119–139. Harlow: Pearson Education.
Samuda, Virginia & Michael Bygate. 2008. *Tasks in second language learning*. Houndmills, New York: Palgrave Macmillan.
Schart, Michael & Marita Schocker. 2013. 'Die Menschen stärken, die Sachen klären': Die Aktionsforschung als praktikabler Weg zur gemeinsamen Entwicklung von Unterricht. In Michael Schart, Makiko Hoshii & Marco Raindl (eds.), 40–59. München: Iudicium Verlag.
Schocker-v. Ditfurth, Marita. 2001. *Forschendes Lernen in der fremdsprachlichen Lehrerbildung*. Tübingen: Narr.
Schocker-v. Ditfurth, Marita. 2002. *Unterricht verstehen. Erfahrungswissen reflektieren und den eigenen Unterricht weiterentwickeln*. Medienpaket zur Förderung reflektierter Unterrichtspraxis. München: Goethe Institut Inter Nationes.
Schön, Donald. A. 1983. *The reflective practitioner: How professionals think in action*. New York: Basic Book.
Van den Branden, Kris. 2006. Training teachers: Task-based as well? In Kris Van den Branden (ed.), *Task-based language education. From theory to practice*, 217–248. Cambridge: Cambridge University Press.
Van den Branden, Kris. (ed.). 2006. *Task-based language education. From theory to practice*. Cambridge: Cambridge University Press.
Van den Branden, Kris, Koen Van Gorp & Machteld Verhelst. (eds.). 2007. *Tasks in action: Task-based language education from a classroom-based perspective*. Newcastle: Cambridge Scholars Publishing.
Van Lier, Leo. 2005. Case study. In Eli Hinkel (ed.), *Handbook of research in second language teaching and learning*, 195–208. Mahwah, NJ: Erlbaum.
Vasquez, Camilla. 2011. TESOL, teacher identity, and the need for 'small story' research. *TESOL Quarterly* 45(3). 535–545.
Wells, Gary & G. L. Chang-Wells. 1992. *Constructing knowledge together: Classrooms as centers of inquiry and literacy*. Portsmouth, NH: Heinemann.
Willis, Jane. 1996. *A framework for task-based learning*. Harlow: Longman.

Jonathan Newton and Trang Bui
12 Teaching with Tasks in Primary School EFL Classrooms in Vietnam

1 Introduction

Task-based language teaching (TBLT) increasingly informs the design and implementation of national language curricula in many parts of the world. Reflecting this real world relevance, scholarship in the field has increasingly taken an ecological perspective, focusing on the role of context in mediating the way teachers interpret the practice of TBLT (e.g., Adams and Newton 2009; Shehadeh and Coombe 2012; Thomas and Reinders 2015). This recent orientation towards the particular stands in synergistic contrast to a well-established experimental/quasi-experimental research tradition focusing on tasks rather than teachers, on learning rather than learners, and on conditions rather than context. It also aligns with M. H. Long's (2015) contention that "true" TBLT is only ever derived from a situated needs analysis, ensuring that tasks are, by definition, local and specific. For this reason, Long identifies "detailed classroom studies of the ways teachers and students perform classroom lessons" (p. 371) as one of the "obvious areas in need of serious research effort" (p. 372).

The study reported in this chapter reflects this classroom orientation. It investigates the 'fertility of the ground' for task-based teaching in a context hitherto under-researched from a TBLT perspective, namely EFL classes in primary school classrooms in Vietnam. In this sector, a new curriculum has recently been rolled out, designed explicitly to improve the English communication skill development of young learners.

The implementation of this new curriculum relies heavily on mandated textbooks which are designed centrally and provided to teachers and students in primary school EFL classes. Teachers are expected to follow the textbook closely as is the common practice in primary school EFL across Asia. Naturally then, the role and nature of the textbook is a central consideration in research into instructional practices in these contexts. Of course the teacher also plays a crucial role in mediating the actual implementation of a textbook and so it is important to also understand the decisions teachers make as they work with textbooks. There is good reason therefore to explore the curriculum in its intended, resourced and enacted forms and to evaluate its congruence with established principles of

---

Jonathan Newton and **Trang Bui**, Victoria University of Wellington

DOI 10.1515/9781501503399-013

task-based teaching and learning. It was for this purpose that the research reported in this chapter was carried out.

2 Teachers, TBLT, and teaching EFL in primary school settings

The question of how teachers engage with and perceive TBLT has been widely researched in recent times (e.g., Carless 2009; East 2012; Erlam 2016; Nguyen 2014; Nguyen, Le and Barnard 2015; Nguyen, Newton and Crabbe 2015; Zhang, 2015; Zheng and Borg 2014). Little of this research has looked at primary school contexts, however. This is not surprising since teaching with tasks is a more established approach in secondary and tertiary contexts. But this is changing. Across Asia we see growing interest in EFL in primary school education and a small but growing body of scholarship looking at how TBLT might serve teaching and learning in this sector. In the remainder of this section we will briefly review research on task-based curriculum reform in Asian contexts and on research in primary school contexts in particular.

Hong Kong led the way in task-based curricular reform in Asia with reforms in the primary school sector beginning in 1999. Carless (2003, 2004) has reported extensively on the implemetation of these reforms, highlighting teacher resistance to TBLT and the contextual constraints that teachers perceived as impeding their capacity and willingness to adopt task-based innovations. In the Chinese context, Deng and Carless (2009) found that despite curriculum reforms designed to encourage task-based teaching, there was little evidence of its uptake by teachers. They attribute this to teachers' limited understanding of how to teach with tasks and to the backwash effect of traditional examinations on teaching practice. These same problems were confirmed more recently by Zhang (2015) in research reporting case studies of three teachers implementing TBLT in primary schools in South China.

In the Vietnamese context, Nguyen, Newton and Crabbe (2015) found congruence between TBLT and the practices of teachers in an elite, urban school. However, other Vietnamese studies situated in non-elite schools have found considerable distance between teachers' beliefs and TBLT principles (Nguyen 2014; Nguyen, Le and Barnard 2015). These contradictory findings highlight the need for research to take account of the influence of specific settings and contextual factors on the dispositions of teachers towards communicative and task-based teaching approaches and on their capacity to adopt these approaches.

We now turn briefly to research focused on tasks for young learners. While as we noted, this is an under-researched learning context, it has attracted a healthy amount of recent interest. Studies in this area are, broadly speaking, of two kinds. Firstly, there are those that focus on how tasks can be used with young learners and the impact of tasks on learning (e.g., Duran and Ramaut 2006; García Mayo and Lázaro Ibarrola 2015; Lee 2005; Pinter 2007; Shintani 2016). Pinter (2007), for example, noted how ten-year-old children in a state primary school in Hungary benefited from systematic repetition of interactive tasks in pairs. Similarly, Shintani (2016) showed how absolute beginner pre-school learners in a private school in Japan were able to engage successfully in input-based tasks and to acquire vocabulary and grammatical knowledge in the process. Overall this research highlights the affordances available for young learners through task-based learning.

Secondly, research on tasks and young learners has investigated the actual implementation of task-based teaching in primary school classrooms in response to specific curriculum innovations (Butler 2015; Carless 2003, 2004; Van den Branden, Koen and Verhelst 2007). For instance, the study by Butler (2015) involved a case study of teachers interacting with elementary school students on task-based assessments and highlighted the limited range of interaction patterns occurring in these assessments when contrasted with child-child interactions.

Carless (2003, 2004) reported on case studies of EFL teachers in Hong Kong primary schools as they struggled to implement a task-based curriculum. The second of these studies highlighted three barriers to the task-based innovation in this context: use of the learners' first language, classroom management, and problems with the quality and quantity of learner language production. Carless argues that these barriers are closely related to how the teachers "filtered and interpreted the innovation" (p. 658) through their understanding of tasks and beliefs about what constituted a productive classroom learning environment. In concluding, he argues that "[t]eachers mold innovations to their own abilities, beliefs, and experiences; the immediate school context; and the wider socio-cultural environment." (p. 659) and that we therefore need more research on these interpretive processes in a wider range of contexts. It is to this end that we have undertaken the research reported in this current chapter.

3 The primary school EFL curriculum in Vietnam

Following a trend evident elsewhere in Asia, Vietnam has sought to boost the teaching and learning of English in primary schools through educational reform, in this case via the National Foreign Languages 2008 – 2020 Project (NFLP). As part of this reform, a new English language curriculum (trial version) was introduced in 2010 which adopts communicative language teaching as a guiding pedagogy for the implementation of the new textbook series (Tieng Anh[1] 3–4–5 2012) currently used in Grades 3–5 EFL classes in primary schools across Vietnam. The curriculum document states that this approach should conform to three guiding principles; the communication, task and meaningfulness principles (Ministry of Education and Training/MOET 2010: 10). Although the communication and meaningfulness principles are further explained in curriculum documents including the teacher's version of the textbook, the task principle is not explained at all in any of these documents although tasks are present throughout the textbook, which we will now describe.

The three textbook series mandated to carry this new curriculum into the Grades 3, 4 and 5 classrooms are each comprised of 20 units covering four themes: Me and my friend, Me and my school, Me and my family, and Me and my community. These themes are repeated in each of the Grade 3 to 5 textbooks but with different lesson topics at each level. Each unit is comprised of three lessons with each lesson typically taught over two 35–40 minute class periods. The first two lessons in each unit contain speaking and listening activities and tasks, and the third, a reading-writing task followed by a 'project' task. Two examples of these project tasks for Grade 4 are (i) interviewing a classmate about what they do in the weekend and reporting to the class, and (ii) designing a birthday invitation card and telling the class about it.

Tasks like these are widely used across the textbooks but with fewer tasks and more language practice exercises in the Grade 3 textbook (for the beginning level). By 'tasks' we refer to activities that reflect the four core features of a language learning task proposed by Ellis (2009), namely: a focus on meaning, the presence of a gap (information or opinion); the requirement that learners draw on their own resources to complete the activity; and the specification of a non-linguistic outcome.

Despite the widespread use of tasks in the textbooks, overall the books conform to a *task-supported* approach in which tasks are used for communicative practice of pre-selected forms rather than a *task-based* approach in which tasks are the central unit of instruction (Ellis, 2003). Accordingly, the teachers' book states that "the student's book follows a sequence of presentation, practice and production to develop English at a basic level" (Sach giao vien tieng Anh[2] 4 2015: 7). Within this PPP approach, the burden of learning new forms falls on the speaking-listening lessons since these are always the first lessons in each

---

[1] English textbook
[2] Teacher's book

unit. As a consequence, these lessons are notably more tightly structured along PPP lines and, as such, represent a weak form of task-based teaching at best. In contrast, the reading-writing lessons and the final project in each unit reflect a much stronger version of task-based teaching. Interestingly, this reverses the more typical pattern of the teaching of speaking being more task-based and communicative compared to the teaching of the other skills, especially the receptive skills (Carless 2009). The research we report in this chapter focuses only on the speaking lessons. An example of a speaking lesson is included in Appendix A.

4 The study

As noted above, curriculum documents for Vietnamese primary school EFL make explicit mention of task and communication principles, and tasks are present throughout the mandated textbooks, albeit often embedded within PPP lesson sequences. Given this orientation to teaching with tasks in the intended and resourced curriculum, our purpose in carrying out the first phase of this two-phase study was to investigate whether teachers in this context were implementing the textbook tasks as intended, and to explore the understandings of teachers concerning their experience of teaching with these tasks and following (or not) the set PPP sequence. In the second phase of the research we investigated how the teachers responded to teaching revised versions of the PPP lessons designed to reflect a stronger version of task-based teaching. This phase directly addressed concerns about the PPP lessons raised by the teachers in phase 1. We also investigated the nature of classroom interaction in the revised lessons. Two research questions sum up the aims of the study:
1. In teaching the textbook speaking lessons, how congruent with TBLT were (i) implementation decisions made by teachers and (ii) their cognition regarding these decisions?
2. What affordances and constraints emerged through the teaching of revised textbook speaking lessons designed to reflect a stronger version of task-based teaching?

4.1 The teaching context and participating teachers

The research took place in primary schools in An Giang province, one of the largest provinces in the south of Vietnam, located approximately 200km far from Ho Chi Minh City. The main author is a primary school English teacher trainer at a university in this province and works in pre-service and in-service teacher training in the province. As part of her work she has been involved in introducing teachers to the Primary Language Curriculum introduced in 2010.

Convenience sampling was used to identify teachers who could participate in the research. Three selection criteria were applied: they had taught the new curriculum for at least two years; were available and willing to participate; and represented a range of urban, rural and semi-rural public primary schools[3]. The latter criterion was important because of the differences in educational opportunities and resourcing of schools across these different contexts, and especially between schools in rural and urban districts. Students in the rural schools, for instance, have almost no access to private classes while for most of their counterparts in the urban schools, additional private English classes are widely accessible.

Seven teachers were selected and invited to participate in the research. All accepted. They were all qualified as implementers of the Pilot Curriculum Policy 2010 and had worked with the new textbook for at least two years. All had obtained a required B2 level in the CEFR. Three were master teachers whose teaching competence is widely recognized. Table 1 summarizes the biodata for each of the teachers. For the second phase of the research involving teaching revised speaking lessons, a sub-set of three of these teachers were invited to participate.

Table 1: Details of the seven participating teachers

Teachers (pseudonyms)	Age (years)	Experience (years)	Qualifications	Gender	School setting	Grade
Lan	24	3	BA (TEFL)	F	Urban	4
Nga	26	4	BA (TEFL)	F	Urban	3
Nhu	35	12	BA (TEFL)	F	Semi-rural	4
Ly	36	13	BA (TEFL)	F	Semi-rural	3
Hoa	26	5	BA (TEFL)	F	Rural	4
Mai	26	5	BA (TEFL)	F	Rural	3
Nam	26	5	BA (TEFL)	M	Rural	4

Note: F = Female, M = Male

4.2 Study design, data collection and data analysis

The research adopted a qualitative case study approach to research design, an approach which has been widely used in research into teacher cognition. An

---

[3] The schools were distinguished based on both the researcher's knowledge of the area and the official categorization of the schools by the local department of education and training.

interpretive research paradigm was also employed because its goal is to "understand the inner perspectives and meanings of actions and events of those being studied" (Anderson and Burns 1989: 67).

Following this approach, in the first phase of the research each of the teachers who had volunteered to participate in the research was observed teaching either a whole unit (three lessons in six 40-minute periods) in the case of the Grade 4 teachers, or two lessons (four 35-minute periods) in the case of the Grade 3 teachers. The lessons were video-recorded and field notes taken. Shortly after each observed lesson (either the same day or the following day) stimulated recall (SR) interviews were carried out following guidelines suggested by Borg (2006) and Gass and Mackey (2000). In the SR interviews, the teachers were provided with samples of recordings from a lesson or a description of part of a lesson and asked to comment about their decision making and thinking processes related to this. Two to three days after their teaching of the entire unit, a follow-up interview was carried out with each teacher. The purpose was to elicit their perceptions of the textbook as a whole and of the PPP-based speaking lessons in particular. All interviews were carried out in Vietnamese.

In the second phase, the first step involved redesigning two of the PPP-based speaking lessons to reflect a stronger task-based approach. These were trialed in classes not involved in the main study and further refined on the basis of this experience. Three of the Grade 4 teachers from the first phase were then invited to teach these lessons as scheduled in the timetable. The first researcher conducted an informal briefing session with each teacher prior to the lessons being taught. The lessons were then observed and recorded, including recordings of 18 pairs of students performing the main task. Follow-up interviews were conducted with the teachers and focus groups of students.

All recorded data from classrooms and interviews from both phases was transcribed for further analysis. The interviews were all conducted in Vietnamese. Once transcribed, they were translated into English. Content analysis was used to analyze the data. This involved identifying emerging themes through an iterative process of analyzing and reanalyzing observation notes, recordings and transcripts (Nunan & Bailey 2009).

4.3 Materials

The redesign of the PPP lessons for the second phase of the study to make them more task-based, drew on principles of task-based lesson design and teaching from Willis and Willis (2007) and Ellis (2003). The redesign involved replacing the listen and repeat activity in the presentation stage with an input processing task, replacing the practice stage with an information gap task, and replacing the performance stage with post-task focus-on-form (FonF) activities. The lesson modifications are summarized in Table 2. These modifications reflect the principles of (i) a primary focus on meaning and on achieving non-linguistic outcomes; (ii) FoF emerging from communicative effort; and (iii) learners drawing on their own resources to achieve task outcomes. The lesson represented here was from the Grade 4 textbook (Unit 8) on the topic, 'What subjects do you have today?'. The aim of the lesson was for students to be able to tell each other about their class timetable.

Table 2: The modification of a PPP lesson into a task-based lesson

Original PPP lesson	Revised TBLT version of the lesson
Presentation (i) Listen and repeat activity using a picture-based dialogue provided in a recording and written form. (ii) After this teacher-led practice, the teacher explains the target structural patterns.	*Pre-task* (i) Brainstorming school subjects in a spider gram for vocabulary priming. (ii) An input-based task in which learners listen to a conversation between two students about their timetables and complete a handout containing partial versions of the timetables.
Practice Q&A drill based on the target structural pattern. Teacher-led practice first and then pair-work.	*Main Task* An information gap task for pair work in which partners share information about two timetables in order to produce final versions and then to find three differences and two similarities between the timetables.
Performance Pair communication activity – ask and answer questions about your partners' timetable using the target patterns provided.	*Post-task* Public performances of the main task by three pairs of learners followed by teacher-led focus-on-form discussion and a language practice game.

5 Findings and discussion

5.1 Phase 1: The PPP speaking lessons

In their classroom practice, the seven teachers all closely followed the PPP sequence for the speaking lessons. In the interviews, six of the seven teachers noted that they did so because program managers expected this. As Nam commented, 'I have to use the traditional teaching method when I teach in my school because it will be a disadvantage for me if I do not follow the established rules.'[4] However, they frequently added more communicative and task-like activities in the presentation and production stages. In the presentation phase, these additional tasks were included to review previous lesson content, memorize the new vocabulary words, and increase engagement. In the production stage these activities were used to increase opportunities for meaningful and communicative practice. The most frequently added activity in the production stage was an interview task in which students interviewed each other to elicit personal information on the topic. The four teachers who often used this activity all highly valued the opportunities for meaningful communication it offered. As Nhu commented, "when I organized the interview activity, my students had [...] more opportunities to communicate with their peers and they did not have to focus their attention on the textbook".

Notwithstanding these enhancements, the overall PPP structure of the textbook lessons meant that most of these tasks were oriented towards form-focused practice of pre-specified language items as is typical of PPP instruction and so reflect a task-supported rather than task-based approach to using tasks for language learning (Ellis 2003).

We now turn to teacher cognition, to the question of what the teachers thought about their teaching practice and specifically about the PPP sequence used in the textbook. Three of the teachers (Lan, Mai, Nhu) expressed somewhat positive views of this sequence. They noted that it provided a predictable lesson structure for lower level classes and conformed to the approach they had learned to use in their pre-service teacher education. As Nhu commented:

> I have followed the PPP approach because I learned this approach from my pre-service education and my colleagues. I find it effective for teaching speaking skills in that following this sequence, new target language items are drawn from contexts. Students learn how to communicate from the contexts. Repetitive practice is needed for the learning of new language items [...] only after a lot of repetition can students develop their fluency in the production stage.

However, even when a positive comment was made, it was often followed by a more negative assessment of the method, as seen in Hoa's comment:

> The advantage when I followed those steps is students had been familiar with the steps, so the teaching was smoother and students could approach the lessons more easily. However, I still feel that students' speaking and listening skills are not fully developed.

Another teacher Ly tended to be somewhat neutral about the value of the approach. Three teachers (Hoa, Nam and Nga), while noting some positive points,

---

4 All excerpts from the interviews have been translated from Vietnamese into English.

were highly critical of this approach. They spoke extensively about its limitations, and expressed a desire to teach in a more communicative way. Criticisms of the PPP lessons converged on how mechanical, time-consuming and boring these lessons could be. As Nam comments,

> I have noticed that some structural patterns in the presentation stage are quite long and if I follow all the steps required, I will have to spend a lot of time and my students will also get bored. As a result, they will refuse to repeat the dialogue. The steps are I ask them, they ask me; then Group A asks group B; then closed pairs and open pairs. I feel this procedure is boring. This repetition does bore my students.

The teachers viewed this issue as particularly problematic for higher level classes. As Nga comments,

> I have based my teaching on the three steps for a year and found it ineffective [...] some lessons were so easy, which bored the students. They even ignored my first step of presenting the language. They did not look at all.

Similarly, Hoa struggled with the rigidity of the lessons, noting that the PPP approach casts students in a passive role. She had this to say:

> I think the steps are so fixed. It's like we arrange and assign things to students. We show them this is what they should say. Then students just have to follow the structural patterns we have taught them. This fails to enhance students' ability to use the language. I also think that here teachers play a more central role and just lead students to what they want them to do.... It is like the learning process is very theoretical. It means we have to provide students something in advance and they have to follow. We provide the theory for students before we get them to practice. I think this can't enhance students' ability to use English language. It is like we force them to do what we want them to do, speak what we want them to speak.

As noted above, the teachers tried to address these deficiencies by increasing the communicativeness of the lessons. Nevertheless, they were dissatisfied with the time allocated for communicative practice. As Hoa commented,

> The time allotted is not enough to maximize the communication ability in students. It is because the production stage just lasts around 10 to 15 minutes. I think it is quite short while this stage is very important. This is when students apply what they have learned in practice and expand their conversation beyond the structures they have just learned in the presentation and practice stages.

Not surprisingly, then, when invited in the interviews to express an opinion on the contrasting PPP and task-based approaches, the teachers were all receptive to a more task-based approach. As Nam commented,

I think it is better when students learned by doing or through activities. I think the students themselves can also learn better in this way than from what we have prepared for them.

In fact, Nga had already gone a considerable distance towards turning the PPP lessons into more task-based lessons by reversing the sequence of activities so that the meaning-focused communication task came first before any attention was given to forms[5]. In Nga's innovation and in the criticisms of the PPP approach by the teachers we saw sufficient justification for initiating the second phase of the research in which we investigated the teaching of two revised PPP lessons re-designed to reflect a stronger version of task-based teaching.

5.2 Phase 2. The task-based lessons

Phase 2 data consisted of (a) classroom observations, (b) recordings of both teacher-fronted classroom talk and peer-peer interaction in the main task, and (c) interviews with the teachers and focus groups of learners. This is a rich data set, but because of space constraints we will focus on two sub-sets of the data only: peer-peer interaction and interviews with the teachers.

In the interviews, the three teachers who taught the revised lessons all reported favourably on the experience, although one teacher expressed qualified support. We address her concerns at the end of this section. These favourable views can be seen in the interview extracts we discuss below. In the lesson transcripts we found abundant evidence of learning processes that confirmed the teacher's positive perceptions. Again, examples are provided below. We now report three main affordances that emerged from our analysis of the transcripts and interviews with the teachers.

Affordance 1. Pushed output

According to Swain (1995), the need to express meanings in a second language pushes learners to use language that they have not yet mastered. She argues that this "pushed output" drives language development in three main ways: it provides opportunities for learners to notice a gap between what they want to say and what they can say; it provides the learner with opportunities to test hypotheses about the language; and it encourages the learner to reflect on linguistic form and thereby to 'control and internalise linguistic knowledge' (Swain

---

[5] Note that Nga's students were stronger than those of other Grade 3 teachers since Nga taught in an urban school in Long Xuyen city where, unlike the other two Grade 3 teachers who taught in rural and semi-rural schools, her students had access to private classes.

1995: 126). We see these processes in Extract 1 (below) from the performance of the main information gap task by two learners. Note in particular the fifth turn in which S1 appears to notice a problem with S2's form of the question, 'Who is English teacher name'. S1 then uses external speech to construct a more target-like version, 'Who is science teacher?' before directing the question to her interlocutor.

Extract 1

01   S1: Ok. English teacher name?
02   S2: Who is...?
03   S1: ...English teacher name?
04   S2: Who is English teacher name?
05   S1: It's Ms Nhung too. Who...who...teach...who Science teacher name? Who is Science teacher? Who is Science teacher? Who is Science teacher?
06   S2: Science? Ms Mai.

Of course, this example of 'pushed output' is also highly collaborative. As Swain (2000) argues, such collaborative dialogue 'allows performance to outstrip competence. It is where language use and language learning can co-occur. It is language use mediating language learning' (p. 97). In the following comment about his experience of teaching the task-based lessons, one of the teachers, Lan, makes a similar point in her observation about how these lessons encouraged learners to "mobilize" their linguistic resources:

> When I used the traditional method, I taught students structural patterns first and then got them to practice the patterns repeatedly using the pictures. This repetitive practice also helped them learn the structures. However, sometimes, the learning was mechanical and did not help students use more vocabulary words. When involving themselves in the task-based lessons [...] students had to mobilise their vocabulary resources to help them express their ideas. [...] This could enable a lot of vocabulary words to be mobilised.

Affordance 2. Peer scaffolding and negotiation of meaning

In the briefing sessions for phase 2, the teachers were encouraged to pair up more capable and less capable peers for the main task. Perhaps as a result of the teachers taking up this advice, the data revealed a consistent pattern of highly collaborative peer-peer interaction in which the more capable peers frequently scaffolded the participation of their less capable peers, helping them complete the task and resolve language problems. An example is provided in Extract 2. Here, S1, the more capable peer, gives instructions to S2 in Vietnamese in line 2 and provides him with the wording of the question (in English) which he needs to ask. She (S1) continues to offer prompts to S2 in lines 4, 8 and 10 to keep the dialogue going. The value of collaborative scaffolding such as this for language learning is well attested in the research literature (e.g. Foster & Ohta 2005; Sato & Ballinger 2016).

Extract 2

01 S2: What...?
02 S1: Ông hỏi là what subject do you have today á. Hiểu không? [*You ask me, 'What subject do you have today'. Do you understand?*]
03 S2: What subject do you have today?
04 S1: on...?
05 S2: Tuesday
06 S1: Tuesday. I have Music, IT, Vietnamese.
07 S2: Music hả? [*You said 'Music'?*]
08 S1: Rồi hỏi tiếp đi. [*Keep asking!*]
09 S2: What subject do you have today?
10 S1: on...?
11 S2: Thursday
12 S1: I have English, Vietnamese and Math.

A subset of collaborative scaffolding involved negotiation of meaning (Foster & Ohta 2005) which was also a salient feature of task-based interaction in the lesson. For example, in line 2 of Extract 3, S2 seeks clarification of the word 'draw'. When S1 is unable to supply the correct word, S2 provides it for him and he then appropriates it.

Extract 3

01 S1: I have Science, Math and draw
02 S2: draw hả? [*Is it 'draw'?*]
03 S1: Um
04 S2: draw hay Art [*'draw' or 'Art'*]
05 S1: Art

The teachers were keenly aware that the task-based lessons increased the kind of productive collaboration seen in extracts 2 and 3, as seen in the following comment from Lan.

> Because they were not provided with the target language items necessary for their communication, they had to make every effort to help their friends understand what they want to say.

Affordance 3. Learner engagement

The term 'engagement' is widely used in education to refer to student interest and participation in learning activities and learning communities such as schools and classrooms. In applied linguistics, Philp and Duchesne (2016) discuss how the construct can be applied to research on classroom language learning tasks, highlighting the multidimensionality of engagement and the implications of this complexity for measuring engagement in task-based interaction. For the purpose of our analysis, we use the term in its broad sense to refer to the extent to which students are "*attracted* to their work, *persist* in it despite challenges and obstacles, and *take visible delight* in accomplishing their work" (our italics) (Schlechty 1994 p. 5). The peer-peer interaction in our data set contained abundant examples of these three characteristics of engagement. As evidence of attraction and persistence, all 18 pairs of learners in our data set successfully completed the task. The third characteristic of engagement, visible delight in accomplishing work, is exemplified in Extract 4 below. In line 2, S1 expresses her satisfaction in completing the task and then, without prompting from the teacher the two learners autonomously appropriate English expressions from the task to engage in a small piece of genuine communication in English (lines 4 to 5) before reverting to Vietnamese to again tell the teacher they have finished the task. We found no evidence of learners engaging in communication like this in English in the PPP lessons from the phase 1 data set.

Extract 4

01 S2: Crazy
02 S1: Cô ơi xong rồi, cô ơi. *[Teacher, we've finished]*
03 S2: Crazy...
04 S1: ... What subject do you like best?
05 S2: Uh... I like Math. What about you?
06 S1: I like Vietnamese. Xong rồi cô ơi *[We've finished, teacher]*

These qualities of engagement were also noticed by Nam who had this to say about the input task used in the task-based lessons to replace the traditional listen and repeat activity.

> When the listening activity was delivered in the traditional way, there was no guarantee that all students would listen. Many students just listened to the recording with no interest. However, the input-based listening task could attract students' attention more effectively because it engaged them in task completion. Students listened with their book closed, so they concentrated better. I noticed that students got more curious and excited.

In summary, the three affordances illustrated above highlight the active engagement of the young learners as they participated in task-based lessons in their Vietnamese primary school classrooms. The teachers were also positive about the learning opportunities provided by the lessons although they noted three concerns: the time involved in materials preparation; difficulty explaining the tasks; and insufficient time for language practice (especially for practising pronunciation). We discuss these concerns briefly below.

The issue of preparation time is a practical concern shared by many busy teachers especially when faced with the choice between a ready-made textbook lesson or preparing original lesson materials from scratch. As one of the teachers, Nhu, noted, "preparing such tasks would take me a lot of time while it is quite easy to just follow the textbooks". Clearly, if teachers are to be encouraged to take a more task-based approach to teaching, ready-made materials will need to be available to alleviate this concern. The second issue of how to give clear task instructions would, we believe, be resolved naturally over time as the teachers and learners became more familiar with working with tasks. To investigate this assumption, however, we need longitudinal research which investigates how teachers' competence in task-based teaching evolves over time.

The third concern (limited practice opportunities) is a more substantive one for task-based teaching. Since there was no shortage of communicative practice in the task-based lessons in our data set, we take this notion of practice to mean controlled practice managed by the teacher and focused on accuracy. Following Willis and Willis (2007), we designed these task-based lessons to include opportunities for controlled practice and FonF in the post-task phase. However, because this phase always occurs towards the end of a lesson, it is the one most likely to be dropped when the main task runs over time, as tasks often do. One of the teachers, Lan, confirmed this point:

> The target structural patterns were not provided until the post stage when the students had completed the target task. However, the time left for practicing the corrected patterns was not enough. More time was needed for explaining and practicing the corrected structural patterns for the students, especially the weak students.

Thus, we would argue that the issue is not one of limited practice opportunities *per se*, but of insufficient time at the end of the task-based lessons to fully realize controlled practice opportunities. Again, for the teachers in this study, this is an issue that may be resolved as they develop expertise in balancing the different phases of a task-based lesson, and perhaps by readjusting their expectations about how much controlled practice is required.

6 Summary and conclusions

Our research showed that despite an explicitly communicative and task-based approach being mandated in the new Vietnamese primary school curriculum, the teachers were required to follow a PPP approach to teaching speaking as laid out in the textbook. Thus constrained, they mostly followed this approach even when strongly critical of it. While some teachers expressed appreciation of the value of PPP for the way it structures learning for lower level classes, other teachers had much more to say about the limitations of PPP, and this is reflected in the widespread practice among the teachers of adding more communicative tasks in the presentation and production stages. In other words, the teachers were naturally going beyond the textbook and fostering a more task-like approach to the lessons. In doing so, the teachers played a pivotal role in mediating the affordances available through textbooks. As Ellis (2015) comments, "[w]hile policy makers and education ministries may set directions and form proposals, it is what teachers do in classrooms which directly affects the success of any reform agenda" (p. 381).

When provided with more strongly task-based versions of the PPP lessons, the three teachers who participated in phase 2 of the research were all positive about the increase in learner engagement that resulted. Evidence from transcripts of peer-peer interaction on the main task in the lessons confirms these impressions. However, we did not collect equivalent interactive data from the PPP lessons which would provide a stronger evidential base to support these claims. Two further limitations of the phase 2 data are worth noting. First, it is possible that the novelty of the new materials may have made the students and teachers more enthusiastic about them. Second the halo affect from being selected to participate in the research may have caused the learners and teachers to invest more effort in the lessons than they otherwise would have.

Despite these limitations, the positive nature of the Vietnamese findings is in contrast to a typically more pessimistic picture painted in many TBLT studies in Asia which reports teachers resisting, avoiding or subverting the task-based requirements of top down task-based policy initiatives (e.g., Carless 2004; Zhang 2015). Often in these studies, TBLT has been mandated without requisite teacher professional learning and support or without due consideration to environmental and social constraints. For instance, Nguyen (2011) who also investigated task-based teaching in primary school English education in Vietnam, claimed that successful implementation of the new curriculum was constrained by teachers emphasizing "mastery of sentence patterns and words rather than stimulating creative or real world communicative use of language" (p. 240), and by teachers lacking the awareness, skills and resources to develop more a more communicative pedagogy.

In contrast, our data shows teachers who are ready and receptive to adopt a more task-like approach to teaching the speaking lessons, particularly one which avoids the repetitive form-focus so typical of the presentation and practice stages in the PPP lesson sequence in their textbooks. We believe that one likely explanation for the contradictory findings between the current study and Nguyen is that Nguyen's research was carried out at a time when the new curriculum had just been introduced and teachers had little experience with it. In contrast, our data was collected four years after the introduction of the 2010 curriculum and all participating teachers had by this time used the new textbook for at least two years. The comparison of these two studies suggests that over time, primary school teachers in Vietnam may be becoming more accustomed to, and at home with, task-based teaching.

Overall, these findings point to the viability of task-based teaching in the context of EFL in Vietnamese primary schools, and show little evidence of the problems implementing TBLT voiced by critics. Lai (2015) argues that research needs to move from identifying constraints on TBLT to exploring how to "push the field forward both in terms of the adoption of TBLT in Asian contexts and in terms of how research in Asian contexts can contribute more to the general field of TBLT" (p. 13). Our hope is that the research we have presented in this chapter contributes to meeting both these aspirations.

References

Adams, Rebecca & Jonathan Newton. 2009. TBLT in Asia: Opportunities and constraints. *Asian Journal of English Language Teaching* 19. 1–17.

Anderson, W. Lorin & Robert B. Burns. 1989. *Research in classrooms: The study of teachers, teaching, and instruction*: Oxford: Pergamon Press.

Borg, Simon. 2006. *Teacher cognition and language education: Research and practice*. London: Continuum.

Butler, Y. Goto. 2015. Task-based assessment for young learners: The role of teachers in changing cultures. In Michael Thomas and Hayo Reinders (eds.), *Contemporary task-based language teaching in Asia*, 348–364. London: Bloomsbury.

Carless, David. 2003. Factors in the implementation of task-based teaching in primary schools *TESOL Quarterly* 38(4). 639–662.

Carless, David. 2004. Issues in teachers' reinterpretation of a task-based innovation in primary schools. *TESOL Quarterly* 38(4). 639–662.

Carless, David. 2009. Revisiting the TBLT versus P-P-P debate: Voices from Hong Kong *Asian Journal of English Language Teaching* 19. 49–66.

Deng, Chunrao & David Carless. 2009. The communicativeness of activities in a task-based innovation in Guangdong, China. *Asian Journal of English Language Teaching* 19. 113–134.

Duran, Goedele & Griet Ramaut. 2006. Tasks for absolute beginners and beyond: Developing and sequencing tasks at basic proficiency levels. In Kris Van den Branden (eds.), *Task-based language education*. New York: Cambridge University Press.

East, Martin. 2012. *Task-based language teaching from the teachers' perspectives: Insights from New Zealand*. Philadelphia: John Benjamins.

Ellis, Rod. 2003. *Task-based language learning and teaching*. Oxford: Oxford University Press.

Ellis, Rod. 2009. Task-based language teaching: Sorting out the misunderstanding. *International Journal of Applied Linguistics* 19(3). 221–246.

Ellis, Rod. 2015. Epilogue. In Michael Thomas and Hayo Reinders (eds.), *Contemporary task-based language teaching in Asia*, 381–384. London: Bloomsbury.

Erlam, Rosemary. 2016. 'I'm still not sure what a task is': Teachers designing language tasks. *Language Teaching Research* 20(3). 279–299.

Foster, Pauline & Amy S. Ohta. 2005. Negotiation for meaning and peer assistance in second language classrooms. *Applied Linguistics* 26(3). 402–430.

Gass, M. Susan & Alison Mackey. 2000. *Stimulated recall methodology in second language research*. Mahwah, NJ: Lawrence Erlbaum Associates.

Lai, Chun. 2015. Task-based language teaching in the Asian context: Where are we now and where are we going? In Michael Thomas & Hayo Reinders (eds.), *Contemporary task-based language teaching in Asia*, 12–29. London: Bloomsbury.

García Mayo, María del Pilar & Amparo Lázaro Ibarrola. 2015. Do children negotiate for meaning in task-based interaction? *System* 54. 40–54.

Lee, Seung-Min. 2005. Training young leaners in meaning negotiation skills. In Corony Edwards & Jane Willis (eds.), *Teachers exploring tasks in English language teaching*, 103–112. New York: Palgrave Macmillan.

Long, Michael H. 2015. *Second language acquisition and task-based language teaching*. West Sussex: John Wiley & Sons.

Ministry of Education and Training (MOET). 2010. *Chuong trinh thi diem tieng Anh tieu hoc [Pilot primary English language curriculum]*. Hanoi: Ministry of Education and Training. http://www.moet.gov.vn/?page=1.24&type=news&view=2545 (accessed 29 April 2016)

Nguyen, G. Viet. 2014. Forms or meanings? Teachers' beliefs and practices regarding task-based language teaching: A Vietnamese case study. *The Journal of ASIA TEFL* 11(1). 1–36.

Nguyen, G. Viet., Van Canh Le & Roger Barnard. 2015. 'Old wine in new bottles': Two case studies of task-based language teaching in Vietnam. In Michael Thomas & Hayo Reinders (eds.), *Contemporary task-based language teaching in Asia*, 68–86. London: Bloomsbury.

Nguyen, T. B. Trang, Jonathan Newton & David Crabbe. 2015. Preparing for tasks in Vietnamese EFL high school classrooms: Teachers in action. In Michael Thomas & Hayo. Reinders (eds.), *Comtemporary task-based language teaching in Asia*, 170–188. London: Bloomsbury.

Nguyen, T. M. Hoa. 2011. Primary English language education policy in Vietnam: Insights from implementation. *Current Issues in Language Planning* 12(2). 225–249.

Nunan, David & Kathleen M. Bailey. 2009. *Exploring second language classroom research: A comprehensive guide*. Boston: Heinle.

Pinter, Annamaria. 2007. Some benefits of peer–peer interaction: 10-year-old children practising with a communication task. *Language Teaching Research* 11(2). 189–207.

Hoang, V. Van, Ha Phan, Ngoc Hien T. Do, Ngoc Loc Dao, Ngoc Minh T. Truong & Quoc Tuan Nguyen. 2012. *Sach tieng Anh 3-4-5 [English textbook Grades 3-4-5]*. Ha Noi, Vietnam: Vietnam Education Publishing House.

Hoang, V. Van, Ha Phan, Ngoc Hien T. Do, Ngoc Loc Dao, Ngoc Minh T. Truong & Quoc Tuan Nguyen. 2012. *Sach giao vien tieng Anh 4 [Teacher's book Grade 4]*. 2015. Ha Noi, Vietnam: Vietnam Education Publishing House & Macmillan.
Sato, Masatoshi & Susan Ballinger (eds.). 2016. *Peer interaction and second language learning: Pedagogical potential and research agenda*. Amsterdam: John Benjamins.
Schlechty, C. Phillip. 1994. *Increasing student engagement*. Jefferson City, Missouri: Missouri Leadership Academy.
Shehadeh, Ali & Christine A. Coombe (eds.). 2012. *Task-based language teaching in foreign language contexts: Research and implementation*. Philadelphia: John Benjamins.
Shintani, Natsuko. 2016. *Input-based tasks in foreign language instruction for young learners*. Amsterdam, Netherlands: John Benjamins.
Swain, Merrill. 1995. Three functions of output in second language learning. In Guy Cook & Barbara Seidlhofer, *Principles and practice in applied linguistics*, 125–144. Oxford: Oxford University Press.
Swain, Merrill. 2000. The output hypothesis and beyond: mediating acquisition through collaborative dialogue. In James. P. Lantolf (ed.), *Sociocultural theory and second language learning*, 97–114. New York: Oxford University Press.
Thomas, Michael & Hayo Reinders (eds.). 2015. *Contemporary task-based language teaching in Asia*. London: Bloomsbury.
Van den Branden, Kris, Koen Van Gorp. & Machteld Verhelst. 2007. *Tasks in action: Task-based language from classroom-based perspective*. New York: Cambridge University Press.
Willis, Dave & Jane Willis. 2007. *Doing task-based teaching*. Oxford: Oxford University Press.
Zhang, Ye. 2015. Task-based language teaching in the primary school of South China. In Michael Thomas & Hayo Reinders (eds.), *Contemporary task-based language teaching in Asia*, 87–102. New York: Bloomsbury.
Zheng, Xinmin & Simon Borg. 2014. Task-based learning and teaching in China: Secondary school teachers' beliefs and practices. *Language Teaching Research* 18(2). 205–221.

Appendix A

A sample speaking lesson from Unit 8 in the textbook 1 for Grade 4

1 Look, listen and repeat.

2 Point and say.

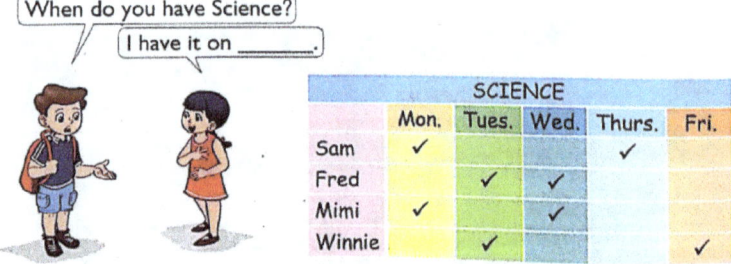

3 Let's talk.

- What subjects do you have today?
- When do you have _____?
- Who is your _____ teacher?

Index

accuracy xvi, 3, 12–26
action research 6, 233, 236, 242
automaticity 219, 220, 224
auxiliary verbs 125, 127

CAF 11–26, 29, 31, 34, 39
– framework 29
children x, 11–26, 80, 222, 261
complexity xvi, 1–5, 12, 14–16, 19–25, 31, 38, 54, 148, 154, 160, 182, 185, 189–190, 206, 236, 237, 246, 272
– theory 1, 4–5, 182, 189–190
concept-based instruction 4, 121
content and language integrated learning (CLIL) ix–xi, 16–17, 202, 205
context vii–xv, 2, 4–6, 11–15, 26, 31, 40, 46, 57, 67, 70–71, 80–84, 86, 92, 94, 99–101, 106, 113, 116, 121, 127, 146–147, 149–150, 152, 156, 167, 170, 172, 175, 183, 186, 189, 195–196, 201, 203, 217–218, 220–223, 228, 233, 235–243, 249–250, 252, 254, 259–264, 267, 275

dynamic assessment 79, 84, 95
dynamic systems 145, 146, 147, 150, 167, 197

ecological
– approach to learning 196
– approach to TBLT 198
– perspective 209, 259
– stance 201
EFL 11–15
English for specific purposes (ESP) ix, xiii, 2
executive model 31, 35
explicit instruction 93–94, 159, 169, 218, 227
exploratory practice 233, 236, 242

face-to-face task-based interaction 63
feedback
– perception 3, 59, 65, 71
– target 55, 62

fluency 3, 12, 14–16, 19–22, 24–26, 30–32, 38, 46, 100, 160, 267
focus on form 4, 79, 95–96, 169–170, 182, 186, 196, 218–222, 225, 228–229, 244, 254, 266
formulaic sequences 3, 5, 29, 31–35, 37–38, 40–46, 167–170, 189
French as a foreign language 105

grammatical accuracy 46, 217, 219, 225
grammatical knowledge 45, 79, 218, 222, 228, 261

historicity 195, 207

input-based tasks 261
intercultural communicative competence 233
interindividual variability 167, 189
intraindividual variability 5

learner-centered instruction (CI) ix, xii, xvii,
limited attention capacity 30

materials preparation 63, 273–275
metacommunicative knowledge 82, 87

noticing 3, 53, 55–60, 62–71, 113, 196, 218, 220, 226–230, 253

oral interaction 11

phonological/executive model 3, 31, 35
pragmatics 102, 149
predictability 145, 163
presentation-production-practice (PPP) 6, 219, 221–222, 228–229, 262–263, 265–269, 272, 274–275
present/practice/produce 219
productive vs. receptive knowledge 168, 171, 182, 185

sociocultural theory 1, 100, 196

strategic interaction scenarios 4, 79, 83
subjectivity 195–196, 201–201
symbolic space 207
synchronous task-based chat 3, 53
syntactic complexity 15–16, 19–25, 30
systemic-theoretical instruction 121

task-based interaction 54, 59, 63, 67, 71, 99, 102, 104, 109, 112, 114, 271–272
task
– performance 3, 16–17, 21, 26, 29, 31, 34–35, 38, 40, 44–46, 153, 159
– planning 3, 29–31, 33–41, 44–47
– repetition 2–3, 11–26, 29, 38, 45, 102
task-supported language teaching (TSLL) 233, 244, 253

TBLT
– implementation viii–xv, 1, 11, 102, 112, 171, 213, 233, 259, 261, 263, 274
– in Vietnam 259–275
– research viii–xvi, 1, 5–7, 29–30, 102
– teacher
– education 154, 233–239, 241, 243, 252, 267
– in-service training 233–255
teaching English to young learners (TEYL)
timing of modified output 59, 61–62, 71
type of modified output 56, 57–59, 61–62, 70

working memory 3, 29, 31, 35, 69–70